'An extraordinarily original and captivating work of detective biography. This is real history, not from the top down or bottom up but from deep inside the heart of living individuals whose stories are all too human'
                                          AMANDA FOREMAN,
              author of *Georgiana, Duchess of Devonshire*

'A marvellous, well-written book, rooted in thorough research on both sides of the Atlantic, which exposes the world of Atlantic trade and slavery through one family's remarkable story'
                                  JAMES WALVIN, author of
   Resistance, Rebellion and Revolt: How Slavery Was Overthrown

'A brilliant work of archival investigation – I was absorbed from start to finish'   IAN THOMSON, author of *The Dead Yard*

'All the detail and character of a Victorian three-volume novel . . . A satisfying popular literary history'
                                  WILL SMITH, *Cumbria Life*

'Rarely has family history been so vivid, following the generations and bravely confronting harsh facts from a colonial past'
                                  JENNY UGLOW, author of *The Lunar Men*

'A wonderful, warm book, which manages to give a new, intimate twist to the epic story of sugar and slavery'
                        ANDREA STUART, author of *Sugar in the Blood*

Mr Atkinson's Rum Contract

THE STORY OF A TANGLED INHERITANCE

Richard Atkinson

4th ESTATE • *London*

4th Estate
An imprint of HarperCollins *Publishers*
1 London Bridge Street
London SE1 9GF
www.4thEstate.co.uk

HarperCollinsPublishers
1st Floor, Watermarque Building, Ringsend Road
Dublin 4, Ireland

First published in Great Britain in 2020 by 4th Estate
This 4th Estate paperback edition published in 2021

1

Illustrated maps by David Atkinson: handmademaps.com
Family tree diagram by Martin Brown

A catalogue record for this book is available from the British Library

ISBN 978-0-00-750923-2

Printed and bound by CPI Group (UK) Ltd, Croydon

MIX
Paper from
responsible sources
FSC
www.fsc.org
FSC™ C007454

This book is produced from independently certified FSC paper
to ensure responsible forest management

Find out more about HarperCollins and the environment at
www.harpercollins.co.uk/green

In memory of my father,
and with love to my sister

CONTENTS

PREFACE

THIS IS THE STORY of my slave-owning, Cumbrian ancestors. It started as a personal research project, an attempt to rectify my ignorance about my father's side of the family and lay to rest some demons which had dogged me ever since his death when I was a child. It would have been pleasing to learn that my Atkinson forebears had been heroes or saints – instead I was confronted by an infinitely more challenging truth.

Clearly, I could not wipe away my ancestors' sins. But I did hope that by telling the unvarnished truth about them, I would be able to help shine a light on a dark episode of history, and show the degree to which slavery was woven into the warp and weft of Georgian society. This is why I made a point of including the most incriminating evidence of their business activities in this book – the most obviously damning of which is the newspaper advertisement for the sale of two cargoes of enslaved Africans by 'G. & M. Atkinson & Co.' that you'll find on page 298. As I gradually gathered and pieced together my sprawling narrative, with its overarching themes of money, trade, politics and war, I realized that I was doing something quite unusual – for it seemed that few tales of British slave-owning families had been written down, or at least not in such detail, let alone by a descendant of the 'guilty' family.

There was a tension at the heart of my project. Some ancestors, most notably Bridget Atkinson, my four-times great-grandmother, cookbook compiler and shell collector extraordinaire, proved easy to love. But her five sons were involved in appallingly exploitative acts; what's more, I found no clue among their plentiful correspondence that they harboured misgivings about the moral foundation of their wealth, even as the anti-slavery movement picked up pace. From today's standpoint, I could see that their behaviour was utterly inexcusable; and yet these were middle-class Englishmen who, in the eyes of their peers, were living well within the bounds of propriety and the law, and were by no means exceptional for their time. Occasionally I found myself wondering what I would have done, had I been in their position.

No one embodied these ambiguities more clearly than the central figure of this book, the founder of the family fortune, my namesake Richard 'Rum' Atkinson. As a businessman, his vast wealth and influence were rooted in aggressive, ruthless trade with the West and East Indies; and yet his private letters revealed him to have a gentle, generous side. Gradually, I came to realize that the 'tangled inheritance' which 'Rum' Atkinson had bequeathed to his nephews and nieces encapsulated, in miniature, the legacy of the wealth that slavery had generated for Britain as a whole. Perhaps, in a way, my struggle to resolve my feelings about my Georgian family is comparable to an ambivalence that many of us feel about this country's past. We may admire our elegant Georgian crescents, squares and terraces – while simultaneously loathing the fact that many of them were built on the back of slavery.

MY BOOK CAME OUT in hardback on 16 April 2020, three weeks into lockdown, at the deadly peak of the pandemic's first wave. The timing was unfortunate, not least because no bookshops were open, but the reviewers were positive, several fulsomely so – although one made an unexpected comment. 'We don't really need another book on the slave trade,' he wrote, 'but a revealing and honest memoir of discovery would be welcome.' I was baffled by this remark, given that I'd made a point of placing my ancestors' worst actions on public record. Moreover, by linking myself to them, I'd positioned myself within their shocking story. *How could I have been any more honest?* But then it dawned on me that maybe the reviewer had a point – maybe I'd shied away from putting my feelings on full display? Perhaps my reticence was open to misinterpretation?

I had no wish to defend my eighteenth-century ancestors. They were participants in a crime against humanity. While telling their story, though, mostly I steered clear of outright denunciation. This was partly to avoid the historical bear-trap of 'presentism' – the misapplication of modern values to past events – and partly because I thought that a sustained bout of authorial hand-wringing would be tiresome for the reader, but mainly because I believed that readers would be capable of making up their own minds.

The book took nearly ten years to write but, as time passed, I became increasingly certain of its relevance – which buoyed me when the going was tough. During the latter half of the decade a succession of books came out that asserted with new confidence the role of people of colour in our national story, from the African-Roman military units garrisoned along Hadrian's Wall onwards. David Olusoga's *Black and British* told a panoramic Black history whose existence had for too long been diminished or even denied, while Afua Hirsch's *Brit(ish)* and Akala's *Natives* explored Black British identity in the shadow of empire. *Mr Atkinson's Rum Contract* was coming from a completely different place and angle, of course, but still I hoped it might offer another perspective on this most painful and sensitive of colonial legacies.

The conversation around race was gathering momentum, but it gained new impetus six weeks after my book was published. On 25 May 2020 George Floyd, an African-American man, died in Minneapolis after a white police officer knelt on his neck for more than nine minutes. This was the latest in a long line of racial atrocities masquerading as law enforcement, and the distressing footage that circulated via social media placed the circumstances of Floyd's killing beyond doubt. This death – this homicide – sent shockwaves around the world. On 7 June, in the former slave-trading port of Bristol, protesters pulled down a Victorian monument to Edward Colston, deputy governor of the Royal African Company from 1689–90, and consigned it to the harbour.

Suddenly, under the bright spotlight of the Black Lives Matter movement, white people were forced to face their privilege, many for the first time. At the British Museum in London, a bust of its founding benefactor, Sir Hans Sloane – much of whose fortune derived from Jamaica – was demoted to a glass cabinet, along with other exhibits showing his links to slavery. In Edinburgh, activists took aim at the statue of Henry Dundas, first Viscount Melville, which stands atop a high stone column in the New Town. Dundas thwarted legislation in 1792 that might have brought the slave trade to an immediate close (see page 242) – he was also a political ally, and love rival, of 'Rum' Atkinson. Elsewhere in the same city, a university tower block named after the Scottish Enlightenment philosopher David Hume – a close family friend of 'Rum' Atkinson's business partner – was renamed as a result of his distinctly unenlightened views on matters of race.

Meanwhile, financial institutions wrestled with their past links to slavery, including the Bank of England, which issued a statement apologizing for 'some inexcusable connections involving former Governors and Directors', and Lloyd's of London, which apologized for its role in the underwriting of slave voyages during the eighteenth and nineteenth centuries. The National Trust, seeking to contextualize the history of its properties, released a detailed report that linked about a third of them to colonialism or slavery, either through the actions of former owners, through fortunes acquired by marriage, or through artefacts and materials (such as mahogany and ivory) that derived from exploitative trade. This proved a highly controversial exercise, interpreted by some on the political right as little more than an attempt to tarnish our finest national treasures. In this febrile, polarised atmosphere, caught between the raw anger of the Black Lives Matter activists and the 'Rule Britannia' patriotism of those 'defending' the beleaguered icons of imperialism, I was doubtful that my voice would be welcome in the conversation.

OUR NATIONAL RECKONING with slavery is so complex not simply because the original sin was so great, but because by leaving it buried for several generations, we have let it put down deep roots in our society. Today Britain is a multicultural nation, the legacy of its global past; in the 2011 census, fewer than half of Londoners identified as 'White British', while nearly one in seven identified as Black. At this juncture, the divisive consequences of empire can no longer be tucked under the carpet. The more awkward a problem, as a rule, the more urgent the need for it to be addressed – and few problems are more discomfiting than that of racial inequality. The frank discussion of historical wrongs is merely the first step on the long road to resolution. Speaking for myself, I felt a tremendous responsibility to put my troubling family story into the public domain. It would at least, I hoped, be a start.

At a governmental level, there's the thorny issue of reparations. In 2013 the Caricom group of fifteen Caribbean states established a commission 'to prepare the case for reparatory justice' for the region's communities 'who are the victims of Crimes against Humanity in the forms of genocide, slavery, slave trading, and racial apartheid'. Caricom's action plan, targeting European governments as the legal bodies that provided the framework for these crimes, includes demands for full formal apologies from the nations involved, the cancellation of international debt, a repatriation program for those of African descent who wish to return to their ancestral homeland, scholarships for indigenous Caribbean people, support in the eradication of illiteracy and other educational goals, investment in cultural institutions, assistance towards the alleviation of a public health crisis, provision of access to technology and science, and recognition of the continuing psychological trauma of slavery.

I believe there's a case for reparations. I can also see that many British taxpayers might balk at picking up the bill, and perhaps argue that it ought to be settled by the descendants of those who profited from slavery. But they might be surprised to discover that this cohort quite possibly includes them – for many more Britons than realize it will have ancestors who participated in some aspect of the slave trade. After all, how many of us know what all our great-grandfathers were up to, let alone their great-grandfathers? You might even make the case that every modern Briton has to some extent benefited from the Georgians' ill-gotten plunder, given that it funded so much of the industry, institutions and heritage upon which our national standing is based. There's no doubt that its slave-generated wealth gave Britain a massive leg-up – as well as creating inequalities that are continuing reminders of this moral stain.

Following abolition in 1833, 46,000 former slave-owners were reimbursed for the loss of their 'human property' through a £20 million compensation package awarded them by parliament, while nothing was given to the 668,000 formerly enslaved men and women. (In February 2018 the Treasury tweeted, with amazing insensitivity, the 'surprising #FridayFact' that the 'amount of money borrowed for the Slavery Abolition Act was so large that it wasn't paid off until 2015', which meant that living British citizens – including millions descended from the enslaved – had 'helped pay to end the slave trade'.) Nearly two centuries later, the disparities perpetuated by this injustice are plain to see. In my own case, although the Atkinson fortune evaporated several generations ago, I still inherited 'cultural capital', represented by the full bookshelves, solid education and family connections that I was lucky to grow up with, in contrast to many of those whose ancestors endured the tragedy of slavery; for just as wealth and privilege pass down the generations, so, often, do poverty and exclusion.

Before I discovered my Georgian family, I knew few of the details of the British involvement in slavery, apart from the fabled achievement of abolition. This book, in a sense, is the story of my personal awakening to the dreadful truth. It has left me with the powerful sense of a chapter of history that is far from ended – after all, it was a mere four generations ago that my great-great-grandfather Dick Atkinson witnessed the last days of slavery in Jamaica. My genealogical odyssey has led me to many new relatives, both living and dead; it has also expanded my sense of what family *means*. I've appreciated the closeness of Britain's connection with its former Caribbean colonies through myriad (mostly long forgotten) ties of blood. I've also understood the degree to which race is a social construct, invented to prop up the institution of slavery and designed to create a legal and cultural gulf between the African and the European.

It's a source of considerable regret to me that I was unable to find out more about the black Atkinsons in my narrative – this was largely a consequence of what might be described as 'archival inequality'. My white ancestors, scattered round the globe, left behind an abundance of correspondence, much of which was stored for posterity in large houses with capacious attics in the north of England, as well as various county and national archives. Sadly, however, the number of records relating to named, enslaved individuals is shockingly small and mostly limited to documents subsequent to 1816, the year that the registration of slaves became mandatory in the British empire. In the case of Betty and her three children, as well as Charlotte Wright, Janet Bogle and their offspring – I won't say more here, to avoid spoilers – I simply reached a dead end, due to a frustrating lack of material.

THIS TALE HAS A FINAL TWIST. Shortly after *Mr Atkinson's Rum Contract* came out, I did an online interview for the Tring Book Festival that was posted on YouTube; it was a long, rambling conversation, and I had no idea who might want to watch it. A few weeks later the festival director forwarded me a message which had just landed in his inbox. 'This is one of the more extraordinary emails we've received,' he wrote.

It came from a woman called Yvette Hewitt, who'd found my interview while doing her own family research. 'My interest was immediately piqued as my family were enslaved by the Atkinson family in Jamaica,' she wrote. 'I am a committee member of the Hennepin County Family History Fair, which is an annual genealogy event in Minneapolis, Minnesota. There is a growing reconciliation and reunification movement in the United States of both enslaved and slave-owning families. My family always spoke about our Caucasian ancestors and part of my genealogical goal is to unify that past in a positive light.'

I leapt at the chance to respond to Yvette. Over several emails, we exchanged stories – it turned out that she was the mysterious 'American woman' whose DNA had matched that of my second and third cousins Renira and Jon Müller in Norway. Yvette's DNA did not match mine (which, given the likely distance of our relationship, was to be expected), but there was another conclusive piece of evidence. Her 85-year-old father, David Wright, came from Galloway, a tiny village within the boundary of the Dean's Valley estate that the Atkinsons had once owned in Jamaica, which I'd passed through on my way to try and find the crumbling ruins of the sugar works there.

I learnt that Yvette and I had more than just a common ancestor in common. We had both embarked on our convergent genealogical paths during the same year, and for similarly personal reasons. There's no way of knowing for sure, but my hunch is that we're descended from Matt, the most promiscuous of Bridget Atkinson's five sons, who lived in Jamaica from 1793 to 1805 – which would make us fourth cousins. Matt was a serial rapist – but without him, neither of us would exist.

One Sunday, shortly before Christmas, my sister Harriet and I met up with Yvette and her husband Craig on Zoom. The four of us had a wonderfully easy, freewheeling conversation, and the warm glow of goodwill was palpable. An hour or so after we finished chatting, I received the following message: 'Dear Richard and Harriet, it was an enjoyable morning for us. Our relationship is special and I cherish it dearly. My parents send their love. Welcome to our big, crazy West Indian family!'

I was touched and humbled by Yvette's generosity. I'd never dreamt, when I first started searching for my eighteenth-century ancestors, that it would lead to such a connection. And while this may not be the final destination on my voyage of family discovery, it feels like a good place to pause along the way.

Richard Atkinson
London, March 2021

'England is not the jewelled isle of Shakespeare's much-quoted message . . . it resembles a family, a rather stuffy Victorian family, with not many black sheep in it but with all its cupboards bursting with skeletons. It has rich relations who have to be kow-towed to and poor relations who are horribly sat upon, and there is a deep conspiracy of silence about the source of the family income.'

– George Orwell, *Why I Write*

The Atkinson family of Temple Sowerby

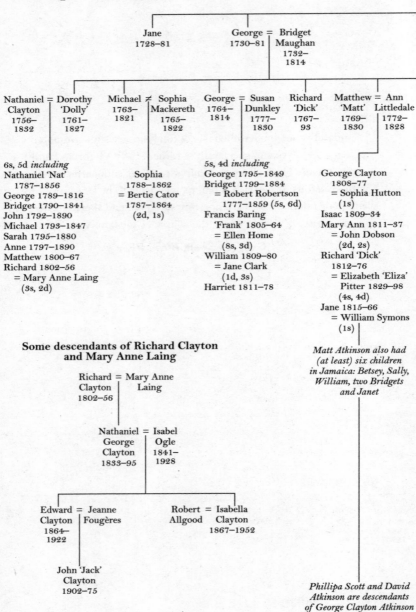

Jane
1728–81

George = Bridget
1730–81   Maughan
1732–
1814

Nathaniel = Dorothy
Clayton   'Dolly'
1756–   1761–
1832   1827

Michael ≠ Sophia
1763–   Mackereth
1821   1765–
          1822

George = Susan
1764–   Dunkley
1814   1777–
         1830

Richard
'Dick'
1767–
93

Matthew = Ann
'Matt'   Littledale
1769–   1772–
1830   1828

6s, 5d *including*
Nathaniel 'Nat'
1787–1856
George 1789–1816
Bridget 1790–1841
John 1792–1890
Michael 1793–1847
Sarah 1795–1880
Anne 1797–1890
Matthew 1800–67
Richard 1802–56
  = Mary Anne Laing
  (3s, 2d)

Sophia
1788–1862
= Bertie Cator
1787–1864
(2d, 1s)

5s, 4d *including*
George 1795–1849
Bridget 1799–1884
  = Robert Robertson
  1777–1859 (5s, 6d)
Francis Baring
  'Frank' 1805–64
  = Ellen Home
  (8s, 3d)
William 1809–80
  = Jane Clark
  (1d, 3s)
Harriet 1811–78

George Clayton
1808–77
= Sophia Hutton
(1s)
Isaac 1809–34
Mary Ann 1811–37
= John Dobson
(2d, 2s)
Richard 'Dick'
1812–76
= Elizabeth 'Eliza'
Pitter 1829–98
(4s, 4d)
Jane 1815–66
= William Symons
(1s)

Some descendants of Richard Clayton and Mary Anne Laing

Richard = Mary Anne
Clayton   Laing
1802–56

Nathaniel = Isabel
George   Ogle
Clayton   1841–
1833–95   1928

Edward = Jeanne
Clayton Fougères
1864–
1922

Robert = Isabella
Allgood   Clayton
          1867–1952

John 'Jack'
Clayton
1902–75

Matt Atkinson also had (at least) six children in Jamaica: Betsey, Sally, William, two Bridgets and Janet

Phillipa Scott and David Atkinson are descendants of George Clayton Atkinson and Sophia Hutton

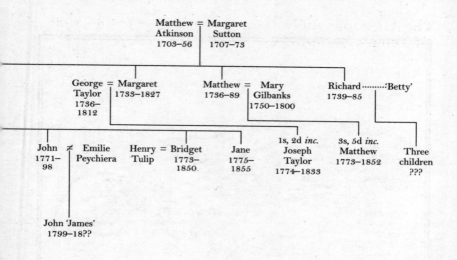

Matthew = Margaret
Atkinson   Sutton
1703–56   1707–73

George = Margaret   Matthew = Mary   Richard ·········:'Betty'
Taylor   1733–1827   1736–89   Gilbanks   1739–85
1736–   1750–1800
1812

John ≠ Emilie   Henry = Bridget   Jane   1s, 2d *inc.*   3s, 5d *inc.*   Three
1771– Peychiera   Tulip   1773–   1775–   Joseph   Matthew   children
98   1850   1855   Taylor   1773–1852   ???
                                                1774–1833

John 'James'
1799–18??

Some descendants of Richard Atkinson and Elizabeth Pitter

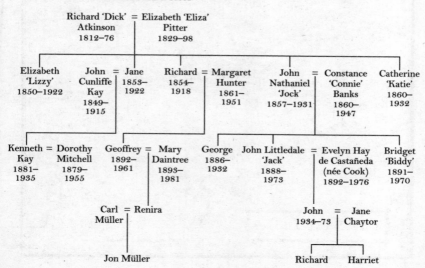

Richard 'Dick' = Elizabeth 'Eliza'
Atkinson   Pitter
1812–76   1829–98

Elizabeth   John = Jane   Richard = Margaret   John = Constance   Catherine
'Lizzy'   Cunliffe 1853–   1854–   Hunter   Nathaniel 'Connie' 'Katie'
1850–1922   Kay   1922   1918   1861–   'Jock'   Banks   1860–
               1849–   1951   1857–1931 1860–   1932
               1915   1947

Kenneth = Dorothy   Geoffrey = Mary   George   John Littledale = Evelyn Hay   Bridget
Kay   Mitchell   1892–   Daintree   1886–   'Jack'   de Castañeda   'Biddy'
1881–   1879–   1961   1893–   1932   1888–   (née Cook)   1891–
1935   1955   1981   1973   1892–1976   1970

Carl = Renira   John = Jane
Müller   1934–73 Chaytor

Jon Müller   Richard   Harriet

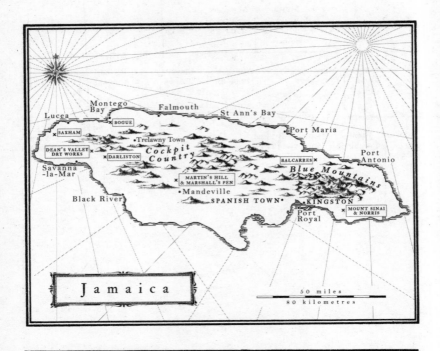

Jamaica

50 miles
80 kilometres

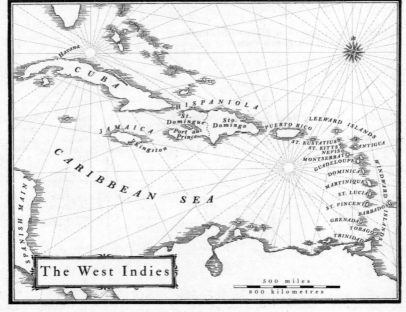

The West Indies

500 miles
800 kilometres

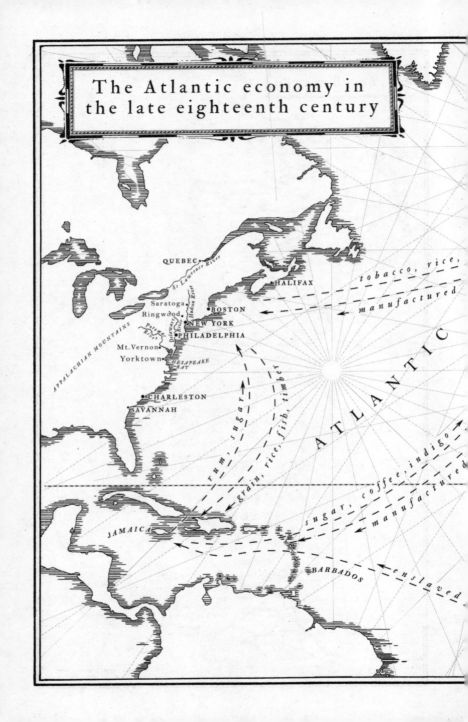

The Atlantic economy in
the late eighteenth century

QUEBEC

St. Lawrence River

HALIFAX

Saratoga
Ringwood
BOSTON

Hudson River

NEW YORK

APPALACHIAN MOUNTAINS

Potomac River

Delaware River

PHILADELPHIA

Mt. Vernon
Yorktown
CHESAPEAKE BAY

CHARLESTON
SAVANNAH

ATLANTIC

tobacco, rice,
manufactured

rum, sugar

grain, rice, fish, timber

sugar, coffee, indigo

manufactured

JAMAICA

BARBADOS

enslaved

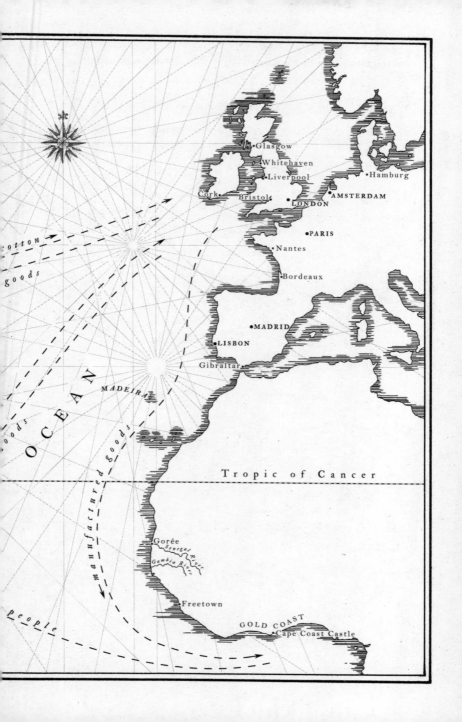

cotton goods

goods

O C E A N

MADEIRA

manufactured goods

people

•Glasgow
•Whitehaven
•Liverpool
Cork•   Bristol•
LONDON
•AMSTERDAM
•Hamburg

•PARIS

•Nantes

•Bordeaux

•MADRID

•LISBON
Gibraltar•

Tropic of Cancer

Gorée
Senegal River
Gambia River

•Freetown

GOLD COAST
•Cape Coast Castle

PART I

The Temperate Zone

ONE

A Tangled Inheritance

SOME OF MY earliest memories are of Temple Sowerby House. I remember the line of tarnished servants' bells in the passage outside the kitchen door, the *tap tap tap* of buckets catching rain-water that dripped through the ceiling, the mint-green porcelain of my grandmother's 1930s bathroom suite; but most vividly of all, I remember the gallery. This was the light-filled corridor up narrow stairs at the back of the house, with three windows looking down on to the overgrown walled garden below. As a small child, on wet days – not unusual in this part of north-west England – I would run up and down the gallery, stomping on the floorboards, pausing only to examine the zoological specimens on display, which included two stuffed crocodiles, a rhinoceros horn and a narwhal tusk. I was par-ticularly drawn to the glass domes filled with birds, their feathers all the colours of the rainbow, although I had no idea where they might have flown from.

This was the early 1970s, by which time dry rot was consuming the Georgian part of the house. In the entrance hall, burnt-orange brackets of fungus bloomed like a ghoulish botanical wallpaper; in the drawing room, many of the floorboards had been pulled up, and much of the ceiling plasterwork had fallen down. My grand-parents, Jack and Evelyn Atkinson, had long since retreated to the rear of the building, the original seventeenth-century farmhouse on to which the handsome front wing had been added during more affluent times. Here the parlour, with its low oak beams and red sandstone chimneypiece, and the kitchen, with its blue enamel range cooker, were the only rooms where they managed to keep the damp remotely at bay.

Jack was quite unfit to be the custodian of such a property. When he moved up to Westmorland from London in the late 1940s, having inherited the 200-acre family farm, he was nearly sixty. Too old and impractical to take the land in hand himself, instead he let it out, and was too soft-hearted to put up the rent for twenty years. As a result, my grandparents were always strapped for cash and invariably in arrears with local tradesmen, who made the classic mistake of confusing gentility with liquidity. They reckoned themselves too poor to have slates replaced or gutters cleared – which is how it came to be that water was coursing through the roof and walls. Even so, every Christmas they ordered a hamper from Fortnum & Mason, London's most exclusive grocer, to make sure they were adequately provisioned during the festive season.

Jack exuded old-fashioned charm; at eighty, as he ambled about the village, tipping his hat to the neighbours, his handsome features were still apparent. Evelyn, on the other hand, had the air of someone constantly disappointed by life, and there was little that did not provide the raw material for complaint. The pair of them rattled around the house, which was largely empty, since most of the contents – beds, tables, sofas, pictures, carpets – had been sold off long ago. They kept strange nocturnal hours, rarely going to bed before three in the morning, and rising in the early afternoon. Sometimes, after breakfast, Jack would wander down to the village shop, only to find that it had already closed for the day. Evelyn, who was obsessed by security – not that there was much worth stealing – roamed the corridors with a big bunch of keys, locking up behind her wherever she went.

My father John, their adored only child, used to dread visiting Temple Sowerby; as the next in a long line of Atkinsons who had inhabited the village for at least four hundred years, he was all too conscious that the house would one day pass to him. Already his parents had started offloading their money problems on to him, often sending begging letters that made him feel guilty and miserable. His salary as a book editor living in London barely met his own needs.

In October 1966 John married my mother, Jane Chaytor, who provided a much-needed burst of energy and hope. She took control of her in-laws' chaotic finances and arranged for a review of the farm rent, which at a stroke doubled their income. She paid their bills – they were amazed to find that the butcher would look them in the eye again. It was she who had the range cooker installed in the kitchen. Jack was captivated by his pretty, practical daughter-in-law, making it all too clear to Evelyn that she was exactly the sort of woman he wished he'd had the good fortune to marry.

A few weeks after I was born, in June 1968, Jack wrote to my father: 'Dear Old Boy, we were delighted with the photos; please thank Jane very much for them. Richard, understandably, didn't show much interest in the proceedings, but you looked, also understandably, as if you were holding the most precious bundle in the world. Quite right too.'[1] Two months later my parents took me up to Westmorland to be baptized in the church at Temple Sowerby.

AROUND THIS TIME, my father started waking in the night with a dull ache in his gut, and hospital tests revealed a tumour; but following surgery his prognosis seemed quite positive. My sister, Harriet, was born in the spring of 1972. That autumn, after four years of good health, my father developed jaundice; the cancer was back. Soon he was too weak to climb the stairs, and a bed was made up for him on the ground floor of our terraced house in Pimlico. He was a sociable man, and over the following weeks a succession of friends and colleagues came to say goodbye. He died at home on 24 February 1973. He was thirty-eight. His funeral took place a few days later, on Harriet's first birthday.

Three months later, Jack too was dead, and buried alongside his son in the graveyard at Temple Sowerby. Suddenly, following the custom of primogeniture, Temple Sowerby House was mine – not that I knew it. As for the farm, the line of succession was not so clear. Under the terms of my great-grandfather's will, written in the 1920s, Jack had been left a life interest in the property, which allowed him to enjoy the income it generated but prevented him from putting it up for sale. This same document stipulated that on Jack's death, the farm would pass to his eldest son or, failing that, his eldest daughter – but no such person now existed. What the will did not anticipate was the possibility that Jack might leave grandchildren who could inherit the farm. So instead the estate was split equally between the principal heirs of each of my great-grandfather's three children: the niece of Jack's elder brother George's late widow; the son of Jack's younger sister Biddy in South Africa; and me. In short, the premature death of my father, and the restrictive language of my great-grandfather's will, meant that the farm passed out of the family's hands.

The bleak practicalities of probate fell to my poor mother. Her first instinct was to hold on to the house, so I might one day have a chance of living there; but given that she had no money for repairs, the idea presented formidable difficulties. The most obvious solution was to pull down the rotten eighteenth-century wing and retain the relatively habitable oldest part. Following the local council's rejection of her planning application, however, my mother realized that only one viable option remained. After moving my grandmother into sheltered accommodation, and suffering many sleepless nights, she called in the estate agents. It was a conclusion for which I will always be grateful.

Temple Sowerby House was by no means an easy sell. Quite aside from its state of semi-dereliction, it had another major drawback. The busy A66 trunk road that crosses the Pennines, linking Penrith and the M6 motorway in the west to Scotch Corner and the A1 in the east, cut straight through the village, not twenty yards from the façade of the house. Just the thought of a thousand lorries thundering past every day was enough to deter most buyers. But finally, in the summer of 1977, the Atkinson family home was sold to a developer who envisioned for it a future as a hotel – the passing trade, for once, counting in its favour.

Apart from the crocodiles, which she banished to a Penrith sale-room, my mother put the contents of the old house into storage; in particular, the three oak court cupboards in the gallery, each carved with the year of its making (1627, 1658 and 1729), which were far too bulky to fit into our small London home. The Atkinson chattels also included two large blanket chests, two broken-down longcase clocks, a well-worn rocking cradle, a spinning wheel and a set of Chippendale mahogany dining chairs, as well as a bookcase full of well-thumbed eighteenth-century volumes on a variety of practical subjects, and heaps of Chinese blue and white porcelain plates, bowls and soup tureens, many of them chipped. Just as I am relieved that my mother got rid of Temple Sowerby House, I'm thankful she kept this motley assortment of objects – baggage they may be, but they are still my most treasured possessions.

My dad's death was the defining event of my childhood; not a day went by when I didn't somehow sense his absence. Because he had been an only child, there were no aunts or uncles to pass on Atkinson stories to my sister and me. (In fact, except for our elderly bachelor cousin in South Africa, who sent us a large, oozingly sticky box of crystallized fruits every Christmas, we were unaware of having any relatives at all on our paternal side of the family.) After the house at Temple Sowerby was sold, the only reason we had to stop off at the village – passing through in the car en route to holidays in the Lake District – was to place flowers on my father's and grandparents' graves. Although these visits lasted a matter of minutes, they loom large in my memory. Every time, as we approached, I would feel fluttering excitement; and every time, as we drove away, I would feel sadder and emptier than before. Temple Sowerby came to represent all that I had lost during my early years; it was a place where it seemed I would always have unfinished business.

WHILE I WAS growing up, people who had known my dad often told me how much I resembled him, so it was perhaps inevitable that I would follow him into a career in book publishing. In many ways I felt blessed to be like him, since it meant I always carried him around with me; occasionally it felt like a curse. In my thirties, I suffered from digestive problems that caused me much discomfort. Bowel cancer can run in families, and for several years I was sure that I was destined to follow my father to an early grave. When I finally celebrated my thirty-ninth birthday, in 2007, it felt as though a weight had lifted, even as another pressed down; for that year Sue and I finally grasped, after seven years of marriage, that we would never have children of our own. This was a fate I had not imagined, and I felt rudderless, as though robbed of my purpose. My emotions turned raw and unpredictable; for no clear reason, I would break down crying in the street. I now realize I was mourning the sons and daughters I would never know.

While my contemporaries looked to the future, and threw themselves into the all-consuming business of raising families, I turned towards the past, and decided that perhaps it was time I found out about those who had preceded me. One day, while rummaging around in my mother's house, I discovered, gathering dust on top of a cupboard, a scruffy old cardboard box which contained several hundred letters tied up in tight bundles with pink legal ribbon. Most of them were addressed to a 'Matthew Atkinson, Esq.' at Temple Sowerby and dated from the first decades of the nineteenth century. At the same time I came across a family tree, mapped out on a roll of graph paper about twenty feet long, which traced the Atkinsons back to the late sixteenth century. It was in my father's handwriting – I guessed he must have compiled it some time before his marriage, since right at the bottom I noticed he had added my mother's name, and then mine and Harriet's, in slightly different shades of blue-black ink. Looking over past generations, I soon realized how presumptuous I had been to assume that I would have children; while some branches of the family tree were ripe with offspring, others withered to nothing. Below the names of all those whose marriages had not borne fruit, my dad had written the sad little genealogical acronym 'd.s.p.' – *decessit sine prole*, the Latin for 'died without issue'.

I found the prospect of delving into the box of letters quite daunting, but one evening I took a deep breath and started reading.

Instantly I felt the exhilarating rush of throwing open a window to the past. Even so, my progress was slow while I got used to the handwriting. For every letter penned in an impeccable copperplate, another resembled a spidery scrawl. Sometimes the ink had faded to a ghostly sepia. Occasionally, to save the cost of a second sheet of paper, the correspondent had simply rotated the page ninety degrees and carried on writing, creating a dense lattice of words. No envelopes were used; sheets were simply folded, addressed on the front, sealed with wax and dispatched, often in evident haste.

I had observed on the family tree that my ancestors were quite unimaginative when it came to Christian names. George, John, Matthew and Richard had been standard issue for Atkinson boys since the seventeenth century. Right from the start, this small pool of names threw me into confusion, for I made the mistake of assuming that the Matthew Atkinson to whom most of the letters were addressed was my three-times great-grandfather, who had died in 1830. Only some months later did I gather that they related to another Matthew Atkinson, his first cousin, who had died in 1852; it would be several years before I discovered how these papers from a collateral branch of the family had ended up in my hands.

Matthew's correspondence mostly concerned business local to Temple Sowerby, and offered tantalizing glimpses of various trades – banking, farming, mining – which the family had been engaged in. Until then, I had always imagined my forebears as head-in-the-clouds types, rather like my ineffectual grandfather, but these Atkinsons were worldly folk. For the first time I was able to piece together the patchy outline of a family narrative. It appeared that something had occurred during the late eighteenth century to disrupt the fortunes of the entire family. Plenty of letters touched on legal matters, with frequent references to the labyrinthine affairs of a late uncle. And then I unfolded a document that made my jaw drop – it was a 'List of Negroes' giving the name, age, employment and value, in pounds sterling, of each of the 196 enslaved workers on a sugar plantation in Jamaica in the year 1801.

*

GENEALOGY IS ADDICTIVE, and I was soon hooked. I signed up to Ancestry, the online portal to an infinitude of parish records, electoral rolls, census lists and telephone directories, all just the wave of a credit card and the click of a mouse away. I spent countless hours googling 'atkinson' and 'temple sowerby' and 'jamaica', and any other combination of words that might summon up evidence of my ancestors. One day I typed 'atkinson' into the search engine of the National Portrait Gallery website (doubtful though I was that anyone to whom I was related would have earned a place in that august institution), and a result popped up for 'Richard Atkinson, Merchant', whose dates matched those of someone on the family tree – my five-times great-uncle.

I clicked through to this namesake's portrait. Instead of the conventional oil painting that I was expecting, what came up on screen was an engraving titled *Westminster School*, dated 4 February 1785, by James Gillray, the most savage cartoonist of his age. In the foreground, portrayed in the role of headmaster, sits the famous politician Charles James Fox, unmistakable with his bushy black eyebrows. William Pitt the Younger, the 25-year-old prime minister, is shown bent over Fox's knee, where he is being given a sound thrashing. Meanwhile a cohort of Pitt's 'playmates', held in place on the backs of prominent opposition figures, line up to await the same punishment, their buttocks bared. Poking out from the pocket of one of these miscreants is a piece of paper bearing two words, 'Rum Contract' – the detail which identifies him as Richard Atkinson. My head was spinning at the thought not only that a relative of mine should find himself in such rarefied company – but that our first encounter should take place at a moment when his breeches were hanging around his knees.

An internet search soon yielded a potted biography of this Richard Atkinson. He had been a West India merchant, director of the East India Company, Member of Parliament, alderman of the City of London, prominent early supporter of Pitt the Younger – and a major government contractor during the American War of Independence. His nickname, 'Rum' Atkinson, apparently originated from a notorious contract to supply a vast quantity of Jamaican rum to the British army headquarters at New York in 1776. He had died relatively young, in May 1785, unmarried, leaving behind an immense, self-made fortune.

BY NOW I WAS in the grip of an obsession, spending all my spare time online in pursuit of my ancestors. One evening during the autumn of 2010, I was browsing the website of Temple Sowerby House Hotel, which included a short page dedicated to the history of the place; and although it was a fairly unexciting account, one paragraph leapt out at me. This was a description of a 'fascinating Recipe or *Receipt* Book', written by Bridget Atkinson for her daughter Dorothy Clayton in 1806, which gave instructions, among other dishes, for collared eels, roasted tench and a sauce to serve with larks. I knew that this Bridget Atkinson was my four-times great-grandmother, as well as 'Rum' Atkinson's sister-in-law. My sister and I had inherited a number of her books – we knew they were hers because she always signed her name on the title page – including *Domestic Medicine: or, a Treatise on the Prevention and Cure of Diseases by Regimen and Simple Medicines*, by William Buchan, MD; *The Scots Gardiners Director, containing Instructions to those Gardiners, who make a Kitchen Garden, and the Culture of Flowers, their Business*, by 'A Gentleman, one of the Members of the Royal Society'; *An Account of the Culture and Use of the Mangel Wurzel, or Root of Scarcity*, translated from the French of the Abbé de Commerell; and *The British Housewife: or, the Cook, Housekeeper's and Gardiner's Companion*, by Mrs Martha Bradley. But this was the first I'd heard of Bridget having written a recipe book of her own. I publish cookbooks for a living; suffice to say my interest was piqued.

So I did something I'd never thought of doing – I stayed a night at the hotel. Arriving at Temple Sowerby around teatime, I parked near the maypole, beside the large stone from which John Wesley was said to have preached in 1782. It was a crisp November day. Across the road, the curtains of the hotel had not yet been drawn, and its brightly lit reception rooms radiated hospitality. Before

Plate I.   Frontispiece to the Compleat English Cook.

Jaques Le Sœur Inv.   *Behold, ye Fair, united in this Book*   B. Cole Sc.
The frugal Housewife, and experienc'd Cook.

The frontispiece of Bridget's copy of The British Housewife.

checking in, I went for a short stroll, as far as the old tannery buildings at the other end of the village. Walking round the green, I found myself appraising Temple Sowerby as if visiting for the first time; with its handsome Georgian houses, coaching inn and red sandstone church, it seemed a delightful place. Much more peaceful than I remembered, too, since a new bypass had diverted all the lorries which had once rumbled through the village.

Over at the hotel, Julie Evans, one of the owners, greeted me warmly. She already knew about my connection to the house, and had reserved a room for me at the back, with a view down the garden. It was nice and cosy, in a chintzy kind of way, and the ensuite bathroom, with its Jacuzzi tub, was a definite upgrade from the spartan facilities of the Atkinson era. Even so, a small, churlish part of me resented the fitted carpets and double glazing, and yearned for the house of my grandparents. As a child, my favourite place had been the gallery, with its clattery floorboards and oak furniture, some of which now dominated my living room in south London. But it seemed that when Temple Sowerby House was turned into a hotel, in the late 1970s, the gallery had been carved up to make bedrooms, including the one I would be sleeping in. To describe my emotions as agitated would be an understatement; as I sat down to dinner, the only guest that night, I had never felt more lonely.

I had almost finished eating when Julie appeared, clutching a scrap of paper. 'I've just remembered something,' she said. 'A few years ago, this person came to stay, and she told me her ancestors used to live here. Perhaps you should get in touch?' She handed me the slip, on which was written an unfamiliar name – Phillipa Scott – along with a telephone number. I was intrigued.

Julie took pity on me after my solitary meal, and we chatted in the parlour. She and her husband Paul had owned the hotel for ten years, and she was clearly so fond of the place that I found myself letting go of the last of my proprietorial feelings. I'd brought a shoebox full of old family papers up from London with me, and we leafed through them together. Then I asked Julie the question I'd been burning to put to her since arriving – what could she tell me about this 'receipt book' that was mentioned on the hotel website? She left the room and returned a couple of minutes later, cradling an old quarter-bound book. She handed it to me; I opened it cautiously, not knowing what might be inside, and was amazed to find almost eight hundred recipes, handwritten in highly legible script.

It was evident from the sheer variety of meat, fish and game dishes in her repertoire that Bridget Atkinson had kept an excellent table. Many of her recipes included spices and flavourings that to this day carry a whiff of the exotic, such as cinnamon, ginger, nutmeg, curry powder, candied lemons and orange flower water. Although the instructions she gave were cursory at best, and her methods on the antiquated side – she was, after all, cooking over an open fire – many of the recipes, especially the puddings and preserves, seemed perfectly relatable to the present. I could imagine trying to make them at home.

Not so the recipes in the last third of the book, where Bridget offered remedies for every conceivable domestic situation or ailment: 'For Berry Bushes infested with Caterpillers'; 'To distroy Moths'; 'To prevent Milk from having a taste of Turneps'; 'A Pomatum for the Face after the Small Pox'; 'To draw away a Humor from the Eyes'; 'For worms in Children'; 'Against Spitting of Blood'; 'To prevent bad effects of a Fall from a high place'; 'To cure the Bite of a Mad Dog'; 'For Insanity'. Some of her preparations sounded downright lethal. On a loose piece of paper tucked into the book I found 'Mrs. Atkinson's Receipt', a concoction of rhubarb, laudanum and gin, all mixed into a pint of milk; it was not clear what condition it was intended for, but it seemed as though it may have been a case of kill or cure.

Bridget would have been in her seventies when she started compiling this volume for her daughter – it was odd to think she might well have written it in the same room in which I was at that moment sitting. For so long, I had associated Temple Sowerby House with death and decay; only now could I sense it as a bustling family home. In all my life, I had never coveted a single object so much as this wondrous book – so I felt crushed when Julie explained that it

belonged to a private collector from Newcastle, and would soon have
to be returned. I must have looked so downcast that Julie insisted I
should immediately write to the owner, Miss Dunn, to ask whether
I might buy the book; indeed, she thrust pen, paper and envelope at
me, and promised to post my letter.

WHEN I OPENED the curtains the next morning, the sky was
a brilliant blue; overnight had seen a heavy frost. After breakfast
I walked across the road to the churchyard, crunching through
glittery grass in search of Atkinson graves; then I set off for
Northumberland, to spend a couple of nights with my godmother
near Corbridge. My route over the Pennines took me on a zigzag
road up the steep side of the Eden valley, through the ancient lead-
mining town of Alston and across an ocean of bronze heather,
dropping down alongside the South Tyne – a spectacular drive.
That afternoon I had a couple of hours to spare, so I visited Chesters
Fort, one of several Roman garrisons along Hadrian's Wall, now
maintained by English Heritage. I knew from my family research
that some cousins, the Claytons, had once lived in the big house near
the ruins, and had been responsible for their excavation – Bridget's
daughter, Dorothy, had married Nathaniel Clayton, the Newcastle
lawyer who purchased the property.

Wandering around the neat stone footings, I struggled to
imagine five hundred Roman cavalry ever having occupied such a
peaceful spot. As drizzle hardened into rain, I took refuge in the
small museum attached to the site. Near the entrance was a glass
case devoted to the life of John Clayton, owner of Chesters for much
of the nineteenth century. Among the objects on display was an old
book which had belonged to his grandmother, Bridget Atkinson –
as usual, her name was inscribed on the title page. Then something
even more extraordinary caught my eye. It was the facsimile of a
letter written by Bridget in January 1758, when she would have been
in her mid-twenties, in which she was begging her sister to placate
their mother, who was furious that she'd got married the previous
Saturday without telling anyone. My heart pounded as I processed

this – did it mean Bridget had eloped? *And how had the museum come by this letter?*

On my return to London, I wasted no time chasing up my leads – within minutes of arriving home, I had dug out the family tree and unfurled it on the kitchen table. First of all, I needed to locate Phillipa Scott, the mysterious woman whose details Julie Evans had given me. There she was, my fourth cousin – our last mutual ancestor was Bridget's son Matthew Atkinson, the one who died in 1830. I googled her, and soon landed on the website of a needlework expert living in Appleby, six miles from Temple Sowerby – with the same distinctive spelling of her first name, this was surely the right person. It was almost midnight on a Sunday, but the urge to make contact with this complete stranger was too powerful to resist. In a short email, I explained who I was and where I'd just been. About three minutes later, Phillipa's reply announced itself in my inbox. Hello! And, yes, she had stayed at Temple Sowerby House some years earlier, but also remembered visiting in the 1960s, as a child. 'Is it my imagination,' she wrote, 'or was there a crocodile on the top landing?'

Phillipa and I spoke on the telephone the following day, and for me it was a cathartic experience. We hit it off immediately, and dis-covered how much we had in common; although we belonged to different branches of the tree, we shared the same deep roots. We chatted for an hour, and afterwards I felt so overwhelmed with joy that I burst into tears. A few weeks later, Phillipa put me in touch with David Atkinson, her first cousin – my fourth cousin – who invited me to stay at his house in Cheshire so that I could search through his collection of family papers. He was trusting enough to let me carry away a suitcase full of them.

I also made contact with the curator of the museum at Chesters, Georgina Plowright, who delivered a surprising piece of news. She had recently unearthed a treasure trove of correspondence between the Atkinson and Clayton families, six large boxes spanning the eighteenth and nineteenth centuries, in the Northumberland Archives, buried among the papers of another family, the Allgoods of Nunwick Hall. (Apparently one of Bridget Atkinson's great-great-granddaughters, Isabella Clayton, had married an Allgood.)

And then there was Bridget's 'receipt book', the scent of which had lured me north in the first place. Two days after my return, I received a call from Irene Dunn in response to the letter I had written from Temple Sowerby. She told me she was a retired librarian with a special interest in books about food; she had found Bridget's manuscript at an antiquarian bookseller's in Bath about fifteen years earlier. It so happened that I had approached Irene at the perfect moment. She was now looking to downsize, and was tickled by the thought of selling the book to me, a descendant of Bridget. One bright Saturday in January I travelled by train up to Newcastle to meet Irene for lunch in a restaurant on the Quayside, and to carry my prize home.

SO THIS IS THE STORY of how I found my eighteenth-century family. It was as though Bridget's cookbook was the key I had been searching for, since doors immediately began to open. The thousands of old letters that fell into my lap as a result of my miraculous trip to Temple Sowerby – they were just the start. Within a few months I had located significant quantities of Atkinson correspondence in more than a dozen public archives and private collections on both sides of the Atlantic. My ancestors, it emerged, had occupied ringside seats at some of the most momentous episodes in British imperial history, most notably the loss of the American colonies, then the economic collapse of the West Indies. When they first sailed to Jamaica, in the 1780s, it was the most valuable possession in the empire; when they left, in the 1850s, it was a neglected backwater. Moreover, through the copious correspondence they left behind, I learnt the intimate details of their lives. Richard 'Rum' Atkinson, in particular, emerged as a brilliant but flawed man who amassed a fabled fortune as well as considerable power, but would have given it up in a heartbeat for the woman he loved.

It became obvious that I had stumbled upon the material for a book. Although I had edited a great many books written by other people, I had never planned to inflict one of my own on the world, being more than happy to remain on the other side of the publishing fence. But I found I couldn't ignore this story which kept me awake at night, so I started rising at six, to spend a couple of hours writing before leaving for the office. It was hard going, and on dark winter mornings it took every ounce of willpower to drag myself out of bed. I soon discovered – perhaps surprisingly, given my professional background – that I had little idea how to go about actually writing a book. So I signed up for an evening class in 'Writing Family History', and it was here that I had another stroke of luck – for the teacher turned out to be the acclaimed biographer Andrea Stuart, who was then at work on *Sugar in the Blood*, the story of her ancestors in Barbados, black and white. One Saturday morning, she took us on a tour of the National Archives at Kew, a vast concrete behemoth where we were inducted into the practicalities of archival research; it was time well spent, for I would become a frequent visitor over the next few years. Andrea encouraged me, at a stage when I really needed it, to pursue my own embryonic Jamaican story.

I look back on this as a strange, transitional period in my life; I felt like a kind of time-travelling commuter, secretly shuttling back and forth between the present day and the world of my eighteenth-century family. It was exciting, certainly, but also emotionally challenging, as I struggled to reconcile my inborn sympathy for these people, my ancestors, with their activities in Jamaica. I was never so naive as to imagine that those activities might be unconnected with slavery, but nor was I fully prepared for the degree to which they were involved. It was not a pleasant discovery.

My eyes were opened, too, to the nature of Britain's culpability. I learned that there were thousands of well-to-do Georgian families, like mine, whose wealth and prestige had derived from the blood, sweat and lives of enslaved Africans. Moreover, individuals from every rank of society had played their part in propping up slavery, from the royal personages who sanctioned the slave trade with West Africa in the first place, to the sailors who crewed the slave ships – even the ordinary working people who consumed the tainted sugar.

Here in Britain, we have tended to keep this disturbing aspect of our national story at arm's length; unlike the United States, where its divisive consequences are plain to see, slavery was not commonplace on these shores. We proudly celebrate our great abolitionists, of course, but we would rather not know *too* much about what they were campaigning to abolish.

Sometimes, after yet another grim discovery in the archives, I wondered what kind of fool would knowingly implicate his own family by writing them into this shocking chapter of history. Yet my instinct told me to press on; in fact, I felt a powerful responsibility to do so. Clearly I could make no amends for my ancestors' misdeeds – but I could certainly attempt to make something positive out of what they had left behind. Since this mostly consisted of old letters, to tell their story made perfect sense to me. But it was essential that I should write it warts-and-all. 'Do not try and make all the ancestors goody two shoes when some were plainly not,' advised David Atkinson, whose messages were a tonic for my sometimes flagging spirits. 'Detach yourself – you have every right to portray some as villains, some as "not sures", some as feckless and some as the heroes. I suspect you might be torn on this – don't be. You have my blessing to treat some of them hard.'

To have my newfound cousins cheering me on was just what I needed as I embarked on a long voyage into our ancestors' past – one that took me all the way from London to the abandoned sugar plantations of Jamaica. But all roads ultimately led to Temple Sowerby, where so many Atkinsons were born and so many are buried. Their tangled inheritance may have scattered them around the world, but the evidence made its way back to that weather-beaten house in the shadow of the Pennines and, eventually, in the form of the curious miscellany of relics and papers that were my inheritance, into my hands.

TWO

The Tanner's Wife

THE RIVER EDEN carves a sinuous line down the valley that bears its name, past ruined castles and ruminating cows, swelling from the countless becks that drain off steep fells; by the time it flows under the red sandstone bridge at Temple Sowerby, it has completed almost half its ninety-mile journey. Cross Fell, highest of the Pennine hills, dominates the skyline at this point; it enjoys the rare distinction of harbouring a breeze with so much bluster that it has its own name. 'A violent roaring hurricane comes tumbling down the mountain, ready to tear up all before it,' was how one eighteenth-century traveller described the 'Helm' wind.[1]

From the summit of Cross Fell – assuming the absence of its usual cloud cap – you can see the hills of Galloway in southern Scotland. Two thousand years ago, the Romans built a wall to keep out the Caledonian people to the north, and legions of soldiers marched through Temple Sowerby on their way to forts along its route; a Roman milestone can be found in a layby just outside the village, although its inscription weathered away aeons ago. Scandinavian immigrants settled in the area during the ninth century. These hardy people left their linguistic imprint across northern England, not just in the words that evoke its landscape – *beck* and *fell* are of Norse origin – but also in its place names. *Sauerbi* is old Norse for 'farmstead on sour ground'. Even the Vikings, it seems, saw Temple Sowerby as a hardship post.

The first tangible evidence of the Atkinsons of Temple Sowerby can be found in the basement of the county offices at Kendal – this is where the records are kept for the historic county of Westmorland, which was absorbed into Cumbria in 1974. William Atkinson – my nine-times great-grandfather – was one of seventeen yeomen who in 1577 were granted thousand-year leases on their land in the village, along with 'reasonable common for the pasturing of their cattle', by the lord of the manor, Christopher Dalston.[2] It feels only fitting that I should examine the legal document in which my ancestors' earliest property rights were enshrined, but the large sheet of vellum is a brute to unfold, so defiantly springy that it resists my attempts to flatten it out. I must be firm with it, I realize, but not *too* firm, since the archivist is watching me like a hawk.

Eventually, after wrestling with it for a minute or two, I have it spreadeagled on the desk, its corners pinned down with iron weights. I now appreciate why calfskin has always been the material upon which parliamentary laws are recorded, for the document remains in superb condition, apart from two holes caused either by rodents or fire – it's hard to tell which. Next comes a still greater challenge – deciphering the script. At first I hold out little hope of being able to read the spiky Elizabethan handwriting. But soon I find that if I stare at them in an abstract way, shapes start to turn into words.

This lease marks the culmination of a conflict that simmered in Temple Sowerby for twenty years. Until the dissolution of the monasteries in the 1530s, the manor was held by the religious orders of the Knights Templar (who gave it their name), and then by the Knights Hospitaller, both of whom interfered little in the lives of the villagers. That all changed in 1543 when the Dalston family acquired the manor from the Crown. It was inevitable the tenants of Temple Sowerby would resent their first resident landlords in nearly four centuries, especially given that both Thomas Dalston and his son, Christopher, made it plain that they intended to claim the common land for themselves. William Atkinson was one of eight villagers who filed a writ against Christopher Dalston in 1559. Their case was rejected by the Lord President of the North at York; next, they took it to Court of Chancery in London.

The 1577 lease was the upshot of this litigation. Dalston gained exclusive use of half the common, and was ordered to grant his tenants possession of the other half. For their part, the villagers undertook to use Dalston's mill at Acorn Bank to grind their flour, and to pay for half of any necessary repairs. Although it was technically a compromise, they nonetheless saw the agreement as a victory against their overbearing lord. Christopher Dalston only conceded to these terms 'because he would be of quietness with the plaintiffs and no further be molested as he by a long time hath been'.[3] He never forgave his tenants their insolence; and they in turn fully reciprocated his ill feelings.

The first mention of the leather-tanning business that kept the Atkinson family busy for at least five generations is found in the will of William Atkinson, second son of William who signed the 1577 agreement. This William never married, and on his death in 1645 he left his elder brother John 'all my leather tubbes and barke and my apparel the bedstead I lye in and one feather bed and one nagge'.[4]

Temple Sowerby was well positioned for the trade in animal skins, being on a major cattle-droving route. Every year, between April and October, thousands of black cows funnelled through the village on their way from the breeding grounds of south-west Scotland to Smithfield market in London; plenty failed to last the distance, falling by the wayside due to lameness or sickness. The 'drovers' who herded cattle were tough individuals, and Westmorland was the harshest terrain they would cross – Daniel Defoe in 1724 described the county as 'eminent only for being the wildest, most barren, and frightful of any that I have passed over in England, or in Wales'.[5] At Temple Sowerby the drovers found a range of services, including a farrier for shoeing horses and cows, two inns and ample pasturage.

Two tanyards lay at a slight remove from the centre of the village – necessarily so, given the stench arising from the tanning process. First, any decaying flesh was cleaned off the raw hides, and any hair removed; next came the stage known as bating, during which the skins were softened in an ammoniac brew of watered-down pigeon shit shovelled from a large dovecote on site. They were then immersed in a succession of clay-lined pits filled with tanning liquor of increasing strength, the active ingredient being the tannin released by ground-up dried oak bark steeped in water. The overall length of the soak determined the toughness of the finished product, but generally lasted a year or more. Finally the cured skins were trimmed, shaved, greased, dyed, rolled, buffed and prepared for market. So many of life's necessities – belts, boots, buckets, harnesses, pouches, saddles, straps and trunks – were fashioned from leather. Its manufacture was by no means a noble activity; but it was a vital one.

THE HEARTH TAX return of my seven-times great-grandfather John Atkinson for 1670 declares just one fireplace – compared to Squire Dalston's nine at Acorn Bank.[6] John died in 1680, and what little I know of him comes from his will, a document noteworthy as the first (but by no means the last) record of friction within the Atkinson family.

The declarative language of John's will suggests it was dictated on his deathbed, the rather melodramatic custom of the day. So close to his final breath, you would hope that John might be making his peace with the world, but it seems he felt the need to mediate between his squabbling offspring. Thus, having apportioned his earthly possessions – he left forty shillings a year to his daughter Barbara, and the bulk of any 'goods and lands moveable and unmoveable' to his son George – John went on to specify some conditions. As long as she remained unmarried, Barbara was to be housed by her brother. 'If the sayd Barbry and Geordge cannot agre,' John went on, 'Geordge is to builde hir a chimley in the backe chamber and she is to live theire and if the sade chamber doe fall to decay then Geordge is to repare the same of his owne cost.'[7] Barbara never did marry, and I haven't been able to discover whether that extra chimney was ever needed. But when George died more than forty years later he left his sister £5 – so perhaps they managed to agree after all.

As I write, George's Latin textbook sits on the desk before me – it's the oldest object I own. Bound in scuffed calfskin, it contains almost five hundred handwritten pages of Latin grammar and syntax. Like the thousand-year lease, the script is in a distinctively Elizabethan hand, which is confirmed by the date: 'anno domini 1595'. For George, too, the book was a hand-me-down, as it pre-dates his schooldays by several generations. Born in 1657, he was a pupil in the early 1670s, by which time the writing style had become rounder and, to modern eyes, much more legible. So how do I know that the book once belonged to him? The impulse to deface textbooks is hard-wired into every small boy's brain. George was no exception, and he wrote his name a few times on the flyleaf, along with this enjoyable doggerel:

> *Hic liber pertinet, deny it who can*
> *Ad Georgeum Atkinson, ye honest young man*
> *In opido Temple Sowerbie he is to be founde*
> *Si non mortuus est, if not laide in ye grounde*

The book is a yardstick of the Atkinson family's social mobility during the seventeenth century. George's grandfather John, who died in 1647, had signed his will with the rudimentary 'mark' of an illiterate man; John's grandson George, on the other hand, could read and write Latin.

History records neither how George met his wife Jane Hodgson, nor when or where they were married, but it must have been relatively late for both of them, since their first child was born in 1701, when he was forty-four and she was thirty-one. Jane came from Threlkeld, near Keswick, in the heart of the Lake District. Perhaps George encountered her on his way to take delivery of a consignment of raw hides at the port of Whitehaven; or maybe he knew her from expeditions to purchase oak bark, a commodity in which the coppiced woods of the Lakeland dales were rich.

The sandy incline known as Whinfell, just across the river from Temple Sowerby, was the most convenient source of the bark that was essential to the tanning process. Around thirty families, including the Atkinsons, cultivated a large open expanse of the fell, although the land was too scrubby – 'whin' being another word for gorse – to be much good. Beyond the villagers' strips, up the hill, lay Whinfell Forest, the domain of the Earl of Thanet. Since medieval times the forest had been renowned for the aristocratic sport of deer hunting, and for its 'prodigious oaks', including a trio known as the Three Brothers.[8]

Sadly, these giants would soon be slain. By the turn of the eighteenth century, Whinfell's oaks had been earmarked for the shipyards of the Royal Navy, which, having consumed vast tracts of ancient woodland in the south, was now sourcing its timber from further afield. Accounts kept by Lord Thanet's steward, Thomas Carleton, record the felling of fifty-four oaks at Whinfell during the winter of 1701, and twenty-three more the following spring. After being peeled and sawn on the spot, the timber was loaded on to sixty waggons that were dragged thirty miles up the old Roman road to Rockcliffe, at the mouth of the River Eden, where it was transferred to two barges and ferried round the coast to Whitehaven, to be warehoused 'till the Queen's Shipp Come for it'.[9] Meanwhile, the bark from these ancient trees was sold to a syndicate of five tanners, one of whom was George Atkinson.

Little went to waste in the rural economy. Animal hair, a by-product of the tanning process, was a commodity in its own right, used to add bulk to the mixture of lime, sand and water that made up plaster. Hair recycled from the tannery at Temple Sowerby found its way into the fabric of some of the area's finest properties; half a ton of the stuff was used in 1718 in the walls and ceilings of the Red House, Thomas Carleton's residence in Appleby.[10]

Over the course of his relatively long life, George's tanning business prospered, and he was able to buy two farms, one at Hilton Bacon, ten miles up the valley, the other at Hesket Newmarket, twenty miles in the other direction. By the time he was ready to be 'laide in ye grounde', when he was sixty-six, he had acquired sufficient property to provide for both his sons.

George's funeral was held on Whitsunday in 1723, and the parish record throws up a curiously intimate detail about his interment. A law had been passed in 1666 requiring corpses to be buried in woollen shrouds, rather than the linen sheets in which they had previously been wrapped; only victims of the plague were exempt. This was a protectionist measure, aimed at reducing linen imports from abroad, with a harsh £5 fine for non-compliance, payable out of the estate of the deceased. (Half the fine went to the informer, the rest to the poor of the parish.) Even so, some fancy folk were prepared to flout the law so that they could be interred in finer fabric. But the Atkinsons were plain people and thus – as the register certifies – George was buried 'in woollen only'.[11]

Following George's wishes, control of the tannery passed to John, his elder son. Matthew, the younger son, inherited the property beyond Temple Sowerby as well as bonds representing money owed to his father. A few years later, after his brother's premature death, Matthew took over the tannery.

SOMETIME IN THE mid-1720s, Matthew bought the farmhouse in Temple Sowerby that would be home to the Atkinson family for the next 250 years, and he immediately embarked upon a programme of building works that included the addition of the upstairs corridor which became known, rather grandly, as the gallery. He married Margaret Sutton of Kirkby Lonsdale in April 1727; as though declaring his intention to establish a vigorous new branch of the family, Matthew ordered his and his bride's initials, and the year of their wedding, to be chiselled into the red sandstone lintel above the front door.

Through this entrance, a narrow passage opened into low rooms on either side. To the left was the main living space, with mullioned windows and a large fireplace, and a ladder leading to a loft. To the right, a cosy parlour led through to the smoky kitchen, where hams and other hunks of curing meat dangled from hooks in the ceiling, and peat smouldered in the hearth; also off the parlour, a creaking staircase led up to the gallery and the sleeping quarters. Matthew

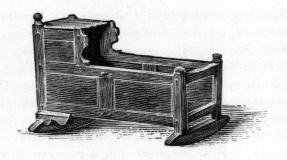

The oak cradle in which the Atkinson children spent their first years.

and Margaret's five children soon filled the house with noise: Jane, who was born in 1728, followed by George, Margaret, Matthew and last, but emphatically not least, Richard in 1739.

Details of their childhood must remain blurry, since the paper trail from this period is non-existent. Much of their growing up would have taken place outdoors, as there were always chores to be performed – cows to milk, pigs to feed, fields to dig, fruit to pick, wood to gather, peat to cut. Certainly, the boys fished in the nearby river; the shooting in the fields and woods around the village was off limits, however, since their father, not being a freeholder, did not have the right to kill game. Likely they played 'Scotch and English', a game in which the players of two teams launched raids into the territory of their opponents in order to steal their coats, meanwhile running the risk of being captured and taken prisoner. This 'active and violent recreation', which was popular in the border country, would have gained further significance for the village lads after 15 December 1745, when a Jacobite force passed through Temple Sowerby – one Atkinson legend tells of family members being forced to give up their pocket watches by the Scots rebels.[12]

What the Atkinson children received by way of education is a matter of conjecture. It's very possible the boys attended the excellent free grammar school at Appleby, but their names are nowhere to be found in the school's (extremely patchy) historical records. The Rev. Carleton Atkinson – no relation – who was a graduate of

Queen's College, Oxford, and rector at Temple Sowerby for forty years, may have tutored them at some point. They were all bright, but the youngest boy, Richard, was exceptionally so. It must have been obvious that his talents transcended the confines of the Eden valley, since somehow – I have no idea what chain of connections might have led to this – he landed a position as a clerk at the house of Samuel Touchet, a merchant of considerable influence based at Aldermanbury in the City of London.

Few traces remain of Richard's earliest years in London. The first evidence I have unearthed of his existence there comes at the end of a legal document relating to the transfer of some land in Temple Sowerby, which he witnessed in London on 14 September 1755.[13] This is also the first sample of his handwriting that I have come across. At sixteen, his signature had not yet developed its ultimate panache, but it already showed considerable self-confidence, underscored by a succession of delightfully superfluous loops – and only slightly undermined by a few blotches, which reveal its author not to be in full command of his ink.

The most conclusive proof of Richard's association with Samuel Touchet would be his contract of apprenticeship. Because stamp duty was imposed on the premium charged by a master, such contracts were registered by the authorities; details of all the apprenticeships entered into between 1710 and 1811 can be found in the National Archives at Kew, contained within seventy-nine bulky volumes that are also, mercifully, searchable online. But here's a puzzle. There's no evidence that Richard was ever apprenticed to anyone. Yet it was while they were both working for Touchet that Richard forged a lifelong friendship with a young man who definitely *was* an apprentice: Francis Baring, the son of a prosperous Exeter wool merchant. (Baring's widowed mother paid £800 for his seven-year apprenticeship, which started on 20 November 1755, when he was fifteen; the hefty premium reflected Touchet's prestige in the City.)[14] So how did Richard manage to get his foot in the door?

In his will, dated 6 March 1755, Matthew Atkinson bequeathed £200 to each of his two elder sons, George and Matthew, and £100 to Richard, which suggests previous expenditure on the latter's behalf. Matthew would die 'of a Jaundice' on 15 April 1756. 'He was not only one of the largest Dealers in his Way in the North,' noted the *Public Advertiser*, 'but also one of the most honourable.'[15]

THE MOTTO ENGRAVED on the face of the longcase clock in the gallery at Temple Sowerby was an hourly reminder of life's brevity – 'Remember Man / That Dye thou must / And after that to / Judgment Just' – and perhaps its message had rubbed off on George Atkinson, who was eager to enter the state of matrimony. He had been visiting his neighbour Biddy Shepard one day in 1756 when he first encountered Bridget Maughan, and was so taken with her that he soon found it convenient to call on her at home in Wolsingham, fifty miles away in County Durham. Theirs would not be a smooth courtship.

Bridget's father, Michael Maughan, had been a mining agent, prospecting for lead and copper on the Duke of Queensberry's estates in Lanarkshire, but died when he was twenty-six. His widow, Dorothy, who hailed from old Cumberland gentry, raised Bridget and her younger daughter Jenny at Kirkoswald, a village twelve miles down the valley from Temple Sowerby, in an extended family surrounded by cousins. Dorothy was a controlling mother who would resort to tears when other methods of coercion failed; as a result, perhaps, both girls were notably secretive when it came to matters of the heart. Apart from a stint at Mrs Paxton's academy in Durham, where they were schooled in the wifely arts of sewing and linen-dressing, the Maughan girls received no formal education. I would guess it was Dorothy who taught them to read and write, for Bridget's writing was almost identical to her mother's; furthermore, her spelling was wildly erratic, and she would remain more or less a stranger to punctuation her entire life.

In October 1755, when Jenny Maughan was nineteen and staying with friends in Newcastle, she fell in love with James Graham, and the couple were hastily engaged. Their idyll lasted a fortnight before Dorothy heard about it, pronounced Graham unsuitable, and commanded her daughter to sever the connection. Jenny's broken heart cast a long shadow over the family during the following months, and it was under its lingering influence that George Atkinson started courting Bridget, a compliment which she rewarded with a robust brush-off:

Sir, I had your Letter and do remember what you said when you were at Wolsingham but you'll excuse me when I tell you I know your Sex a Little better than belive one word of it. When I was Last at Temple Sowerby I was told you courted Miss Thomson of Bowes and I belive it is so. I have the greatest reason to respect you for your great civility both to my Sister and myself. I shall always esteem you as a friend but no pitty for I am very sure your Heart is as safe as ever it was at Least for me.[16]

As a matter of fact, Bridget liked George more than she let on, but was afraid to encourage him, foreseeing her mother's disapproval. Dorothy, who was proud of her pedigree – which included a smidgen of Plantagenet blood – would no doubt say the Atkinsons smelled of trade, and an odoriferous one at that. Gentry they most definitely were not. There was, however, another reason for Bridget's guardedness during the summer of 1756 – for her heart was already under siege.

Earlier that year, Dorothy had moved to Wolsingham, the home of her parents-in-law, perhaps after falling out with one or more of her sisters. In these new surroundings, she might have felt that two unmarried daughters reflected badly on her; in any case, when a local gentleman started courting Bridget, Dorothy pressed her to accept his hand. So far as the daughter was concerned, though, the match was unthinkable. In the ensuing battle of wills, Bridget's friends feared she would be the one to give way first.

In August 1756, Bridget received a diverting parcel of books from her cousin James Tinkler, a merchant in London, accompanied by a letter full of family gossip and news of the opening salvos of a war with France. James was clearly worried about Bridget, for the letter to his 'Dear Coz' opened with the admission that he had been 'perplexed with a Thousand Fears' for her welfare. With regard to an ongoing commission, he could report only modest success: 'I have Collected a Few more Shells which I shall Send with the Other Things, and I Promise you I Lett nothing of that kind Slipp that I Can Procure. But it's now Fashionable for the Ladies to decorate their Rural apartments with Them, which makes them Both Scarse and Dear.'[17]

James Tinkler was not the only one with concerns about Bridget's beleaguered state of mind. By September, she had still not decisively turned down her suitor's proposal, and her standoff with her mother was now the subject of local tittle-tattle. 'How hard it is to think that people might be quite happy and there own parents make them quite miserable,' wrote Biddy Shepard, who knew that Bridget was soft on George Atkinson, and was keen to promote his suit:

> If you can only try for a littel bitt of More Spirit and Resolve
> to fight throw it and not Sink under the weight of what Some
> people would only Look on as trifels and who knows but you
> may yet make that worthy fellow happy that would be willing
> to be seven times hanged and let down agane for you, and if not
> him Some body else that disarves you. Never however throw
> your Self away on a *munkey* that all the World agrees is not
> worthy of you.[18]

*

TEA ARRIVED IN England in the 1650s, and was initially a luxury enjoyed only by the very rich. Over the following century, however, tea drinking turned into a British obsession, so much so that high-minded individuals began preaching against the moral consequences of the habit. One forthright critic of the beverage was the reformer Jonas Hanway, whose *Essay on Tea*, published in 1756, pinned many social ills on it, including rotten teeth, a soaring suicide rate and a loss of bloom in chambermaids. (He had a point about the teeth; the growth of tea drinking went hand-in-hand with a boom in the consumption of the sugar used to sweeten it.) The East India Company, as the holder of the monopoly on trade with the Orient, ought to have entirely fulfilled the nation's demand for tea; but the commodity was so exorbitantly taxed that around half of the leaves landing on British shores were imported illegally from the continent. James Corbet, a merchant and ship-owner from Dumfries, is known to have smuggled tea from the Swedish city of Gothenburg via the Isle of Man. His business ledgers record that George Atkinson – a regular visitor to Dumfries – purchased a pound of 'Singlo green tea' from him for 8s 6d on 30 September 1756.[19]

For George, the following winter was purgatorial, for he heard not a word from the object of his affection. On 4 March 1757, after months of silence, he could stand it no longer, and decided to enlist Bridget's sister Jenny to his cause, placing a small package addressed to her on a cart to Wolsingham. 'Good Tea I know is a thing not very common in your country, yet an article which I think Ladies ought always to be Indulged in,' George wrote in his accompanying letter. 'I have lately met with a parcell which takes my fancy vastly, yet knowing my Deficiency of Judgement in those things, I have sent a sample which I hope you'll give me your opinion of the first time I see you. I have every week since Christmas been expecting News from your Place of some Conquest this Winter,' he continued, a note of despondency creeping in, 'but I find you keep these things too closely amongst yourselves. Oh Jenny (as the Scotchman says) keep a good gripp of your heart, for after that's gone I now find (by Experience) uneasyness, Jealousy &c follows, and always assure yourself of this, that it's much easier for a person not in Love to persuade his Mistress he has a Passion for her, than for those who Loves with the greatest Sincerity.'[20]

Poor, lovelorn George – such an appeal carried its risks, but perhaps he felt he had little to lose. Certainly, his petition appears to have done him no harm. Over the following months, Bridget made it clear that one way or another, whether her mother liked it or not, she would marry George Atkinson.

On the morning of 7 January 1758, George rode out from Temple Sowerby, following the Eden ten miles downstream, past the ancient standing stones known as Long Meg and her Daughters, to St Michael's Church at Addingham. The village itself no longer existed, having been washed away when the river changed course in the fourteenth century; only the parish church remained. There he met Bridget, who was staying with her Tinkler relations in Kirkoswald and had stolen away for a few hours. Their wedding ceremony could not have been more discreet. At this solemn, lonely place, in the low midwinter light, they must have believed their secret to be safe.

They had hoped to keep it under wraps until Whitsunday, but news of their marriage somehow reached Wolsingham a few days later. Bridget, in palpable distress, dashed off a note to her sister: 'I beg Dear Jenny you will use your intrest to paceffy my Mother and to prevaill with her to alow me to come home a Little whille indeed my happyness depends upon it. I beg you'll write soon and tell me the worst.'[21] Her aunt Barbara Tinkler also wrote to Dorothy: 'Dear sister, Whether the News of your Daughter Bridget's being married to Mr. George Atkinson may be so Gratefull to you, as I could wish, I cannot Conjecture. But as I understand, She formerly acquainted you with her intentions I hope it will not be so Surprising to you. The man has a very good Character, and we all hope will make a kind and indulgent husband.' On the reverse, Bridget added a mournful paragraph of her own. 'Dear Mother,' she implored, 'till I have a Line from you I can never be easy. Alowe me once more to desire your Blessing and Leave to come over which if you do not grant will make me very unhappy perhaps to my Lives end.'[22]

MOTHER AND DAUGHTER made their peace. The *Gentleman's Magazine* recorded the match in the mercenary language of the day:

> Mr. Atkinson, tanner, near Appleby – to Miss Maughan of
> Wolsingham, Durham £3000.[23]

Bridget brought a tidy dowry to the marriage. George immediately set about enlarging the house at Temple Sowerby, which must have felt gloomy and old-fashioned. If his aspirations or his budget had been greater, he might have opted to pull the whole thing down and start again from scratch; instead he tacked on a symmetrical front extension built of brick, two storeys high and five bays wide. The new front door opened into a double-height hall; to either side was a well-proportioned reception room, and on the floor above were two commodious bedrooms. The old and new parts of the house connected to each other via a narrow corridor. The extra living space would soon prove its worth, but from an architectural point of view the overall effect was clumsy. It was as though two very different houses were huddled too close together, each treading on the other's toes.

While George supervised a succession of bricklayers, carpenters, plasterers and painters at Temple Sowerby over the spring and summer of 1758, Bridget stayed at Wolsingham, where she greatly missed her warm-hearted husband. George soon made a favourable impression among the Maughans' circle in Wolsingham by sending over some leather to help a struggling cobbler. 'He was stunned and could not tell how to express his gratitude and I hear says he never had so much given in his Life,' Bridget reported back. 'In short my Dear George has made a poor Family happy which is to me a greater pleasure than I can express, much more so than when you tell me you have Wainscoted the parlour to Oblidge me.'[24]

By the autumn, the house at Temple Sowerby was habitable. Newly installed as its mistress, Bridget duly received and then returned social calls from all the neighbours, which necessitated much sipping of tea. Such proprieties were especially tiring for her now that she was in the early stages of pregnancy. In mid-November, George wrote to sister-in-law Jenny at Wolsingham to say that while Bridget was well and cheerful, she was so busy completing her local visits before winter set in that she hoped her mother would forgive the lack of a letter that week.

In January 1759, the entire Atkinson family converged on Temple Sowerby to celebrate the feast of Twelfth Night. Matthew, who was George's partner at the tannery, had picked up a cask of West Indian tamarinds for Bridget at Whitehaven on his way back from a business trip to Dublin. Richard had come up from London, stopping off to meet sister Margaret (a woman of almost suffocating piety) and her husband George Taylor at Bowes in County Durham; the three of them had travelled together the last thirty miles over the desolate pass at Stainmore and down into the Eden valley. Two hours after the arrival of the Bowes contingent, Bridget wrote to Jenny with a pithy assessment of her youngest brother-in-law, whom she was meeting for the first time: 'Dicky is a very Smart Youth.'[25]

Over the winter Bridget kept Jenny occupied making baby clothes. 'As I knew you were very busy working for me,' Bridget wrote in late January, 'I shall say nothing about your not answering my Letter. I fancy you will be at a Loss for directions about the Little things. The Long Lawn I intend for skirts and some ordinary caps which you may border with what Leaves of the Cambrick of which you may make six caps, four Laced ones of the fine and two plain ones of the coarse. You need be in no hurry as I hope if all be well we shan't want them before May.'[26]

A boy was born in June 1759, but would die in infancy. A second child followed in February 1761, a girl called Dorothy. Two weeks after his daughter's arrival, George sent off a bulletin to Jenny, reporting on the happy progress of Bridget and 'her little Dolly'.[27] Alas, at this point in the narrative, the family correspondence dries up, a drought that would last more than a decade. To state the obvious: for old letters to provide the basis for a story, they need not only to have been written, but also to have been preserved. Now that George and Bridget were living under the same roof, they no longer had reason to write to one another; meanwhile most of the extended Atkinson family were in regular contact with each other in or around Temple Sowerby. Richard's communications from London were rare and wondrous happenings. 'I am glad that you have heard from Brother Richard,' wrote Margaret to eldest sister Jane on such an occasion. 'I think you are highly favoured.'[28]

As for the Maughan side of the family, they were touched by tragedy. Jenny never got over her forced separation from James Graham, and his death three years later – he left her his gold watch – further lowered her spirits. She died at Temple Sowerby in January 1762, at the age of twenty-five – a melancholy event that deprived Bridget of her only sibling and closest correspondent.

THREE

Atlantic Empire

LONDON IN THE 1760s. From the ashes of the great fire a century earlier had risen a sprawling metropolis of three-quarters of a million people; the gabled timber houses which kindled the devastation had been replaced by flat-fronted terraces of fireproof brick, while stone edifices such as the Mansion House trumpeted mercantile prestige on an imperial scale. The Lord Mayor was chosen each year from among the twenty-six aldermen of the City of London, an ancient office held in 1762 by William Beckford, the inconceivably wealthy owner of three thousand slaves in Jamaica.

London was a filthy place, notable for its pall of coal smoke that smeared the sky and caught in the back of the throat. Pedestrians took care to avoid treading in the contents of chamber pots strewn across the cobbles. 'Except in the two or three streets which have very lately been well paved,' observed a Frenchman visiting in 1765, 'the best hung and richest coaches are in point of ease as bad as carts; whether this be owing to the tossing occasioned at every step by the inequality of the pavement, or to the continual danger of being splashed if all the windows are not kept constantly up.'[1] The back alleys of the city clanked and clattered with the workshops of craftsmen – bootmakers, cabinet-makers, confectioners, cutlers, gunsmiths, haberdashers, hatters, mercers, milliners, perfumers, printers, saddlers, silversmiths, sword-cutters, tailors, watchmakers, wigmakers – while glass-fronted emporia lined its main thoroughfares.

'The shops in the Strand, Fleet-street, Cheapside, &c. are the most striking objects that London can offer to the eye of a stranger,' wrote the same Frenchman. 'They make a most splendid show, greatly superior to any thing of the kind at Paris.'[2]

Driving London's prosperity was trade, underpinned by the Navigation Acts. The first of these laws had been passed during the 1650s, to challenge Dutch commercial dominance, but they had since grown into the regulatory system that governed Britain's trade with the rest of the world. The guiding purpose of the Navigation Acts was to keep the benefits of trade within the empire, and they enshrined the basic principle that raw materials produced in the colonies, such as sugar, cotton and tobacco, could only be conveyed to Britain or another of her colonies in a British ship, while all foreign-produced goods bound for America or the West Indies had to be shipped first to Britain to be taxed, then carried onwards in a British ship. It was axiomatic that the role of the colonies was to generate wealth for the mother country.

The privileged status conferred upon British shipping by the Navigation Acts gave rise to a mighty merchant fleet; and nowhere was its strength more visible than on the four-mile stretch of the River Thames from London Bridge downstream as far as Deptford. In summer months the 'Upper Pool' near the Tower of London resembled a dense forest of masts, and it was often remarked that you might walk from one side of the river to the other, stepping from deck to deck.

On the north bank of the Thames stood the Custom House, the portal through which so much of the nation's taxable wealth passed in the form of sugar, coffee and indigo from the West Indies; tobacco, rice and cotton from America; timber, hemp and iron from the Baltic; and tea, silk and porcelain from China. The busiest period, from May to September, was marked by the arrival of hundreds of West Indiaman ships, heavy with muscovado sugar that would first be processed in one of the capital's eighty refineries, then stirred into the tea on which everyone was so hooked; there was often such a backlog that a cargo might sit around for two months before

The crowded quays fronting the Custom House.

clearing customs. Meanwhile, in the maze of streets behind the quays, hundreds of clerks sat hunched over ledgers in the dim light of their masters' counting houses, totting everything up.

Which is where young Richard Atkinson, albeit tentatively, enters the frame. Even by the standards of the day, his employer Samuel Touchet was a ruthless capitalist – not that this word had yet entered the lexicon. The eldest son of Manchester's wealthiest manufacturer of linen and cotton goods, Touchet had moved to London in the 1730s to gain better access to the market for the commodities needed by his family firm. The Touchets were early investors in Lewis Paul's roller-spinning machine, whose operation required so little skill that anyone would be capable of spinning 'after a few minutes' teaching', as the 1738 patent application boasted – 'even children of five or six years of age'.[3] During the late 1740s, Samuel Touchet was responsible for importing more than a tenth of England's raw cotton, and rivals suspected him of attempting to create a monopoly; by 1751, he and his three brothers together owned about twenty ships, some of which plied the infamous 'triangular' trade.

*

THE ROYAL AFRICAN COMPANY had been established under charter from Charles II in 1672, with the purpose of setting up trading posts and factories along the Gold Coast – modern-day Ghana – and exploiting the continent's ready supply of gold and slaves. By the 1750s, Britain had eclipsed Portugal to secure dominance in the slave trade; every year during that decade, British ships carried about 25,000 enslaved Africans across the Atlantic, destined for the colonies of the West Indies and the American mainland. The 'African trade' was largely accepted as a necessary evil; the economist Malachy Postlethwayt declared it to be of 'such essential and allowed Concernment to the Wealth and Naval Power of Great Britain, that it would be as impertinent to take up your Time in expatiating on that Subject as in declaiming on the common Benefits of Air and Sun-shine'.[4]

Brightly dyed, striped and checked cotton textiles, like those made by the Touchets in Manchester, were in great demand in West Africa. Indian fabrics were the benchmark against which all others were judged, but knock-off versions were fast gaining market share, and the Touchets' were among the best. (British manufacturers continued to use the Indian names – *calico* and *chintz* would enter the English language.) As Thomas Melvil, the governor of Cape Coast Castle, the principal British slave trading post on the Gold Coast, informed the Company of Merchants Trading to Africa in August 1754: 'If the Ashantee Paths open the Goods wanted will be Guns, Gunpowder, Pewter Basons, Brass Pans, Knives, Iron, Cowries, Silks. The Bejutapauts will go out. Of these Touchet's are here preferred to India.'[5]

At the same time, while merchants in Liverpool, Bristol or elsewhere packed their vessels with goods to be bartered for human cargo, West African men, women and children snatched from inland villages were marched to European forts on the coast, to be sold by their captors on to a Danish, Dutch, French, Portuguese or (most likely) British slave ship. It might take a ship's captain weeks, or even months, to purchase enough human cargo to fill its hold; two Africans per ton (bearing in mind that in shipping terms, tonnage

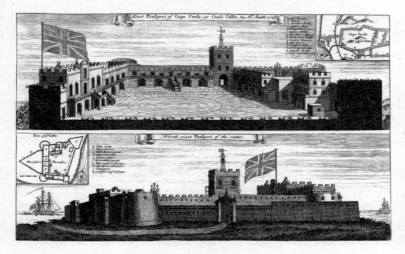

Cape Coast Castle, the main British slave trading fort on the Gold Coast.

is a measure of volume) was considered the 'right' load. The transatlantic leg of the voyage – known as the 'middle passage' – lasted around two months, and never was so much suffering crammed into so little space. Shackled and naked in the stifling heat of the ship's belly, unable to relieve themselves except on the bare boards where they lay, rolling in blood, vomit, excrement and urine, occupying less space than a coffin, it is hardly surprising that many captives sought to end their own lives. Some tried drowning themselves, others refusing food; but it was dehydration, caused by a water ration of just one pint a day, hastened by sickness and dysentery, that would prove most deadly of all. The crew simply tossed the corpses over the side without giving them a second thought. Roughly one in ten Africans died during the middle passage.

On arrival in the Americas, the survivors were prepared for sale. Their dark skin was slathered with a mixture of gunpowder, lemon juice and palm oil, then polished with a brush, to create the illusion of glistening good health. Grey hair was either shaved off or dyed black. The backsides of those suffering from dysentery were bunged with oakum, the tarred fibre used for filling gaps between timbers in wooden ships. Human cargoes were often sold by the method known as a 'scramble', in which the Africans were taken to a merchant's yard, the gates were suddenly thrown open, and the buyers rushed in, grabbing hold of their prey 'with all the ferocity of brutes'.[6] At this point, families were often separated for ever. Afterwards, the newly purchased men, women and children were branded with the initials of their master or estate, and assigned 'slave names' to strip them of their previous identities; the men were often given names of generals or gods from classical antiquity, such as Apollo, Brutus, Cupid, Hannibal, Jupiter and Ulysses, as if to mock their degraded state.

Once the ship's decks had been swabbed, then loaded up with sugar, coffee, tobacco and other commodities, it was ready to make the third side of the triangle, and return to Britain, to start this appalling cycle all over again. A triangular slave voyage typically lasted around eighteen months. The export of manufactured goods to West Africa, then the purchase of the labour with which to produce the raw materials, then the import of those raw materials from the Americas – as a business model, the diabolical logic of the triangular trade could hardly be faulted. Archive records indicate that ships owned by Samuel Touchet and his brothers took part in at least four triangular slave voyages. The first three vessels sailed to the Gold Coast between 1753 and 1757; there they embarked a total of 541 Africans, subsequently disembarking 455 in Jamaica.[7] The statistics of the Touchets' fourth voyage mark it out as a catastrophic venture. The *Favourite* sailed from Liverpool in January 1760, taking on board seven hundred Africans at Malembo in what is now Angola; by the time of its arrival at the sugar island of Guadeloupe the following January, only four hundred were still alive.[8]

TRADE AND WAR have always been energetic bedfellows. During the global conflicts of the eighteenth century, ministers regularly consulted merchants for their superior knowledge of distant lands, as well as their practical experience of shipping and finance. Meanwhile, for the business community, war represented opportunity. One manifestation of this murky symbiosis between merchants and ministers was privateering, an activity considered by some to be 'but one remove from pirates'.[9] At least two of Samuel Touchet's vessels carried 'letters of marque' – the licences granted by the Admiralty to British merchant ships, permitting them to seize vessels belonging to enemy subjects. One of Touchet's ships, the *Friendship*, was about to sail to the West Indies when it received its letter of marque in October 1756, shortly after the start of the Seven Years' War; the weaponry allocated to its crew of forty men included 'sixteen Carriage Guns, thirty six Small Arms, thirty six Cutlaus, twenty five Barrels of Powder, thirty Pounds of great shot and about fifteen hundred weight of small shot'.[10]

But Touchet had his eye on altogether greater spoils. He and a fellow merchant, Thomas Cumming, cooked up an audacious, secret scheme to invade the French colony of Senegal, fitting out and arming five ships at a personal cost of more than £10,000. Touchet's ships sailed from separate English ports on 23 February 1758 and rendezvoused at the Canaries; from here, by previous arrangement with his friend Admiral Anson, First Lord of the Admiralty, they continued in convoy with three warships. A bar at the mouth of the Senegal River proved impassable to the naval vessels, but Touchet's merchant flotilla landed two hundred marines and covered their march eleven miles upriver to Fort Saint-Louis. The French capitulated on 1 May. The adventurers returned laden with booty, including 400 tons of gum arabic – the sap of the acacia tree – a product essential in the printing of linens and calicoes, for which British textile manufacturers had previously been forced to pay premium rates.

So where, you might be wondering, has Richard Atkinson been all this time? There he is in the background, absorbing the rudiments of his trade; conversing with brokers and dealers at the Royal Exchange, or 'Change, the most cosmopolitan spot on earth; frequenting coffee houses, chiefly the Jamaica for West Indian business, Jonathan's for stocks and commodities, and Lloyd's for shipbroking and insurance; supervising the unloading of cargoes down at the

View of the TOWER of LONDON.

View of the CUSTOM HOUSE, LONDON.

View of the ROYAL EXCHANGE, LONDON.

Some places well known to the young Richard Atkinson.

quays; and generating reams of correspondence. Sadly, little evidence of Richard's personal life has survived from his twenties. I imagine he was less raffish than his contemporary, James Boswell, who left behind a journal of his first extended stint in London that is replete with tales of encounters with writers and prostitutes – yet this is pure supposition on my part. It's ironic and not a little frustrating that Richard, whose professional life was taken up with the meticulous recording of the smallest details, should have proved so mysterious in his private affairs – but happily, this would soon change.

We might infer that Richard attempted to smooth off the rough edges of his northern diction, for in May 1761 he attended a series of talks given by the Irish actor Thomas Sheridan, held at Hickford's Concert Room on Brewer Street, on the subject of elocution. Sheridan, who was the godson of Jonathan Swift, not only advocated the 'polite pronunciation' of the court, but believed that regional dialects carried 'some degree of disgrace' about them.[11] 'The letter R,' he declared, 'is very indistinctly pronounced by many; nay in several of the Northern counties of England, there are scarce any of the inhabitants, who can pronounce it at all. Yet it would be strange to suppose, that all those people, should be so unfortunately distinguished, from the rest of the natives of this island, as to be born with any peculiar defect in their organs.'[12] The price of admission – one guinea – included an 'elegant Edition' of the lectures in a single quarto volume, and Richard's name is listed (as are those of 'Mr. Francis Baring' and 'James Boswall, Esq') among the book's six hundred or so subscribers.[13]

At the general election in the spring of 1761, Samuel Touchet was elected MP for Shaftesbury. Weeks later, a financial crisis almost engulfed him. As the merchant Joseph Watkins wrote to the prime minister, the Duke of Newcastle, on 28 May 1761: 'Private credit is at an entire stand in the City, and the great houses are tumbling down one after the other, poor Touchet stopped yesterday & God knows where this will end.'[14] Touchet's merchant house ultimately came crashing down in October 1763, with debts of more than £300,000.

After Francis Baring's apprenticeship expired in November 1762, he went on to set up a London office for his family firm. Business was precarious at first, and his mother Elizabeth, alarmed by his speculations, counselled him to 'let Mr. Touchet's example of grasping at too much and not being contented with a very handsome profit which he might have had without running such enormous risks, be a warning to you'.[15] Richard Atkinson, on the other hand, helped wind up Touchet's affairs – a task he was said to have performed 'with great ability' – before taking up a position as a clerk to the West India merchant Hutchison Mure, who was based at Nicholas Lane, off Lombard Street.[16]

SAMUEL FOOTE'S COMEDY, *The Patron*, opened at London's Haymarket Theatre in June 1764. It featured Sir Peter Pepperpot, a West Indian plantation owner with an 'over-grown fortune', drooling at the thought of a 'glorious cargo of turtle' and dreaming of a girl as 'sweet as sugar-cane, strait as a bamboo, and her teeth as white as a negro's'.[17] Such men were ripe targets for satire – although they usually had the last laugh, for their money bought them land, status and power.

Richard Atkinson's new boss, Hutchison Mure, was one of those men who sought to convert the base metal of their West Indian fortunes into the gilded trappings of the landed aristocracy. Hailing from the younger branch of a well-connected Renfrewshire family, Mure had come to London in the 1730s. After a short spell as a cabinet-maker, he entered the West India trade, having acquired some Jamaican property through his marriage. Soon, by his mid-thirties, he had made enough money to purchase the Great Saxham estate in Suffolk. His growing portfolio of Jamaican properties, meanwhile, included one called Saxham, after his English country seat, and another called Caldwell, after the Mure ancestral home in Scotland.

It seems that Mure, who is listed in the *Register of Ships* for 1764 as the owner of eighteen vessels, was an enthusiastic participant in the slave trade. Between 1762 and 1766, over the course of eight voyages, 2,959 Africans embarked on the middle passage aboard his ships, and 2,527 disembarked in the West Indies, all but 521 of them landing in Jamaica.[18]

The first of these voyages was the anomaly, in that it diverted at the last moment to Cuba, which on 14 August 1762 had fallen temporarily into British hands; Mure's ship, the *Africa*, landed its human cargo at Havana on 18 October. Two months later, presumably feeling flush from the profits that would follow, Mure commissioned Robert Adam to design a new house for him at Great Saxham. Adam dreamt up a vast Palladian villa with a *piano nobile* featuring a suite of rectangular, square, circular and octagonal state rooms – the plans are kept at Sir John Soane's Museum, and they are magnificent. For reasons unknown, however, Mure's palazzo never made it off the drawing board; instead he settled for the lesser option of incorporating some Adam interior designs into the old Jacobean house.

Now in his mid-fifties, Mure hoped to retire from active trade and live out the rest of his days in rusticated splendour. He was a practical man, and fascinated by agriculture; the philosopher David Hume, an old family friend, described Mure as 'a Gentleman of a very mechanical Head', as well as 'one of the most judicious Farmers and Improvers' to be found in the eastern counties.[19] And so his West India merchant house required a succession plan. Although one of Mure's three sons, Robert, was already a partner, he lacked the flair to head such an operation; but Richard Atkinson might just be the man for the job. In 1766, aged twenty-seven, Richard became Hutchison and Robert Mure's junior partner.

Mure, Son & Atkinson, as the new partnership would be known, began in the wake of the Seven Years' War, when Britain was for the first time the truly dominant global power. An almost indecent number of colonial territories had been seized from France and Spain during that conflict – to the extent that Lord Bute, the prime minister, realized that concessions would be necessary to avoid a peace so humiliating to the losers that they would soon be spoiling for another fight. The question was, which of the captured colonies should Britain keep, and which ones should be given back? The debate – on which much journalistic ink was expended – focused

mainly on the relative merits of Canada versus the islands of Guadeloupe and Martinique.

The argument for holding on to the tiny West Indian territories
and ditching Canada was obvious to most people – Guadeloupe's
exports alone were worth twenty times more than the fur trade of
'barren' Canada. 'What does a few hats signify, compared with that
article of luxury, sugar,' sniffed one gentleman.[20] But the West India
lobby, not enjoying the competition provided by the former French
islands – the wholesale sugar price had fallen 20 per cent since their
capture – pushed hard for their restoration to their previous owners.
The American colonists favoured the same outcome, albeit for different reasons. Benjamin Franklin, the agent of the Pennsylvania
Assembly in London, wrote:

> By subduing and retaining Canada, our present possessions in
> *America*, are secured; our planters will no longer be massacred
> by the *Indians*, who depending absolutely on us for what are
> now become the necessaries of life to them, guns, powder,
> hatchets, knives, and cloathing; and having no other *Europeans*
> near, that can either supply them, or instigate them against us;
> there is no doubt of their being always disposed, if we treat
> them with common justice, to live in perpetual peace with us.[21]

In the end, the colonists prevailed. Under the Treaty of Paris,
which came into effect on 10 February 1763, Guadeloupe and Martinique went back to France, while Cuba was returned to Spain;
Britain held on to Canada, Florida and the sugar islands of Grenada,
Saint Vincent, Dominica and Tobago.

The Seven Years' War had started in America, escalating out
of all imaginable proportions from skirmishes in the Ohio valley
between colonists loyal to the British flag and an alliance of French
settlers and Native American tribes. Victorious Britain now found
itself mired in a national debt of historic proportions, and unable to
afford adequate protection for its newly acquired American territory, as was soon proved by a series of Native American attacks on

British forts and settlements to the south of the Great Lakes. As a result, in October 1763, George III issued a proclamation forbidding colonial settlement beyond a line drawn along the Appalachian watershed – much to the fury of land speculators who were intent on expropriating Indian territory.

Lord Bute resigned from the premiership after less than a year; George Grenville, who was said by the king to have the 'mind of a clerk in a counting-house', took over as prime minister and set about putting the nation's finances in order.[22] It would only be fair, he argued, for American colonists to help pay for the troops needed to defend the newly enlarged empire; while each Briton contributed about twenty-six shillings to the imperial coffers every year, each American gave about a shilling.

But American colonists always made a point of challenging the mother country's efforts to squeeze money out of them. The only revenue-raising taxes to which they would readily agree were those voted by their local assembly, while the only 'external' taxes remotely palatable to them were those used to regulate the trade of the British empire in its entirety, such as the import duties that fell within the Navigation Acts. Yet the Americans had signally failed to enforce the Molasses Act of 1733, which aimed through a duty of six pence per gallon to make molasses from the French West Indies prohibitively expensive, and thus tie the rum distillers of New England to the produce of the British sugar islands.

Grenville reckoned that if this duty were cut, making it cheaper to import French molasses legally than to pay the bribes and run the risks that attended smuggling, it would have the counter-intuitive effect of raising revenue; and so parliament voted to halve the tax on foreign molasses, to three pence per gallon, from April 1764. The Sugar Act sparked outrage in America. 'There is not a man on the continent of America,' fumed Nathaniel Weare, the comptroller of customs in Massachusetts, 'who does not consider the Sugar Act, as far as it concerns molasses, as a sacrifice made of the northern Colonies, to the superior interest in Parliament of the West Indies.'[23] A writer in Rhode Island's *Providence Gazette* ranted that

American interests had been trampled by a 'few dirty specks, the sugar islands'.[24] Their common hatred of the Sugar Act united the New England colonies for perhaps the first time, and set them on a collision course with the mother country.

BRITANNIA RULED the waves, for the time being, and her navy patrolled the waters of the North Atlantic and Caribbean, watching for French and Spanish attempts to violate her citizens' interests. To give one trivial example, tensions had long festered over British loggers' claims to the timber in the Spanish-held territory of Honduras. It is amid such rumblings that Richard Atkinson makes a fleeting appearance, in the earliest letter that I have found in his hand, dated 29 June 1764. He writes to the Secretary to the Treasury, Charles Jenkinson, with information from the merchant grapevine: 'As any Intelligence concerning the Bay of Honduras will I presume be acceptable I take the Liberty to send you an Extract of a Letter from the Same Hand as the former . . .'[25] The letter may not make for stirring reading, but it proves that Richard was already cultivating contacts at the very highest political level.

Meanwhile, George Grenville announced a new tax on the American and West Indian colonies. A stamp duty – such as had existed in the mother country since 1694 – would be payable on a range of paper items, from almanacs, newspapers and playing cards to conveyances, diplomas, leases, licences and wills. Each colony would appoint its own stamp distributor, who would take a small cut of the proceeds, but otherwise the tax would be largely self-regulating, since without its stamp any official document would be null and void. The bill passed through the House of Commons 'almost without debate'. Only Colonel Isaac Barré, a fearless orator whose left eye had been shot out during the capture of Quebec five years earlier, punctured the chamber's complacency with a 'vehement harangue' in which he argued that the very reason the colonists had emigrated to America was to flee such measures.[26] The king gave his assent to the Stamp Act on 22 March 1765. No one could have predicted its consequences.

Resistance erupted in Boston on 14 August, when the newly appointed stamp distributor for Massachusetts was hanged in effigy from the 'Liberty Tree'. It was unsurprising that the Bostonians should be foremost among the 'Sons of Liberty' – who took their name from a phrase used by Colonel Barré – since theirs was a literate and litigious mercantile community upon which the duty would weigh heavily.

By the time the Stamp Act came into force on 1 November, it was clear that the Americans' refusal to accept the duty would have a disastrous effect on trade, since without legally stamped port clearance papers their merchant ships might be seized at any time. Relations between the American and West Indian merchant communities were already frayed; now the mainland contingent resolved to cut off trade with all those sugar islands that submitted to the Stamp Act. The Jamaicans were the most acquiescent of all – they paid more stamp duty than all the other colonies put together. One Canadian newspaper, reporting an outbreak of yellow fever in Jamaica towards the end of 1765, quipped that 'the Inhabitants of the Town of Kingston fed so voraciously on the stamps, that not less than 300 of them alone died in the Month of November'.[27]

Although the Jamaicans certainly disliked the Stamp Act, pragmatism deterred them from rejecting it. Whereas the mainland assemblies resented being asked to pay for their own defence, the Jamaican Assembly actively volunteered a financial contribution, at the same time lobbying for an enhanced military presence on their island. The British sugar islands were surrounded by French and Spanish territories, and common sense dictated that these old enemies would soon seek to avenge their humiliation in the Seven Years' War. Most of all, however, the planters feared attacks from within. As the ratio of blacks to whites increased on the islands – in Jamaica it was roughly ten to one – so did the danger of slave insurrections. In November 1765, as the Stamp Act started to bite, an uprising broke out in the parish of St Mary, on the north side of the island; although it was soon quashed, it must have concentrated the colonists' minds.

Six prime ministers would hold office during the 1760s. The Marquess of Rockingham, replacing Grenville, adopted a more conciliatory tone towards the Americans – but it would be William Pitt's denunciation of the Stamp Act which finally persuaded Rockingham that repeal was the only way out of the crisis. Over three weeks, from 28 January 1766, a committee of the whole House considered the proposed repeal bill, with a succession of merchants coming forward to describe the negative impact of the Stamp Act on both sides of the Atlantic. The star witness was the 'celebrated electric philosopher' Benjamin Franklin, as the minutes describe him – his experiments concerning the nature of lightning had made him one of the scientific establishment's most venerated figures. Before 1763, Franklin testified, there had always been 'affection' among Americans for the mother country; but recently he had begun to be 'Doubtfull of their Temper'.[28]

Early on the morning of 21 February, MPs started bagging seats in the House of Commons in anticipation of the afternoon's debate. Pitt warned that parliament's failure to repeal the Stamp Act would lead to civil war, and cause the king 'to dip the royal ermine in the blood of his British subjects in America'.[29] For the time being, His Majesty's robes remained snowy-white; for both houses passed the repeal bill, along with a face-saving 'declaratory bill' that asserted parliament's right in principle to tax the colonies, and the king gave his assent on 18 March. American and West Indian merchant ships moored on the River Thames marked the news by hoisting their colours and blasting off their guns.

THE AMERICANS HAD MANAGED to overturn one piece of hated legislation; now they took aim at the Sugar Act. On 10 March 1766, at a gathering of colonial merchants held at the King's Arms Tavern in Westminster, the West Indian contingent agreed that the three pence duty that Americans paid on foreign-produced molasses could drop to a single penny. This was a massive climbdown on the West Indians' part; and yet, to their great dismay, when the American Duties Act passed into law in June 1766, it imposed a penny per

At its 'funeral', the Stamp Act is taken in a tiny coffin to a burial vault reserved for especially detested laws.

gallon duty on *all* molasses imported into the mainland colonies, thus eliminating any advantage possessed by the British sugar islands over the French. These reforms were too technical to be of much public interest, but they marked a further cooling in relations between the colonial merchant lobbies. By now the West Indians wholly distrusted the Americans, believing them to be motivated by treacherous ambitions to trade freely with the French.

Until the 1760s, the West Indian interest in the City of London had been informally managed. The Society of West India Merchants emerged as a lobbying organization sometime during this decade; its precise origins are obscure, since the minutes taken at its meetings before 1769 no longer exist. Under its chairman, Beeston Long, the society usually met on the first Tuesday of the month at the London Tavern, a dining establishment on Bishopsgate Street; attendance ranged from three (a quorum) to many more when feelings about some issue were running high. As the merchants tucked into turtle flesh – these gentle beasts lived in the cellars, in tanks painted with tropical scenes to make them feel at home – they chewed over the concerns of their trade. According to parliamentary records,

Richard Atkinson was among a delegation from the society summoned by Alderman William Beckford to the House of Commons in May 1766 in a last-ditch attempt to steer the arguments around the American Duties Act in the West Indians' favour.[30] The society's records show that during the 1770s Richard attended around six meetings every year; unfortunately the minutes are so cursory, and so devoid of descriptive colour, that it is impossible to gain much sense of his contribution.

The association between a merchant house such as Mure, Son & Atkinson, and the West Indian planters it served, rested on mutual confidence – not least because an exchange of letters between London and Jamaica often took four months or more. The merchant conveyed a planter's sugar crop back to England and brokered its sale, taking a 2½ per cent cut of the proceeds. It also sourced and shipped out any tools, provisions and other items required for the smooth operation of the planter's estates, subject to a mark-up; it recruited his overseers and book-keepers, and arranged their outward passage; it acted as his banker, paying bills of exchange drawn on his account, and advancing credit whenever necessary; it even oversaw the education of his children and ran his shopping errands. In short, it took care of his every need in the mother country.

But it was not quite a relationship of equals. So long as his account remained in credit, the planter maintained a degree of control; as soon as his expenses exceeded his remittances, however, the merchant gained the upper hand. The sheer precariousness of the sugar business – where hurricane, drought or rebellion could wipe out the year's produce at a stroke – drove many proprietors deep into debt, as what started out as modest loans ballooned into unsustainable mortgages secured against their property. The merchant could foreclose whenever he chose, and many men, including Hutchison Mure, were guilty of seizing clients' estates by this means.

John Tharp, who owned a number of estates in north-west Jamaica, retained Mure, Son & Atkinson as his London agents from 1765 to 1772. A cache of the firm's letters sent to Tharp's plantation house in St James Parish has survived, heavily watermarked and discoloured from years of storage in the tropics. Most of the correspondence is in Richard's handwriting, and it is illuminating about the seasonal rhythm of the West India trade and the volatility of the sugar market. The cane crop was cut and processed during the early months of the year. Gradually, over the summer, merchant ships returning from the West Indies appeared in the Thames, weighed down with their sticky cargo; if too many ships came at once, the glut drove down the price of sugar, while a scarcity early or late in the season pushed it upwards. The letters stamped on the large hogshead barrels in which the sugar was transported identified the estate on which it had been produced; its quality could be highly variable. 'Those of the Mark PP were much better than those of the same Mark last Year,' Richard wrote to Tharp on 13 July 1767, 'for these were only *very brown*, those of last Year were *black*.'[31] ('PP' signified Pantre Pant, a plantation that was managed by Tharp in the parish of Trelawny.)

Each autumn, Mure, Son & Atkinson sourced John Tharp's plantation 'necessaries' and other domestic goods, which were shipped out to Jamaica once the hurricane season had safely passed. In December 1767, in time for Christmas, the enslaved population of Tharp's estates were lucky enough to receive 1,107 yards of coarse Osnaburg linen and the needles with which to stitch the cloth into garments; meanwhile, for the master and his wife, there were tailored frock coats with gold buttons and braid, kid mittens, a 'very Neat Demi peak Sadle with red morrocco Skirts and doe Skin Seat neatly stitched stirups Leathers & Girths', a pair of brass pistols, a 'Copper Tea Kitchin with 2 heaters', twelve canisters of hyson tea, a 'Gadroon'd Cruit frame', a case of pickles containing 'Capers Girkins Olives Mangoes Mustard Oil Soy Wallnutt French beans Colly flower Anchovies', a hogshead of claret, casks of lavender and rose water, a selection of wallpapers, fine grey hair powder, guitar strings and the score of the *Beggar's Opera*.[32]

NO CENSUS EXISTS to permit more than a guess at how many black people were living in London at this time. 'The practice of importing Negroe servants into these kingdoms is said to be already a grievance that requires a remedy,' reported the *Gentleman's Magazine* in 1764, 'and yet it is every day encouraged, insomuch that the number in this metropolis only, is supposed to be near 20,000.'[33] This figure seems likely to have been an overestimate, but not wildly so. Among the wealthy, black servants had cachet, while black children were often treated as toys, to be returned to the colonies once they grew up or their owners tired of them. Samuel Johnson – who was more enlightened about these matters than most – famously employed a black manservant, Francis Barber, to whom he would leave the residue of his estate.

In clarification of the Navigation Acts' requirement that all merchandise must be transported to and from the colonies in British ships, the Solicitor General had ruled in 1677 that 'negroes ought to be esteemed goods and commodities' under the law.[34] But while the institution of slavery was woven into the fabric of colonial law, its status was not so certain in the mother country. According to one famous Elizabethan ruling, England was 'too pure an Air for Slaves to breath in', and many contradictory opinions had since been offered up.[35] In 1749, Lord Chancellor Hardwicke pronounced that a slave in England was 'as much property as any other thing'; whereas in 1762, Lord Chancellor Henley declared that 'as soon as a man sets foot on English ground he is free'.[36] It seems baffling that such men, the greatest legal minds of their time, could be so changeable in their judgements on a question that could surely be seen as none other than the choice between right and wrong.

In September 1767, David Laird, the captain of one of Mure, Son & Atkinson's ships, the *Thames*, was caught up in a dispute arising from the ambiguous status of a human 'commodity' destined for Jamaica. The episode had its origins two years earlier, however, when Granville Sharp, a clerk in the ordnance department based at Tower Hill, found a young black man of about sixteen injured outside the Mincing Lane premises of his brother William Sharp, a surgeon well known for treating the poor. It seemed that David Lisle, a lawyer who had brought the youth – whose name was

Jonathan Strong – from Barbados, had beaten him with a pistol so repeatedly that he had almost lost his sight and could hardly walk. William Sharp had Strong admitted to St Bartholomew's Hospital; Granville Sharp later found work for him as the delivery boy for an apothecary on Fenchurch Street.

One day during the summer of 1767, Lisle spotted Strong by accident and tricked him into entering a public house. There, backed up by two burly officials, he sold him to James Kerr, a sugar planter who was one of Mure, Son & Atkinson's clients. Kerr insisted he would only pay the £30 purchase price once Strong was securely on board the *Thames*, which was then preparing to sail for Jamaica. In the meantime the young man was thrown into the Poultry Compter, one of several small prisons dotted about the City. It was from here that, on 12 September, Granville Sharp received Jonathan Strong's letter begging for help.

Sharp called upon Sir Robert Kite, the Lord Mayor, in his capacity as London's chief magistrate, and requested that all those with an interest in Strong should argue their claims in open court. At the hearing on 18 September, Captain Laird and James Kerr's lawyer both insisted that the young man belonged to Kerr by virtue of a signed bill of sale. After heated debate, Kite stated that 'the lad had not stolen any thing, and was not guilty of any offence, and was therefore at liberty to go away'. Laird immediately grabbed Strong by the arm, saying that 'he took him as the *property* of Mr. Kerr', whereupon Sharp threatened to have him arrested for assault. Laird released Strong's arm, and all parties left the courtroom, including Strong, 'no one daring to touch him'.[37] Kerr subsequently pursued a court action against Sharp, seeking damages for the loss of his property; he persevered with the suit through eight legal terms before it was dismissed.

The thought that right here, on the streets of London, black people could have been lawfully snatched, sold and transported against their will to the colonies, seems almost unfathomable today; but such was the reality of the Atlantic empire. This particular incident was noteworthy only in that it galvanized the man who would come to be seen as the father of the anti-slavery campaign, twenty years before Wilberforce and Clarkson took up the cause. Granville Sharp subsequently became a formidable expert in habeas corpus, and his book, *A Representation of the Injustice and Dangerous Tendency of Tolerating Slavery*, would be the first major work of its kind by a British author. Which is how, in a blink-and-you-missed-it kind of way, Richard Atkinson came to be a bystander at the dawn of the abolition movement.

FOUR

Four Dice

THIS WAS AN AGE of polymaths, a time when gifted amateurs made strides in the fields of astronomy, botany, chemistry, mechanics and physics. Two of Richard Atkinson's closest friends in the early 1770s were George Fordyce and John Bentinck, both Fellows of the Royal Society, founded in 1660 for the purpose of 'improving natural knowledge'. Fordyce, a physician and lecturer in chemistry at St Thomas's Hospital, was also a member of Samuel Johnson's Literary Club, where his shambolic manner inspired various anecdotes. On one occasion, following a bibulous dinner, Fordyce was supposedly called out to attend to a fine lady. Unable to locate her pulse, he muttered under his breath 'Drunk, by God!'; the next day he received a letter from his patient containing £100, begging him not to disclose the intoxicated state in which he had found her. Bentinck, a naval captain, was also a skilled engineer, best known for developing a ship's pump that became standard issue throughout the Royal Navy. Some believed him underrated; Benjamin Franklin thought his 'ingenious Inventions' had not always 'met with the Countenance they merited'.[1] Captain Bentinck would die in his thirties, in 1775 – Richard was his executor.

Robert Erskine was another engineer who was much in Richard's orbit around this time. He had moved to London from Edinburgh in the mid-1750s, and for six years had used Hutchison Mure's premises as his postal address in the capital. Erskine's talents as an

inventor seem to have been offset by bad luck in his financial dealings; in 1762 he was briefly committed to the debtors' prison. Soon
afterwards he began work on a new pump, calling it the 'Centrifugal
Hydraulic Engine'.[2] Only two were ever sold – one to the Venetian
ambassador and the other for use in a salt mine belonging to the
King of Prussia – and when Erskine fell out with an investor over
their losses, Richard and his friend Captain Bentinck stepped in as
arbitrators. Subsequently Erskine set up as a surveyor with a particular expertise in hydraulics, and established a practice at Scotland
Yard in Westminster. By 1770, the year that he published 'A Dissertation on the Rivers and Tides, to Demonstrate in General the
Effects of Bridges, Cuttings, or Imbankments, and particularly to
Investigate the Consequence of such Works, on the River Thames',
he had acquired some impressive clients, and his luck – like the tide
– seemed to be turning.

Richard, however, had other plans for Erskine. Since 1765,
Mure, Son & Atkinson had been part-owners of an ironworks at
Ringwood, New Jersey, about forty miles north-west of New York.
This enterprise had started at great tilt a few years earlier under
its founder, Peter Hasenclever; by the summer of 1766 its assets
included four blast furnaces, seven forges, ten bridges, thirteen mill
ponds and more than two hundred workers' dwellings. Before long,
Hasenclever had run through the £54,000 capital he had raised in
England to fund the venture. He returned to London in November
1766 after learning that one of his partners had declared bankruptcy.
In May 1767 Richard Atkinson was appointed a trustee of the business; Hasenclever was demoted to the position of agent, and soon
resigned in disgust.

Following Hasenclever's departure, the ironworks struggled.
The trustees' monthly letters of instruction to Reade & Yates of
Wall Street, their New York agents, carrying Richard's signature as
the managing partner in London, are a sorry catalogue of setbacks.
Disobeyed instructions, delayed shipments, impatient creditors and
accounting discrepancies – such are the perennial frustrations of
long-distance business relationships. By January 1770 the trustees

distrusted both the ironworks' managers, one of whom had been caught embezzling their money, and the other squandering it. 'An honest & a capable man is what we want,' they told Reade & Yates.[3] Robert Erskine answered such a description – but it is something of a mystery why he accepted Richard's invitation to cross the ocean to run a failing ironworks. Perhaps he perceived the American colonies as a place where he and his wife, who had recently lost their only child, might start again; maybe the salary of two hundred guineas, plus 5 per cent of the profits, was after years of financial troubles too powerful a lure to resist.

To remedy his lack of experience in the iron trade, Erskine gave himself a crash course in its practicalities during the autumn of 1770, when he spent two sodden months touring Britain's most prominent ironworks, including Coalbrookdale in Shropshire and the Carron Company in Stirlingshire. Often he turned up at sites unannounced, finding workmen more than happy to show him round in return for a few shillings. ('A very agreeable present to men who with families of 6 or 7 Children earned only 12s. a Week,' he would observe.)[4] Along the way, Erskine gathered dozens of lumps of iron ore which he boxed up and sent back to London for chemical analysis by George Fordyce.

Every few nights, by the guttering candlelight of his lodgings, he wrote a long letter to Richard in London, describing all he had seen; thirteen of these dispatches have survived, and they paint a vivid picture of iron production at the start of the industrial revolution, as the charcoal furnaces producing soft, malleable iron suitable for the blacksmith's forge were superseded by the hotter coke-burning furnaces of the coalfields. At Bersham in Denbighshire, for example, Erskine watched white-hot iron flowing from a furnace into the sand mould for one of fifty cannons ordered by the King of Morocco, protecting his eyes from the glare by 'Cutting a small hole in a letter and looking through it', and observed the barrel of another cannon being bored by a drill bit fixed to the axis of a water wheel, a procedure that 'made a very disagreeable noise which at a distance was much like that of Geese'.[5]

In late October, en route to Scotland, Erskine broke his journey at Temple Sowerby. During his stay, perhaps seeking respite from George and Bridget Atkinson's noisy brood, he worked out the height of Cross Fell, using his quadrant and a dish of mercury to provide a reflective 'false horizon'. It was a rare cloudless day. 'The Old Gentleman was so civil as to remain uncovered,' he told Richard, referring to the mountain, 'which was the more polite, as he had not been so long bare headed for many days before.' By Erskine's reckoning, Cross Fell stood 3,731 feet above the meadow by the bridge over the River Eden; while a benchmark chiselled into one of the quoins of Temple Sowerby church states the village itself to be 348¾ feet above sea level. He believed his measurement to be 'pritty accurate', but it turns out he was off by more than a thousand feet, for Cross Fell in fact stands 2,930 feet tall.[6]

During his final weeks in London, Erskine must have wondered whether he had made an error in accepting Richard's offer of employment, especially when turning down a commission from the Dean and Chapter of Westminster to survey their estates. In January 1771 he was elected a Fellow of the Royal Society; one of his nominees was Benjamin Franklin. Before sailing to America, Erskine wrote Richard a heartfelt note: 'I cannot have forgot the abject state to which I was reduced some years ago, nor can I ever fail calling to mind your kindness in suffering me to be a burthen to you. I am thus free in acknowledging my sentiments & obligations to prevent the most distant suspicion of ingratitude, which were it to rise in the bosom of such a friend would hurt me as much as anything I ever met with.'[7]

ALEXANDER FORDYCE was a banker well on his way to becoming one of the wealthiest men in the land; he was also the uncle of Richard's physician friend George Fordyce, although just six years separated the older man from his nephew. It was Alexander who, having witnessed the deft way in which Richard dealt with Samuel Touchet's unravelling affairs, had urged his associate Hutchison Mure to take on this impressive young clerk. Richard repaid the favour by offering Fordyce his unswerving loyalty.

Perhaps Fordyce saw something of himself in his protégé, for both men were the youngest children of provincial middle-class families. Fordyce had started out as the apprentice to an Aberdeen hosier, but soon leapt over the haberdasher's counter and moved to London, where he found work as the outdoor clerk to a well-known banker. He started gambling in the public funds and stocks, and made a small fortune in 1762, towards the end of the Seven Years' War, 'at the time of signing the preliminaries of the late peace, of which he gained intelligence before the generality of the bulls and bears at Jonathans'.[8] He was less risk-averse than his peers and, for a while, a good deal luckier.

By 1768, Fordyce was managing partner of Neale, James, Fordyce & Down of Threadneedle Street. It was said that his 'pride kept pace with the increase of his fortune', and when the firm moved to premises opposite the Bank of England, he insisted that his name should be listed first on the brass plate, even making hollow threats to terminate the partnership if his senior partners did not comply.[9] Fordyce stood for Colchester in the general election that year, and Richard canvassed alongside him for several weeks. After spending £14,000 on wooing the townsfolk – a lavish sum, even by the venal standards of the day – Fordyce lost by twenty-four votes, an outcome he attempted fruitlessly to reverse by raining down charges of bribery and corruption on his opponents. 'I really think we shall *force* the Mayor to return Mr. Fordyce,' wrote Richard from the battlefield, with characteristic vim.[10]

At the height of his pomp, Fordyce purchased a princely country house at Roehampton, nine miles south-west of London, filling it with fine furniture and works of art – Raphael cartoons and suchlike – that gave every appearance of riches and sophistication. He landscaped its spacious grounds, which adjoined Richmond Park, in the naturalistic style promoted by Lancelot 'Capability' Brown, felling an avenue of sixty mature elms using a contraption of Captain Bentinck's devising 'for drawing up trees by the roots' – after wrapping a long chain around the trunk, it took four men about twenty minutes to prise each tree from the earth.[11]

Now, to complete his ascent to the pinnacle of society, Fordyce was on the hunt for a suitably dazzling wife. His brother James, a Presbyterian minister, was courting the governess to the children of the newly widowed Countess of Balcarres. (James Fordyce's ponderous *Sermons to Young Women*, published in 1766, would later achieve dubious fame when Jane Austen had Mr Collins read them to the less-than-enthralled Bennet sisters.) Shortly after his brother's engagement, Alexander Fordyce called upon Lady Balcarres while passing through Edinburgh, and was struck by her second daughter, Lady Margaret Lindsay, an auburn-haired girl of fifteen. The countess, at first appalled by the thought of such a vulgar connection, was soon won round – the Lindsays were poor by aristocratic standards, and the pecuniary advantages of the match were obvious. (By supporting the Jacobite uprising of 1715, the third Earl of Balcarres had ended his days under house arrest, leaving his estates deep in debt.) Fordyce married his noble bride in June 1770 at her ancestral home on the Fifeshire coast; he was forty, she was seventeen. They set off for London the next day.

IT IS AT THIS POINT in the story that Richard Atkinson comes at last into sharper focus; because Lady Anne Lindsay, the elder sister of his patron's wife, was a dedicated lady of letters, and would go on to write about him at great length.

Anne Lindsay was a defiantly independent young woman who refused to conform to many of the conventions of submissive female behaviour. During her early years in Edinburgh, she had acquired a keen interest in literature and the arts, and a reputation as an accomplished conversationalist; she had also turned down a fair few proposals of marriage. She was thought very pretty, although perhaps not quite as arrestingly so as Margaret, from whom she had hitherto been inseparable. (The playwright Richard Brinsley Sheridan would call them 'Beauty's twin-sisters'.)[12]

Anne would later describe how, during the lonely months after Margaret's marriage, she daily climbed up to her little closet where, with pen in hand, she scribbled away 'poetically and in prose' in pursuit of 'artificial happiness'.[13] That winter Anne wrote a ballad that may have reflected her own ambivalent feelings about the state of matrimony. 'Auld Robin Grey' told the story of a simple country girl who, believing her true love to be dead at sea, marries an old man out of duty; a few weeks later her sweetheart returns from his unexpectedly long voyage. This bitter-sweet song would become famous – William Wordsworth called it one of the 'two best ballads, perhaps, of modern times' – although Anne was always reticent about revealing herself as its author.[14]

During the spring of 1771, when she was twenty, Anne left Scotland to take up residence with the Fordyces in London. After five days on the road, her carriage pulled up at a small door in Holywell Lane, a narrow street off Shoreditch. The Fordyces were away at the time, at their country house, and Anne was ushered into the drab apartment by servants. As first impressions go, this did not augur well; had she not known that her brother-in-law was in the midst of building a splendid mansion in Grosvenor Square, she later commented, she would have been mortified by these surroundings, which offered no clues of elegance, apart from a pair of beeswax candles on the table 'instead of the mutton-fats' she was accustomed to.[15] At noon the following day, Anne spied the Fordyces' coach with 'three well-powdered footmen behind it' pulling up outside the house; she ran downstairs, and the sisters tearfully embraced.[16]

She soon noticed a young man standing nearby, 'his arms crossed, and with an expression of benevolence, admiration, and what the French call bonté in his countenance'. From this moment on, Anne Lindsay and Richard Atkinson – who, at thirty-two, was twelve years her senior – would get along famously. She immediately felt him to be a 'sort of family friend', with whom she was on the same 'footing of ease' as if she had always known him: 'I was convinced I had done so, his countenance assured me of it; it was hearty, open, intelligent to the greatest degree, and it was impossible not to forgive the familiarity of his manners when ineffable good-humour and zeal was the basis.' Social deference was not one of Richard's habits. 'Zooks,' she recalled him saying, 'life is too short for bowing and scraping. When people esteem one another beforehand, it should make short work of the business of introduction.'[17]

Even so, an earl's daughter, arriving in London for the first time, was expected to observe certain formalities, foremost among them her presentation at court – it being reckoned 'improper' to be seen out in public until 'their Majesties had had the first glance'.[18] Until then, Anne had been quite innocent of the distinction drawn by fashionable people between 'the Man of the World and the Man of Business', but she now perceived the gulf dividing 'even the plain Country Gentleman' from the 'inhabitant of Cheapside'.[19] She also realized that her brother-in-law was a bore, and that the reason they did not receive many dinner invitations was because those who would have been delighted to welcome the sisters 'would not consent to pay the tax of his company for the *agrément* of ours'. The dinners hosted by the Fordyces were dreary affairs, generally attended by a 'few unpleasant men relieved only by the excellent Atkinson'. At one such gathering, Anne caught Richard gazing at her and Margaret with 'an expression that had an esteem and reverence in it, that I thought was almost accompanied with a sad feeling that such a pair should be no better associated'.[20]

DURING THE SPRING of 1772, Richard began to notice that Fordyce was preoccupied; on top of the 'hard bravery of manner and false spirits' that he habitually projected, a certain wildness in his behaviour suggested something was wrong.[21] When Richard voiced his concerns, Fordyce burst into tears and confessed to business problems, then tried to laugh them off. Pressed further, Fordyce revealed that only a miracle would prevent his bankruptcy.

Early on the morning of 9 June, Fordyce, without warning, told Margaret and Anne that they must leave town immediately; he then bundled them into the coach 'like frightened hares', slammed the door and ordered the coachman to deliver them to the country house at Roehampton.[22] That evening, he returned to Holywell Lane and packed up his papers. Richard stayed with him through the night. Fordyce left shortly after dawn, instructing his clerk to inform his partners that it was 'impracticable to carry on business'.[23] At noon on 10 June, the bank of Neale, James, Fordyce & Down stopped making payments.

While Fordyce lay low in an obscure corner of the city, Richard rushed to Roehampton. At about six o'clock he entered the parlour, finding Anne busy with her needles and silk; his face, she saw, was 'pale and haggard'.[24] He took her hand and was silent for a moment, before revealing that Fordyce was ruined, and that bailiffs would soon be arriving to take possession of the house. The sisters hurriedly stuffed their clothes into bed sheets and set out for London in two coaches, the second of which was full of dresses. Richard did his best to buoy their spirits, but Anne soon realized he was masking his own fears. When she asked whether he had been caught up in Fordyce's misfortunes, he replied 'no' with an agony that pierced her soul: 'I saw that ruin hung impending over his own head, and that he spared to Margaret at that moment the knowledge of what would have added to her distress.'[25] Fordyce's bachelor brother William, an eminent doctor, had offered the sisters sanctuary at his house in Sackville Street, off Piccadilly. In the gloaming of the physician's parlour, Richard at last explained what had led to this catastrophe.

During the Falklands crisis of 1770, when it had briefly seemed that a diplomatic standoff between Britain and Spain over those remote South Atlantic islands might lead to war, Fordyce had gambled heavily on the stock market, paying handsomely for inside information from secret negotiations that were taking place on the continent. The news with which his spy had set sail ought to have made him a fortune; but a thick fog descended at sea, forcing the ship into port for twenty-four hours. Fordyce lost his advantage, and instead incurred large losses. More recently, Fordyce had received letters from India, sent by the faster but less reliable overland route via Basra, Aleppo and Constantinople, describing events that were almost guaranteed to bring down the East India Company's stock price. He had quickly 'borrowed' an enormous quantity of stock and sold it short, intending to buy it back at a lower price and pocket the difference. But the stock price stubbornly refused to drop – instead it rose – so that when the day of settlement for Fordyce's transaction arrived, he had a 'difference of ten per cent to pay on half a million, some say, a million and a half, of India stock'.[26]

At the beginning of June 1772, the Bank of England, alarmed by a sudden decline in its gold reserves due to excessive demand from Scotland, announced that it would no longer accept many Scottish bills of exchange. These were the indispensable tools of credit of the time, pieces of paper on which one merchant made a promise to pay another a certain sum on a fixed date several months down the line. Bills of exchange were entirely transferable – they could be used by the recipient to pay a third party, or could be cashed sooner than the stated deadline, at a small discount, by a banker acting as a 'bill broker'. They kept the wheels of commerce turning; the economist Adam Smith would vividly describe the role of paper bills, in providing a substitute for gold and silver coin, as 'a sort of waggon-way through the air'.[27] Since much of the business of Neale, James, Fordyce & Down was with Scottish accounts, Fordyce could no longer obtain funds to cover his liabilities, and his opulent façade crumbled to dust.

RICHARD VISITED THE SISTERS the next morning, bringing the latest news from the City; so far there had been five major bankruptcies, and many more were expected. For now, Mure, Son & Atkinson held firm – but so closely intertwined were the affairs of the mercantile community that it was impossible to say whether it would survive. Later that day the wife of one of Fordyce's partners, unhinged by her nine children's reduced prospects, cut her own throat with a razor.

By now Fordyce was universally reviled, especially since it was rumoured he had hidden large sums from his creditors. With many bailiffs out to take him into custody, it was decided that the following Sunday, 14 June, by the light of the full moon, he would ride down to a port on the south coast and slip away to France; for his ledgers were in such disarray that to open them up to scrutiny at this point would only further blacken his name. On the continent he would have time to smooth out any irregularities within his accounts; and then, within the three months' deadline imposed by the bankruptcy laws, he could return to London and face justice.

Fordyce had not seen his wife since before the crisis began, and a last visit was fixed for ten o'clock on the night of his departure. Margaret begged Richard to be present – both sisters had come to rely upon his support – but asked him to delay his arrival by half an hour so that Fordyce, who would doubtless be in great distress, might have time to compose himself. When Richard turned up at Sackville Street – tactfully late as requested – he found the sisters, as well as William and George Fordyce, anxiously waiting in the parlour. At last there was a hammering at the front door, and Alexander entered in a mood of such exuberance that 'had a cannon-ball swept us all low, the company would not have had their powers more annihilated than by his manner'. Watching Fordyce drain great bumpers of port, as though celebrating some triumph, Anne wondered whether he had been 'deranged by his misfortunes', but on balance thought not, for she could detect 'no phrenzy in his eyes'. Richard had noticed some 'ugly fellows' lurking on the street corner as he was arriving, and he went home just before midnight, wearing Fordyce's clothes to act as a decoy.[28] Fordyce himself departed several hours later, after arguing violently with his wife. Later that morning all were relieved to hear that he had left for Dover, taking £100 advanced by Richard to cover his expenses.

The crisis came to a head in London on 22 June. 'It is beyond the power of words to describe the general consternation of the metropolis at this instant,' reported the *Gentleman's Magazine*. 'The whole city was in an uproar; many of the first families in tears.'[29] The day started with the news that one of the City's greatest banks had stopped payment, having rashly accepted £100,000 worth of Scottish bills, and a false rumour was circulating that the Bank of England would soon follow suit. At the Adam brothers' ambitious Adelphi housing development near Charing Cross, where the largely Scots workforce were entertained by perambulating bagpipers, two thousand men were laid off.

Horace Walpole, the wittiest commentator of his day, offered a characteristically lively appraisal. 'Will you believe,' he wrote, 'that one rascally and extravagant banker had brought Britannia, Queen of the Indies, to the precipice of bankruptcy!' A story, repeated by Walpole, did the rounds that Fordyce had visited a Quaker banker, begging for a loan. 'I have known several persons ruined by *two dice*,' the old man was said to have replied, 'but I will not be ruined by *Four dice*.'[30]

Relative calm only returned to the London markets later in the week, after the Bank of England stepped in to offer credit to some of the City's most reputable merchants and financiers. But it would not prop up the Ayr Bank, a splashy new operation underwritten by two dukes – Queensberry and Buccleuch – which had over the

Alexander Fordyce, clutching a purse full of gold and a 'Scotch Bill' for £10,000.

previous three years pumped out some £200,000 in paper notes. The Ayr Bank stopped payments of coin for their notes on 25 June. 'We are here in a very melancholy Situation,' wrote David Hume, in Edinburgh, to Adam Smith, who was hard at work on *The Wealth of Nations.* 'The Carron Company is reeling, which is one of the greatest Calamities of the whole, as they gave Employment to near 10,000 People. Do these Events any-wise affect your Theory? Or will it occasion the revisal of any chapters?'[31]

LADY ERSKINE, a young widow with a highly developed sense of social decorum, took pity on the Lindsay sisters in the last week of June, and invited them to stay with her in Hanover Square. After breakfast on their first morning there, a 'visitor of considerable fashion' called on their hostess; a few minutes later, Richard's arrival was announced. The sisters squirmed with embarrassment. He clearly had no idea that an invitation from Lady Erskine might be necessary, or that he should at least have asked them to pave the way for his call by mentioning that he might wish to see them – such delicacies as these 'his heart would have scouted as the frippery of politeness'. As he strode across the drawing room to greet them, Anne noticed the reaction of their hostess. 'The chill of Lady Erskine's regard, I might say the contempt,' she recalled, 'might have driven all the warm blood of Atkinson's body into his heart, like the drop of brandy which is above all proof, had he perceived it; but he was not thinking about her, and was blind as a beetle.'[32]

Richard had come with the latest news from the City. Now that the worst was over, he said, it was time 'to bury the dead, and support those who have survived it'. Soon the first visitor left, and since Lady Erskine's frostiness had been 'only to mark to the other that he was not one of *her set*, being a citizen, and one of the people employed to stop if possible the fall of the Stocks', she was now perfectly civil towards him. 'Your Mr. Atkinson,' she remarked to the sisters after he had taken his leave, 'I really take to be a good creature.' Her loftiness vexed them; as Anne later wrote:

To have been angry would have placed us in the wrong; was he not a good creature? And the best of all good creatures? He was not a man of fashion. Why then be angry at Lady Erskine for calling him what he was? Because we wished her to respect him both on our account and his own, and she would not give a particle more than was barely due to him whom she esteemed *mauvais ton*, which was with her the greatest nuisance it was possible to bring into society. His smile, his bow, his method of walking straight down the throat of the person he talked to, all put her more out of temper than I thought her collected manner would have condescended to be.[33]

Soon afterwards, the Countess of Balcarres arrived to take her daughters home to Scotland. 'It was the kind Atkinson who had our last sorrowful look on departing,' Anne recalled. 'He stood at the door of the carriage as if he was losing his all for the first time.'[34] Before heading north, the sisters spent a month with their uncle in Hertfordshire. The summer had been hot and dry, and a haze of dust lingered over the fields. One day, as her stay was drawing to a close, Anne was taking a 'little melancholy walk' in a shrubbery that opened on to the road, when a carriage stopped and Richard jumped out: 'I screamed for joy, and ran up to him as to our good Angel, could one be supposed stepping out of a Post-chaise.' So busy had Richard been salvaging his own affairs that he had barely left his desk during the intervening weeks. Anne asked him how much the partnership of Mure, Son & Atkinson had lost. 'By everything I can guess,' he replied, 'the sum will be above two & forty thousand pounds.' When she wondered what proportion of this amount he was personally liable for, he grasped her hand. 'Such a part,' he said, 'as sweeps bare every foundation on which presumption might have dared to build her castle.'[35]

AFTER A SUMMER of speculation about the whereabouts of the rogue banker – 'Mr. Fordyce must be a most compleat Ubiquarian,' observed one newspaper, 'since he possesses the strange power, if we credit what the public prints assert, of his being almost at the same instant in Holland, Italy, France and England' – he returned on 6 September.[36] He was lucky to be alive. A mile off the coast at Rye, the cutter on which Fordyce was crossing had snagged a wreck, gouging a hole in its bottom; the leak was temporarily plugged by a barrel of salt beef, and he and his fellow passengers had been rescued by a passing boat.

At midday on 12 September, passing with difficulty through the crowd gathered to jeer at him, Fordyce entered Guildhall. For the first two hours of his bankruptcy hearing, a succession of debts were proved before the commissioners, including £16,000 to the Bank of England and £35,000 to Mure, Son & Atkinson. Then the creditors began to interrogate Fordyce, first wishing to know how much of their money he had absconded with – to which Fordyce tearfully responded that, far from this being true, he had been obliged 'to borrow a small trifle from a friend, to pay for a few pair of stockings which he had occasion for on his journey'.[37] Some of the creditors were suspicious of Richard's role, observing that Fordyce had transferred large sums of money into his account during the week leading up to 9 June; but Fordyce accounted for this, explaining that Richard was a 'particular friend' who had 'on emergencies, given him bills on the Bank, which he gave in payment to the Bank Clerks in the morning and refunded the money to Mr. Atkinson in the afternoon'.[38]

The commissioners proved compassionate; they even returned Fordyce's pocket watch and Margaret's jewellery. 'The benevolent temper of the English nation never appeared more strongly than at Mr. Fordyce's examination last Saturday,' reported the *London Chronicle*. 'Calumniated as he had been in all the public prints, the moment he shewed himself only intentionally upright, resentment gave way to commiseration; his misfortunes even added dignity to his character, and the very rabble grumbled pity.'[39]

After the trial, the contents of the Fordyce residences were sold off at auction. Richard purchased a pair of horses, which he presented to Margaret; another kind creditor bought back her carriage. The playwright Samuel Foote acquired a single pillow; on being asked what possible use he could have for such an item, he was said to have answered: 'Why, to tell you the truth, I do not sleep very well at night, and I am sure this must give me many a good nap, when the proprietor of it (though he *owed so much*) could sleep upon it.'[40] Foote's next production, a satire called *The Bankrupt*, would draw heavily on Fordyce's woes.

THE BANKING CRISIS of 1772 was short-lived, but its ill effects would soon ripple around the empire, bringing a spell of optimism in the Atlantic economy to a close. Many American merchants found themselves with warehouses full of goods imported from Britain, and debts they could no longer discharge. This, in turn, ruined many businesses in the mother country. One British politician would later observe that the long credit terms allowed to merchants in the colonies, and the difficulty of recovering debts from them, had 'made bankrupts of almost three-fourths of the merchants of London trading to America'.[41]

Despite Robert Erskine's best efforts, the ironworks at Ringwood continued to test Richard and his fellow trustees' patience, and they finally resolved to put it up for sale. Advertisements appeared in the *New-York Gazette* in September 1772, but there were no takers. Meanwhile they instructed their American agents to sell off their pig iron warehoused in New York 'as fast & as far' as possible, only to find that Reade & Yates, themselves in deep financial trouble, had been stockpiling it for use as a currency with which to settle their own bills. 'Had your object been to destroy us as a Company,' the trustees wrote in December 1772, 'you could not have held a Conduct more likely to effect your Purpose.'[42]

Richard would with hindsight look back on 1772 as a year of 'horrors'. On a personal level, he had been working towards a larger share of the partnership, which he had hoped might assist a cause as yet unarticulated, but extremely close to his heart. Alexander Fordyce's bankruptcy not only demolished Richard's 'castles in the air'. It also had consequences that would ultimately lead to a great diminution of the Atlantic empire.

FIVE

All the Tea in Boston

TWICE A YEAR, great auctions of tea and other luxurious goods took place at the headquarters of the East India Company in London. The Bank of England invariably granted the Company a short-term loan before each sale, to ease its cash flow as it waited for accounts to be settled – £300,000 was the sum advanced in the spring of 1772. But with many merchants unexpectedly strapped for funds that summer and unable to pay their bills, even the almighty East India Company was snared in the financial crisis. When the Company defaulted on a payment to the Treasury in August, its wobbling finances became public knowledge and its stock price started to slide; within weeks it had tumbled from £225 to £140. The collapse, of course, came too late for Alexander Fordyce; had he been able to hold out till then, as one journalist pointed out in late September, he would have made as much money 'as not only would have settled all his affairs, but have left an handsome fortune for life'.[1]

The East India Company's problems stemmed partly from the American public's widespread reluctance to consume its tea. Back in 1767, after the repeal of the Stamp Act, parliament had introduced taxes on various items – glass, paint, lead, paper and tea – imported into the colonies. While bearing a superficial resemblance to the taxes used to regulate the flow of trade throughout the British empire, the purpose of these so-called 'Townshend duties' (named after Chancellor of the Exchequer Charles Townshend, their originator) was to raise money for the Treasury, which made them quite as unpalatable to many colonists as the Stamp Act.

The Americans had retaliated against the duties with the powerful weapon of non-importation, which kept out around 40 per cent of British imports. Their tactic worked. In April 1770, shortly after Lord North became prime minister, all the duties were repealed, apart from the one on tea – which was kept in order to assert parliament's authority to raise tax from the colonies. After the subsequent collapse of the non-importation movement, goods from the mother country flooded the colonies. Even so, contraband Dutch tea continued to dominate the American market; less than a quarter of the tea consumed there came through legal British channels. By the end of 1772, there were said to be seventeen million pounds of surplus leaves rotting in the East India Company's warehouses around the City of London.

The British government had for some time wished to rein in the overbearing East India Company, and its financial woes provided Lord North with vital leverage. Through the Regulating Act, passed in June 1773, ministers gained some control over the management of India; in return, the Company was granted a loan of £1,400,000, as well as concessions to help reduce its tea mountain. Under the Tea Act, all duties previously charged on leaves imported to Britain and then re-exported to America were cancelled; the saving could be passed on to consumers. Suddenly, a pound of the Company's fully taxed tea cost Americans a penny less than the smuggled variety. Ministers were confident that the lower prices would persuade American consumers to swallow their pride, but they were quite wrong; the colonists saw the Tea Act for what it was, a clumsy attempt to trick them into accepting the Townshend duty and thus the principle of parliamentary taxation.

On 20 August 1773, Lord North and his Treasury Board issued a licence for the export of 600,000 pounds of tea to the ports of Boston, New York, Philadelphia and Charleston. The *Dartmouth*, laden with 114 chests of tea, entered Boston harbour on 28 November; from then its captain had twenty days to pay the duty on his

The 'Mohawks' empty the tea chests into Boston harbour.

cargo, or else the vessel would be impounded. Leading merchants of the town, insisting that the tea must be rejected, requested a special clearance to allow the ship to leave port without unloading its cargo – but the governor of Massachusetts, Thomas Hutchinson, declined to grant permission. Soon two more vessels filled with tea arrived from London and moored alongside the *Dartmouth*.

On 16 December, the day before the *Dartmouth*'s customs payment was due, a crowd of several thousand gathered to hear the ship's owner, a local merchant, reveal that Governor Hutchinson remained adamant in his refusal to let it depart. As the meeting broke up in the late afternoon, a number of men dressed as 'Aboriginal Natives', their faces blackened with coal dust, 'gave the War-Whoop', a pre-arranged signal to hurry to the three vessels.[2] Over several hours, by the light of lanterns, these self-styled 'Mohawks' smashed open 342 chests of tea and threw them overboard. Next morning, at high tide, the broken-up tea chests could be seen bobbing above a vast slick of briny sludge that stretched across the bay.

BRITISH PARLIAMENTARY ELECTIONS during the eighteenth century were notorious for their bribery, bullying and other skulduggery – sins which could undoubtedly be laid at the door of Sir James Lowther, who owned great tracts of Cumberland and Westmorland, and whose sense of entitlement was so inflated that he saw the parliamentary seats returned by those counties, and all the boroughs within, as his personal property.

Much more importantly – at least for the purposes of this story – John Robinson was Lowther's law agent, land steward and chief stooge. Born in 1727 the son of an Appleby draper, Robinson had been articled to his uncle Richard Wordsworth, attorney-at-law to the Lowther family, at the age of seventeen. Over the years he had upset numerous people while executing his employer's orders, and many blamed the 'dirty attorney of Appleby' for the baronet's obnoxious behaviour in general.[3]

Lackey though he may have been, John Robinson did not lack political ambitions of his own. In January 1764, he was returned through Lowther's influence as MP for the county of Westmorland. He would (at least in the beginning) faithfully support his patron's interests, while forging a close friendship with another of Lowther's men, Charles Jenkinson, the MP for Cockermouth, who was at that time Secretary to the Treasury. In 1765 Robinson acquired a long lease on the White House in Appleby, which he remodelled in Venetian style; its ogee-arched windows remain to this day an incongruously exotic feature of the town's handsome main street.

George Atkinson was only three years younger than Robinson, and they must have moved in overlapping local circles; so it seems likely that they were already well acquainted when, in 1769, George applied to Robinson to sponsor a parliamentary bill permitting the enclosure of the common at Temple Sowerby. Indeed, Robinson may have urged George to make the application – for the enclosure of common land was a well-worn method of forging political allegiances, through the creation of freeholders who would gain the franchise. George had hitherto been ineligible to vote, for what land he owned was held under a thousand-year lease from the lord of the manor, Sir William Dalston. It certainly served Sir James Lowther's interest to facilitate the enclosure at Temple Sowerby, for he was at the time tussling with the Duke of Portland for political supremacy in the area. Dalston, for one, detected mischief in the scheme. 'The Lowtherians Resentment is so great,' he told the duke, 'as to spirit up my Lease-hold Tenants of Temple Sowerby to the Honourable House of Commons against me, for liberty to take up a large Quantity of waiste Ground where I am Lord, without consulting or acquainting me with it, and directly against my Opinion.'[4]

John Robinson's focus shifted from Westmorland to Westminster in 1770, on his appointment as Secretary to the Treasury under Lord North. The new prime minister – whose courtesy title, as the heir to an earldom, meant that he sat in the Commons, not the Lords – was one of the warmest men in politics, with a quick wit and a nice line in self-deprecation. In his appearance, North cut a clumsy figure, of which Horace Walpole offered this uncharitable description: 'Two large prominent eyes that rolled about to no purpose (for he was utterly short-sighted), a wide mouth, thick lips, and inflated visage, gave him the air of a blind trumpeter.'[5]

Robinson had been warned that his post at the Treasury would involve 'a Sea of Troubles', and it certainly required the mastery of several briefs.[6] There was the nation's financial administration, which tied him up in correspondence with officials throughout the land; there were twice- or thrice-weekly Treasury Board meetings, chaired by Lord North, after which Robinson was responsible for issuing all the necessary orders, contracts and payments of money; and there was the role of chief whip in all but name, through which he managed the prime minister's parliamentary business. Although the Secretary to the Treasury operated behind the scenes, he wielded great influence.

In the spring of 1773, four years after George Atkinson's application, Robinson at last placed his private bill to enclose 'Temple Sowerby Moor' before parliament; royal assent was granted on 28 May.[7] Now the commissioners appointed to oversee the division of the common could get to work. The 360 acres were distributed between the heads of twenty-four households in Temple Sowerby, and the resulting fields demarcated with hawthorn saplings; the area was then mapped out on parchment and executed as a legal document. George, who bankrolled the process, was allotted fifteen acres in lieu of his expenses, taking his overall share of the land to fifty-one acres.

GEORGE III OPENED PARLIAMENT on 13 January 1774 with a 'gracious speech' outlining his government's priorities for the coming session.[8] News of the Boston 'tea party' arrived a week later, however, and the unruly state of the American colonies suddenly trumped all other concerns. On 29 January, the cabinet agreed that strong measures would be needed to bring the colonies back into line; as a result, the passing of a series of 'coercive' acts would occupy parliament over the coming months.

Lord North announced the measures that would be contained within the Boston Port Act on 14 March; the town's harbour would be shut up for business until its people had made 'full satisfaction' to the East India Company for the destruction of the tea.[9] The House of Commons almost unanimously welcomed the legislation; even Colonel Barré, a hero to the Sons of Liberty, gave it 'his hearty affirmative'.[10] Three more coercive acts were nodded through before the summer recess, one of which revoked Massachusetts' 1691 charter and restricted the people's right of assembly; another allowed the governor to move a trial to Britain if he believed a fair hearing was unlikely in the colony; and a third permitted uninhabited houses, outhouses and barns to be requisitioned as accommodation for British soldiers. Meanwhile a law extending the boundaries of Canada, and guaranteeing the free practice of Catholicism there, angered many Americans, who saw it as an assault on their territory and their faith.

The 'intolerable acts', as they soon became known throughout the thirteen colonies, turned hordes of wavering loyalists against the mother country. In New Jersey, Robert Erskine continued to enjoy a frank correspondence with Richard Atkinson – 'I write to you as a brother & as a friend, and it is a relief to give you my sentiments naked open & undisguised,' he wrote on one occasion – but from this time onwards, his tone is one of noticeable disaffection.[11] 'I have had a great deal too much business on my own hands to think of, much less to write on politicks till now,' he wrote in June 1774, 'but things draw fast to a Crisis if the news be Confirmed that an obsolete Act of Henry the VIII is to be extended to this Country whereby people obnoxious to the Governor here or Government at home may be transported for trial to Britain. I have no doubt that a total suspension of Commerse to and from Great Britain and the West Indies will Certainly take place.'[12]

THESE ILL WINDS from America did not entirely blow the domestic agenda off course during the parliamentary session of 1774. As the king had heralded back in January, his government introduced bold measures to improve the 'state of the gold coin', and not before time, because guinea, half-guinea and quarter-guinea coins had become so debased – through 'clipping' (filing metal from a coin's circumference) and 'sweating' (collecting metallic dust from coins shaken in a bag) – that they were on average one-tenth lighter than their legal weight.[13] The Recoinage Act passed on 10 May 1774; by a Royal Proclamation pinned to the door of every church in the land, the order went out that all 'light' gold should be passed over to the official collectors for the district. They would take it at face value, cut and deface it, and transport it to the Bank of England in London, returning with pristine coin of the correct weight. Over the following four years, gold coins worth £16,500,000 would be renewed by this process.

John Robinson ran the operation out of the Treasury in Whitehall, commissioning 130 local money changers and settling terms with them. It was necessary that they should be men of substance, since the payments they would make to those handing in defective coins would need to come out of their own coffers – they would be reimbursed for their services later. 'The Allowances are from a third to one per cent in lieu of all risque, trouble, loss of Interest and Expences,' Robinson told prospective changers.[14] He appointed

George and Matthew Atkinson to oversee the recoinage in West-morland; the county was so remote from the capital that he allowed them a special commission of 1¼ per cent on all the money they exchanged.[15]

Robinson's choice of the Atkinson brothers for his home county may have been rooted in old acquaintance, but they were also emi-nently qualified for the task, for banking had overtaken tanning to become their primary line of business. The difference between the two occupations was not so great as it might sound, for tanning was a capital-intensive trade, and large sums of money passed through the brothers' books. Moreover, they permitted their customers what would these days be considered excessively long payment terms – often a year or more – and it was a relatively small leap from pro-viding credit to offering bank accounts.

During the early stages of the industrial revolution, when coin was often scarce, manufacturers regularly relied on brokers to con-vert the bills of exchange that they received for their goods into gold and silver with which they could pay their workers. Since the 1750s, George and Matthew Atkinson had been performing this service for the proprietors of Backbarrow ironworks, at the southern tip of Lake Windermere, where it was the custom to hold a grand payday at the feast of Candlemas. Every year, in January, the partners of the iron-works would make the eighty-mile round trip to Temple Sowerby to exchange paper bills for coin; the delegation generally consisted of at least half a dozen armed men, passing as it did through some truly desolate terrain. Towards the end of 1774, however, gold was in such universally short supply – £4,500,000 had been withdrawn from public circulation over the summer – that the Atkinson brothers' usual banking contacts in Newcastle and Glasgow could not provide the £14,000 in coin needed for the Backbarrow payday.

Over the autumn, George had conveyed several loads of 'light' gold – on two occasions, more than £20,000 – down to London to be recoined, and he now proposed to his friends at Backbarrow a scheme that would have to be kept secret. He wrote from Temple Sowerby:

The only method that we can think of to be on a certainty is to fetch about £8000 from London in this way – that two of your people must come here the 29th day of January with all the bills that have come to your hands then, and they shall have £4000 home with them next day. And I will go off in that night, fly to London, get there on Wednesday night, stay Thursday and Friday to get the bills discounted, and set out on Saturday or Sunday morning and be here on the 8th or 9th with as much as will make your payments easy. The only objection to this plan is the short days and dark moon, and to balance that we will take 4 days to come down instead of 3 which was our limited time last August, and after one is 60 or 80 miles from London the danger of robbery is over.[16]

Such a mission entailed a good deal of risk, for the lonely roads surrounding the capital were haunted by highwaymen legendary for their brazenness; only two months earlier the prime minister had himself been held up at gunpoint and relieved of his pocket watch and a few guineas.

LORD NORTH CALLED a general election in September 1774, six months sooner than strictly necessary, for it made sense to get this business out of the way – a 'Continental Congress' had recently assembled at Philadelphia to debate the colonies' collective response to the 'intolerable acts', and trouble was looming. John Robinson assisted the prime minister with the purchase of seats for those men whose presence in the House of Commons the ministry deemed necessary. (With patrons of 'pocket boroughs' demanding around £3,000 per seat, the Treasury spent nearly £50,000.) Sir James Lowther, having quarrelled with Robinson, chose to represent Westmorland himself – George Atkinson, as a newly minted free-holder of the county, dutifully awarded Lowther his vote.[17] Robinson secured a Treasury-sponsored seat at Harwich in Essex.

Twelve of the thirteen American colonies, all apart from Georgia, sent delegates to the First Continental Congress; the sibling territories had not always agreed, but their anger towards the mother country now bound them together. 'The Oliverian spirit in New England is effectually roused and diffuses over the whole Continent,' Robert Erskine wrote to Richard Atkinson on 5 October. 'The rulers at home have gone too too too far: the Boston Port Bill would have been very deficient of digestion, but Altering Charters, the due course of justice & the Canada Bill are emitents which cannot possibly be swallowed and must be thrown up again.'[18]

Congress published its resolutions on 20 October. The import of any goods from Britain, and sugar, coffee or pimento from the British West Indies, would be banned almost immediately, and no American goods would be sent to Britain or the West Indies after 10 September 1775 unless the coercive acts were repealed. On its final day, Congress issued a 'loyal address' to the king, listing its grievances in carefully deferential language; but since His Majesty viewed Congress as an illegal body and the imperial relationship as non-negotiable, he did not see fit to dignify the petition with a response.

The West India lobby took particular fright at the resolutions of Congress, since sugar planters looked to the American colonies for much of the basic food on which their enslaved workforce subsisted. On 18 January 1775, more than two hundred men gathered at the London Tavern to discuss what to do next; Richard was present, and he argued firmly (but with little effect) against a proposal to send parliament a petition warning of the calamity threatened by the resolutions, pointing out that since it 'was only meant to recommend to the consideration of Parliament, what Parliament would certainly consider of themselves, it was a futile measure'.[19] His assertion would be proved correct. The government, inundated with merchants' entreaties on the subject, set up a special panel for their assessment, which was dubbed the 'Committee of Oblivion'. It was two months before the West Indians' petition reached the top of the pile; by this time the ministers had already made the policy decisions that the petitioners had been hoping to influence.

It was alarming that West Indian planters should rely so much upon American grain and rice, and crucial that a substitute for these starchy crops was found – one that would grow on the islands. Thus, in March 1775, the Society of West India Merchants announced the reward of £100 for anyone who brought 'from any part of the World, a plant of the true Bread Fruit Tree, in a thriving Vegetation, properly certified to be of the best sort of that Fruit'.[20] Captain Cook had enthused about this plant after visiting Tahiti five years earlier. 'The fruit is about the size and shape of a child's head,' he had written, a rather unsettling description. 'It must be roasted before it is eaten, being first divided into three or four parts: its taste is insipid, with a slight sweetness somewhat resembling that of the crumb of wheaten-bread mixed with a Jerusalem artichoke.'[21]

BOSTON, THE HUB OF colonial discontent, remained calm for the time being. 'The winter has passed over without any great Bickerings between the Inhabitants of this town and His Majesty's Troops,' General Thomas Gage reported to Lord Dartmouth, the Colonial Secretary, on 28 March 1775.[22] Two weeks later, though, Gage received orders from Dartmouth to use force in disarming any rebels. Before dawn on 19 April, seven hundred soldiers marched from Boston to seize a stockpile of weapons from the village of Concord, some seventeen miles away. The mission was meant to be secret, but everyone living along the route had somehow been alerted. At Lexington, a skirmish blew up between redcoats and rebel militia that left eight local men dead. By the time the British reached Concord, the colonists' stash was no longer in evidence; and as they withdrew, a running battle started that continued all the way back to Boston. Harassed by crossfire, about 250 redcoats were either killed or wounded, versus ninety rebel casualties.

These clashes signalled a new escalation of the conflict. Within days, an army of fifteen thousand rebel volunteers had mustered to block access to the peninsula on which Boston was built, and where the British were garrisoned. On 3 May, Robert Erskine informed his employers in London that he had received an application for gunpowder from the 'principal people of the County of Borgen in the Jerseys, in which your Iron Works are situated', and that these men were forming a militia to defend themselves against the British. He no longer believed that a reconciliation between America and the mother country was possible – unless, that is, 'Blood seals the Contract'.[23]

Congress convened again at Philadelphia on 10 May; among the delegates was Benjamin Franklin, recently returned from London. On 14 June Congress voted to establish its own fighting force – the 'American Continental Army' – and appointed George Washington, a wealthy Virginia planter, as its commander-in-chief. Meanwhile at Boston, on 17 June, a British force led by General William Howe attacked the Charlestown peninsula – the closest promontory across the water from the town – and captured it from rebels occupying Bunker Hill. This was a tactical victory for the British, for it secured control of Boston harbour, but a Pyrrhic one, too, with more than a thousand redcoats dead or wounded – twice the casualties of their opponents. Only recently, ministers had sneered at the 'raw, undisciplined, cowardly' colonists, but General Gage advised them to think again: 'The Tryals we have had shew that the Rebels are not the despicable Rabble too many have supposed them to be.'[24]

BY NOW, GAGE was finding it near impossible to obtain food for the eight thousand men under his command. 'All the ports from whence our supplies usually came,' he wrote to the Treasury on 19 May, 'have refused suffering any provision or necessary whatever to be shipped for the king's use.'[25] The Treasury was the Whitehall department with responsibility for army provisions; which is why Lord North, as First Lord of the Treasury (and therefore, according to convention, prime minister), needed to attend to the minutiae of feeding a garrison more than three thousand miles away. On 13 June the Treasury Board ordered their usual contractors to ship 4,000 barrels of salt pork, 6,000 barrels of flour and 1,000 firkins of butter to Boston.

News of the Battle of Bunker Hill reached London on 25 July; the following day, Lord North solemnly informed the king that the conflict had now grown 'to such a height, that it must be treated as a foreign war'.[26] At some point it must have dawned on the prime minister and his colleagues at the Treasury that if the soldiers cooped up at Boston were to remain healthy over the winter, they would need better than salt rations to sustain them; and yet, given the onset of the hurricane season, it was perilously late in the year to start planning the dispatch of fresh food supplies. At the Treasury, it fell to John Robinson to procure the shipping that would be needed for such an operation. He soon discovered that the army's most robust transport vessels had already left for America; meanwhile his next port of call, the London merchants who specialized in the America trade, refused to charter their ships to the Treasury, fearing the consequences for their colonial property if they were seen to be aiding the authorities. Sometime during August, it seems that Robinson sought Richard Atkinson's advice on this knotty problem. The partnership of Mure, Son & Atkinson had never undertaken government business before, but Richard readily offered his assistance.

On 8 September, Robinson confirmed that the Treasury wished to send large quantities of food and fuel to Boston before the arrival of winter; later that day, Richard attended Lord North at Downing Street, and offered to obtain and ship the necessary items. The prime minister agreed to his terms – a commission of 2½ per cent, as was the mercantile norm – with one notable exception. Given that the price of rum was almost as volatile as the spirit itself, Lord North preferred to fix its cost beforehand; so the two men agreed to use the price quoted in the standing contract for supplying the navy with rum in Jamaica, adding on the 'usual freight of 6 pence per gallon', and allowances of 4 per cent for insurance and 10 per cent for leakage.[27]

The rushed manner in which Lord North engaged Richard's services reflected the emergency. No contract was drawn up; no record of the agreement made it into the Treasury Board minutes.

Richard at once committed four of Mure, Son & Atkinson's vessels to the expedition, swaying fellow merchants to volunteer ships. These were the items on the prime minister's 'shopping list':

4375 Chaldron of Coals
468,750 Galls of Porter
2,000 Sheep
2,000 Hogs
Potatoes
Carrots
Sour Crout
Onions
Sallad Seed
Malt – a small Quantity for the Hospitall
Vinegar – a reasonable Quantity for six Months Consumption
20 Boxes of Tin Plates
33,320 Pounds Wt of Candles to be shipt from Cork
100,000 Gallons of Rum – to be sent from Jamaica next Spring
400 Hogsheads of Melasses – ditto[28]

The list was largely compiled through guesswork. 'We are busy sending out every Comfort & Conveniency for the Troops,' Robinson wrote to Charles Jenkinson on 19 September, 'but since Gen. Gage does not tell us anything they want or may be useful, we are obliged I may say to grope for it.'[29] The *Thames* set sail for Boston at the end of September, the first of thirty-six ships that would depart over the following two months as soon as their holds were packed and winds permitted. The captain of the *Thames*, David Laird, was not only one of Mure, Son & Atkinson's longest-serving employees – it was he who had eight years earlier been involved in the altercation over Jonathan Strong's fate – but was also known to General Howe, the new commander-in-chief of the British forces in America, both men having fought at the Battle of Havana back in 1762.

As is clear from his correspondence with General Howe, Richard took great pains to make sure the supplies arrived in optimum condition. Five hundred tons of potatoes were loaded gently into the ships 'so as not to bruise them', and onions were stored in hampers for the same reason. To guarantee the safe passage of livestock, Richard ordered generous pens to be built in the ships' tween decks. The Lincolnshire breed of sheep was chosen as fittest to undergo the voyage, in preparation for which the animals were kept on dry food for ten days before being taken on board; the pigs were the 'half fed kind from the Country & of a large Size, such as will pretty certainly get fat upon the Voyage, a Plentiful Stock of Beans & Water being provided for their Consumption'.[30] As a further incentive to take care of the animals, Richard offered the ships' captains a bonus of 2s 6d for each one they landed alive.

Scurvy, which we now know to be caused by a lack of vitamin C, was by no means limited to seafaring men; it often afflicted those subsisting on salt rations. Sauerkraut, or 'sour crout', was widely believed to be effective against the disease, and its main ingredient, cabbage, was just then coming into season. Richard planned to send up to 300 tons of the stuff out to America. 'We are informed that in general the Sailors have disliked it at first & afterwards grown extremely fond of it,' he told General Howe. 'This first dislike may we hope be lessened by our having left Juniper berries & Spices out of the composition which appear to contribute nothing to its Preservation.' Normally, it would be unwise to seal and ship casks of sauerkraut during its six-week fermentation period, as they were likely to rupture – but such obstacles did not faze Richard. 'We have caused Valves to be made (which cost a mere Trifle) to fix in the Bungs of the Casks which Valves being kept down by a Spiral Spring strong enough to resist any thing that can happen in rolling the Cask, will at the same time give way to a Pressure far less than sufficient to burst it & so let out the expanded air,' he explained to Howe. 'By this means we shall be able to ship the Sour Krout within a week or ten days of gathering the Cabbage.'[31]

John Robinson kept the king updated on the progress of the Boston expedition. 'Mr. Robinson,' starts one of his memoranda, 'has the Honour to send, by Lord North's Directions, for His

Majesty's Inspection, two Casks of Sour Crout, put up with Valves, in the same Manner as the Casks shipped for America; and also one of the Valves – The Cask marked No. 1 has been sometime made and may be nearly fit for use, that marked No. 2 is at present in a state of Strong Fermentation.'[32] No detail affecting the comfort of His Majesty's troops was beneath royal scrutiny.

All the while, the press provided a sardonic commentary on these goings-on. 'One person has contracted for several thousand cabbages at 3d. each, which, were they brought to market at home, would barely fetch half that price,' reported the *Evening Advertiser* on 5 October. 'It is computed, that, by the time the above sheep and hogs arrive at the places of their destination, they will stand the government (or rather the public) in no less than *two shillings* per pound, bones included, which occasioned a Wag to remark, that the Ministry have brought their pigs to a *fine market.*'[33]

DURING THE SUMMER of 1775, Congress ordered all able-bodied men to form into companies of militia – an edict that presented Robert Erskine with a headache, for he knew that were his forgemen, carpenters and blacksmiths to enlist in different units from each other, production at the ironworks would soon seize up. He therefore applied to the New Jersey Congress for permission to raise his own company of foot soldiers, and gained his captain's commission in mid-August.

Erskine explained the situation in his next letter to Richard, neglecting to mention that the owners of the ironworks would bear the cost of the muskets, bayonets, flints, powder and shot with which their employees would, if necessary, fight the British. He also expressed his disappointment at not having received a personal letter from Richard for the best part of a year: 'You would add greatly to my satisfaction were you to favour me oftener with a few lines directly from yourself – I know, my Dear Sir, the multiplicity of your engagements and that you have no time to throw away in letters of mere Compliments – but I cannot help wishing to hear from you were it ever so short, especially since I heard of your bad state of health.'[34] (This is the earliest mention I have found of Richard's fragile constitution.)

It was not long before Erskine faced a crisis at the ironworks, after the London-based proprietors decided they would no longer honour his bills drawn on them. With little coin circulating in New Jersey, Erskine started dipping into his stock of iron – 'a commodity which neither fire nor vermin can destroy' – to settle with tradesmen.[35] As he informed Richard on 6 December:

I have between 6 & 700 Ton of pig & 20 & 30 Tons Bar at the Works and expect to make 50 more before the frost sets in. I have no reason to despair, it gives me some satisfaction to tell you so, because I have no doubt it will give you pleasure. I know it would pain you to see anyone in distress, much more one who has had so many proofs of your regard – Distress did I say? Oh my country! To what art thou Driving – this gives me poignant distress indeed. How long will madness and infatuation Continue?[36]

The first four ships of Richard's provisioning fleet limped into Boston harbour on 19 December, with the *Thames* at their head, having experienced atrocious storms during the twelve-week crossing. On 31 December, General Howe wrote to John Robinson with a description of the cargoes of the nine ships so far arrived. The supplies of porter, malt, vinegar, salad seed and sauerkraut had held up well, but most of the potatoes had putrefied in the heat of the hold. Only forty out of 550 sheep and seventy-four out of 290 pigs had landed alive; their pens had proved too spacious, and they had repeatedly been 'thrown upon one another by the Violent motion of the Ship'.[37] Most of the carcasses were too badly crushed to be fit for consumption and had been thrown overboard.

The expedition's goal had been to bring home comforts to the besieged garrison over the winter, but it proved an abject failure. A foot of snow had fallen in Boston on Christmas Eve, and fuel was in such short supply that Howe authorized the scrapping of old wharves, houses and ships for firewood. The general would be forced to place his troops on short rations in mid-January 1776. In the end, just twenty-four of the thirty-six provisioning ships made it to Boston, including seven stragglers that arrived too late for their rotting cargoes to be unloaded, since by then the garrison was on the point of departure. (The remaining twelve ships were forced 'by Stress of Weather' to put into Antigua for essential repairs.)[38]

On the morning of 5 March, Howe discovered that Washington's Continental Army had, overnight, occupied the Dorchester Heights, a lofty no-man's-land across the water. Twenty American cannons now pointed towards Boston. The next ten days saw the packing up of the British garrison. Any ordnance that could not be carried away was destroyed or dumped in the sea; seventy-nine horses and 358 tons of hay were also left behind.[39] On 17 March, with the arrival of a fair wind, 120 ships carrying more than ten thousand troops and loyalists set sail for Halifax, Nova Scotia.

SIX

The Rum Contracts

AN ARMY THAT LACKS a strong supply of food, clothing and shelter will be fatally weakened; and yet military historians have often ignored the behind-the-scenes contribution of those working to provide these necessities. As Professor Arthur Bowler, one of the few academics to have studied the logistical minutiae of the American conflict, has written: 'Since human society began, minstrels and historians have told over and again the exploits of men on the field of battle while condemning to limbo by the process of neglect the more prosaic activities of contractors, commissaries, quartermasters, subtlers, and administrators generally.'[1] Presumably these story-tellers have considered the deeds of such people to be too boringly deficient in that stirring narrative quality, jeopardy, to merit their attention – but what greater jeopardy could there be than knowing that a vast army, struggling to save an empire on the other side of a wide ocean, looks to you for its every need? This was the burden that Richard Atkinson would bear for the next six years.

By the start of 1776, it was clear that the redcoat army fighting the American rebels would have to be almost entirely provisioned from home. The shortcomings of the system by which the Admiralty was the government department with responsibility for shipping the troops out to America, while it fell to the Treasury to organize the delivery of their supplies, were perfectly obvious – but the Navy Board categorically refused to offer assistance.

Custom dictated that each British soldier in the field received the same basic ration: one pound of bread and either one pound of salted beef or nine ounces of salted pork every day, plus items issued on a weekly basis, typically eight ounces of rice or oatmeal, six ounces of butter or cheese and three pints of pease. On 9 February, the Treasury Board settled terms with six merchant syndicates who would between them, over the following year, supply provisions for 36,000 men in America and 12,000 men in Canada, at a cost of 5¼d for each daily ration. Richard was the managing partner of the group that won the contract to feed the army in Canada.

Two weeks later, the Treasury agreed to engage Mure, Son & Atkinson to 'take up a sufficient Quantity of Shipping to carry the Provisions ordered from Time to Time by this Board for the Supply of the Forces in America'.[2] The individual contractors would arrange for supplies to be taken to Cork, on Ireland's south coast, where under the direction of a Treasury commissary they would be loaded into ships chartered by Mure, Son & Atkinson. The provisions would be sent to America in quarterly batches, with ships making two return crossings every year; that, anyhow, was the theory.

During the spring of 1776, the Treasury Board and the Navy Board – which was preparing to take 27,000 infantry, plus a cavalry regiment and 950 horses, out to America – were in fierce competition for the limited pool of merchant shipping that was available to hire. By the end of April, Richard had succeeded in chartering fifty-two ships on the Treasury's behalf; but then the Navy Board, urgently needing vessels to carry horses, unilaterally hiked the previously fixed hire rate of 11s to 12s 6d per ton per day. This placed Richard, who was still obliged to offer the lower rate, at a serious disadvantage, and over the next six weeks he managed to charter only nine more ships. On 12 June Richard expressed his concerns at a meeting between Lord North and Lord Sandwich, First Lord of the Admiralty; afterwards the Treasury Board put up its rate to 12s 6d, while the Navy Board dropped its rate back down to 11s. The manoeuvre enabled Richard to hire seventy-six more vessels over the next seven weeks, although merchant shipping was so scarce by then that he was forced to cast around in ports as distant as Amsterdam and Hamburg.

Once chartered, the Treasury required Mure, Son & Atkinson to have the merchant ships armed 'in due Proportion to their Burthen', meaning that a large number of cannons in a variety of sizes had to be found at short notice.[3] Thus (to give two examples) the *Locke*, an ex-East Indiaman of 685 tons' capacity, was furnished with twenty nine-pounder and six four-pounder cannons, while the *Lyon*, a vessel of 170 tons from the port of Leith, was fitted with ten two-pounders and eight swivel guns. 'You are already, Sir, apprized of the Disappointment we have met with in Guns,' Richard wrote to John Robinson at the Treasury. 'This has driven us to ransack this Town and its Environs for light six Pounders.'[4]

Although rum did not fall within the standard army ration, it was still considered essential. It provided warmth on cold nights; it made bad water drinkable; it offered relief from pain; and it prevented wounds from turning septic. On 2 May, the Treasury Board settled terms with five West India merchants, each of whom was to supply 100,000 gallons of rum from the sugar island with which he was closely connected. Richard's tender for Jamaican rum was the winning bid for that colony. Each island distilled its rum to a different strength, and Jamaican rum was most potent of all – a distinction which did not, however, quite account for the discrepancy between the 5s 3d per gallon that the Treasury agreed to pay Richard, and the 3s secured by a Barbados merchant. The suspicion that Richard had negotiated an outrageously good deal for himself by underhand means would follow him around like a bad smell for the rest of his days.

THE ABSENCE OF any surviving letters between Richard and his siblings at Temple Sowerby has left a glaring gap in the family correspondence, and I have little sense of the dynamic that existed between them. But they were by no means estranged. George Atkinson saw his youngest brother quite often during the mid-1770s, when his duties as the Treasury's money changer in Westmorland regularly took him to the capital; the task of replacing the nation's defective gold coinage would take four years to complete.

As for Bridget, who we last met in 1762 – it's fair to say she had been far from idle, not only having given birth to ten children (two of whom died in infancy), but also running the family house and farm. During the late 1760s, Bridget and George had taken the lease on one of Lord Thanet's new farms across the river at Whinfell; it was just as well that she did not mind getting her hands dirty, for it was a condition of the tenancy that the land should be cleared, and she often came home reeking of gorse smoke.[5] (One lucky day, while turning over an old rabbit warren, Bridget's plough unearthed a gold 'fede-ring' brooch – two pairs of arms joined together with clasped hands, with a devout message in raised letters on the sleeves – that dated back to the fourteenth century, when Whinfell had been a deer park belonging to the great Clifford family.) Bridget abhorred waste of any kind, and made a point of planting apple trees in the corners of her fields where the plough could not reach – it became a kind of signature of her occupancy. The topographer William Hutchinson, who toured the northern counties in 1774, observed the Atkinsons' farm approvingly. 'We then passed Whinfield Park,' he wrote, 'where we had the pleasure of viewing a large tract of ground, lately enclosed from the park, and growing corn. There is not any thing can give greater satisfaction to the eye of the traveller,

The gold brooch that was ploughed up on Bridget's farm.

than to behold cultivation and industry stretching their paces over the heath and waste, the forest and the chase – population must follow, and riches ensue.'[6]

So far as I know, Bridget only visited London twice – and her second visit, as an old woman, would be a miserable business. The first time, in May 1776, when she was forty-three, George brought her down with him after the weaning of their final child. George returned to Westmorland a week later; Bridget, on the other hand, decided to stay put until her husband came back with another consignment of 'light' gold. It was, in fact, her brother-in-law Richard who urged her to remain in the capital, as Bridget explained in a letter to her eldest child, fifteen-year-old Dorothy:

> Your Uncle was not willing I should return with your Father.
> He purposed my seeing the King go to the House of Lords and
> two or three Little jaunts into the country. I have been foolish
> enough my Dear Dolly in buying you a peice of Checked
> Muslin for a Gown and also a peice of striped Lutestring for
> another it is not very fashionable but I got it cheap. I durst not
> sent your Hatt and cloak by your Father I am sure they would
> have been quite spoiled. I have almost spent all my Monny,
> many Temptations are here.[7]

Bridget must have spent a good deal of her 'Monny' on shells, for a cart would soon arrive at Temple Sowerby, delivering a box that contained, among other things, '54 pretty shells in a Bag & 4 mighty ugly ones loose'.[8] Her collection was acquiring a global dimension; her latest coup had been to persuade George Dixon, a Kirkoswald man who was appointed armourer of the *Discovery* on Captain Cook's third voyage, to keep an eye out for specimens. 'Hear is sum smal Qurosetes such as large Locusts, small spotted snakes, but no shells of any account,' Dixon would report from Cape Town on 24 November 1776. 'What is qureas I shall get, if our stay will Permit (but ounderstand we must sail on Wednesday first from this for New Zealand, in the South Sees).'[9]

Shortly after returning from London, Bridget would oversee the 'inoculation' of her four youngest children against the smallpox.[10] This nerve-racking procedure involved scratching the skin with a needle, then rubbing the contents of a smallpox pustule into the wound. Within days, symptoms including a high fever, a painful rash and pustules might start to appear, and the danger period could last a fortnight; the possible side effects of this treatment ranged from disfigurement to death.

This, of course, was some twenty years before Edward Jenner's famous experiments of the 1790s, which confirmed the common rural belief that an infection from cowpox conferred immunity to smallpox, and explained why milkmaids were possessed of such flawless complexions. As a young man, in 1772, Jenner had attended George Fordyce's courses on the 'practice of Physick', the 'Materia Medica' and chemistry.[11] A brief sentence in a letter written by Bridget to her husband George around this time (she neglected to give the date) offers an obscure hint, tucked among chit-chat about prison visits and church pews, that she knew about the connection between cowpox and smallpox, and might even have discussed it with George Fordyce. 'I shall go to the Gaol to see poor Mr. Bird,' she wrote. 'I was sure Dr. Fordice would be of my Opinion in regard to Matts Cow but all the World could not convince my Sister. I am glad you have got the Seats in the Church made up I hope our Rector and you are sitting in it today it is a great acquisision and a good thing as I saw no use that piece of Space was to any one and now we shall have room enough for all our Family.'[12]

I LIKE TO IMAGINE Bridget and Richard, the two pivotal characters in this story, standing side-by-side in the crowd that watched George III travel in his golden coach to the House of Lords to close parliament on 23 May 1776. (I cycle along the processional route, past St James's Park, on my way into work every day.) The king addressed his subjects solemnly on that occasion, expressing regret that he had recently found it necessary to ask his 'faithful Commons' for extra money to pay for the American conflict, and still holding out hopes that his 'rebellious subjects' would yet be 'awakened to a sense of their errors'.[13]

But it was too late for that. In Philadelphia, on 4 July, Congress ratified the final text of the 'unanimous declaration of the Thirteen United States of America'. The document, which started by stating the 'self-evident' truth that all men were 'created equal', went on to list the 'Injuries and Usurpations' to which the colonists had been subjected, before drawing the following conclusion: 'A Prince, whose Character is thus marked by every Act which may define a Tyrant, is unfit to be the Ruler of a free People.'[14] The text was in large part drafted by the Virginia planter Thomas Jefferson, and its pretensions to moral authority did not go unchallenged. 'If slavery be thus fatally contagious,' pondered Samuel Johnson, 'how is it that we hear the loudest yelps for liberty among the drivers of negroes?'[15]

The withdrawal of British forces from Boston in March 1776 had left them without access to a port between Nova Scotia and Florida. Now the British high command aspired to make New York their headquarters, since it held the key to the American interior, as the gateway to the mighty Hudson River; for the time being, though, the Continental Army controlled the island of Manhattan. General Howe sailed from Nova Scotia with nine thousand men, seizing Staten Island – five miles south of Manhattan – at the end of June. Two weeks later Admiral Howe, the general's brother, arrived at the head of a fleet carrying eleven thousand troops. Thirteen thousand more would soon follow, including a large contingent of Hessians – German mercenaries hired to serve alongside the redcoats.

When Robert Erskine learnt, on 12 July, that five British warships had outrun rebel batteries defending the mouth of the Hudson, and were now anchored only twenty miles from Ringwood, he set to work on a contrivance to prevent further incursions. Erskine's 'Marine Chevaux de Frise' – along the same lines as the wooden frames with spikes that were used to head off cavalry charges – was a tetrahedron made of oak beams tipped with iron points that would pierce the hull of any ship passing over it. Eight days later, he presented a scale model for General Washington's inspection; he also

Robert Erskine's device to prevent the British from penetrating the Hudson River.

wrote to Benjamin Franklin in Philadelphia, offering it for use on the Delaware River. In the end, similar devices of a rival design were used to defend the Hudson, although it appears that the ironworks at Ringwood provided the spikes – Erskine's cash book records a debit of £1,022 against 'the United States' for eleven tons supplied to make 'Chevaux-de-frise'.[16]

During the autumn of 1776, the British advance seemed almost unstoppable. Four thousand redcoats landed at Kip's Bay, on the east side of Manhattan, on 15 September; within hours they had taken New York. By the end of November, General Howe was confidently predicting the expulsion of the Continental Army from New Jersey; this territory, with its abundance of 'covering, forage, and supplies of fresh provisions', would make fine winter quarters for his troops.[17] '*I think the game is pretty near up,*' General Washington told his brother on 18 December. 'No Man, I believe, ever had a greater choice of difficulties and less means to extricate himself from them.'[18]

A week after writing these words, on Christmas night, Washington led a straggling column across the icy Delaware River. The next morning, after a short battle, they captured two-thirds of the Hessian brigade garrisoning the small town of Trenton, New Jersey. This modest victory marked a turnaround for the rebels; another morale-boosting win followed ten days later at Princeton. Howe's hopes that his army might achieve self-sufficiency were dashed; from now on, he told the Treasury Board, all provisions must come from Britain – since America could be relied upon for nothing.

'WE ARE IN FORCE sufficient to enter upon offensive Operations,' General Howe had written to ministers in London on 6 August 1776, 'but I am detained by the Want of Camp Equipage, particularly Kettles and Cantines, so essential in the Field, and without which too much is to be apprehended on the Score of Health.'[19] Consequently, on 14 September, the Treasury ordered Richard Atkinson to supply 'barrack furniture' for 25,000 men, uniforms for 5,000 loyalist militia, and a pair of 'thick milled woollen mittens for every man', as well as to 'take up & arm shipping sufficient to carry the whole together with the Camp Equipage Shoes Stocking & Linnen for the next Campaign'.

Richard's clerks immediately set about sourcing thousands of beds, bolsters, blankets, candles, candlesticks, rugs, pokers and tongs. 'We are obliged to obtain goods of all Sorts from the Makers as matter of favor & preference,' he commented, 'whilst their workmen are universally Engaged in Combinations & all the Licentiousness arising from a Superabundance of employment.'[20] (A collective demand for improvements in pay or conditions was known as a 'combination'.) With winter coming, shortcuts were needed, and Richard warned General Guy Carleton, commander-in-chief in Canada, that he had ordered 30,000 yards of 'legging dyed at Leeds to be sent unpressed'; the material might seem coarser than usual, but it would not be any 'less durable or less warm'.[21]

The sheer unpredictability of the business of provisioning the army in America was already abundantly clear. The idea that each of the Treasury's ships would make two return crossings a year had proved hopelessly optimistic. In August 1776, a westerly wind confined several Canada-bound ships to the English Channel for three weeks, giving rise to fears that they would fail to reach Quebec before the annual freezing of the St Lawrence River. Such setbacks were intensely stressful for all concerned. 'I am sorry to find Lord North by his letter so uneasy at all the Victualling ships being not yet sailed for Canada,' the king wrote to John Robinson, 'as I attribute part of it to his not being in good spirits.'[22] By 26 September, when the last of the twenty-nine ships destined for Quebec that year sailed from Cork, Richard and his partners in the Canada contract had supplied 591,500 pounds of salt beef, 2,366,000 pounds of salt pork, 3,458,000 pounds of flour, 1,274,000 pounds of bread, 253,496 pounds of butter, 610,985 pounds of oatmeal, and 27,420 bushels of peas for the consumption of the troops.

The mounting cost of feeding the army soon began to attract scrutiny. Richard's name was not mentioned during a robust parliamentary debate about the subject on 21 February 1777 – surprisingly, perhaps, given that more than one-third of the Treasury's expenditure on the war over the previous year had passed through his books and those of his various partners. Colonel Barré did, however, observe that 5s 3d per gallon for the 100,000 gallons of Jamaican rum supplied by Richard was a 'most unheard of and exorbitant price' – but Lord North insisted it had 'left little or no profit for the contractor'.[23]

The prime minister's annual budget, delivered on 14 May, revealed a shortfall of £5 million that would have to be met with a public loan. When, by way of response, the opposition launched a stinging attack on the cost of the war, Colonel Barré returned to the cost of the rum; the contractor, he suggested, must be a 'very good friend of the treasury indeed'. Not so, said Lord North: 'The contract with Mr. Atkinson was for rum of the very best proof, the finest that could be had in Jamaica.' Indeed, he continued, once freight, leakage, insurance and commission were taken into account, the 5s 3d agreed by the Treasury Board, 'so far from being a bad bargain, was evidently a very favourable one'. Barré replied sarcastically that on such terms the poor contractor 'must be ruined', and it was cruel of the Treasury to treat him so unfairly: 'He now plainly saw the reason why people of all sorts were so shy of taking government contracts. But this Mr. Atkinson must be the greatest idiot in the whole contracting world: did he make his contracts for sour crout and porter upon the same principles?'[24]

At one point during these proceedings Lord North tripped over his numbers and confessed that he was not certain whether the values he was quoting were in pounds sterling or Jamaica's local currency – a hugely embarrassing slip-up. Afterwards the *Morning Post* gossiped that Sir Grey Cooper – John Robinson's fellow Secretary to the Treasury, who sat beside the prime minister during debates and was meant to feed him with facts and figures – had received a 'private whipping' for the blunder.[25]

Decisive action was clearly needed to head off a brewing political scandal. The next time Richard was summoned before Lord North and his Treasury Board, on 3 June, it was agreed that some independent merchants should be asked to evaluate whether the rum might reasonably have been cheaper and, if so, how much it ought to have cost. Beeston Long, the chairman of the Society of West India Merchants, and two other City of London grandees, were appointed referees.

THE TREASURY BOARD had already given General Howe the go-ahead to order more rum direct from the merchants who had shipped such large amounts of it to New York during the summer of 1776. It was typical that Richard should have been the only one of the five original suppliers who was far-sighted enough to appoint an American agent. He wrote to Howe on 14 January 1777 offering to furnish as much rum as necessary: 'We have by various Conveyances ordered our Agents in Jamaica to secure a sufficient Quantity to enable them to execute your Excellency's Commands to what extent soever they may receive them.'[26] The same day he informed Joshua Loring, the merchant acting as his agent in New York: 'Doubting as we do whether any of the other Contractors have made proper dispositions for a supply in the West Indies, we think it probable that the General may call upon us for more than one fourth part of his whole supply.'[27]

In the event, this would prove quite an underestimate. On 1 April, Howe and Loring concluded an agreement for Mure, Son & Atkinson to provide 350,000 gallons of rum. This colossal order – equivalent to one-sixth of the volume that would be exported from the West Indies to Britain that year – was the entire quantity required by the army for the year ahead.[28] (General Howe told John Robinson that he had thought it advisable to confine the order to Mure, Son & Atkinson, rather than divide it between several contractors, so that 'there might be no disappointment in the main Object'.)[29] Unfortunately Howe and Loring chose not to specify the cost. Instead they declared: 'Whereas the price of Rum is very fluctuating and it is impossible to obtain sufficient Information on that Head, it is agreed by & between the Partys that the same be referred as a Point hereafter to be settled upon the most reasonable Terms between the right Honourable the Lords Commissioners of his Majesty's Treasury and the said Messrs Mure Son & Atkinson.'[30]

The Lords of the Treasury heard about the new contract in early June, shortly after Lord North's humiliating budget speech, and they soon told Howe that they were unable to 'ascertain here the price to be paid for Rum', instead ordering him to settle the matter from New York.[31] Unsurprisingly, Richard saw things differently; he believed a clear understanding had existed that any top-up order from America needed only to specify the quantity of rum, since the price had already been fixed at the time of the previous contract in May 1776.

The Lords of the Treasury would spend many hours considering the rum contracts over the summer of 1777, and Richard would be repeatedly summoned to appear before them. On 10 July they ordered him to cut his agency rate from 2½ to 1½ per cent, an indignity to which he 'chearfully' submitted, while voicing concerns that his rival merchants might see this as a scheme of his own devising to undercut them. 'These things are not reckoned reputable in the City,' he told John Robinson.[32]

Sometime in mid-July, Beeston Long and the other referees filed their report on Richard's previous rum contract, the one from May 1776. They concluded that the spirit had been too expensive at 5s 3d per gallon, and proposed it should be priced at 4s ¾d – a reduction of nearly a quarter. Richard disputed this figure on grounds that they had incorrectly estimated the cost of the insurance premium at 13½ per cent – despite having seen the *actual* policies, which showed that of the 1,126 puncheons of rum which Mure, Son & Atkinson had arranged to be shipped to America, the premium paid on 826 barrels had been 15 per cent of their value, and on 100 barrels it had been 25 per cent. On 200 barrels Richard had been unable to secure cover – too bad that this last consignment had been seized by privateers. According to Richard's calculations, these costs and uninsured losses were equivalent to an insurance premium of 31½ per cent – which proved that, far from having profited by the contract, as was claimed, he had lost by it.

After the referees refused to concede that he might have a point, Richard's tone turned combative. On 23 July he wrote to the Treasury Board, hoping they would 'consider the increased price of 5s. 6d. as the very lowest' fair price for the rum.[33] By mid-August his patience was all but exhausted, and he wrote an exasperated letter to the Treasury, reeling off some of the unforeseeable events that 'every Contractor not meaning to ruin himself' was obliged to factor into his prices:

Short Crops in Jamaica. Combinations against him. Negligence of Agents. Misconduct of Masters of Ships. Want of supply of Lumber. Long Detention & consequent Leakage and Expences in following the army from Port to Port in America; but *above all* that imminent Danger inseparable from the nature of the Undertaking, by which so heavy a Loss has been actually sustained, *the Danger of uninsurable Risques.*[34]

It was a howl of frustration from a man whose considerable powers of persuasion seemed for once to have deserted him.

LIKE ALL CIVIL WARS, the conflict in America created fault lines that severed families and friendships; such was the rift between Benjamin Franklin and his loyalist son William, the last colonial governor of New Jersey, that they never made their peace. Suffice to say, Robert Erskine could not have foreseen that within five years of his arrival in New Jersey he would find himself on the opposite side of a full-blown war from his friend Richard Atkinson.

Before his move to the colonies, Erskine had been a surveyor of some repute. The first map he drew for George Washington, which charted adjoining districts of New Jersey and New York, was small enough to be folded in a pocket; Erskine handed it to the general himself. Shortly afterwards, on 19 July 1777, Washington wrote to Congress: 'A good Geographer to Survey the roads and take sketches of the Country where the Army is to Act would be extremely useful and might be attended with exceeding valuable consequences.'[35] Which is how Erskine came to be appointed Surveyor General to the Continental Army, with the rank of colonel. However, his sense of obligation towards Richard and the other owners of the ironworks prevented him from taking up the position until he had made arrangements for his absence. 'The great Confidence my employers have all along placed in my integrity and honour, has demanded my best endeavours on their behalf,' Erskine explained to Washington. 'What ever feuds and differences take place between States and nations yet these cannot alter the nature of justice between man &

man; or cancel the duty, one individual owes to another.'[36] Despite the political chasm dividing him from the men who had sent him to America in the first place, his loyalty towards them did not falter.

During the next three years, Erskine and his team of assistant surveyors, draughtsmen and chain-bearers traversed New Jersey, New York, Connecticut and Pennsylvania, creating more than 250 maps that would prove of inestimable value to the revolutionary cause. He would never meet Richard Atkinson again; for a heavy cold contracted in the field soon turned into a fever, and he died at Ringwood on 2 October 1780. Less than two years later, the New Jersey legislature would pass an act confiscating the ironworks from its British proprietors and vesting control in Erskine's widow and her second husband.[37]

ALTHOUGH THE FRENCH loudly protested their neutrality, it was an open secret that they were providing all manner of supplies to the American rebels – cannons, rifles, gunpowder, clothes, leather, salt, brandy and wine. American privateers, meanwhile, were welcomed at French ports. 'I trust the different Vessels that hover round the Island will be put on their guard particularly to protect Liverpool, Whitehaven, the Clyde and even Bristol,' the king wrote to John Robinson in May 1777, 'for I do suspect that the Rebel vessels which have been assembling at Nantes and Bordeaux mean some stroke of that kind which will undoubtedly occasion much discontent among the Merchants.'[38]

Sure enough, in August, at the mouth of the English Channel, American privateers managed to pick off two ships from a 160-strong merchant convoy returning from Jamaica, and sailed them to Nantes, where they were plundered, stripped of their rigging and abandoned on mud flats. One of the vessels, the *Hanover Planter*, which belonged to Mure, Son & Atkinson, had 360 hogsheads of sugar and eighty-seven puncheons of rum on board. Lord Stormont, the British ambassador to France, personally negotiated the return of the ships and their valuable cargoes, an outcome which prompted Lord North to write, on 25 September, that he was 'more sanguine' than he had been for a while in his 'expectations of the continuance of peace'.[39]

The main thrust of the British campaign in America for 1777 was to isolate the rebellious New England colonies from the more loyalist middle colonies by securing the Hudson River; General Burgoyne would lead a southbound expedition from Montreal, with General Howe leading a northbound one from New York, and the two forces would converge on Albany. 'Gentleman Johnny' Burgoyne's push started well, with the capture of Fort Ticonderoga on 6 July. Howe changed his mind, however, and instead sent his army south to take Philadelphia. An inveterate gambler, Burgoyne chose to press ahead, but his luck ran out at Saratoga on 17 October; surrounded by the Continental Army, he was forced to surrender with nearly six thousand men. The defeat would prove a turning point of the war, for it persuaded the French that it might be worth openly backing the American cause. 'This unhappy Event,' Lord Stormont reported from Paris, 'has greatly elevated all our secret Enemies here, and they break out, tho' not in my Presence into the most intemperate Joy.'[40]

RICHARD'S RUM CONTRACTS would go down as a footnote in the history of the American war, yet they consumed an undue quantity of ministerial time, and generated a mind-numbing amount of paperwork. I could well imagine how all those beleaguered clerks must have felt; after weeks spent sifting through hundreds of Treasury and Colonial Office box files and letterbook volumes in the bunker-like confines of the National Archives at Kew, I myself felt heartily sick of the business.

A letter in which General Howe refused to suggest a price for the rum reached Whitehall from Philadelphia in January 1778; he merely expressed his regret that the affairs of Mure, Son & Atkinson, who had 'exerted themselves so manifestly upon every occasion which has fallen under my Observation', should have been left undetermined for so long 'from a Chain of Difficultys they could not foresee'.[41] Richard continued to press the Treasury Board for

two dozen witnesses – under-secretaries, chief clerks, insurance brokers, sugar brokers, planters and merchants among them – were called upon to analyse its every last detail.

It was soon revealed that Richard had managed, almost by accident, to make an excellent bargain for himself. As it turned out, the price paid by the Royal Navy for its rum in Jamaica, which was the basis for his deal with the prime minister, was surprisingly high. John Robinson had only later worked out why this should be so, when he discovered that rum was just one component of a much more extensive naval provisioning contract. Whereas the Treasury Board treated rum as a separate item, in the navy 'grog' was part of the standard daily ration. Three merchants in Jamaica had bid for the navy's provisioning contract, quoting individual prices for each item – bread, beef, pork, pease, oatmeal, butter, vinegar, rum – from which a total cost per man, per day had been calculated. While the winning tender had been the cheapest overall, for rum it had been on the high side.

THE LONG-DREADED ALLIANCE between America and France finally materialized in a treaty signed on 6 February 1778. No longer was the war at arm's length, on the other side of a wide ocean; now it threatened British shores. On the night of 23 April, Captain John Paul Jones of the *Ranger*, an American naval vessel sailing out of Brest, raided Whitehaven, the Cumberland port where he had once served his apprenticeship, disembarking thirty men who spiked the town's cannons and set fire to ships in its harbour. Meanwhile, down south, where the threat of invasion was all too real – French troops were reportedly massing in Brittany and Normandy – a series of tented cities sprang up to accommodate the newly mobilized county militia.

The Treasury Board invited tenders for supplying the camps with bread, wood, forage and straw; the winning bid came from Simon Fraser, one of Richard's close friends. In its contract with Fraser, the Treasury specified that the army's 'ammunition bread' should be baked from whole wheat into loaves of six pounds. But many of the soldiers refused to eat this coarse bread; Colonel Henry Herbert of the Wiltshire Regiment, camped at Winchester, complained to John Robinson that it contained 'Bran capable of purging a Horse'.[50]

When the tradesman sub-contracted to supply the bread unilaterally took it upon himself to provide bran-free loaves for the troops, Richard, who was Fraser's hitherto silent partner in the contract, reluctantly intervened. He wrote to the baker:

> I understand that you have agreed to deliver Bread of Better
> Quality than the Contract specifies without increase of Price
> or diminution of Weight. This I am confident Mr. Fraser will
> have put a stop to, but lest he should have missed you, or by
> any other accident this letter should find you still undecided,
> I am to desire, and Expressly to direct that on no account
> whatsoever you deliver any other Bread than is described in
> the Contract.[51]

A few days later Richard visited Coxheath camp, near Maidstone, to smooth over the matter with its commander, General William Keppel. 'I have this morning seen Mr. Atkinson, and If he is as Honest as he *appears* Sensible; & *is* Clear – The Camps will be very well furnished with Every Article he is Contractor for,' Keppel told General Amherst, the British commander-in-chief, on 18 June. 'We parted very Good friends as he may tell you; and perfectly satisfied with each other.'[52] But Keppel, after going without bread for two days, soon downgraded his opinion of Richard and his ilk. 'The Contractors deserve to be hanged,' he wrote to Amherst on 23 June. 'It is Mr. Atkinson or Mr. Frazar that is to supply Bread, and good Bread, every delivery in Camp, and they must be made answerable notwithstanding they are under the Protection of Mr. Robinson altho' he perhaps deserves hanging as much as either of them.' Keppel, whose political allegiances lay with his cousin, the Duke of Richmond, added a telling postscript: 'I beg this Letter may be considered as a publick one.'[53]

As was bound to happen, the press picked up the story and mangled the facts. 'The contracts for serving all the camps with *bread*,' reported the *Evening Post*, 'are executed by Mr. Atkinson, partner with Lord Bute's agent, and brother-in-law to Mr. Robinson, of the Treasury. The bread has been scandalously bad, but how should it be otherwise. Every thing is now an arrant *job*. Mr. Atkinson is a Scotchman.'[54]

All this time, of course, Richard was making a fortune. Of the £1,406,923 expended by the Paymaster of the Forces for the twelve months up to February 1778, some £495,020 had been billed by Mure, Son & Atkinson, and £133,772 by Richard on behalf of the Canada contractors – although how much of this was profit is impossible to say.[55] But he was also under constant pressure; in particular, the burden of managing the transport fleet that shipped the army's supplies across the ocean lay heavy upon his shoulders. His partners, the Mures, offered negligible support, for they rarely came to town. Clearly Richard was unable, or unwilling, to delegate the fine details of the government contracts to his clerks, for the hundreds of letters, reports and bills from Mure, Son & Atkinson which are scattered throughout the public archives are mostly in his handwriting. He made himself so indispensable to Lord North and the Treasury Board that he became their first port of call for any business requiring special speed or discretion. He had a heroic capacity for work, often writing, writing, writing late into the night, and his letters generally convey boundless energy and optimism. The issue of the rum contracts, still unresolved, enveloped his activities in a cloud of opprobrium – and yet here he was, pulling off astonishing logistical feats in the service of king and empire. At times he must have felt close to buckling beneath the intolerable weight of it all.

SEVEN

Jamaica Imperilled

FRANCE'S ENTRY INTO the war forced a rethink of Britain's military strategy. Suddenly, due to the produce of the mainland contributing so much less to the national purse than that of the sugar islands, saving the American colonies was a lower priority than defending the West Indian ones. Lord North and his cabinet immediately ordered the evacuation of Philadelphia, to free up a large force for redeployment in the West Indies. On 18 June 1778, after nine months' occupation, General Sir Henry Clinton – Howe's successor as commander-in-chief in America – led his army out of the city, marching overland to New York to avoid a confrontation with the French fleet.

One of the most serious provisioning crises of the war would unfold over the following months. The efficiency of the transport fleet that Richard ran on behalf of the Treasury was greatly dependent on its ships being swiftly unloaded in America, then released immediately to return to the main depot at Cork, to pick up another batch of supplies. But the process had been hindered right from the start by difficulties at New York. During the first year of the war, after a fire destroyed much of the town, thirty-nine vessels chartered by Mure, Son & Atkinson were pressed into service as floating warehouses. Following this episode, General Howe had recruited David Laird, erstwhile captain of the *Thames*, to act as agent and supervisor for the transport ships arriving in America;

but their slow turnaround was a problem Richard continued to grapple with.

A few weeks after the British withdrawal from Philadelphia, a French naval squadron appeared on the horizon outside New York harbour. 'Captain Laird is now and has been so bussie since his return from Philadelphia that he has no time to write,' Thomas Skelton, Laird's deputy, wrote to Richard on 14 July. 'The Count De Estaing has been these three days past at Anchor off Sandy Hook with 15 Sail of men of war, 11 of them line of battle Ships.' Now that New York was under blockade, Skelton cautioned, there was 'no saying' when ships might be able to depart for Ireland.[1]

The panic presently subsided, for the French fleet sailed away after eleven days. Already that summer, however, with so many vessels having failed to return, the Treasury Board had directed Mure, Son & Atkinson to take up '3,000 Tons of the stoutest & strongest ships they can meet with, & send them to Cork, & arm them immediately'.[2] When Richard received Skelton's letter, on 24 August, he passed it to John Robinson; the Lords of the Treasury were sufficiently rattled to order a further 5,000 tons of shipping. Six weeks later, Richard had managed to charter the ships, although finding crews for them was proving more of a challenge. 'The difficulty of this part of the Service increases with the Scarcity of Seamen,' he told Robinson, 'and we fear admits of no remedy, as the Men cannot be kept on board against their Consent.'[3] By the end of October, however, twenty-two vessels with a capacity of 7,965 tons, crewed by 1,608 sailors, were ready for loading at Cork.

General Clinton, meanwhile, warned that stores in New York were running low. The hold-up of ships in America was undoubtedly the nub of the problem; yet poor communications were also to blame, for the baffling reports of the commissary in New York meant that John Robinson could barely work out whether the troops were eating 46,000 rations a day, as allowed for, or considerably more than that. (Somehow, in seven months, they had managed to consume an extra three and a half million pounds of bread and flour, and an extra two million pounds of meat.) In November,

Robinson penned a blistering eleven-page reprimand to the commissary – such was the gravity of the situation that he ran the letter past George III himself. 'The Drafts seem highly proper but oblige me again to repeat that the inaccuracy in stating the Rations in N. America is most extraordinary and encourages the opinion of fraud or great negligence,' wrote the king. 'Nothing can be more proper than the part taken by Mr. Robinson in the whole of this transaction.'[4]

By mid-December, the warehouses in New York were near empty. Clinton told the Colonial Secretary, Lord George Germain:

> Your Lordship will be startled when I inform you that this Army has now but a fortnight's Flour left. I hear no accounts that can give me hopes that Supplies are on the Coasts, and the North West Winds which blow violently and almost invariably at this Season make the arrival of any Fleet in this Port very precarious indeed. Our Meat with the assistance of Cattle purchased here will last about forty days beyond Xmas, and a Bread composed of Pease, Indian Corn and Oatmeal can be furnished for about the same time. After that I know not how We shall Subsist.[5]

This episode was a striking reminder of the extent to which the redcoat army relied upon the exertions of the Treasury Board, and Mure, Son & Atkinson, and many more links in the extended supply chain. Fortunately for General Clinton, the first of the previous autumn's intake of shipping sailed into New York harbour on 4 January 1779, and the crisis was averted.

Now, more than ever, John Robinson wished that the Treasury could be shot of its responsibility for shipping the army's supplies to America, and he reopened talks on the subject with the Admiralty; in February, the Navy Board agreed to take on the role. It was settled that the Navy Board would start shipping the army's provisions from May 1779, and would replace the Treasury Board's policy of sending individual armed vessels with their own system of dispatching large convoys of merchant ships under naval protection. Richard received instructions to discharge from service the 130-odd ships under his management; these new arrangements terminated a large portion of his government business, and he was clearly annoyed to be presented with a *fait accompli*. 'Having heard of no Imputation of Misconduct on our part or dissatisfaction on that of the Board,' he wrote to Robinson, 'it was not without some Degree of surprize that we thus received Information of a treaty so far advanced.'[6]

Meanwhile the fog surrounding Richard's rum contracts was no closer to lifting. Stephen Fuller, the agent of the Jamaican Assembly in London, had failed to come up with a formula for pricing the additional 350,000 gallons ordered by General Howe back in April 1777; now the Lords of the Treasury proposed passing the matter to two new referees, who would themselves have the power 'to name an umpire, If they shall see occasion'.[7] Richard consented to the plan, choosing his old friend Francis Baring to act on his behalf; the Treasury Board nominated the merchant John Purrier. But the arbitration process once again stalled in May 1779, when Baring and Purrier wrote to the Treasury stating 'their Inability to proceed to the award', and requesting further directions.[8]

On 20 July, Lord North chaired a special meeting about the rum contracts; it was attended by all five Lords of the Treasury, as well as the Attorney General, Alexander Wedderburn, a notorious bully. The terse language of the minutes – 'Mr. Atkinson is called in & heard and Mr. Attorney General states to him some Ideas for the settling of this Business for his Consideration' – masks what Richard would later recall as one of the most bruising encounters of his life.[9] As for the Treasury Board's proposed solution, which was to lump all three of his rum contracts together and judge them on criteria that he regarded as 'feigned' – it offended his sense of justice. The following day, Richard reiterated his position: 'I beg leave to repeat that I consider the three Contracts as things perfectly distinct and unconnected with each other.' He could hardly believe, having 'invested his Fortune in a most arduous & essential Service to the Army', that the Treasury was now attempting to browbeat him into submission.[10]

DURING HIS PREMIERSHIP, Lord North suffered from debilitating bouts of what would nowadays be diagnosed as depression, and he made repeated failed attempts to quit his office. 'Lord North cannot conceive what can induce his Majesty, after so many proofs of Lord North's unfitness for his situation, to determine at all events to keep him at the head of the Administration,' the prime minister had written in March 1778, in the third person as was customary for letters to the monarch.[11] He again tried to break free in June 1779, but Spain was by now on the point of entering the war, and the king responded that his resignation 'would be highly unbecoming at this hour'.[12]

The French and Spanish allies planned a naval assault on the British Isles that summer, to be followed up with a land invasion by an army of more than thirty thousand men. In the event, the Spanish navy arrived six weeks late at the agreed rendezvous off the coast of north-west Spain, and as the French fleet sweltered in the heat, many sailors fell sick. The Bourbon allies at last headed north on 25 July, but their bad luck continued; as adverse winds slowed their progress, they missed out on the plunder from two British merchant convoys returning from the Leeward Islands and Jamaica. On 16 August the combined fleet, numbering sixty-six ships of the line, was spotted off Plymouth; two days later a great easterly gale scattered them into the Atlantic. Like its predecessor of 1588, the Armada of 1779 ended in failure.

Still, the mood in Britain remained sombre. 'Never did a deeper political Gloom over-spread England, than in the Autumn of 1779,' Nathaniel Wraxall would later recall in his *Historical Memoirs*.[13] And few men were gloomier than Lord North. In November, John Robinson told Charles Jenkinson about a harrowing conversation in which the prime minister had confessed that he could not bear to be thought 'the Cause of the destruction of His Majesty's Power' and perhaps the collapse of his country: 'He then My Dear Sir fell into such a Scene of Distress, I assure you as made my Heart bleed for him, & drew Tears from my Eyes.'[14]

Even as Britain's own shores were threatened, its gravest concern remained the West Indies. 'Our Islands must be defended even at the risk of an invasion of this Island,' the king wrote in September 1779. 'If we lose our Sugar Islands it will be impossible to raise Money to continue the War.'[15] These colonies, unfortunately, were highly vulnerable to attack; most of them were dotted among the Lesser Antilles, a chain of islands enclosing the Caribbean Sea, and surrounded by enemy possessions, while Jamaica, the largest and most valuable, lay a thousand miles to the west.

Dominica had been the first island to fall prey to the French, and its capture horrified all those who held an interest in the West Indies. On 3 December 1778, at a packed meeting of merchants and planters held at the London Tavern, a vote was carried to petition the king to cease the 'predatory war' in America. Richard led the minority who opposed the petition, claiming that many of its assertions were 'absolutely false'.[16] The news soon afterwards that Saint Lucia had been wrested away from the French temporarily calmed the merchants' nerves. In June 1779, however, Admiral d'Estaing took Saint Vincent without a shot being fired, followed days later by Grenada, and reportedly swore that by the time he was finished, the King of England would not have enough sugar 'to sweeten his tea'.[17]

On 25 September, word reached London that d'Estaing had sailed his fleet to Saint Domingue, the French colony to the east of Jamaica. Four days later, twelve of Jamaica's most prominent merchants and planters – including Richard – met to prepare a statement to be placed before Lord George Germain. They reminded the minister that there were fewer than two thousand regular soldiers stationed in Jamaica, and suggested that its militia, a corps made up of all able-bodied white males, was quite unequal to the task of its defence. Not only were these men 'unused to discipline' and 'unfit to undergo fatigue', but their absence from the workplace left 'all the Women & Children, all the boiling Houses, & Distillerys, and all the Plantations desolate, & abandoned to the Mercy of the Slaves;

a grievance in some respects but little inferior to that of being left to the Mercy of the Enemy'.[18]

Ten days later came news that six thousand French troops were headed for the Caribbean. While ministers vacillated, the merchants took command of the situation. On 15 October, a fund was established to provide a bounty of five guineas to each man enlisting for a new Jamaican regiment, payable on 'his being approved by the commanding officer'.[19] Richard subscribed £100, as did each of his partners, and donations soon flooded in from many prominent Jamaican proprietors.

As it happened, a regiment of eight hundred infantry, the 88th Foot, had been ready to embark for Jamaica since the summer, but the Navy Board had not yet found vessels to carry them in. On Saturday 23 October, Richard and his fellow merchant Samuel Long called upon Germain and offered to provide transport ships for the regiment. They found a sympathetic audience in the Colonial Secretary — indeed, he had personal reason to be concerned for Jamaica's safety, having three years earlier appointed his six-year-old son to the lucrative office of Receiver General of the island. Germain agreed to find an extra 750 recruits, and informed the Admiralty that transport would be required; the Admiralty ordered the Navy Board to provide the necessary vessels; the Navy Board found merchants willing to undertake the service; and the merchants told the captains to cease loading commercial goods and instead take on board provisions for the troops.

All was in hand, it seemed, until the commander-in-chief, General Amherst, declared himself unwilling to commit so many men to the defence of Jamaica. 'What think you of Lord Amherst disavowing the directions given last Saturday concerning the recruits,' Richard asked his friend William Knox, who was Germain's deputy at the colonial office. 'The ships are all engaged, the provisions laid in, and the whole expence incurred; nothing will move him.' As Richard was finishing his letter to Knox, another arrived, prompting the following postscript: 'Since writing what precedes I have (near midnight) received Lord Amherst's letter in answer to one we

wrote him to-day as a last effort, in which he maintains his character, and all the recruits we are to get are a hundred and twenty-five.
A thought strikes me by which I think the shame of this transaction
may be hid. I will see Lord North upon it in the morning if he is not
gone (as Lord George is) into the country.'[20]

In the end, through determined lobbying, Richard managed to
have the number of recruits raised to 350 – two hundred of whom
were immediately press-ganged at Chatham. Samuel Long, Richard's collaborator during these operations, rode down to Gravesend
on 5 November to see them all embarked.

The merchants' forwardness soon became public knowledge.
'The following extraordinary notice of the sailing of the Jamaica
fleet, was stuck up at Lloyd's coffee house yesterday evening,' the
Evening Post reported, in droll mode:

> *Admiralty, Nov. 12, twelve o'clock.* Mr. Atkinson presents
> compliments to Mr. Long, and acquaints him, that the fleet
> will sail from Portsmouth in the first fair wind after Sir Geo.
> Rodney's ship is ready, without waiting for any thing that is
> not then got round; Sir George goes down tomorrow. Mr. A.
> submits to Mr. Long, whether notice should not be sent to both
> coffee houses.[21]

The threat to Jamaica appeared to lift when the news came soon
afterwards that the French fleet had been sighted off Georgia. Even
so, on 8 December 1779, the Jamaica agent Stephen Fuller presented
a petition to Lord George Germain, complaining that too little
was being done for the island's defence. The Colonial Secretary
replied that although the king and his ministers appreciated the
'very great value & importance of Jamaica', they were not prepared
to disclose the 'amount or the nature' of measures adopted for its
safety.[22] Germain's lofty response caused a rift in the Jamaica lobby
between those inclined to condemn the ministry and those who
favoured a more collaborative approach. On 17 December, at a meeting from which Richard was conspicuously absent, the planters and

merchants appointed a sub-committee to campaign for greater naval and military protection for their island. 'I see the Proprietors of Jamaica after all the attention shewn to them shew still a disposition to give trouble,' the king observed to John Robinson.[23]

Before Christmas, news came of a great victory at Savannah, the capital of Georgia, where the occupying British had repelled a much larger besieging force supported by the French navy; subsequently Admiral d'Estaing had limped back to France with his fleet. On Christmas Eve, the cabinet resolved to send three thousand more troops to Jamaica, in addition to five thousand men who were about to embark for the Leeward Islands. Only Lord Amherst objected, maintaining that the loss of men would leave the kingdom 'in too defenceless a State' – but the king overruled his commander-in-chief, and four regiments were ordered to ready themselves.[24]

Although more troops would be dispatched to the West Indies over the winter of 1779–80 than had been sent to America since 1776, many of the Jamaica lobby continued to harp on about the previous autumn's invasion scare. 'The safety of such a possession as Jamaica ought not to have been left to chance,' they moaned in a petition placed before the Commons on 10 February. During the parliamentary debate that followed, the absentee planter Richard Pennant accused the prime minister of caring so little about Jamaica that he never bothered to read its governor's reports, an act of negligence for which he 'deserved to be impeached'. (At which point North was said to have bellowed across the chamber: 'Impeach me – impeach me now.') Germain questioned the legitimacy of the lobbyists' petition, given that the 'meeting at which it had been resolved upon, had never been advertised' – a claim denied by Pennant, who said he 'had the advertisements in his pocket, and he was very sure, that Mr. Atkinson was the only one present, who had any objection at all'.[25] (This was a lie, for the minutes of the meeting on 17 December prove that Richard was not there.)[26] Thomas Townshend, a vocal opponent of the war, suggested that Richard's censure of the petition was quite meaningless, given his manifold connections with the ministry: 'He held the greatest number of contracts, and was to be heard of at the Admiralty Office, the Navy Office, the Victualling Office, the War Office, and, in short, at every place where money was to be gotten. In fact, he appeared to be the principal Minister, and perhaps he was the most *active* Minister we had.'[27]

THE POLITICAL CAMPAIGNER John Horne Tooke, released from prison after serving a short sentence for seditious libel, chose to channel his anger into a polemical investigation of the public finances. *Facts Addressed to the Landholders*, which Horne Tooke co-wrote with the radical economist Dr Richard Price, came out in January 1780; it soon ran to eight editions. The activities of Mure, Son & Atkinson had come to epitomize the profligacy of the ministry, and Richard's rum contracts received the dubious honour of their own chapter. They were an easy target, a throwaway line – 'as cheap as Mr. Atkinson's rum', Horace Walpole would write, describing something that wasn't cheap at all.[28] On 8 February, the freeholders of Yorkshire, hobbled by heavy taxes and the low value of grain, presented parliament with a petition demanding 'economical' reforms – this would soon be followed by similar petitions from twenty-eight counties and eleven boroughs. Three days later, in an epic speech that Lord North admitted was 'one of the most able he had ever heard', the Irish statesman Edmund Burke demanded a root-and-branch reform of every category of national expenditure.[29]

The press, as ever, greatly enjoyed the prime minister's discomfiture. The *London Courant* waggishly proposed that he should set up a 'new Board' to restore parliament 'to its proper purity', whose first task would be to dispose of the largest vermin. 'The Duke of Richmond and Lord Shelburne,' the journalist suggested, 'will take a great deal of killing; so will Barré and Fox (the latter already judged, like Shelburne, pistol-proof). As for the inferior class, including all the apostate country gentlemen, they had better be executed by contract. Mure and Atkinson will of course offer proposals to the Board; and as in their extensive undertakings they must necessarily have many expert cut-throats under them, they will probably do the business per head as reasonably as they do any other.'[30]

Fenchurch Street, looking west. The Ironmongers' Hall dominates the foreground; Richard's house was set back behind gates on the left-hand side.

The mood of pent-up public fury spilled over in London on 2 June 1780, when a march against Catholic emancipation led by Lord George Gordon disintegrated into a five-day orgy of looting and arson. Richard had recently moved to 32 Fenchurch Street, a mansion set back behind a gateway and courtyard on one of the City's main thoroughfares – as was usual at this time, it acted as both his home and place of business. Its location was midway between flashpoints at the Bank of England and the Tower of London, and I wondered whether he was caught up in the violence. I was excited to find a report in the *Morning Chronicle* of a bishop whose carriage had been surrounded and had its wheels taken off; this prelate had found refuge in 'Mr. Atkinson's house', but thirty men had subsequently broken down the door, forcing him to escape from a rear window.[31] Disappointingly, after further digging, I learnt that the 'Mr. Atkinson' in this story was not Richard, but a lawyer in Westminster – such are the minor hiccups of historical research.

On 15 June, as the capital was clearing up after the riots – some put the number of dead and wounded at seven hundred – a measure of good news arrived from South Carolina. After a siege lasting six weeks, the American garrison at Charleston had surrendered to General Clinton, who had taken five thousand prisoners. Reports from the West Indies, however, were less cheering. An outbreak of fever in Saint Lucia had killed hundreds of soldiers and left many too feeble for duty. The best medicine was believed to be claret – but dispensing it to the men would involve a thicket of red tape. William Knox, under-secretary at the colonial office, asked Richard for his ideas about the best way to supply it. 'By the Act of Navigation, no Wine can be imported into our Colonies from Europe, unless from Great Britain, Madeira or the Azores,' Richard advised. 'Guernsey, Jersey & Ireland are equally prohibited to send Wines directly to the Colonies. A neutral Ship might be sent to Bourdeaux or any other Port in France, to clear out for Holland & stop in Great Britain, & might tranship the Wine by License as abovementioned.'[32]

On 9 August, in a major setback for the merchant community, the Spanish fleet intercepted a convoy recently departed from Portsmouth, seizing fifty-five ships mostly headed for the West Indies; their cargo was valued at £1,500,000. The plunder also included five East Indiaman ships – a loss from which Richard managed, in a letter to Knox dated 12 September, to spin a silver lining of sorts:

> You desired Information some time ago about the means of
> supplying Wine to the Army in the West Indies, which leads
> me to communicate to you an Offer that has just been made
> me of the Refusal of about four thousand Dozen of Claret in
> Bottles at Madeira which had been sent thither to meet
> the outward bound India Ships which are taken. The only
> Objection there can be to the Quality is that it is too good,
> but I am confident that no such speedy Supply can be sent by
> any other Mode.[33]

When the Treasury Board next met, Mure, Son & Atkinson were ordered to send a ship to Madeira to pick up the claret and 'proceed with it to Saint Lucia with the utmost expedition'.[34]

*

SPAIN HAD PLACED the Rock of Gibraltar under siege from both land and sea within a week of declaring war on Britain in June 1779. The following spring, Admiral Sir George Rodney had managed to sidestep the blockade to deliver provisions to the eight thousand men trapped there; but letters since smuggled from Gibraltar reported dwindling stores of beef, butter, oats, pease and wheat, as well as coal, candles, lamp oil, rum and vinegar. In September 1780 John Robinson received instructions from Lord George Germain to procure two years' worth of every necessity while maintaining the strictest secrecy, to prevent whispers of the mission from reaching Spain. Naturally, the Treasury Board awarded the contract to Mure, Son & Atkinson.

But a complication with the coal supply threatened to expose the operation. At the start of the siege, the Treasury had cancelled various standing contracts for the supply of the garrison; it had not, however, revoked the contract held by the powerful Fox family to provide coal, since this fell within the remit of Charles Jenkinson, the Secretary at War. The Foxes' agent, anticipating an expedition to Gibraltar, had already filled a number of collier vessels which were now ready to leave. Robinson asked Jenkinson to lay them off immediately. 'To put in Motion the Ships avowedly taken up by your Contractor for carrying Coals to Gibraltar,' he explained, 'loaden as such, & known to be so by every Man on board – would I fear at once make the discovery.'[35] It was Richard who came up with a solution; so as to 'preserve the secret, and avoid giving offence to the contractors', he offered to procure the coals himself, while passing on the benefit of any mark-up and commission to 'the Mr. Foxes'. (William Knox would tell this story years later, in his memoirs, 'in justice to the memory of a man who possessed the best talents for executive business that I ever was acquainted with'.)[36]

Admiral George Darby received orders to sail for Gibraltar on 1 January 1781, but repairs prevented his fleet from leaving until mid-March. Fortunately, as Darby rounded Cape St Vincent with twenty-nine ships of the line and almost a hundred store ships, the Spanish navy was nowhere to be seen. The British fleet swept into the Bay of Gibraltar on 12 April, swiftly unloaded its cargo, and departed nine days later.

Because the expedition was so hush-hush, the paper trail was minimal, which is why it barely appears in the official records; but it was clearly a mammoth undertaking. Mure, Son & Atkinson billed the Treasury £266,858, which John Robinson tucked away in the public accounts under the heading 'Provisions and Stores shipped for Special Service'.[37] By way of comparison, Richard had invoiced £108,487 for the supplies sent out to Boston in the autumn of 1775.[38] Unlike the earlier mission, however, the relief of Gibraltar was a resounding success – not least because it provided the fuel for a conflagration, eighteen months later, that would help bring the war to a close.

GENERAL WASHINGTON'S MOOD was sombre during the latter months of 1780; with the Continental dollar almost worthless, deemed 'fit for nothing But Bum Fodder', his troops were restless.[39] 'We have been half our time without provision & are likely to remain so,' he wrote on 5 October. 'We have no Magazines, nor money to form them. And in a little time we shall have no men, if we had money to pay them.'[40] The national finances of the French were also fast unravelling; from a British perspective, a strategy of attrition offered the best odds of winning the war.

In December, Richard and his fellow contractors agreed terms with the Treasury to provision the army in America over the following year; they would supply rations for a total of 86,000 soldiers at $5\,^{27}/_{32}$d per day. Richard's Canada syndicate would feed fifteen thousand men.[41] But beasts even more voracious than humans also relied upon the Treasury for their rations – the army's four thousand-odd horses, each of which daily chomped through about nine pounds of oats or twenty pounds of hay. During the war, Mure, Son & Atkinson would invoice £219,271 for oats alone. This species of grass grows best in a cool, damp climate; so it was fitting that Richard should turn to sub-contractors from such a region – namely, his brothers at Temple Sowerby.

Evidence of George and Matthew Atkinson's involvement in the enterprise lies in a scuffed leatherbound book that I inherited, which appears to be their main business ledger, under an account headed 'Oats, Meal, Sacks, Casks'. No letters exist on the subject, or at least none that I have seen, so it is left to the numbers to do the talking – and they are large numbers. In March 1781, for example, the Treasury ordered Mure, Son & Atkinson to supply General Clinton with 50,000 quarters of oats. The Navy Board was unable to provide transport on this occasion, so Mure, Son & Atkinson also chartered 10,000 tons of shipping (around thirty vessels) to carry the load to New York. Richard invoiced the Treasury £36,956 for the oats and £43,181 for the shipping; his brothers, meanwhile, having settled with the suppliers of the grain, made a profit of £9,800, as is revealed by the transfer of this sum from the 'Oats, Meal, Sacks, Casks' account into their profit and loss account.[42]

The high price of the oats did not go unremarked. In the House of Commons, Sir Philip Jennings Clerke – a sworn scourge of contractors – commented that an 'ingenious gentleman had calculated what the real cost of oats was to government on their arrival in America, and it had been found to be exactly three oats for a halfpenny'.[43] Edmund Burke 'shuddered' at the expense, pointing out that the money spent on buying and shipping the oats would have purchased two new frigates for the navy.[44]

I was exhilarated to uncover the Temple Sowerby connection to the oat supply – even if it looked suspiciously like profiteering. When I started writing the story of the Atkinson family, I had hoped to connect them to the big events of the time. Here, in miniature, was exactly what I'd wanted to achieve, for in tracing a route through the various documents – from General Clinton's letter from New York to the colonial office in London, via the Treasury Board minutes and Mure, Son & Atkinson's invoices, finally to the handwritten ledger on the desk in front of me – I was able to follow the trail from the British headquarters in America, via Westminster, all the way back to Westmorland. And I knew exactly where nearly £10,000 of public money had gone – straight into my ancestors' pockets.

EIGHT

A Heartbreaking Letter

LADY ANNE LINDSAY'S self-imposed exile in Scotland, following her brother-in-law Fordyce's bankruptcy, would last four years. In Edinburgh, that great city of the Enlightenment, she would shine in the company of some brilliant older men, notably the philosophers David Hume and Lord Monboddo. At one memorable dinner, hosted by the physician Sir Alexander Dick in 1773, she even managed to impress Samuel Johnson.

The famous doctor of letters, then sixty-three, was touring Scotland at the time with the 'faithful Bozzy, his friend, adorer and biographer'. The old Countess of Eglinton, Johnson told the spellbound company, always called him 'Son', since he had been born the year after she was married. James Boswell interrupted to correct the great man – no, he said, it was the year *before* she was married. 'Had that been the case,' Johnson retorted, 'she would have had little to boast of.' At this point Anne piped up: 'Would not the *Son* have excused the *Sin*?' Prior to her interjection, Anne noticed, Johnson had been 'disposed to be sulky', but afterwards he became 'excessively agreeable & entertaining'. Most pleasingly, she had later watched Boswell 'steal to the window to put down the *Jeu de mot* in his commonplace book'.[1]

It was during these years that Anne would make the acquaintance of Henry Dundas, an ambitious young lawyer who had lost much of his fortune in the banking crash of 1772, and had recently been elected to parliament for the first time. Anne's friendship with Dundas was never quite straightforward; the 'partiality' he formed for her 'had for its basis *nothing at all*', as she recalled it. 'It was a hearty, serviceable, admiring, gallant good-will, such as was in his nature for all womankind, old and young, tho' more particularly for the young.'[2]

Lady Margaret Fordyce's time in Scotland had been curtailed by the unwelcome discovery that the £500 a year settled on her by her husband before their marriage, while safe from the grasp of his creditors, was dependent on their living together. She returned to London, and they set up home at Harley Street in Marylebone, on the unfashionable north side of Oxford Street. Their reconciliation proved merely perfunctory, but luckily he was often away. In a typically outlandish bid to make a new fortune, Alexander Fordyce was busy setting up a chemical works at South Shields, near Newcastle, to harness a method of manufacturing 'fossil alkali' (sodium carbonate) and 'marine acid' (hydrochloric acid) which had recently been discovered by his chemist nephew George.

It was only in 1777, when she was twenty-six, that Anne decided to move back to London, after a modest legacy from her grandmother endowed her with some financial independence. Despite their connection to the notorious bankrupt Fordyce, the sisters still had an entrée into the smartest salons, where as Anne would recall they were 'prized by many and welcomed like little holidays into society'.[3] Often they were asked to sing, at which they were both extremely accomplished. 'Lady Margaret Fordyce is at this time confessedly the first voice in the list of *fashionable amateurs*; she is a pupil of the *Italian school*, and executes the most difficult passages in the most finished manner,' reported one newspaper. 'Lady Anne Lindsay has likewise a charming pipe, but her style is quite the reverse of her sister's being entirely confined to the plaintive melody of *Scotch ballads!*'[4] The novelist Fanny Burney described the sisters' late arrival one evening at a lavish party at Lady Gideon's: 'I had hopes they would have sung, but I was disappointed, for they only looked handsome.'[5] It goes without saying that Richard was delighted to have them both back in the capital – Anne remembered him welcoming them 'like boons sent from Heaven'.[6]

Anne's male admirers tended to follow a pattern – as she herself described it, 'starting up with zeal . . . vanishing like meteors'. She attributed this to her relative poverty: 'I had nothing for my lovers to pay their debts with, or to appropriate to younger children.'[7] Viscount Wentworth was one of the few who stuck around. They first met at a musical soirée in 1778, where he was charmed by her singing, while she was taken with his flute-playing, not to mention his fine figure, which 'spoke him more decidedly the man of rank' than most of his sex.[8] But Anne would soon learn that Wentworth was less available than he appeared. For more than a decade, he had been living with a mistress, Catharine Vanloo; she had come over from Flanders as the governess to his younger sisters, seducing him when he was virtually a boy, and had since borne him two children. He was also in regular attendance at the gaming tables of St James's, where he was diligently squandering his inheritance. The on-off relationship between Anne and Lord Wentworth would cause them both considerable anguish over the coming years.

One day in 1779, Richard overheard the Lindsay sisters discussing the pension for which their mother, Lady Balcarres, had unsuccessfully applied to the king, and he discreetly asked Anne ('pardon me the presumption of the question') where she kept her money. 'In the Moon! We are all as poor as Church mice,' she answered. 'I am the only person of fortune in the family as I had a legacy left me in money, of £300, not long ago, by my Grandmother.' Richard went on to explain that there were many ways in which such a sum might be put to work, and he begged Anne to entrust it to his care. "Tis so little, my good friend, that it is scarce worthy your troubling yourself about it,' she said. 'We must teach it then to become bigger,' he replied with a smile.[9]

The worst hurricane in memory tore through the West Indies in October 1780; the western parishes of Jamaica took a particular pounding. This was yet more dire news for Richard's partner Hutchison Mure, whose Suffolk residence, Great Saxham Hall, had burnt down the previous year. Financial troubles now forced Mure into the confession of an 'alarming and disgraceful secret', hidden for fifteen years. Back in 1766, when Richard joined the partnership, Mure had neglected to mention private debts of £30,000 for which they would be jointly liable, an omission which had caused the old man so much stress during the intervening years that 'he had sometimes feared for his reason'.[10] His creditors were closing in; unless he could quickly sell off a couple of his sugar estates, he would be undone.

Although the revelation came as a profound shock to Richard, it also presented him with the opportunity to acquire Jamaican property of his own for a good price. In raising the capital to buy Dean's Valley Dry Works in Westmoreland Parish, he was assisted by a loan of half its value from his friend Captain David Laird; while he purchased the Bogue estate in St James Parish as a joint venture with a slippery financier named Paul Benfield.[11] Through these transactions, Richard became the co-owner of some five hundred enslaved men, women and children. A few months later, in April 1781, Hutchison Mure folded his Suffolk landholdings into the assets of the partnership, paving the way for another of his sons – William, who had previously been living in Jamaica – to join the firm.[12] Thus Mure, Son & Atkinson became Mures, Atkinson & Mure.

THE TREASURY WAS FORCED to borrow vast sums of money during the American war, the national debt nearly doubling in seven years. Doom-mongers predicted economic collapse; but the enormity of these sovereign debts paradoxically confirmed the strength of the British financial system. It was the Treasury's practice to pay a low interest rate on government loan stock, but to sell it to investors at a generous discount on its nominal value – this, in time, guaranteed a handsome return on their initial outlay. The close-knit relationship between the Treasury and the most powerful men of the City of London ensured the ministry's access to funds for pursuing the war. A slice of the national debt was the most secure possible investment, and financiers selected by the Treasury to partake of the loan stock gained the power to bestow considerable largesse on family, friends and associates.

When Lord North announced to the House of Commons, on 7 March 1781, that he would need a £12 million loan for the following year, he neither expected an easy ride, nor did he receive one. Charles James Fox, who took an opposing view to the prime minister on almost all matters, sourly accused him of raiding the public purse in order to prop up his parliamentary majority through bribes for supporters. Sir Philip Jennings Clerke suggested that North had parcelled out the loan to his private friends as a reward for past services: 'In particular, he was well informed that Mr. Atkinson the contractor, and partner with Mr. Mure, had no less than £3,300,000 to his own share.'[13] The prime minister rubbished the 'very idea' of such a sum being allocated to one man: 'Great bankers, the House well knew, applied for many other persons, as well as on their own account, but no person would have such a proportion as the hon. gentleman had mentioned.'[14]

This was far from the end of the matter. In a fierce debate the following week, the opposition let rip about the mishandling of the loan, and the role of a certain notorious rum contractor. George Byng, MP for Middlesex, complained that the list of individual subscribers and their allocations had not been sent to the Bank of England, as was customary, before the loan was presented to parliament; instead, he claimed, it had been held back at the Treasury for three days, where it had 'undergone many garblings, and many corrections'. Moreover, he knew of 'very suspicious' circumstances relating to the part played by Richard in the distribution of the loan: 'It was pretty certain that he was in a room at the Treasury by himself, with the list, while many respectable and responsible men had it not in their power to converse with the noble lord on the subject.'

John Robinson, in a rare speech, admitted that Richard had been consulted about small-scale applicants from the City whose names were unknown to the Treasury – lottery-office keepers, tailors and suchlike – but 'as to Mr. Atkinson having the list in a room by himself, the fact had never happened, he had neither settled the list, nor had he the list to interfere with at all'.[15]

When the full list of subscribers was published, Mures, Atkinson & Mure's official portion was found to be £200,000 – a sizeable chunk, but by no means unprecedented. Richard had also quietly set aside loan stock worth £30,000 for Anne Lindsay's personal benefit. The financial markets were buoyant. 'The stock has risen greatly already,' he told her shortly afterwards, 'but a week hence it will overtop expectation: *have you nerves to stand it?*'[16] On 13 March, the noise of cannon fire at the Tower of London reverberated around the City. Admiral Rodney had captured the Dutch island of Saint Eustatius in the West Indies, cutting off a crucial source of supplies for the Continental Army; almost half the ships entering Philadelphia and Baltimore over the previous year had come from this supposedly neutral port. 'What an unlooked-for piece of good fortune,' wrote Richard to Anne.

A few days passed, and the markets climbed even higher: 'All remains steady.' Then came news of failed peace negotiations with France and Spain, and the stock tumbled. When Anne heard what had happened, she put on her 'oldest bonnet', strolled up to the open fields at the top of Harley Street, and 'walked and reasoned and fatigued' herself into accepting her diminished expectations: 'I have not lost all (thought I) if I can feel in this manner, and if I still possess the friendship of Atkinson.'[17]

Richard called at Harley Street early the next day. Fordyce was away, and Margaret indisposed; as he had hoped, he had Anne all to himself. 'You are a philosopher indeed,' he smiled as he entered the room. 'I had fortunately reason, from a friend of mine who crossed with the messenger, to suspect how this was likely to be.' He had cashed in her loan stock, if not at the very top of the market, then not far off it. 'Here is your little gain,' he said, handing her a printed certificate for 'long Annuities' worth £3,475, which promised her £200 a year.

It was the first time she had ever felt herself to be 'decidedly rich', and she reacted by bursting into tears.[18] 'The more I reflect on the generous proof you gave me this morning of your friendship & zeal for the interests of one who is so destitute of every means of shewing her gratitude but by her words,' she would write to him later that day, 'the more vexed I am with this vile tongue that did not do my feelings Justice.'[19]

The City of London was abuzz with rumours of staggering gains. 'It is reported upon 'Change,' said the *Gazetteer*, 'that the *celebrated* Mr. Atkinson's *clerks* are complimented with upwards of £150,000 of the new loan.'[20] Meanwhile, at Westminster, Sir George Savile introduced a parliamentary motion for a committee to look into the allocation of the loan, on grounds that a 'certain gentleman' had been allowed to doctor the lists 'in what manner best suited his own interest'.[21] George Byng, seconding the motion, pedantically read out to the chamber the names of the loan's 1,147 subscribers; among those that caught his eye were Messrs. Smith & Sill, who were well known as Richard's lawyers, and David Laird, whose £10,000 allocation was most surprising, since he had only arrived from America 'a few days before the noble lord opened his budget; but Captain Laird is the friend of Mr. Atkinson'.[22]

To avoid the scrutiny of her peers and – worse still – the clutches of her brother-in-law, Anne kept her newly acquired fortune a secret. Alexander Fordyce bragged endlessly about the riches that would soon spew forth from his soap-making factory in County Durham; but he was up to his old tricks again, bullying associates into lending him money, and flying into a rage if anyone had the temerity to question his dealings. 'He has drained the best powers of every friend he has,' Richard told Anne. 'Our House has suffered (if a mercantile interest is included) above a Hundred thousand pounds by him, he holds it as his worst enemy because it will go no further. Apart from this I have lent him (which I consider as gone) £13,000, and by what shifts and duplicities has it been obtained!'[23]

Once more, during a tearful two-hour tête-à-tête that dredged up unwelcome memories of that fateful day, nine years earlier, when he had brought word of her husband's impending bankruptcy, it fell to Richard to break to Margaret the unwelcome news of these debts.

The following morning, as the sisters were eating breakfast, bailiffs turned up at Harley Street to seize the contents of the house; but Richard was already on the spot, waiting to intercept them, and immediately took charge of the situation, paying off the sum for which Fordyce was being pursued. As Anne would recall: 'When he returned to us (gentle and unostentatious in all his modes), he sat down on his chair as if he thanked the friendship of those who allowed him to occupy it. This painful business over for the present, he departed, leaving a letter which he said he had forgot to deliver to Margaret, containing Two hundred pounds to discharge her own immediate bills.'[24]

GIVEN THE RUMPUS surrounding Richard's rum contracts, their settlement was a surprisingly low-key business. What ought to have been the routine matter of agreeing a fair price for this most ordinary of commodities had mutated into a full-blown political scandal, the subject of at least twenty-seven Treasury Board meetings. But on 31 May 1781, after a hiatus of almost two years while waiting for the Attorney General to determine the principles by which they should be guided, the referees Francis Baring and John Purrier were ready to deliver their verdict.

They marked down both Richard's first contract (100,000 gallons at the price paid by the navy in Jamaica, plus freight, leakage and insurance, agreed with the prime minister in September 1775) and his second (100,000 gallons at 5s 3d, agreed with the Treasury in May 1776), compelling him to refund £9,171 of the £61,608 that he had already received. (Even so, the judgement offered Richard vindication of sorts, for during the first failed attempt at arbitration, four years earlier, Beeston Long had refused to take the soaring cost of insurance into consideration; Baring and Purrier, on the other hand, factored it into their calculations.) With the referees' ruling on his third contract (350,000 gallons at a price to be determined by the Treasury, agreed with General Howe in April 1777), Richard had cause for satisfaction, for they set the price at 5s 2d per gallon – only a penny less than the much-criticized second contract.

Furthermore, Captain Laird certified that 499,738 gallons had been delivered to New York in fulfilment of the third contract, in nineteen ships unloaded under his supervision – a colossal over-delivery which valued the rum at £129,099.[25] Mures, Atkinson & Mure had already been paid most of this amount; the remaining £24,767 was authorized by royal warrant on 26 July, in the dead of the summer recess, when anyone who might have kicked up a fuss was out of town.[26] The final settlement of the rum business marked the end of one difficult chapter of Richard's life, and the start of another, more emotional one.

IT WAS SOON after my discovery of Bridget Atkinson's 'receipt book' – at a time when it was first dawning on me that I had somehow unearthed an astonishing family story, but as yet had little sense of where it might lead me – that I learnt about Richard's correspondence with Lady Anne Lindsay, in an old volume which I came across online. How many such letters existed, the book did not divulge; to find out more, I would need to visit the National Library of Scotland.

One Thursday evening, just before midnight, I boarded the sleeper train at Euston; seven hours later it trundled into Edinburgh Waverley station, on a gleaming spring morning. I arrived at the library as it opened – I had already been warned by the curator of manuscripts that the reading room would close at lunchtime, and there was a great deal for me to get through. I started with the printed catalogue of the Lindsay family archive, and was amazed to learn that the collection included hundreds of letters written by members of the Atkinson family over three generations – Richard had merely initiated a correspondence which had continued into the 1830s. I had an inkling that these later letters might relate to Jamaican property, but this would need investigation another time – the twenty-six letters written by Richard to Anne would keep me busy for one morning. Three hours later, I emerged on to the cobbles of Edinburgh's Old Town, into bright sunshine, feeling giddy, elated, and just a little besotted with my namesake.

Until this moment in the story, Richard's most heartfelt sentiments have remained under wraps – which might, perhaps, have caused you to draw the conclusion that he was not the marrying type. You would be mistaken, though, for Richard had fallen in love with Anne Lindsay the moment he first laid eyes on her, and had ever since been working towards a day when he might have sufficient wealth to transcend the social gulf that separated them.

One Sunday in July 1781, when he was forty-two, Richard sat down to write the letter on which his future happiness would hinge. He had already primed Anne to expect a note about a 'matter more interesting' to him than any other, hoping that she might be able to offer him 'very salutary counsel' on a point where he confessed himself 'at a loss how to decide'.[27] That evening Anne was alone at Harley Street, and expecting a visit from her fickle suitor Lord Wentworth, when Richard's letter was delivered – her first impression was that 'it was a thick one'.[28]

When Anne (much, much later) wrote her life story, she cherrypicked quotes from hundreds of old letters so that they slotted neatly into her narrative – rather as I have tried to do. When the time came to recount the circumstances surrounding this particular letter, however, her powers of précis deserted her; instead she chose to present Richard's words unabridged. As she would explain to her readers: 'It is so much my duty to do justice to that excellent man, that you must forgive me if on this occasion I sacrifice your patience to him.'[29] Two hundred years on, I find myself facing a similar predicament – the main difference being that I am not quite so willing to test my readers' patience. So I will only say that Richard's letter, as an account of how he had reached this pivotal moment, is as revealing a self-portrait of the man as exists, and can be found in its entirety on page 419. But here is its tremulous final paragraph:

And now, by what *tenderest* Epithet, shall I adjure *My Counsellor* to tell me whether my Desires ought to be laid at my fair Friend's Feet or not! I tremble from the fear of diminishing the Share I at present hold in her Esteem, but the Knowledge

I have of the Generosity of her Heart supports me in the Hope that she will not put an unkind Construction upon any part of my Conduct. And altho' I suspect her in one particular to be *an Economist* yet I am sure she is *no Niggard*, but that her Heart will feel the *inestimable* Value of a frank Avowal – and that if *your happy* Counsel at eleven tomorrow (if not forbid) is to embolden me to submit my Passion – *she* will with *one* Look of Kindness at our *first* Interview extend to me the Golden Sceptre and tranquilize my Spirits by *that* assurance that there exists no absolute & insurmountable Bar to my Happiness; beyond which meaning I will not attempt to interpret her Goodness till she gives me leave. How many Blessings does my Heart wish to pour upon her![30]

Anne had not quite finished reading this 'heart-breaking letter' when she heard Margaret come in through the front door, and she hastily retreated to her bedchamber, for she did not want her sister to know that she had been sobbing. Anne realized, from the 'delusion of hope' which pervaded Richard's letter, that 'no report respecting Lord Wentworth' had reached his ears; and it was with deep sadness that she sat down at her desk and revealed her attachment to another man. 'Never did I find a letter so difficult to write, every feeling in my nature was at jar,' she recalled. 'Loaded with obligations, in my own person and in Margaret's, yet returning nothing, disappointing the constant heart that had been so long devoted to me . . . The Watchman called one . . . and two . . . and three . . . and four; and five found me with the pen still in my hand, & my letter unfinished.'[31]

At eight on Monday morning, a messenger delivered Anne's letter to Fenchurch Street. 'Could I only find words, gentle without conveying Illusion, unreserved yet consoling how eagerly would I not use them,' she had written,

But there I must stop – if you will permit to make him who calls himself my client my confidant perhaps I may in the course of a day or two find courage to paint the situation of

a heart which has long strayed from home into the possession
of one who I hope has by degrees learnt to value it – there it
rests and ever will remain. I would not have hurried this point
to my friend had I not learnt at one time from a painfull
experience how severe a moment that of uncertainty is. God
bless you, I pray for your happiness.[32]

Richard called at Harley Street on Wednesday, at Anne's invitation, and was shown up to the drawing room. 'Ten years seemed
added to his appearance, which made me start, and filled my heart
with something like remorse,' she remembered.[33] The conversation
was general, for he was one of several callers that morning, and was
thus unable to say what he had wished to be able to say. That evening he wrote to Anne:

Escaped at length from the tiresome Task of talking about one
thing whilst my mind is wholly intent upon another, I fly to the
Relief which an undisguised communication with my Friend
alone can give me. I hope I did not betray myself today to
Lady M, altho' I am not sure of it. I do not misinterpret your
Intention in not seeing me alone, but you had very near taxed
my Fortitude too high. The Wind & the Dust for these two
days (of which from the Impossibility of excusing myself from
seeing multitudes if I staid at home I have spent a great part in
the Streets) have been my very good Auxiliaries in preventing
observation.[34]

Richard's great dread, having revealed his innermost feelings to
Anne, was that she might henceforth shun his company, to avoid
'adding fresh Fuel to a hopeless Flame'; so he set out to prove that
any such qualms were unnecessary. 'For the Inquietude I have given
you I will not attempt a *common* Apology which you would despise,'
he wrote to her the following week. 'I rather dare flatter myself with
your approbation of my having *disclosed* my Sentiments under the
circumstances in which I did it; and that *bearing* Adversity like a

Man, my Friend will not think hardly of me for having *felt* it as a Man.' Now, as he explained, he hoped to foster a relationship of a fraternal kind:

> My *Hopes* are *dead*. I know too well the force of a true
> attachment in a strong and virtuous Mind to expect a change
> whilst any thing like a proper conduct is reciprocally held.
> I solemnly repeat therefore that all my *Hopes* are at an end.
> That I feel I can rejoice in your happiness with another, and
> when the proper time arrives can *cordially* court his Friendship.
> I entertain not a Sentiment at this Moment that ought to alarm
> or offend him. *Let* me not then upon mistaken Ground *be held
> distant!* Let me have leave to cultivate the Affection of a Brother,
> and to watch over your Welfare as far as my Knowledge
> extends, with a kind Brother's Care![35]

NINE

Mortal Thoughts

THE RELENTLESS WORKLOAD of the war years, as well as the recent blow of his failed marriage proposal, had taken their toll on Richard's health. He would spend much of the autumn of 1781 at Brighthelmstone, a resort in vogue ever since the publication of *A Dissertation on the Use of Sea-Water in the Diseases of the Glands* by Richard Russell, a local physician, nearly thirty years earlier. (The town's altered status – from sleepy fishing village to princely destination – would be accompanied by a change of name, with 'Brighton' soon replacing its more cumbersome precursor.) Richard had managed to secure a good house at the bottom of West Street, overlooking the steep shingle beach. 'The Place as full as can be conceived,' he told Anne on 22 August. 'All the World now resorting to the Rooms since the D & Ds of Cumberland have led the way.'[1] (The duke was a younger brother of the king, who had caused a great scandal by marrying a commoner.)

The Lindsay sisters stayed several weeks with Richard at Brighton during the season, and they made it their mission to launch him into the best society. As Anne afterwards recalled: 'I now saw that the only way in which I could be of present use to Atkinson was by impressing on Margaret that we owed it to his friendship to give him every aid on entering more into company than his habits had hitherto led him to do.' Music and dancing were the principal diversions at Brighton. Richard himself laid on entertainments, engaging some 'choice Catch-singers' from London to stay a few days of every week down in the resort; meanwhile the sisters sang at the soirées of their royal friends, the Cumberlands.[2] Anne watched Richard moving uneasily among the fashionable set, showing his discomfort in their society: 'The manners of the excellent Atkinson were so unlike those of the day that while his heart was glowing with benevolence, ten to one his manner was astonishing all around, and creating a sensation of pain from its familiarity to the persons in the world he felt most respectfully towards.'[3]

Richard's melancholia increased after the deaths, in quick succession, of his two eldest siblings. Jane, who had never married, died at Temple Sowerby on 26 August, aged fifty-three. Six weeks later George, suffering from a 'large tumour on his neck', came down to London to submit to the knife of John Hunter, the king's surgeon; he died two days later in 'excruciating pain', aged fifty-one, and was buried in the little church at Rood Lane, a stone's throw from Fenchurch Street.[4] Sadly, I have no way of finding out whether Bridget was there to hold George's hand during his final hours, nor whether Richard was at his brother's bedside – this event is not recorded by any family letters, only in a brief newspaper report.

Thus mortal thoughts were uppermost in Richard's mind, and he now set about writing his will. 'If ever Man was entitled to dispose of his fortune according to his own sentiments, it is myself,' he would tell Anne, declaring it his intention not only to make ample provision for her in the event of his death, but also to remove any financial obstacles to her marriage to Lord Wentworth:

> I am clearly convinced that the probability of enjoyment in
> Life is *with me* at an end. All my Hopes are therefore centred
> in standing as high as I can in your Esteem, and promoting
> your Happiness in the way it can be pursued; and strange as
> it would sound to the multitude, yet I trust my Friend will
> find nothing *to reprove* in the strong Wish I express that her
> Happiness were in its own way completed, and even that
> *I* could be made instrumental in accelerating it.[5]

ON 25 NOVEMBER 1781, a messenger drew up outside the house of Colonial Secretary Lord George Germain in Pall Mall, conveying a report that a Franco-American army had encircled a British force of nine thousand men at Yorktown in Virginia, and on 17 October, following ten days' bombardment, General Cornwallis had capitulated. Germain immediately went to see Lord North at Downing Street, who received the news 'as he would have taken a Ball in his Breast', repeatedly exclaiming 'Oh, God! it is all over!' as he paced up and down the room.[6]

The Battle of Yorktown ended British hopes of holding on to the American colonies, and unleashed a tide of recriminations back home. Of all the events which had contributed to the catastrophe, a consensus formed that Sir George Rodney's deeds on the island of Saint Eustatius had been among the most discreditable. Britain had declared war on the Dutch Republic in December 1780, infuriated by the partiality shown by this supposedly neutral nation towards its enemies. Admiral Rodney had seized the Dutch freeport of Saint Eustatius in February 1781; according to prize protocol, he was due a one-sixteenth share of all captured goods, and he chose to spend the next three months auctioning off the contents of the Dutch warehouses, rather than giving chase to his French adversary, Admiral de Grasse. In July, as the hurricane season approached, naval operations in the West Indies were suspended as usual, and Rodney decided to return to England, leaving behind a reduced fleet to follow the French towards the American mainland.

Admiral Graves had arrived at the mouth of Chesapeake Bay on 5 September, hoping to bring relief to Cornwallis's besieged army, only to find its entrance blocked by Admiral de Grasse. The two squadrons traded fire throughout the afternoon, causing heavy damage on both sides, and Graves subsequently retreated to New York. It was the correct decision, even if it did seal the fate of the American colonies; for the destruction of the fleet would have led to the obliteration of Britain's interests in the West Indies.

Meanwhile, in London, Sir George Rodney set about defending himself against accusations of avarice. His claims of ill health won him scant sympathy. 'Spending so much Time in the damp Vaults of St Eustatia, in taking a minute Cognisance of their Contents, even to a single Pound of Tub Butter and Stockfish, must have affected a Constitution much more athletic than that of the *gallant* Admiral,' scoffed the *Public Advertiser*.'[7] During the autumn, Rodney admitted a stream of visitors to his house in Hertford Street; Richard's name appears twice in the visitors' book, on 16 and 30 November, but we can only guess at what they discussed.[8]

Lord North's ministry quickly unravelled following the disaster at Yorktown. The prime minister could no longer hide his ambivalent feelings about the war, long suppressed out of duty to his monarch. On 12 December, Sir James Lowther placed a motion to end the conflict before the House of Commons. North objected to the wording of Lowther's motion, claiming that it would undermine the country's ability to forge an advantageous peace; while Germain, as Colonial Secretary, vowed he would never sign any document recognizing America's independence. Two days later, in a mute display of ministerial disagreement, halfway through a heated debate on the subject, North stood up from the front bench and sat down behind it, 'leaving Lord George Germain alone in that conspicuous Situation, exposed to the Attacks of the Opposition'.[9]

The Christmas recess ought to have offered Lord North respite from his political foes; instead he found himself a hostage to his so-called friends. Henry Dundas, now Lord Advocate of Scotland, was a powerful debater who also commanded a sizeable contingent of Scottish MPs. So long as Lord George Germain continued to hold office, Dundas told the prime minister, he and his supporters would stay away from the House. At a time when the ministry's majority was ebbing away, this ultimatum could not be ignored – and soon Germain was gone.

On 25 February 1782, Lord North announced a new loan to plug the hole in the national finances; this time £13,500,000 would be needed. To avoid a repetition of the previous year's controversy – when Richard was alleged to have sat in a room at the Treasury where he apportioned the loan to subscribers of his choosing – the prime minister invited tenders from two groups of City men. The *General Advertiser* announced the winning team:

> The conductors of this grand operation are no other (take them as they are) than Edward Payne, Esq., a wealthy linen-draper; the Right Honourable Thomas Harley, contractor for cloathing and remittances; the Scotch banker, Mr. Drummond, contract-copartner with Mr. Harley, and the renowned, immaculate, and undaunted Richard Atkinson, the famous rum-contractor. On the three first there needs no comment; but surely the Minister must have been drunk with contract rum, who could presume to bring the last personage forward again to public inspection . . . Atkinson, the former disciple, and now the fair representative of Samuel Touchet! Atkinson! of whom a late Alderman emphatically said, *Samuel Touchet will never die while that fellow lives.*[10]

This last was a cruel jibe – for Touchet, who was Richard's earliest mentor, had some years before hanged himself from his bedpost, a despised and broken man.

'We have agreed for the Loan on the same Terms we should have offered had there been no opposition,' Richard told Anne, at the end of a long day of negotiations at Downing Street. '*Low*, but in my opinion *safe.*'[11] Although Mures, Atkinson & Mure this time took a £2 million share of the loan, Hutchison Mure wished to hold on to just £200,000 for the direct benefit of the partnership. Richard was free to distribute the remainder of the loan stock as he saw fit, and he chose to place much of it under his friends' names without telling them – planning only to reveal what he had done once he could pass on 'the gain with the intelligence'.[12] He showed this list of secret beneficiaries to Anne; her own name, naturally, came at the very top.

LORD NORTH'S MINISTRY suffered its first outright parliamentary defeat on 27 February. The following week, news came of the surrender to the Spanish of the Mediterranean island of Minorca. This event was not unexpected, for the fortress of St Philip was riddled with scurvy, and Mures, Atkinson & Mure had recently been ordered to dispatch emergency supplies of lemons, rice, molasses, essence of spruce, 'portable soup', salt, sugar, tea leaves and strong red wine; but still, it harked back to a dark moment in 1756 when, as Charles James Fox taunted the prime minister, the 'loss of Minorca alone' had been considered 'sufficient grounds for the removal of an administration'.[13]

Shortly afterwards, what seemed like better news arrived from the West Indies – Admiral Hood had apparently trounced Admiral de Grasse's squadron and rescued Saint Kitts from invasion. Richard obtained this information on 8 March, via a ship returning from Jamaica, and immediately passed it to Philip Stephens, the first secretary of the Admiralty. The opposition were sceptical, however, suspecting the story to be a fabrication 'coined on purpose' to provide relief to the failing ministry.[14] 'That Messrs. Muir and Atkinson should fly with alacrity to Government with any thing in the shape of good news, will not be wondered at, when it is considered how deeply they are interested in it,' commented the *London Courant.*[15] When official word reached the Admiralty on 12 March, it was clear that the earlier report had been an exaggeration. Hood had indeed outmanoeuvred de Grasse's superior fleet, but still the French had managed to capture Saint Kitts.

On 15 March the ministry scraped through a motion of no confidence by just nine votes. 'The rats were very bad,' complained John Robinson, whose job it was as chief whip to keep the sinking ship afloat.[16] To everyone except the monarch a change of ministry seemed inevitable. For a few days the king bleakly pondered his own abdication, before reluctantly granting Lord North permission to resign.

Late on the afternoon of 20 March, Lord Surrey, from the opposition benches, stood up in the packed chamber of the House of Commons to propose a motion for the removal of the ministers; at the same time Lord North rose to make a short statement of his own. After an hour's wrangling over which noble lord should take the floor first, North prevailed and announced the end of his ministry. Parliament adjourned immediately. Outside snow was falling, and MPs impatiently thronged Old Palace Yard while their carriages were summoned from afar. Lord North, on the other hand, had told his coachman to wait outside, so his was the first carriage to roll up. 'Good night, Gentlemen,' he said as he climbed in, 'you see what it is to be in the Secret.'[17]

The following week was marked by the customary scramble to reward the loyal supporters of the outgoing ministry. One of these, James Macpherson, was a Scotsman notorious for his 'discovery' of an epic poem by the third-century bard Ossian, which he had 'translated' from the Gaelic. Published to great fanfare in 1761, *Fingal* had soon been exposed as a literary hoax – Samuel Johnson denounced its author as a 'mountebank, a liar, and a fraud'. Macpherson had served the Treasury first as a pamphleteer (a role for which he was eminently qualified, given his proven ability to make things up), and latterly from the back benches of the House of Commons. Lord North wished to award Macpherson a pension, but was unable to do so unless he vacated his parliamentary seat; Richard provided a solution to this predicament, at the same time turning it to the Lindsay sisters' advantage, by offering to pay Macpherson a lump sum of £4,200 from his own money, in return for pensions of £150 a year for each of them, to come out of a special fund set aside for 'indigent young women of quality'.[18]

Lord North's handwriting was dreadful at the best of times, but the letters from his final day in office betray the sheer intensity of his haste. Among the warrants sent over to St James's Palace for royal signature on 26 March were those for the Lindsays' pensions, and also for John Robinson's pension of £1,000 a year. 'In order to produce £1,000 nett, the Pension must be of £1,500,' observed North in a scrawled postscript.[19] At nine the next morning the king wrote: 'I can by no means think Mr. Robinson should have the fees paid out of his Pension of £1,000 per annum; I therefore return it unsigned that it may be altered, but it must be here before eleven this day and antedated some days.'[20] And two hours later: 'Where is Robinson's Warrant?'[21] By the afternoon, the Marquess of Rockingham had kissed hands and was again prime minister, some sixteen years since last holding the office.

Entirely unmerited though they were, no one thought to pass comment on the pensions awarded to the Lindsay sisters. John Robinson's pension, on the other hand, generated a barrage of abuse. John Sawbridge, an MP for the City of London with a republican reputation, launched a vindictive attack on Robinson in the Commons. Why did Robinson need this lavish sum, when he already owned a 'very fine house' in St James's Square and a 'most superb villa' just outside the metropolis? And how had he been able to buy these valuable properties in the first place? In response, Robinson disclosed that he had sold his 'paternal estate' in Westmorland for £23,000, and had given the proceeds to his daughter on her recent marriage; that he had borrowed £12,800 to buy his 'small house in the country'; that he did not own the house in St James's Square, but had taken it on a repairing lease for the annual rent of £150; and that he had a backlog of bills and two families to support.[22]

Sawbridge's insinuation was that Robinson had derived financial benefit from his connection to his favourite contractor – but whether Richard ever paid backhanders to the Secretary to the Treasury, we'll never know. Certainly, though, Richard had recently assisted his friend with a delicate money problem. In August 1781, Robinson's only child Mary had become engaged to Henry Nevill, the heir to Lord Abergavenny. Much to the future father-in-law's disappointment, however, the young blood had turned out to be a gamester. Robinson, having already settled a dowry of £25,000 on his daughter, agreed to bail Nevill out, but insisted on a full reckoning of his debts. Richard had gone down with Robinson to Sussex, and then to Monmouthshire, to perform the due diligence that preceded the marriage. When Nevill, having sworn he owed no more than £18,000, discovered the true figure to be £26,000, he persuaded his attorney to present a false account to Robinson, and agreed to repay the secret balance from his wife-to-be's marriage settlement. After the wedding, Robinson cleared all the debts admitted by Nevill, and Richard paid off tradesmen's bills worth more than £400. All this expense would almost ruin Robinson; he gave up the house in St James's Square, and sold his coach-horses. Unsurprisingly, he chose not to divulge these details in the House of Commons.

WHILE LORD NORTH'S ministry was fading away, France plotted its annexation of Britain's sugar islands. Faced with such a clear danger, the West India lobby put aside their political differences and on 2 January 1782 presented a grand petition to George III in which they begged for 'reinforcements, naval and military' to be sent without delay. The king, it was reported, received the petition with a respect that had not always been 'shewn to his people' when they had 'presumed to approach him on the subject of public grievances'.[23] Unusually for a document that implied criticism of the ministry, Richard was one of the signatories.

Violent winds in the English Channel prevented Admiral Rodney's fleet from setting out for the West Indies until mid-January 1782. All this time, the French navy under Admiral de Grasse continued to pick off the Leeward Islands; the fall of Saint Kitts was swiftly followed by the surrender of Nevis and Montserrat. On 25 February, Rodney finally joined up with Admiral Hood, and the combined fleet anchored at Saint Lucia, where it was well positioned to keep watch over the enemy at neighbouring Martinique. By 8 April the French were on the move, and believed to be planning a rendezvous with the Spanish at Santo Domingo before heading west to Jamaica; the French flagship, the *Ville de Paris*, was rumoured to have fifty thousand manacles on board, to be used for restraining the island's enslaved population.

Early on 12 April, the British caught up with the French off the coast of Dominica, near the rocky islets known as Les Saintes. The engagement started in the time-honoured manner, with the warships of the two nations – thirty-six British, thirty French – sailing in parallel lines in opposite directions while blasting away at each other. But after several hours' battle, when the smoke was at its

Admiral de Grasse relinquishes his sword to 'the Gallant Admiral Rodney'.

thickest, the wind changed, which suddenly divided the French line. A number of British vessels were able to glide through the gap, and proceeded to bombard the enemy at close range from both sides. By evening, five French ships had been captured, including the *Ville de Paris*, with Admiral de Grasse on board. The fatalities ran into thousands; the sharks fed well that night.

The story of this great British victory, by which Jamaica was rescued from the clutches of the French, electrified the nation. The Battle of the Saintes was the first time that 'breaking the line' was recognized as a naval tactic, and in its aftermath the theoreticians squabbled over whose idea it had been. It's possible that Richard played a small role in its conception.

John Clerk of Eldin, the Scottish author of an influential text-book about naval tactics despite never having been to sea, was the first to take credit; he claimed to have attended a meeting with 'Richard Atkinson, the particular friend of Sir George Rodney' in January 1780, at which he had communicated his 'theories of attack from both the windward and leeward', in particular his 'doctrine of cutting the enemy's line', all of which Richard had promised to tell the admiral.[24] The playwright Richard Cumberland, on the other hand, believed the idea had occurred to Rodney while they were both the guests of Lord George Germain during the autumn of 1781; Cumberland recalled the admiral rounding up a heap of cherry stones at the dinner table and arranging them 'as two fleets drawn up in line and opposed to each other', before animatedly steering the pips representing his warships among those of his enemy.[25] Both accounts were later disputed by Sir Howard Douglas, who insisted that his father, Rodney's Captain of the Fleet, had been the 'original suggester' of the manoeuvre.[26] In any case, through his brilliant deployment of this tactic at the Battle of the Saintes, Admiral Rodney was reinvented as the great saviour of the empire, a silhouette to be found gracing countless commemorative medals, tankards and punchbowls.

DESPITE HIS FAILURE to unite the Atkinson and Lindsay lines through marriage, Richard continued to promote the interests of both families. Through the patronage of Sir William James, one of his partners in the contract to provision the army in Canada and chairman of the East India Company in 1779, Richard had obtained a coveted Bengal writership – a junior clerical position – for his nephew Michael Atkinson, George and Bridget's eldest son.[27] Richard's next nephew, George, had meanwhile joined Mures, Atkinson & Mure's counting house at Fenchurch Street in order to learn the rudiments of the West India trade, with a view to joining the partnership at some future date.

As for the Lindsay family – Richard's devotion to their cause was almost limitless. Anne was by now the mistress of a £30,000 fortune after he managed to sell her 'secret share' of the 1782 loan for a 'princely gain'.[28] Richard also loyally served the interests of Anne's brothers, in particular guiding the older ones through the complex negotiations for army commissions – the going rate for a lieutenant-colonelcy being at that time around £5,000. Alexander, sixth Earl of Balcarres, who was Anne's junior by thirteen months, had served under General Burgoyne in America, proving his mettle (and good fortune) during fierce fighting near Ticonderoga, where 'thirteen balls passed through a jacket, waistcoat, and breeches' without inflicting so much as a scratch.[29] Soon afterwards, at Saratoga, Balcarres had been captured and paroled to New York in exchange for a Continental Army officer of the same rank.

Colin Lindsay, Anne's third brother, had also served in America before landing at Gibraltar with Rodney's expedition in the spring of 1780. Two years later he was still cooped up there, and the garrison's supplies were once again running low. So impregnable was the Rock that the French and Spanish allies could find no way of taking it by land; instead they planned a grand assault from the sea. A French engineer devised a system of floating batteries, built from the hulls of old vessels; ten of these monsters, each armed with fifteen cannons, were anchored in a line five hundred yards from the shore. The offensive started on the morning of 13 September 1782, and the batteries went to work blasting away at the fortress.

But one commodity of which Gibraltar did have plenty was coal, left over from Richard's supply eighteen months earlier. By late afternoon the garrison's forges had built up a blistering heat, and it was time to unleash the British secret weapon – more than a hundred cannons which rained down red-hot shot on the floating batteries. Within hours they were destroyed, and nine enemy warships had also been consumed by fire. The following month, Admiral Howe sailed unchallenged into the bay with thirty-four warships and thirty-one transport ships, bringing relief to Gibraltar for the third and final time. Richard played no role in this mission; for the new Treasury Board showed no desire to engage his services.

THE YOUNGEST OF the Lindsay sisters, nineteen-year-old Elizabeth, married Philip Yorke, heir to the Earl of Hardwicke, in July 1782; Richard helped draw up her marriage settlement.[30] Announcing the nuptials in its gossip column, the *Morning Herald* also suggested that another marriage was imminent, though 'not with quite so much advanced certainty', between Lady Anne Lindsay and Viscount Wentworth.[31] But this was no longer true; for the death of Catharine Vanloo several months earlier had dealt their engagement a fatal blow. Anne now felt that were she to marry Wentworth, it would be merely to fill the vacancy left by his late mistress.

Nor had he curbed his gambling. Late one evening that summer, Wentworth turned up at Harley Street in great distress and confessed to Anne that he had spent the previous three days and nights at his club, where he had squandered such a vast sum that he had been forced to borrow from moneylenders on terms 'usurious beyond the common pitch of usury'. Anne's decision to free him from the grip of these men derived more from pity than love; and he could never know that it was she who had saved him. With some reluctance, for it would not be easy to explain her motives 'without opening ill-healed wounds', she asked Richard to carry out the business on her behalf.[32] Wentworth accepted Richard's offer of a loan with complacent civility, and unwittingly borrowed £4,500 of Anne's fortune. 'I have been very busyly employed in *paying money* lately, & this morning have washed my hands of all Israelitish connections,' he told his sister on 20 August. 'I am now as poor as a Rat, tho' hope I have laid in a fresh stock of credit, which I shall use sparingly.'[33]

A few months later, Richard rescued Anne from another unpleasant situation. 'Leon', a blackmailer who appeared to have inside knowledge of Wentworth's rackety private life, perhaps through a connection with the late Mrs Vanloo, threatened to publish all the love letters Anne had ever written to him, and thus reveal to the world the 'Villanous art' that she had practised against his dead mistress: 'how you endeavourd by every means in your power to push her away from his house from his Children to send her abroad – in short what did you not do to make her miserable that you might triumph as Lady W – a title his Lordship never meant to bestow upon you'.[34] Richard drafted a sharp reply, which was duly left at Seagoes Coffee House in Holborn. 'Your threatening Letter has been laid before Counsel,' he wrote, 'and it appears that by Act of Parliament the punishment for *sending it* is *Death*. From circumstances known to one of the Persons mentioned you are already in part traced, and to push the Enquiry to your compleat Detection and punishment is far from difficult. The smallest publick Impertinence will at once fix that purpose and facilitate its execution.'[35]

Although Richard always insisted that Anne's fortune was hers to treat entirely as she pleased, and pressed her to spend more, she had mixed feelings about doing so. She appreciated the luxuries it bought, such as the well-appointed box at the King's Theatre in the Haymarket, within nodding distance of the Duke of Cumberland and Prince of Wales's boxes – her subscription was in Richard's name, but she had all the benefit.[36] She did not, however, enjoy the secrecy surrounding her money; and nor could she shake the feeling that it was slightly ill-gotten. 'I often wished,' she later wrote, 'I could have possessed my pension and a quiet £5,000 only, rather than be subjected to the censure of people who might blame me for deriving any advantage from the Funds, thro' the means of a rejected lover.'[37]

For various reasons, Richard was short of ready money during the latter months of 1782, and Anne was happy to tie up half of her capital, some £15,000, to relieve him of the burden of a loan to the estate of the late Captain John Bentinck. But when Richard tried to persuade her to accept documents that would identify her as a mortgagee on the Bentinck estate in Norfolk, she refused, feebly protesting that she did not have a writing desk to lock them in. When he offered to buy her such an item, a fear that he would make an expensive present of it tyrannized over her better judgement. 'I promised I would procure myself a bureau,' she recalled, 'but without intending to do it.'[38]

The will that Richard began planning in the wake of his siblings' deaths had meanwhile swollen into an ambitious document; it had taken him and his lawyers more than a year to prepare. On 22 December 1782, the day before he signed it, Richard sent the final draft over to Anne, along with a covering letter, to make sure he had her concurrence 'in the propriety' of every part of it:

I cannot say that I am sorry to find a necessity for changing the Plan we before talked of and tying up the Estates for the present Generation. I think it will be the means of their doing the more good. I have no Wish that any Nephew of mine should be put above being the Builder of his own fortunes, for I do not think it would contribute to his happiness. Assistance therein I would afford him, but not enough to make him dream that he was to plant himself there, and live a vegetable Life upon the Income. As the matter now stands arranged, I solemnly declare I think I have left as much to my own family as will do them any good, and that my own Sentiments are somewhat wounded by leaving so little in your power, and I sincerely ask it of your friendship to tell me truly your thoughts thereon.

At this point, Richard enters into a rather tortuous declaration of the 'ardor' with which his soul rushes 'to a communication' with hers 'in points where I feel they are made to embrace each other in spite of all the empty formalities of Life' – before acknowledging that he is 'wandering' from his purpose, and continuing:

Let us my dear Friend talk all this fully over & put it into such form as may be most to the purpose if the Event of my Death should happen – and forgive this ill connected Letter – when I took the Pen I meant only to write half a dozen Lines . . . but I am some way got into a way of writing straight forward to you, without forethought or attempt at Correction of what I have wrote, that *indeed* is not a careless contempt of my Friend – but (as I think) a part of that extreme desire which possesses me to throw my whole Heart open to her, to throw its most secret Sensations unveiled before her. The Consciousness that her Eye must review it would be sufficient to keep out all the *black* Family, & as to human Frailties, the Heart knows much less than mine that does not know that under the Influence of a generous confidence they would become the very Cement of its best Happiness. But there's no end of Dissertation. And so – it being near two in the morning, I say – *Fingers* be at rest – & *Mind* take thy chance of being so to.[39]

TEN

A Royal Coup

SHELVES EITHER SIDE of my sitting room fireplace display blue and white Chinese porcelain of a pattern representing flowers and butterflies – plates, bowls, sauceboats and soup tureens – the remnants of a much larger dinner set which evidently saw plenty of active service in its day. I had always wondered how this china might have come into my family, but it was only when I found out about Richard Atkinson's ship, the *Bessborough*, that its provenance began to emerge.

Launched at Rotherhithe on 27 November 1772, the *Bessborough* held one of the East India Company's valuable licences to carry porcelain, silk and tea back from China. Such ships were the supertankers of their day – the *Bessborough* was 144 feet long and 39 feet broad, with three decks and 907 tons' capacity. Richard commissioned the building of the vessel and acted as its managing owner, a role known as 'ship's husband'. Shipping on such a scale and over such epic distances carried grave risks, too great for an individual to bear, and East Indiaman vessels were typically owned by syndicates, their holdings divided up into one-sixteenth shares.

When the *Bessborough* returned from its second voyage, in October 1781, it was in need of a total overhaul. (It had been caught up in conflict on the Indian subcontinent during the four years it was away, having assisted in the blockade of the French enclave of Pondicherry in August 1778.)[1] Some prickly correspondence about the repairs reveals tensions between Richard and another of the *Bessborough*'s owners, the globetrotting botanist Sir Joseph Banks. On one occasion, when Banks sent a note complaining how long it was taking to put the ship into dry dock at Deptford, Richard's reply conveyed a clear flash of irritation. 'I very frankly confess to you,' he shot back, 'that I think the Distrust expressed by your Letter of this Date might have been spared till you had better foundation for it than the Suggestions to which you seem lately to have paid attention. I know of no reason but the want of Water for the Bessborough's not getting into Dock, and believe that no other exists.'[2] By December 1782, the newly copper-bottomed *Bessborough* was once again seaworthy and ready to embark upon its third voyage to China.

One afternoon at the British Library I was scrutinizing a hefty tome called *Chinese Armorial Porcelain*, hunting through thousands of pictures for a match with my own china. I turned a page, and there it was – a plate exactly like mine, apart from the coat of arms painted in its middle. (The Atkinson version has a humble monogram.) '*Montgomerie* quartering *Eglinton*,' read the caption. 'This service was undoubtedly made for Captain Alexander Montgomerie of the Hon. East India Company who commanded the East Indiaman *Bessborough* at Canton in 1780.'[3] It was a eureka moment – I could only imagine that Montgomerie must have purchased my porcelain at the same time as his own.

This explanation, already plausible, was later reinforced when I found Captain Montgomerie's papers relating to the *Bessborough*'s second voyage in the library of the National Maritime Museum at Greenwich. The East India Company allowed its ships' officers generous personal trading allowances – eighty tons going out, sixty tons coming home – and the first of Montgomerie's invoice books records that his outward cargo included beads, buttons, gold thread, ribbons, canvas, cordage, saddlery, claret, port, Jamaica rum, glassware, hats, linseed oil, tar, ironware, sheet copper, knives, sword blades, pianofortes, sheet music, stationery, prints, periodicals and books. It also shows that he bought 262 chests of opium in India,

A soup tureen, brought back from China on board the Bessborough.

to be exchanged for tea in China.[4] A second invoice book records that on the return passage, Montgomerie's personal goods included hyson tea, cassia bark, rhubarb, wallpaper, silks, nankeen (a kind of cotton cloth), 'Gambouge' (a deep yellow pigment) and porcelain. More specifically, listed among his buys at Canton in November 1780, from a merchant called Synchong, are '3 Table Setts of the Best Blue & White Stone China, scolloped border, Gold Edge, & Landscape pattern consisting of 170 Pieces', as well as another set of the same pattern bearing 'Captn. Montgomerie's Arms'.[5] This, I am certain, is the record of my china's purchase.

THE HEADQUARTERS OF the Honourable East India Company – to use the official title of this most morally dubious of corporations – were on Leadenhall Street, two minutes' walk from Richard's premises in Fenchurch Street. Behind a deceptively narrow façade, East India House stretched back some three hundred feet, and included rooms for the twenty-four directors and their clerks, a garden and courtyard, warehouses, and a General Court Room for the meetings of stockholders, known as 'proprietors'. The East India Company's politics had grown ever more rancorous over the previous decade, despite the supposed restraining influence of Lord North's Regulating Act of 1773. This legislation had subsumed the presidencies of Madras and Bombay under Bengal's control; but Warren Hastings, promoted to Governor General of Bengal, had proved a divisive figure, and Lord North's attempts to dismiss him had been thwarted by the proprietors. Meanwhile, John Robinson had set about building a government power base within the Company by actively encouraging the ministry's supporters to purchase stock, holding out the possibility of rewards for those who made themselves useful in the General Court of Proprietors. Richard had owned stock nominally worth £1,000, enough to qualify him to vote, since October 1773.[6]

It was inevitable, given the extent of his commercial interests, that Richard should cross paths with some shady characters, and the aforementioned Paul Benfield, co-purchaser of the Bogue estate in Jamaica, was perhaps the shadiest of the lot. How Richard first got mixed up in his affairs is not entirely clear, but the two men likely met in late 1779 or early 1780; it would be an exaggeration to call them friends, but they must have seemed useful to one another. Benfield – nicknamed 'Count Rupee' – was a key player in one of the East India Company's most toxic scandals, which had originated in Madras during the 1760s. The business centred on the spiralling debts of the Nawab of Arcot, ruler of southern India's Carnatic region, who had borrowed vast sums at exorbitant rates of interest from many local Company officials.

Benfield, who was foremost of the old man's creditors, was among a handful of Company servants recalled to England to account for their disruptive activities. John Macpherson was another; he arrived in London in July 1777, joining forces with his cousin, James 'Ossian' Macpherson, on a press campaign to justify his actions. (It was James Macpherson whose pro-ministry pamphleteering would later be rewarded with a lump sum paid by Richard on Lord North's behalf.) Benfield purchased a Wiltshire estate that included an electoral interest in Cricklade, a borough with notoriously bribable voters; at the general election of September 1780, he and John Macpherson were returned as the town's two MPs. Three months later, the directors of the East India Company cleared Benfield of wrongdoing and granted him leave to return to Madras. However, a group of irate proprietors led by Edmund Burke pressed for a hearing of their own. At the subsequent inquiry, on 17 January 1781, the

Richard 'Rum' Atkinson, whose tangled legacy
is at the heart of this story. This miniature – here
much enlarged – was painted by Richard Cosway
in 1783, and belonged to Lady Anne Lindsay.
Do I detect a certain sadness in its subject's eyes?

Temple Sowerby House in 1930. The original farmhouse squats behind the Georgian extension; the bay window and porch are clumsy Victorian add-ons.

The legal document, inscribed on vellum and dated 1577, that granted my nine-times great-grandfather William Atkinson a thousand-year lease on the land he occupied at Temple Sowerby.

My grandparents, my father and me in the walled garden at Temple Sowerby in 1968; and me again, this time on my own two feet, outside the house three years later.

Two views of the gallery at Temple Sowerby in about 1915. This light-filled corridor no longer exists, having been subdivided into hotel bedrooms. Eagle-eyed viewers will spot John Robinson's portrait above the chair in the top picture.

George Atkinson, probably painted in London in the 1770s while he was down on Treasury business. Close inspection reveals George, who was a tanner by trade, to be holding a volume of poetry. This portrait hung in the dining room at Chesters until the great sale of 1930 – I have no idea where it is now.

Bridget Atkinson's 'receipt book', and her cure for insanity. Approach with extreme caution.

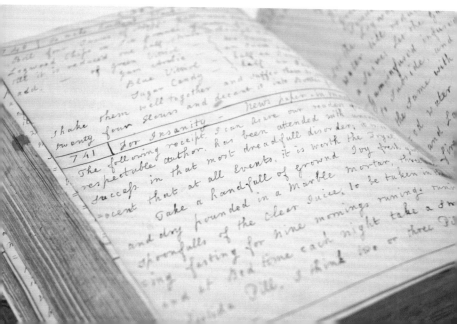

Lady Anne Lindsay, the love of Richard Atkinson's life.
Not only was she a great beauty, but also a gifted writer,
singer, painter and conversationalist.

The *Bessborough*, of which Richard was 'ship's husband', depicted
in three positions in the English Channel, its decks crowded with
people. Launched in 1772, this East Indiaman undertook four
voyages to China before being sold as a hulk in 1788.

John Robinson in later life, portrayed in his capacity as Surveyor General of Woods, holding a letter addressed to the king. Between 1788 and 1802, Robinson oversaw the planting of more than eleven million acorns in Windsor Great Park.

A crowd outside a print shop jostling for a glimpse of its latest wares. Political and social visual satire flourished in the late eighteenth century; James Gillray (1756–1815) and Thomas Rowlandson (1756–1827) were the masters of the genre.

Gillray's *Westminster School*. Pitt the Younger is birched by Fox.
Richard Atkinson (whose 'Rum Contract' pokes out of his pocket)
awaits punishment, clinging to the bespectacled Edmund Burke;
as does John Robinson (identified by the rats fleeing his garments),
piggy-backing the corpulent figure of Lord North.

motion was carried in Benfield's favour by a narrow margin; a week later he set off for India.

It was in the midst of all this clamour, on 31 December 1780, that Richard and Benfield had each signed the legal instrument with which Hutchison Mure vested in them the joint ownership of the Bogue estate.[7] Benfield had no wish to become a sugar baron; his share of the investment was simply a vehicle for his East Indian loot. He would gradually pay for his half of the Jamaican property with bills, gold and diamonds remitted from Madras.

In March 1781, eighteen-year-old Michael Atkinson – George and Bridget's eldest son – sailed to Calcutta to take up his East India Company writership, travelling on the same ship as John Macpherson, recently appointed by Lord North to the Supreme Council of Bengal. Michael's family connections would prove of great value on the subcontinent. 'Our friend, Mr. John Macpherson, will explain to you how much we all owe in these disagreeable times to the ability, friendship and exertions of Mr. Atkinson,' James Macpherson wrote to Governor General Hastings on 22 April 1782. 'Mr. Atkinson has a nephew, under your government, who went out last year under the protection of Mr. Macpherson. In policy, as well as gratitude, decided support and a marked attention are due to that young gentleman on account of his Uncle.'[8]

TIME AND AGAIN I would marvel at Richard's uncanny knack of positioning himself, if not at the epicentre of major events, then extraordinarily close by. Often it feels as though he is just offstage, pulling strings – something that James Gillray suggests in an early engraving, *Banco to the Knave*, which was published on 12 April 1782, just after the fall of the North ministry. Lord North is depicted presiding over a large card table, looking down dolefully as he acknowledges that it is all over; Charles James Fox has a huge pile of gold guineas in front of him, Lord Rockingham a smaller one. A cheering crowd of supporters throngs round them; and at one end of the table sits a croupier, representing (though looking nothing like) John Robinson, who

Banco to the Knave, in which the change of ministry is likened to a game of cards.

says simply: 'Atkinson cut the cards.' Richard's political skills would come into their own during the two years of intense turbulence that followed the demise of Lord North's government.

Lord Rockingham's ministry was short-lived, for he died from influenza in July 1782. The most pressing business of his successor, the Earl of Shelburne, was to end the war; the provisional terms of an Anglo-American peace treaty were signed in Paris on 30 November. The new land boundaries between the British territory of Canada and the fledgling United States of America were drawn on terms that were noticeably generous to the latter. 'The English buy peace rather than make it,' the French foreign minister sniped from the sidelines.[9]

Many MPs agreed with this assessment – the prime minister had given too much away. John Robinson was troubled to learn that

Lord North was planning to vote against Shelburne's peace treaty, and drafted a memorandum to his old master, warning that such an action might 'shake the Government and the Constitution of this Country to its Foundation'.[10] He asked Richard for his thoughts on the document. 'Upon the best consideration I can give the matter, I cannot help feeling an Indelicacy towards an *old* Friend, in the communication,' Richard replied on 6 February 1783.[11]

As Shelburne's grip on power weakened, it was clear that he would need to join forces with one of the other main parliamentary factions, but he failed to form a coalition with either Lord North or Charles James Fox. Instead something unthinkable happened. Fox sent a 'civil' message to North, and these once-mortal enemies met to coordinate tactics for a forthcoming debate. Only recently, Fox had declared that he would not 'for an instant' consider working with Lord North or his allies – men who 'in every public and private transaction' had shown themselves 'void of every principle of honour'.[12] Now MPs were flabbergasted by the spectacle of Fox and North sitting side-by-side on the opposition front bench. On 24 February, the weight of adverse parliamentary numbers bearing down upon him, Lord Shelburne tendered his resignation.

At this time, broadly speaking, there were two political parties – Whig and Tory – but they were not monoliths in the sense that we know today, instead loose social alliances sharing a general outlook, clustered around strong individuals. Aristocratic Whigs had engineered the Glorious Revolution, and they saw political power as emanating from the people through a 'contract' existing with their monarch, who was to be opposed if he overrode their interests. Lord North was, if anything, a moderate Tory – a grouping associated with the landed gentry – but would not have been fenced in by this label. By the 1780s, however, the political parties were starting to become more clearly defined, with economic reform and the reduction of royal power at the heart of the revitalized Whigs' ideology.

Charles James Fox, their leader, was a colossus of the House of Commons – the subject of more political cartoons than any other man of his time. A hostility existed between Fox and the king that was more deep-seated than mere partisan difference, for they were also polar opposites in temperament – while the monarch was a man of markedly moderate habits, Fox was the 'hero in Parliament, at the gaming-table, at Newmarket'.[13] According to the king, Fox was someone 'who every honest Man' would wish 'to keep out of Power'; which is why the prospect of such an individual leading his government was almost too painful to contemplate.[14]

It was Henry Dundas, the Lord Advocate, who first proposed William Pitt, the Chancellor of the Exchequer, as a candidate to replace Shelburne. As the second son of the late Earl of Chatham – Pitt the Elder – the younger Pitt certainly had pedigree, even if he lacked experience. He had entered parliament only two years earlier, aged twenty-one, as a protégé of Sir James Lowther. ('Appleby is the Place I am to represent,' he had written to his mother, 'and the Election will be made (probably in a week or Ten days) without my having any Trouble, or even visiting my Constituents.')[15] Shelburne, while resigning from office, suggested to the king that he might consider inviting Pitt to form a ministry. After putting this idea to the young man, the king reported that he had responded with a 'spirit and inclination that makes me think he will not decline'.[16] Pitt spent the evening of 24 February with Dundas, trying to work out whether a working majority in the Commons was within his grasp. 'I feel all the difficulties of the Undertaking and am by no means in Love with the Object,' Pitt told his mother the following day. 'The great Article to decide by, seems that of numbers.'[17]

Dundas next asked John Robinson, whose knowledge of the shifting sands of parliamentary loyalties was unrivalled, to compile a breakdown of those MPs who were likely to support Pitt, and those who would likely oppose him. The plot to bring Pitt into power was a profound secret. To avoid raising suspicions, Robinson asked Richard, as a mutual friend – for Richard knew Dundas fairly well, not least as another of Anne Lindsay's admirers – to carry the completed document from his house at Sion Hill, near Brentford, to Dundas's residence in Leicester Square, so that he himself 'might have no communication with the Advocate'.[18]

If Anne Lindsay's account of 27 February is to be believed, the day might have ended quite differently. She would describe the following story as a 'whimsical little instance to prove on what trifling circumstances important matters in the line of politicks often hinge'. That morning Richard, on his way from John Robinson's house into town, had unexpectedly dropped in at Harley Street while she was getting dressed, and sent up a note asking her to come down immediately, since he had something important to tell her:

> One pin was necessary to tuck up my hair, and to change a gown all over with powder for a clean one. I hurried below, and found him with his watch in his hand, departing. 'O! what may not these five minutes delay have cost,' said he. 'Pitt has not seen this canvass . . . I have this instant got it, it is triumphant! He promised to be with the King as 11 o'clock struck, it wants but three minutes of it; if he is not gone, he is our Minister . . . God bless you!' And off he rushed. Half an hour brought him back with a dejected air. 'Alas!' said he, 'I was too late. He had set off five minutes before I reached his house, leaving this note: *Had the canvass been favourable you would have been here. I must decline; perhaps 'tis best.*'[19]

Far-fetched though this tale might sound, it seems likely that some version of it took place. John Robinson himself, in a letter to Charles Jenkinson, alluded to a last-minute setback when he described how a 'ray of Light' which might have persuaded Pitt to form a ministry 'came forward a *few* Hours too late'.[20] George III now approached Lord North, who refused to lead, but agreed to serve in a coalition cabinet; all of which is how, on 3 March, the king came to offer the reins of government to his arch-enemy Fox, on condition that an independent peer nominally headed the ministry. But Fox would not serve under any prime minister except the Duke of Portland, who was unacceptable to the monarch.

During this nail-biting time, Robinson was confined to his country residence by gout. (Anyone wondering how gout might justify

*The gout, which tormented many eighteenth-century gentlemen
of a certain age.*

his absence from Westminster at such a critical moment need only
examine Gillray's depiction of the illness, in which some infernal
creature sinks its fangs and talons into the swollen foot of a sufferer.)
On 14 March, after the nation had been without a prime minister for
three weeks, Robinson wrote to Jenkinson, who was in close contact
with the king, suggesting that he make one last attempt to 'set the
Wheel a-going thro' Atkinson, with the Advocate & Pitt'.[21]

Two days later, the king reluctantly agreed to let the Duke of
Portland form a ministry, but refused to deal directly with him, only
through Lord North. Portland was at last granted an audience on
20 March, but admitted he could not yet name his cabinet; George
III, sensing an opportunity, dispatched a one-line letter: 'Mr. Pitt,
I desire you will come here immediately.'[22] The next day, Portland
again waited on the monarch, who refused even to glance at a partial
list of the cabinet, insisting on every post being filled before he would
look at it. 'The D. of P. has been with the King & they have parted
angrily,' Richard told Robinson that night. 'Demands, no less than
Honours & Power *unlimited*! If the Parties quarrel *clearly* between
themselves, the thing *will do*. If the King quarrels *with them*, it will

not do.'[23] Pitt, meanwhile, was hoping for signs of support in the Commons, but none were forthcoming, and he again turned down the premiership. Richard wrote on 25 March:

The blossoms of yesterday are finally *blasted*. Upon a very recent conversation between Mr. Pitt and the Advocate, the latter gives the business up as wholly at an end. All that can remain will be to give such support as one can to the Government, for by Heaven I am convinced there are not materials in the country to form another. This young man's mind is not large enough to embrace so great an object, and his notions of the purity and steadiness of political principle absolutely incompatible with the morals, manners, and grounds of attachment of those by whose means alone the Government of this country can be carried on.[24]

The king held out for another week as he pondered the 'cruel dilemma' of being forced to appoint a ministry made up of men 'who will not accept office without making me a kind of slave'.[25] Not for the first time, he contemplated abdication. On 1 April, after five weeks of political deadlock, George III signalled that the new cabinet would be expected at St James's the following day to kiss hands. John Robinson commented: 'Poor King, how very very much does His Situation deserve pity.'[26]

BEFORE THIS DISRUPTION, Henry Dundas had been working on a bill to place the East India Company and its territories under tighter government control. It would be hard to overstate the importance of the Company to the commercial life of Britain at this time. Some historians have characterized it as the first multinational corporation, but it was so much more powerful than even this description might suggest, possessed of a vast private army with which it had subjugated emperors and princes; and thus huge swathes of the Indian subcontinent were effectively ruled from nondescript offices in the City of London.

Dundas had been taking an interest in Indian affairs since 1781, when he was appointed chairman of a secret committee set up to investigate the war against Hyder Ali, the great Sultan of Mysore; before long his scrutiny would extend to every aspect of the Company's activities. But when he finally placed his India Bill before parliament, on 14 April 1783, the new ministers made it clear that they would not give it their support, and thus it was still-born.

Although the Duke of Portland was officially prime minister, his 'indolent habits and moderate capacity led him to relish power rather than to seek it' – this was Anne Lindsay's pithy analysis – which meant that Charles James Fox was leader in all but name.[27] In those days, before the existence of a professional civil service, or salaries for MPs, ministers relied upon royal patronage to reward those who laboured on the government's behalf. The king so hated this particular ministry, however, that he simply shut down the supply of offices, sinecures, titles and pensions that were needed to keep the cogs of administration well greased. 'I do not mean to grant a single Peerage or other Mark of Favour,' he told Lord Shelburne.[28]

It would turn out there was good reason why Fox had given Dundas's India Bill such short shrift in the spring, as he harboured plans for legislation of his own. Fox placed his India Bill before the House of Commons on 18 November. One measure alone contained enough powder to touch off a massive blast in the cellars of East India House; this was the plan to establish a board of seven commissioners, nominated by parliament, who would have the 'power to appoint and displace officers in India'.[29] To those who detested Fox, or owned East India Company stock, the bill seemed like the 'boldest and most unconstitutional measure ever attempted', a brazen scheme to steal the patronage of the Company and put it to work for his personal political ends.[30] The bill's first reading was on 20 November, and Fox made it clear that he intended 'to take the House, not only by force but by violence'.[31]

Richard led the East India Company's resistance to Fox's India Bill from the start. On 21 November, at a Grand Court held at the Company's headquarters on Leadenhall Street, he was appointed to

*A Transfer of East India Stock, in which Fox makes off
with East India House.*

a committee of nine proprietors tasked with defending its rights and
privileges; but the chairman of the group immediately fell ill, leaving
Richard to step into his shoes. The committee's first undertaking
was to compose a strongly worded petition, objecting to the seizure
of 'lands, tenements, houses, warehouses, and other buildings; books,
records, charters, letters, and other papers; ships, vessels, goods,
wares, merchandizes, money, securities for money, and other effects'
that was threatened by Fox's bill.[32] This document was placed before
the Commons three days later.

The committee's next task was to disprove Fox's claim that the
Company was £8 million in debt – an assertion which had caused
the price of its stock to slide from £138 to £115 in just three days.

By the time of the bill's second reading, on 27 November, Richard had compiled a detailed report on the Company's finances – by *his* reckoning, it was almost £4 million in credit. At the start of the debate, two lawyers presented Richard's conclusions from the bar of the House of Commons. Fox then stood up to give his response. The report, with 'many things inserted, which ought to have been omitted, and many things omitted, which ought to have been inserted', was a staggering distortion of the Company's affairs, he asserted, and he condemned the men who had dared to produce 'an account so full of imposition and absurdity'.[33] Fox's display of righteous indignation dazzled his enemies; William Pitt, leading the opposition, complained that he had 'run through the account with a volubility that rendered comprehension difficult, and detection almost impossible'.[34] When the House divided, at 4.30 a.m., the ministry prevailed by a decisive 229 votes to 120. 'The shameful impositions of the Company, in the printed state of their affairs, were completely detected and exposed,' said one newspaper. 'Opposition seemed planet-struck.'[35]

I find this incident fascinating because it shines light on a critical flaw in Richard's character, one that might be considered the source of many of the Atkinson family's future troubles. Francis Baring, writing to Lord Shelburne two days later, pinpointed Richard's role in the drubbing:

> Atkinson has brought Mr. Pitt into a scrape by endeavouring
> to prove *too much*, & of which he was warned at the outset; but
> it ever was the case with him, his talents & imagination are
> so rapid that they always run away with judgment; & at this
> moment instead of taking ground which is sound, defensible
> against every attack, & sufficient for the purpose; he is
> endeavouring to elucidate & support, various articles which
> he must know himself to be moonshine.[36]

On 3 December, as Fox named his board of seven commissioners – all of whom, it was muttered, were better known at Brooks's Club than in Bengal – Pitt conspicuously stayed away from Westminster. At its final reading in the lower chamber, on 8 December, the India Bill passed by a majority of more than two to one, and Fox was able to carry it up triumphantly to the House of Lords.

JOHN ROBINSON HAD stayed away from Westminster while the India Bill passed through the Commons, conveniently blaming his absence on a further attack of gout, in part to avoid the very public treachery of being seen to vote against Lord North. Once again, Richard acted as Robinson's go-between with Henry Dundas and others; this explains why much of the tiny amount of correspondence to have survived from this deepest of political intrigues is in Richard's handwriting.

The India Bill's passage through the Lords, it would seem, was a foregone conclusion. 'We are informed that Ministers have an ascertained majority of two or three and thirty Peers,' reported the *London Chronicle*.[37] However the king, and many others, saw Charles James Fox as a dangerous man who had to be stopped; and so the battle lines were drawn for the greatest test of the respective powers of the monarch and parliament since the Glorious Revolution. On 1 December, Lord Chancellor Thurlow – who strongly opposed the bill – placed a memorandum before the king which professed 'to wish to know' whether the legislation appeared to 'His Majesty in this light: a plan to take more than half the royal power'. Thurlow's message also suggested that were the king to take the highly unusual step of revealing his feelings on this matter, 'in a manner which would make it impossible to pretend a doubt', the bill would face defeat in the House of Lords.[38] Two days later, Richard learnt that the Chancellor's communication with the king had produced the desired effect. 'As far as I can learn or judge,' he told Robinson, 'every thing stands prepared for the blow if a certain Person has Courage to strike it.'[39]

That 'certain Person' was, of course, George III. But he would not strike the 'blow' until William Pitt had indicated his readiness to take office; and first Pitt needed to be sure that a parliamentary majority lay within his reach. On the evening of 5 December, Robinson received a message from Dundas, urgently requesting an analysis of the House of Commons. 'That Night I worked until past 2 & the last Night until towards 3 this Morning, & both Days, except some little Interruptions, until this Moment that it is finished as well as may be in such a Hurry for my Pen has been constantly driving all the above mentioned space of time,' Robinson wrote to Jenkinson, in evident haste, two days later.[40]

What Robinson omitted to say was that Richard was also present at Sion Hill, his pen likewise 'driving' round the clock to compile the document. We know as much because a rough version of this highly speculative survey, in Richard's handwriting – one page is splashed with what looks like strong black coffee – exists in the family archive of John Robinson's descendant, the Marquess of Abergavenny. The two men drew up a list of all 558 parliamentary seats, dividing them into four columns headed P, H, D and C, for 'Pro', 'Hopeful', 'Doubtful' and 'Contra', according to the sitting member's likely stance towards a Pitt ministry.[41]

Richard carried the finished document across town to Dundas on the evening of 7 December. 'I found our Friend last night & looked over the Paper with him,' he reported back to Robinson, in deliberately veiled language. 'Although at the first Blush it had not appeared quite so favorable as had been expected, yet on fuller consideration and going through the whole it was admitted that the turn was throughout strongly given to the unfavorable Side & that there was no *manly* ground of apprehension.'[42]

THE INDIA BILL received its first reading in the House of Lords on 9 December. Richard, who had prepared a petition from the East India Company for presentation during the debate – another 'Bomb from the India House', as John Robinson put it – briefed Lord Thurlow first at his house in Great Ormond Street.[43] The following day, after learning that Pitt was ready to 'receive the burthen' of office, George III instructed Lord Temple to make peers aware of his strong aversion to the India Bill. Richard summarized these manoeuvres for Robinson, ending with the royal trump card: 'He has given authority to say (when it shall be necessary) that whoever votes in the House of Lords for the India Bill is not *his* friend.'[44]

The king's intervention had an electrifying effect. On 15 December, the East India Company's lawyers gave evidence in the upper house for eleven hours before seeking permission, as it neared midnight, to continue the next day; somehow the opposition managed to muster a majority of eight votes on a motion to adjourn the debate, in effect postponing the decisive division on the second reading. Around thirty peers, it seemed, had switched sides.

That same evening, four conspirators – William Pitt, Henry Dundas, John Robinson and Richard Atkinson – discussed tactics over a secret dinner hosted by Dundas at Leicester Square. In a note calling Robinson into town, Richard explained that the covert nature of the gathering was 'lest the measure in agitation should be guessed at'.[45] This 'measure' was a general election, and their objective was to identify the means by which a majority in the House of Commons might in due course be obtained.

It is at moments such as this that the gulf between parliamentary democracy then and now seems at its most unbridgeable. The minutes of this and subsequent meetings, which are in Richard's handwriting, identify thirteen landowners who between them controlled forty-one seats that might be purchased with royal patronage; sixty-nine seats that might be bought using a combination of money, offices and honours; and sixty-five seats for which money alone would suffice. Even Robinson, no wide-eyed innocent, was horrified by the projected expenditure – £193,500 for 134 seats to ensure a majority – and he would distance himself from the figures. 'Parliamentary State of Boroughs and their Situations with Remarks, preparatory to a New Parliament in 178- on a Change of Administration and Mr. Pitt's coming in,' he noted on the minutes. 'Sketch out at several Meetings at Lord Advocate Dundas's in Leicester Square and a wild wide Calculate of the money wanted for Seats but which I always disapproved and thought very wrong.'[46]

For Communication

		These are supposed to be partly accessible in one way & part in other ways which till communication cannot be well judged of.
D. Northumb. 7.	Launceston 2 Newport 2 Bevalston 2 Northumberland 1	
Mr Elliot 7.	Lisheard 2 S. Germans 2 Grampound 2 Cornwall 1	Suppose 10,000
Lord Falmouth. 3	Tregony 2 Mitchell 1	9,000
Sir F. Bassett. 5	Mitchell 1 Truro Queer 2 Penryn Queer 2	12,000
Lord Orford. 4	Ashburton 1 Callington Queer 2 Castlerising 1	
D. of Newcastle 6.	Aldborough 2 Boroughbridge 2 Retford 1 Newark 1	
Lord Sandwich 3	Huntingdon 2 Huntingdonshire 1	Suppose Office
Mr Howard (Bagot)	Castlerising 1	
Mr Hooper	Christchurch 2	
Lord Hertford 3	Orford 2 Coventry 1	Suppose Office
Lord Sackville 2	East Grinstead 2	
Sir Jno Honeywood 2	Steyning 1 Himself 1	
Lord Aylesbury 4	Marlbro 2 Great Bedwin 2	Suppose 1 Seat 3000
Mr Selwin 2	Luggershall 1 Himself 1	do 3,500
Mr Shaftoe 2	Downton 1	do 3,500
Lord Lisburne 2	Himself etc	
Government Influence 3	Portsmouth Dartmouth Harwich	Arrangement rather than Expence
×× Lord Powis 2	Montgomery Ludlow	Donnecan & Cashion Aldborough Suffolk 2
Lord Galway N. Walsh 2	Pomfret 2 Winchester 1 ××	

Sixty-nine parliamentary seats and their proprietors, in Richard's handwriting.

The struggle reached its climax on 17 December. Fox had tabled an emergency resolution to protest against the king's flagrant violation of the rule that he could only operate through his ministers, and this business in the lower chamber would coincide with the crucial vote on the India Bill along the corridor in the House of Lords. At midnight, while both houses were still in the throes of debate, Richard dashed off a note to Robinson with some unexpected news. 'My dear Sir,' he wrote, 'I am dragged into the India Direction.' Earlier that day, during a meeting of the proprietors at East India House, while Richard was in a side room dealing with an urgent query from Lord Thurlow, he had without warning been nominated to fill one of two vacancies caused by the resignation of Foxite directors. 'Tomorrow I will breakfast in Leicester Square & take a Servant with me to send out to you. You stand high with Mr. Pitt about which I have more to tell you than I can well write,' he concluded.[47]

At noon the following day, Richard sent Robinson a high-spirited message to say that the India Bill was demolished, defeated in the Lords by a majority of nineteen: 'What a constitution of Character this is!'[48] That evening, as Portland, Fox and North were in conference, a messenger brought a letter from George III demanding the surrender of their seals of office. 'I choose this method,' explained the king, 'as Audiences on such occasions must be unpleasant.'[49]

ELEVEN

Secret Influence

LADY ANNE LINDSAY was firmly of the opinion that Richard received insufficient recognition for his role in the slaying of Fox's India Bill. 'Abilities in a certain rank of life have not always fair play granted them,' she would later comment:

> On several occasions when he showed me able statements prepared for Mr. Dundas and for Lord Thurlow to convey to the King, I could discover that they would be transcribed over by themselves before they reached the Royal eye. I expressed an idea of this kind to Atkinson. He smiled, and said it might be so . . . Men were men; providing he could do good, it was the same thing to him who had the credit of it.[1]

To this day, Richard's part in the 'coup' that would usher William Pitt the Younger into power – a watershed event in British political history – has not been fully acknowledged by historians. John Robinson's survey of the House of Commons, and the papers estimating the cost of parliamentary seats, are among the most revealing documents dating back to this drama – and yet, so far as I am aware, no researcher has detected Richard's hand in them, either because they have not identified the handwriting as his or, more likely, because they have seen them in transcript only. The papers are held by Lord Abergavenny at his family archive in Sussex; another way to access them is through a book, the *Parliamentary Papers of John Robinson*, compiled by Professor W.T. Laprade in 1922. But he was working from transcripts made in the 1890s: 'The task of preparing these papers for publication has been the more difficult in that the editor has never seen the originals.'[2] Since then, biographers of Pitt the Younger have relied upon Laprade as their primary source, which meant that I was maybe the first researcher to recognize Richard as the actual *author* of the documents – a genuinely thrilling discovery for an amateur historian.

WILLIAM PITT took office on 19 December 1783, aged twenty-four, and set about cobbling together a cabinet. He had few heavyweight candidates at his disposal, especially since he chose to forgo the services of Lord Shelburne, under whom he had served as Chancellor of the Exchequer. He also purposely distanced himself from those who had cleared his path to power; Henry Dundas was appointed to the relatively junior post of Treasurer of the Navy.

The newly deposed coalition greeted Pitt's premiership with barely disguised mirth. 'We are so strong,' wrote Fox, 'that nobody else can undertake without madness, and if they do I think we shall destroy them almost as soon as they are formed.'[3] As yet, Pitt plainly lacked the parliamentary majority that he needed; but there was no greater practitioner of the dark art of luring MPs across the floor than John Robinson. 'No Man in the House of Commons knew so much of its original Composition; the Means by which every Individual attained his Seat; and in many Instances, how far, and through what Channels, he might prove accessible,' Nathaniel Wraxall would observe.[4] With the king's blessing, the vaults of royal patronage were thrown wide open. The sparkle of honours, offices and pensions was too much for most men to resist, and Robinson now set about deploying these baubles to devastating effect.

Over the Christmas holidays, Robinson had so many letters to write, and the weather was in any case so bitterly cold, that he did not leave home once in nine days. He first set about securing the great political proprietors – an earldom was promised to his old patron Sir

James Lowther in return for the nine seats under his control. Word soon got around. The *Morning Chronicle* portrayed 'Jack' Robinson as a kind of magician of the gutter: 'Jack can shew wonderful tricks with Rats, he can turn their skins and fur into ermine, and make them appear outwardly much nobler creatures than common Rats.'[5] The *Public Advertiser* printed an 'IMPORTANT WARNING!!!' that one Robinson, 'Secretary to the Secret Influence', was grubbing around for seats, and that gentlemen should be 'on their Guard against the Grand Corruptor or his Agents'.[6] Soon afterwards the same newspaper hinted at the identity of Robinson's chief accomplice: 'To my certain Knowledge there are TWO *Rats*, one of whom has for twelve Years burrowed in the Treasury; the other in a dirtier Place, yet shall be nameless. These have been seen lately gnawing some valuable Parchments in Leadenhall Street, and are supposed to have committed many daring Depredations on the Public.'[7] I think we can guess the name of that second rat.

Already Richard was liaising with Dundas about the fine detail of a new India Bill, with a view to smoothing out any potential objections beforehand. 'I saw Mr. D today who is confined with a complaint in his head, whether Rheumatick or Tooth Ach is not quite clear,' Richard told Robinson on 31 December. 'His Bill does not go to all the Objects we had in view; but in as far as it goes to them, it does not materially differ from ours.'[8] Pitt revealed these plans to a secret committee of the directors of the East India Company on 5 January 1784; broadly speaking, political control over the Company's affairs would pass to the Crown, while its commercial business and patronage would remain intact.

Parliament assembled to debate the 'state of the nation' on 12 January. It promised to be a historic occasion, and as many people 'as ever were wedged together in the same place' crowded into the public gallery of the Commons.[9] '*The Battle is at this moment joined*, and the Debate of the night determines King George or King Charles,' Richard declared. 'My opinion of the Result is, a small majority for the present ministry tonight, a Dissolution this Week & *King George for ever*.'[10] For sixteen hours, the prime minister faced down intense abuse from the benches before him about the underhand method of his installation. When the House rose, past six in the morning, the false optimism of Richard's prediction was revealed; the opposition carried the vote by 232 to 193. 'King Charles' reigned – for the time being.

Richard was formally elected a director of the East India Company on 14 January. Pitt placed his India Bill before parliament that same day, at pains to stress that the legislation had been 'chiefly founded on the resolutions of proprietors of India-stock'.[11] After its second reading, the bill was defeated on 23 January by eight votes – an event that terminated John Robinson's long friendship with Lord North. Robinson had been secretly plotting against his former master for the best part of a year, but had hitherto refrained from openly voting against him. The next day, Robinson called upon North at his Grosvenor Square residence, but was refused entry. 'I do not desire any explanation of your conduct,' North wrote afterwards. 'You are so good as to say that you felt some difficulty in making the option between being my friend & my enemy; you have chosen the latter, & your choice has put it out of my power to make any: your option has necessarily determined mine.'[12]

The Infant Hercules, in which Pitt strangles two snakes representing Fox and North.

After the defeat of Pitt's India Bill, the confidence of some of his closest supporters started to falter. 'Whilst the King, Mr. Pitt, & Mr. Dundas are I really believe untainted with Timidity,' observed Richard on 27 January, 'I fear there may lurk some Sparks of it in other members of the Cabinet.'[13] Beyond Westminster, however, the populace began voicing their support for George III and his new minister. The first stirrings were on 16 January, in the City of London, when a cavalcade of dignitaries – the Lord Mayor, aldermen, sheriffs and other bigwigs – waited upon the king to congratulate him for exerting his prerogative 'in a manner so salutary and consti- tutional'.[14] Soon, similarly approving addresses started trickling in from places as far-flung as Penzance and the Orkneys, turning into a torrent over the following weeks.

IF ANY OF THESE events were of the least interest to Dorothy Atkinson, she did not think to mention them in her correspondence. Richard's eldest niece, now twenty-two, had earlier that winter come to live with her uncle at Fenchurch Street, joining her younger brothers George and Dick, who were both learning to be merchants. It was Anne Lindsay who, for reasons not entirely selfless, had urged Richard to invite Dorothy down from Temple Sowerby. She would later explain:

> To marry Lord Wentworth was no longer in my intention. To marry any other person and break the heart of my best of Friends by a new attachment, I felt impossible. To remain single, or to marry himself (which I could not bring myself to do) was my sole alternative, and in Truth it contained so little Happiness to me either way, that I sometimes wished I had five thousand pounds only and the liberty I had lost. By one means only I saw I might regain it & of this there was but a poor chance – if I could get the Happiness of Atkinson made up from some other quarter by some amiable woman then I saw I should be my own mistress again.[15]

Dorothy made a favourable impression on the Lindsay sisters. 'She was a tall fine girl,' Anne recalled, 'of a sweet and ingenuous countenance, and resembled himself in a manner that rendered her the more interesting to us.' She would need schooling in the ways of society, for 'she was awkward, being from the wilds of Westmoreland', but there were few instructors more qualified than the Lindsay sisters.[16] Dorothy kept up a delightfully artless correspondence with her mother, Bridget, about her new life in the capital. Here is a letter dated 2 March 1784:

I think I left off my dear mother with telling you that we were to dine at Mr. Mure's on Sunday. My uncle and I accordingly went in the coach about two to Lady Balcarres' where I was received by her, Lady Margaret and Lady Ann with that politeness which always distinguishes people of real fashion – and with particular kindness upon my uncle's account. We stayed till four and made an appointment for me to go to the opera with the Ladies on Tuesday – we then went to Mr. Mure's where George and Dick joined us there was none but ourselves and a very pleasant day we spent *no cards introduced.*

On Monday morning I went out in the carriage to call upon Lady Ann who by my uncle's desire went a shopping with me. I was to get whatever she thought proper for me – and so in the first place we bought of Mr. Alanson one & twenty yards of white satin at 10d. per yard for a night gown & petticoat, bespoke a pair of stays of rose colloured tabby – next we got a piece of fine Linnen for a morning gown, also bespoke an hoop and last of all a balloon hat for the opera.

On Tuesday I went to Miss Williams and fixed upon two Vallancine edgings for the plain muslin. I have also had from her a long white sattin cloak & muff the cloak trimmed with white skin a black hat and two caps. I will send you patterns of the Gowns when they come home. I went from Miss Williams to Lady Balcarras's where I had my hair dressed and the Lady's equipped me in my Balloon & for the opera. I dined with them and my uncle joined us at the opera house. It was very agreeable indeed – the Ladies have the Duke of Cumberland's box during his absence it is adjoining to that of the Prince of Wales (who was there) and is the next best to his – Vestris is still here and performed wonders. Lord Wentworth, my uncle and I supped at Lady B's. We set his Lordship down and then came home.

There is one thing which will confine me a little. My uncle does not chuse that I should go out at all but in the coach – and one of the Footmen always attends me – but when I go to buy my aunt's gown and to execute my other commissions I mean to take a hackney coach least I should make bad bargains. I forgot to tell you that Miss Fordyce came of Sunday morning and breakfasted with us. She says she is quite weary of the pursuit of shells not having got any new ones these twelve months. I must I think keep this letter till the house sends a frank as all this scribble is scarcely worth paying postage for.[17]

THROUGHOUT THE WINTER, John Robinson continued to chip away at Fox's parliamentary majority through the sustained deployment of royal patronage. Meanwhile, preparations were under way for the general election that might be called at any time. On 29 February, Pitt's election committee met at Dundas's house in Leicester Square. Some papers from this gathering still exist; they are mostly in Richard's handwriting. One document lists seventy boroughs whose seats were likely to be actively contested, and a 'measures to be taken' column records what was agreed about each place: 'Callington – Mr. Pitt to learn of Lord Orford whether he sets up one or two members . . . Chippenham – Lord Weymouth to be spoke to by Mr. Dundas about Sir Edwd Bayntun's Interest . . . Northampton – Mr. Robinson to consult H. Drummond about opposing Lord Lucan . . . Poole – Mr. Atkinson to converse with F. Baring on this Subject.' Another paper sets out forty-two seats

*John Robinson, portrayed as a rat catcher, snaring MPs
with money and honours.*

reckoned 'certain for Money', and the names of thirty-four potential candidates – Francis Baring and Nathaniel Wraxall are among
eleven men listed as Richard's nominees. Yet another document, this
time written by Robinson, suggests 'Persons who will pay £1,500 or
perhaps somewhat more' for seats, and those who will pay '£2,000
or £2,500 or perhaps £3,000'.[18] Here is the first clue that Richard was considering a political career – for his name is to be found
within this last category of men with very deep pockets indeed.

On 1 March, in the House of Commons, Fox tabled a motion
urging the king to dismiss his ministers; it passed by just twelve
votes. A week later, Fox moved to communicate to the monarch
that 'no administration, however legally appointed, can serve his
Majesty and the public with effect, which does not enjoy the confidence of this House'.[19] When this motion passed by a single vote,
Fox must have known his time was up, for the next day he permitted
the Mutiny Act – a law to prevent the existence of a standing army
without parliament's consent, renewed annually and about to expire
– to pass without opposition, thus removing the final impediment to
a general election. On 22 March, the king borrowed £24,000 from

the banker Henry Drummond to fund the purchase of parliamentary seats by the Treasury; two days later, he dissolved parliament.

Richard agreed to stand for the City of London – how much coaxing he needed is not clear, but Anne Lindsay recalled a certain reticence on his part: 'It gave him eminence, but to be its Member he thought would interfere too much with his private business.'[20] As a necessary preliminary to his candidacy, on 24 March, Richard was admitted to the freedom of the Goldsmiths' Company. Two days later a group of supporters, led by Edward Payne, a former governor of the Bank of England, met at the London Tavern, where they passed a resolution to recommend him to the electorate. Of the City's four sitting MPs, John Sawbridge was most vulnerable to challenge, and it was his seat that Richard hoped to snatch – for it was Sawbridge who had two years earlier shown such malice on the subject of Robinson's pension.

Nowadays, a general election campaign usually lasts about five weeks, while the polls remain open for just fifteen hours, but during the eighteenth century, almost the reverse was the case – a short canvassing period was followed by an extended poll. Also unlike today, votes were cast publicly – which meant that numbers could be totted up along the way.

The moment Richard's candidacy was announced, personal attacks upon him started appearing in the press. First came the story of two merchant ships, the *Venus* and the *Monarch*, both of which he had chartered in 1780 to bring sugar from Jamaica, but which had subsequently been requisitioned to serve as army transports. After all but one of its crew perished through sickness, the *Venus* had been abandoned and burnt by order of its commanding officer, and Mure, Son & Atkinson had received damages of £3,500 from the governor of Jamaica. The ship's owner, however, had successfully prosecuted a claim against Richard for this compensation money. ('A more gross violation of justice never was attempted,' thundered the *Gazetteer*.)[21] A similar action regarding the *Monarch*, which foundered in the disastrous hurricane of October 1780, had been settled out of court. 'They have attacked me on the Rum, & on the Story of two Ships lost on the Spanish Main,' Richard complained to Robinson. 'On Rum, henceforward *Silence!*'

Francis Baring and John Purrier, the ultimate referees of the rum contracts, offered their support through a handbill in which they declared that they had been fully satisfied by 'the Uprightness of Mr. Atkinson's conduct' – not that Richard expected this message to be treated with any great respect by the citizenry of London. 'You will believe that the pissing Posts will not be uncloathed with it,' he told Robinson.[22]

The twenty thousand-strong electorate of the City of London, comprising the membership of the ancient livery companies, had one week in which to cast their votes. Richard's appearance on the hustings at Guildhall, as polling opened on 30 March, was greeted by 'hisses and groans' from the crowd.[23] That same day, the *Gazetteer* published a vicious denunciation:

Is it possible that the Livery of London can be so utterly destitute of common sense, common honour, and common spirit – so drunk with ignorance of their real interests, so dead to every thing that renders a public body respectable, as to elect Richard Atkinson in preference to John Sawbridge? What is Atkinson? A man hackneyed in whatever renders a public man infamous, a private man contemptible. In this man's dealings with the public, he has perpetuated an act of such an extraordinary nature, that the base trick is grown into a proverb; his original obscure name is forgotten; and he is elevated into the notorious distinction of '*The Rum Contractor*' – added to this you find him high upon all lists of *loans, contractors,* &c. and never known but in some of those numerous *jobs* by which, in a time of public calamity, he has made a considerable fortune from the distresses of the nation. In private life what is he? A being who has progressed from the very lowest and meanest sphere, through all the gradations of a various life, to the accession of great wealth; steady to the object of *making money* . . .[24]

At the end of the second day of polling, Richard was running fifth, having received 419 votes, with Sawbridge eighty-nine votes ahead; but still he remained upbeat. 'In spite of News Papers & Reports depend upon it I am safe for the City,' he assured Robinson that evening.[25]

The following morning, a handbill pinned up throughout the City smeared Richard's name still further. Its author was one John Berens, who identified himself as an assignee of the estate of Peter Hasenclever, founder of the ironworks of which Richard had been a proprietor before the American war. Without offering a shred of evidence, Berens linked Richard to a forged bill of exchange, accused him of perjury, and claimed he had deceived Hasenclever's creditors. Next morning, in an open letter to the 'worthy Liverymen', Richard offered a concise explanation of the Hasenclever business. 'Gentlemen and fellow-citizens,' he concluded, 'you can be at no loss to judge of the purpose for which these repeated attacks are made upon me, and I most cheerfully commit myself to your generosity and spirit to turn them on the heads of their fabricators.'[26] On the fourth day of polling, for the first time, Richard received more votes than Sawbridge.[27]

At the start of the seventh and final day, the first three candidates – Brook Watson, Sir Watkin Lewes and Nathaniel Newnham – were safely ahead, but the fourth seat hung in the balance. On this day Richard received 434 votes and Sawbridge 357 – which overall left Richard short by just seven votes. Indeed, he almost pipped Sawbridge, since soon after 3 p.m., when poll books closed, 'three postchaises, each containing three voters, who had been brought up from distant parts of England by Atkinson, arrived at the hustings'.[28] The *Morning Herald* gleefully imagined Pitt receiving the news of Sawbridge's victory during dinner at Downing Street, and the ensuing rumpus causing the contents of the soup tureen to end up 'in the Rat-catcher's breeches'.[29]

But Richard and his supporters, after such a dirty campaign, were in no mood to concede; at a crowded meeting on 9 April, they demanded a scrutiny of the votes. (An unusual step – the last time a scrutiny had taken place in the City of London was fifty years earlier.) The Lord Mayor ordered the livery companies to provide lists of their membership, and the two rival camps set up headquarters to gather information about the electorate; Richard's followers sat daily at the King's Head Tavern in the Poultry, while Sawbridge's supporters took up residence at the Guildhall Coffee-house on Cheapside. Had any liveryman been impersonated? Had any liveryman voted twice? Were all liverymen up to date with their company fees? The *Morning Post* reported: 'Bets run much against Mr. Sawbridge in the city.'[30]

WHILE THESE ENQUIRIES were in progress, Richard was taken up with the annual elections at East India House, working closely with Francis Baring, who had been a director of the Company since 1779. The careers of the two men, friends for almost thirty years, had run along parallel tracks since they left Samuel Touchet's employment in the early 1760s. Richard had been the first to achieve prominence through his services to Lord North's ministry; but Baring had been later favoured by Lord Shelburne's ministry with contracts to provision the army at the tail end of the American war, more or less picking up where Richard had left off.

The East India Company elections of 1784 would prove unusually contentious. Under rules set by the Regulating Act, directors held office on a revolving four-year basis, which meant that each year six of the twenty-four stood down, to spend a year 'out by rotation'. John Robinson wrote to 220 proprietors soliciting votes for Pitt's favoured candidates. Richard, meanwhile, was plotting to oust the 'slow & languid' chairman, Nathaniel Smith; he and Baring had already agreed with Laurence Sulivan, an influential director, that they would have free rein to 'settle the Chairs' if Pitt's candidates prevailed in the election on 14 April.[31]

Richard envisaged Baring as chairman, and taking the deputy chair for himself. Sulivan changed his mind, however, and decided to put himself forward. While Richard considered Sulivan not only an ally, but 'by far the fittest Man for the Office', Pitt and Dundas refused to countenance his election as chairman so long as his friend

Warren Hastings held power in Bengal.[32] Robinson tried to dissuade Sulivan from standing, claiming that Fox would table a hostile motion against him, and Pitt could not prevent such a measure 'lest he should be suspected of screening any Man improperly'; but then Sulivan arranged a meeting with the prime minister, who falsely denied objecting to his candidacy. Sulivan would write, somewhat bitterly, after losing by a single vote to Smith, the incumbent mediocrity: 'Atkinson and Baring have been smothered in their own Pit – and instead of sharing Power with me which they might have done they are now of no consequence whatever.'[33]

RICHARD'S ELECTORAL SCRUTINY, before the Sheriffs of the City of London in the domed Council Room at Guildhall, began on 26 April. With little precedent to follow, the opposing teams agreed that they would examine doubtful votes from each of the eighty-odd livery companies in alphabetical order – from Apothecaries to Wheelwrights. Sawbridge had hired an expensive legal team; Richard preferred to represent himself, believing lawyers 'were unnecessary, tending to create delays'.[34]

On the first day the tally was even, with three invalid votes struck off each candidate's score. 'Mr. Atkinson had of himself singly to contend against the Quirks and Quibbles of experienced Lawyers,' reported the *St James's Chronicle*, 'and in some Instances appeared an Over-Match for them.'[35] After the second day, when Richard queried the votes of a cooper, a dyer, a painter-stainer and two innholders, and Sawbridge's legal team those of a joiner, a wine-drawer, a gunsmith, a grocer, a blacksmith and a girdler, the tally stood at five bad votes for Richard and three for Sawbridge. The scrutiny inched forward in this pettifogging mode until 3 May, by which time Richard had been docked thirteen votes and Sawbridge eleven, and Richard's supporters gave notice that they would take part no further. 'In six days you have decided upon 33 or 34 votes only,' they told the Sheriffs. 'To continue a proceeding at once troublesome, expensive, inadequate, inconclusive and dangerous, appears very improper.'[36] On 4 May, John Sawbridge was declared MP for London.

As it happened, a still more rancorous contest was under way in Westminster, where one of the two sitting members, Charles James Fox, was in danger of losing his seat. (An idiosyncrasy of this constituency was that polling lasted forty days.) In this frenzied atmosphere, even members of the 'gentle sex' turned into violent partisans. One night in the coffee room of the opera house on the Haymarket, Lady Margaret Fordyce, with a 'ferocity truly *clannish*', reportedly snatched the laurel sprig denoting Foxite allegiance from another woman's bosom. 'Has *secret influence* entirely subdued her Ladyship,' wondered the *Morning Herald*, 'that decency and good manners is no longer to be attended to?'[37]

Fox would hold on to his seat, by a whisker, but dozens of his acolytes were not so lucky – they came to be known as 'Fox's Martyrs'. When, on 24 May, the Commons divided for the first time after the election, Pitt was able to savour the sweet sensation of a three-figure majority. It was a triumph for which John Robinson, in particular, reaped his reward. The *London Gazette* announced the creation of ten new peerages, the most senior of which was the earldom of Abergavenny, to be conferred upon Robinson's daughter's ailing father-in-law – meaning that she would soon become a countess. Lowther's earldom of Lonsdale came lower down the list, and he felt the affront keenly, for Robinson had once been his servant. 'I am told that Sir James Lowther is very much discontented & violent about his peerage, on account of the precedence which John Robinson's grandson will have over the Lowthers,' Francis Baring gossiped to Lord Shelburne. 'They even apprehend that he may join opposition upon that account.'[38]

The corrupt nature of eighteenth-century politics meant that Richard did not have to wait long for a parliamentary seat. When it seemed that he might not succeed in London, Pitt asked Sir Edward Dering – described by Horace Walpole as 'a foolish Kentish Knight' – to put a seat aside for him.[39] Richard's lawyer John Smith was duly returned as MP for the tiny Cinque Port of New Romney in *locum tenens*, before vacating for his client in mid-June. (Years later, Dering would write to Pitt citing his consent to this arrangement, 'though much against Sir Edward's inclination as not liking Mr. Atkinson's Character', as a reason why he deserved a peerage.)[40] It seems that Pitt placed a high value on Richard's expertise – many thought too high a value. As the *Morning Herald* bellowed: 'The *Rum* Mr. Atkinson – strange as it may sound to the ears of the world – is at this moment *Minister of finance* for this insulted empire! – not a single measure is adopted without his approbation.'[41]

TWELVE

A Dose of Vitriol

WILLIAM PITT THE YOUNGER'S sheer youthfulness when he came to power was a gift to satirists; many portrayed him as a callow schoolboy, running the country under the watchful eye of his Cambridge tutor George Pretyman. One 'anecdote' from the *Rolliad*, a collection of squibs first published in the *Morning Herald*, describes a typical day at Downing Street in June 1784:

> Mr. Pitt rises about *nine*, when the weather is clear, but if it should rain, Dr. Prettyman advises him to lie about an hour longer. About *ten* he generally blows his nose and cuts his toe nails, and while he takes the exercise of his *Bidet*, Dr. Prettyman reads to him the different petitions and memorials that have been presented to him. About *eleven* his valet brings in Mr. Atkinson and a *warm shirt*, and they talk over *new scrip*, and other matters of finance. Mr. Atkinson has said to *his* confidential friends round change, that Mr. Pitt always speaks to him with great *affability*. At *twelve* Mr. Pitt retires to the water closet, adjoining to which is a small cabinet from whence Mr. Jenkinson confers with him on the *secret instructions* from Buckingham House . . .[1]

Now the House of Commons lay at his command, Pitt wasted no time in placing a new India Bill before parliament. As a prelude, a select committee conducted an investigation into the East India Company's accounts; its report, which came out on 22 June, cast doubt on some numbers submitted by Richard on behalf of the directors.[2] Two days later, Charles James Fox warned MPs not to be 'led by Forgeries and false Calculations' into forming a positive impression of the Company's financial health – causing Richard, in what appears to have been his maiden speech, to defend himself against 'so foul an imputation'.[3] By the time of the next debate on the Company's affairs, a week later, Richard had presented the prime minister with a paper rebutting seventy-three negative assertions made by the select committee.[4] 'I am really almost knocked up with the matters which are & have been in hand,' he told Robinson.[5]

On 6 July, during a stifling heatwave, Pitt introduced his India legislation to a listless House. A Board of Control would be appointed by the Crown, and vested with powers to supervise all aspects of the East India Company's civil and military governance at home and in India. The proprietors would lose much of their clout, since they would hold no veto over joint decisions of the Court of Directors and Board of Control. The directors would keep their valuable patronage, which included the appointment of 'writers' to the Company's administration in India, and cadets and assistant surgeons to its armies. The bill passed its second reading, without division, a week later.

ANNE LINDSAY SPENT much of the early summer of 1784 making arrangements for an expedition to the continent. The Lindsay sisters' circle of friends included the 'lovely, soft' Maria Fitzherbert, who had experienced the misfortune of being widowed twice before she was twenty-five. It was in Anne's box at the opera house that the Prince of Wales was said to have 'first beheld' Mrs Fitzherbert. 'He soon took me aside,' Anne recalled, 'to ask me what Angel was it that sat beside me in a white hood? I told him, and from that moment he appeared to live but in the hope of meeting her again and again, and of drowning himself like the poor fly in the sweets he should have shunned.'[6]

The match was ill-starred from the start. Mrs Fitzherbert was certainly gratified by the attentions of the prince, who was six years her junior, but too proper to consent to be his mistress, and her status as both a commoner and a Catholic made it unthinkable they could marry. Such hindrances did not deter the 21-year-old prince, though, and his assault upon the virtue of *La Belle Veuve* was soon tittle-tattle everywhere.

Anne's decision to go abroad was in part motivated by the fact that she could now afford to do so; for it was two years since, 'through Atkinson's kindness', she had been 'blessed with independence enough to venture to form a wish of amusements beyond the common habits' of her past life. She also felt an urge to cut loose from her benefactor. As she later explained: 'There was a set of invisible ties of restraint . . . which I wished to relax, not to break. I thought Atkinson might profit by my absence.'[7] She started casting around for travel companions; one day in June, Mrs Fitzherbert called upon her and proposed they set off as soon as possible.

Richard had grave doubts about the propriety of such a trip. 'I do not reason upon the measure itself in which there can be nothing wrong but upon the opinions of the World,' he told Anne on 2 July. 'Whatever may be *our* Conviction that a desire *to avoid* the pursuer is your friend's Motive, the general opinion will I fear remain fixed that if that purpose had been very sincere the means of carrying it into effect might long since have been found & might still be found without going abroad for two or three Months. Were there any Gentleman of your own family or connection of the Party, I should think nothing of it, but in truth I fear that the fair young Widow so circumstanced makes no Chaperon at all.'[8]

Prince George, for his part, tried to dissuade his *inamorata* from leaving by means of an absurd display of histrionics, which included swallowing physic – a purgative – to make himself look pale and drawn, and other tactics that Anne considered unworthy of 'any honest man'. Finally, the evening before Mrs Fitzherbert was due to depart, the prince stabbed himself with a sword. Although he did himself no serious harm, he 'bled like a calf', and subsequently threatened to rip off his bandages unless she solemnly promised to marry him when she returned from France. The next morning Mrs Fitzherbert fled for the port of Dover. Anne followed two days later in her newly purchased dark chocolate post-chaise, having 'bade adieu' the previous night to the 'excellent friend' who had made her adventure possible.[9]

ON 12 JULY, while Anne's carriage bounced along the turnpike to Dover, Richard was speaking in a parliamentary debate about a bill to suppress smuggling that would – in his view unfairly – make the owner of a ship answerable for an attempt by one of its crew to import even the smallest amount of contraband spirits or tea. Afterwards a writer in the *Morning Chronicle*, who confessed he had hitherto not been 'in the habit of admiring Mr. Atkinson's political character', commented that Richard's speech on the subject had been 'replete with sound reasoning, unanswerable argument, great commercial knowledge, and above all, the present principles of the constitutional laws of the land'.[10]

Certainly, smuggling had reached epidemic levels. In coastal areas, large bands of armed men operated in plain sight; even in London it was 'no unusual thing to see Gangs of 10, and 15, and 20 Horsemen riding even in the Day time with Impunity'.[11] Law enforcement was too blunt an instrument with which to combat criminality on such a scale. Instead Pitt and his advisors hit upon the tool of tax reduction – for if, they reasoned, the duties on contraband items were lowered so as 'to make the temptation no longer adequate to the risk', then smugglers would go out of business.[12] Tea, taxed at an eye-watering 119 per cent, was the obvious commodity on which to test this theory.

Pitt's proposal was to cut the duty on common Bohea tea to 12½ per cent, and on finer varieties to between 15 and 30 per cent; at the same time, the reduced tea duties would be offset by a marked increase in the window tax. Richard's fingerprints can be found all over this initiative; several documents in his handwriting crop up among Pitt's papers, now in the National Archives, with titles such as a 'Computation of the Average Price of each Species of the Tea now laying in the Company Warehouses uncleared by the Buyers – when the old Duties shall all be deducted & a new one of 12½ per Cent imposed' and a 'State of the actual Cost of the Tea to be imported by the India Company this present Summer 1784, with the new Duties payable thereon'.[13]

The measure worked. At a stroke, demand for the East India Company's legally imported leaves doubled, and its stock soon ran low. While the directors waited for new shipments of tea to arrive from China, they set up a committee – Richard was one of three active members, Francis Baring another – to plug the gap through purchases from European merchants. The smugglers attempted to sabotage the first of the Company's tea sales in the autumn; a number of strange men with 'Silk-Handkerchiefs round their Necks, and Weather beaten Countenances' descended on Leadenhall Street and forced up the auction prices to levels that threatened, but ultimately failed, to wreck the scheme.[14]

Richard had been far from happy with the state in which Pitt placed his India Bill before parliament. 'I cannot my dearest friend describe to you to how great a degree the publick business has incommoded me since you left us,' he would write to Anne on 21 July, as the legislation underwent line-by-line scrutiny during the committee stage. 'The India Bill was brought in *without communication* and full of Errors & Infirmities. I induced the Directors as a body to make private Representations setting them to rights & prepared all the Remarks & Amendments. They are every one in the course of being adopted & we shall make the Bill a good Bill at last & consistent in its Principle.'[15] The bill passed through the Commons without division on its third reading; apart from some choice invective from Edmund Burke, who had been the chief architect of Fox's India Bill, it was all quite unremarkable. The king wrote to Pitt the following morning to express his relief: 'I trust now little more trouble will be given in finishing the business of this Session, as Mr. Fox's Speech yesterday was I suppose his last Words on the Occasion and that He will retire to his new purchased Villa.'[16]

Pitt's India Act of 1784 would settle the constitution of British rule in India for more than seventy years – until the demise of the East India Company.

WHILE THE SUMMER reached its dog days, and the ranks of 'country gentlemen' thinned out as they left town for the shires, Richard remained dutifully at Westminster. Following the smooth passage of the India Act, the opposition were gripped by the conviction that Pitt's parliamentary majority had been purchased with East India Company money. During a lengthy monologue on 30 July, Edmund Burke pointed to the seats directly behind the ministerial front bench, where Richard and other MPs with Company connections were seated. 'The India bench,' Burke proclaimed, 'was very properly placed *above* the Treasury Bench, because the latter was subordinate to the former, and ruled by it.'[17] Richard wrote to Robinson late that evening. 'I think the fates have set a Spell upon me to prevent my getting to Sion Hill,' he sighed. 'I cannot describe to you how the India business at both ends of the Town has harassed me. We have fixed the Dividend in the Committee tonight at 8 per Cent without either Fox or Eden making their appearance. *They have unchained Burke who raved like a Bedlamite for two hours & I consider this as a proof that the sober Men of the Party mean to absent themselves.*'[18]

Early on Sunday 1 August, Richard set out with his niece Dorothy for Hamels Park, the Hertfordshire home of Lady Elizabeth Yorke, the youngest of the Lindsay sisters. He returned to Fenchurch Street that night on his own, carrying a bundle of correspondence addressed to Anne, who had recently arrived at the fashionable resort of Spa. Before forwarding her family's letters on to Anne, he added one of his own, which serves as an expression of his general world-weariness at this point in his life:

I have since been almost worn out with a new point that has
arisen in East India matters which will be managed right,
and will I hope in a very few days close our Campaign on India
Affairs in Parliament. I cannot attempt to give you in any

compass of a Letter the least Idea of the particulars, & shall
therefore only say that whilst I am conscious of having done
essential Service both to the Company & the Publick, I am
equally certain that nobody will thank me in either department.
Such is the vile nature of publick business! This my dearest
friend I say to *yourself.* I become every day more & more
convinced of the justice of an opinion I long ago gave you that
publick business may serve for an amusement, where the Grasp
at happiness has failed, but contains nothing in it that comes
home to the Heart.[19]

On 18 August, John Robinson hosted a grand party to celebrate the end of the parliamentary session. As Richard told Anne:
'We all dine tomorrow at Sion Hill viz. Mr. Pitt, Dundas, & the
Chancellor.'[20] It was, in fact, Richard who provided the centrepiece
of the politicians' feast that evening, but its carriage across town
presented a distinct challenge, as his letter to Robinson suggests:
'I am lucky enough to have a Turtle under my Command – about
lb 60, or 70 – & if I had the means of sending it out to you, should
be glad to spare you the trouble of sending for it, but I know not of
any Conveyance by which it can be sent with safety therefore shall
trust to your sending for it in the course of tomorrow and whether
I am at home or not my servants will have instructions where to
find it.'[21]

The preparation of a 'turtle dinner' was one of the most daunting
challenges of the eighteenth-century culinary repertoire. Hannah
Glasse opens her recipe for turtle prepared 'the West India Way'
with the following instructions: 'Take the turtle out of the water the
night before you dress it, and lay it on its back, in the morning cut
its head off, and hang it by its hind fins for it to bleed till the blood
is all out, then cut the callapee, which is the belly, round, and raise
it up; cut as much meat to it as you can, throw it into spring-water
with a little salt, cut the fins off, and scald them with the head . . .'[22]
The custom was to serve the turtle in five dishes that showed off
its fleshy charms to the greatest effect – the 'calipash' (baked back

meat), the 'calipee' (boiled belly meat), the guts (stewed in a creamy sauce), the fins (served in a clear broth) and, the climax, a tureen of luxurious turtle soup. Oh to have been a fly on the wall – or in the soup – at that particular dinner.

THE PASSING OF THE INDIA ACT by no means restored harmony to Leadenhall Street, for bitter differences would arise that autumn among the directors of the Company and the newly established Board of Control over an issue which had poisoned Indian politics for twenty years – namely, the Nawab of Arcot's debts. As Paul Benfield's agent, Richard supported the claims of the men, including several of his fellow directors, who had lent the prince vast sums at what many considered usurious rates of interest; but the chairman of the Company, Nathaniel Smith, took an opposing view. At a meeting of the directors on 23 September, Smith pushed through a draft dispatch to Madras which contained 'some very extraordinary Complimentary Paragraphs' about its governor, Lord Macartney, an enemy of the Arcot creditors, as well as drafting a 'most cruel and insulting Letter' to the nawab that was highly critical of Benfield.[23]

Richard was one of seven directors who signed a strongly worded dissent from this correspondence on 6 October, absolving themselves from 'all Responsibility for the Consequences to ensue therefrom'.[24] Two days later the Board of Control, headed by Henry Dundas, decided to radically rewrite Smith's dispatch to Madras so that it recognized the validity of all the nawab's debts, and established a sinking fund to settle them with his territorial revenues. To those who believed, like Edmund Burke, that the so-called 'Arcot Squad' had exerted undue influence during the general election – here, in the form of payment for services rendered to the ministry, was corroboration.

In the midst of this scheming, on 2 October, Richard was elected an alderman of the City of London. Although a tremendous honour, he felt rather pressed into service – 'the Devil has at length directed these Aldermen to resign,' he wrote about the two vacancies which had arisen – but his refusal to stand would have generated too much censure.[25] Following the election, Richard threw an entertainment for his Tower Ward voters at the Ship Tavern. Newspaper accounts suggest there was no shortage of refreshments: 'One gentleman was picked up and placed in a baker's basket; he was then carried in state to his own door, preceded by a choice band of choristers smoking their pipes, and chaunting, "*he was drunk, he was drunk, he was drunk when he died!*" Another tippling rogue was *served up to his wife and family* on a window shutter, covered over with tobacco pipes arranged in beautiful order.'[26]

Richard wrote to Anne in the Netherlands on 12 October; he had not heard from her in a while. 'Still is the Oracle of Brussels silent although Devotions are performed,' he declared, his heartfelt words suggesting that he was still deeply in love with her:

> Keeping within my *Heathen* Creed, I must say that Destiny has hitherto directed the Views of my Life to *Hope*. To her therefore I will still burn Incense; alas *without hope* that a superior Deity will ever assume her rightful Throne. News of our Friends I have none. For the private reason you know of (*and for no other*) I went to Brighthelmstone on Saturday – returned last night at Midnight. Was *sworn in* as Alderman today. Dined with the Lord Mayor, in a Company so stupid that Wilkes (who honestly tried) could not enliven it, *et me voici*, at nine o'Clock waiting for an Interview on India matters which grow infinitely entangled and intending again to take the Command of my Battery as much before the end of the Week as I can.[27]

The 'private reason' for Richard's visit to Brighton was to lobby Pitt, who had taken a house there. Dundas was pressing for Sir Archibald Campbell, recently governor of Jamaica, to be appointed commander-in-chief in India; Richard meanwhile hoped to man-oeuvre Anne's brother, Lord Balcarres, into the colonelcy of the 78th Highlanders, which would make him Campbell's second-in-command. But his tête-à-tête with the prime minister failed to bear the intended fruit. A member of the Board of Control, Lord Sydney (the recently ennobled Thomas Townshend), an arch-critic of Richard's contracts during the American war, had warned Pitt to distance himself from Campbell's nomination: 'You will find a Combination of the most insatiable Ambition & the most sordid Avarice & Villany at the bottom of this base Work.'[28]

Richard broke the news to Lord Balcarres in a letter dated 29 October:

I am sorry to acquaint you that our India Politicks have
gone very perversely, and that by means of Lord Sydney's
persevering in a ministerial recommendation, whilst Mr. Pitt
disavowed all interference on the part of the Ministry, the
Court of Directors was ensnared & in vindication of what the
majority of them thought their own honour, have appointed
General Sloper Commander in Chief in India. Your Lordship
will have seen some impertinences in the News papers about
your being appointed second in command. It is impossible for
me to guess how that Report got about for I assure you I never
opened my Lips on the subject to any body out of the small
Circle that was originally in the knowledge of our Castle
building on that subject.[29]

According to rumours in the press, Richard would soon be made a baronet. The *Gazetteer* reported on 17 November that John Robinson, as a reward for 'rendering the House of Commons a cypher in the constitution', had been offered the honour for any friend he cared to name, and had nominated 'one Atkinson, distinguished for his sagacity in making the rum contract'.[30] Whether this was true or not, the two men hardly saw each other during the autumn of 1784. 'I think it an age since we met & wish most ardently for an opportunity, though no particularly pressing matter occurs,' Richard wrote on 2 December. 'I have been since Sunday confined (mostly in bed) with a Fever, taken I believe just in time to prevent its becoming rather a serious one. It is almost gone but not quite; and I am today for the first time able to sit up the whole day, and hope there is little doubt of my getting clear of it very soon.'[31] Richard's own assessment of his illness was characteristically sanguine. East India Company minutes hint at its gravity, however, for he was absent from all but two of the fourteen meetings of the directors held in December.

Richard spent January 1785 in Brighton, convalescing beside the wintry sea; by the end of the month, he felt sufficiently recovered to write Dundas a lengthy private memorandum about 'necessary reforms' in the Court of Directors.[32] Soon he was back in London.

He next attended East India House on 16 February, where a critical decision – the choice of the next Governor General of Bengal, a successor to Warren Hastings – was scheduled for the following day. According to a report in the *Gazetteer*, the prime minister summoned Richard, along with Laurence Sulivan, to Downing Street on the eve of the vote, and declared that he wished them to nominate Lord Macartney for the post. Both directors were said to have been dumbfounded at this intervention; Richard apparently replied that the 'proposition was so contrary to his feelings, and so contradictory to the principles on which his friends had hitherto embraced the interests of Mr. Pitt, that he should exert himself in the Court of Directors, and elsewhere, to oppose the appointment of Lord Macartney'.[33] Whether or not this exchange took place (for it was later denied) would in any case prove immaterial, since Richard was prevented from casting his vote by the 'most extraordinary accident in the World'.[34]

Next morning, his servant mistakenly gave him the wrong medicine – oil of vitriol, known today as sulphuric acid, instead of the physic that was intended. Without George Fordyce's swift intervention, the blunder would have killed Richard, and it certainly left him too weak to attend the Court of Directors.

All but two of the twenty-four directors showed up at East India House that day, and when the motion was put 'that Lord Macartney succeed to Bengal on the Resignation or Removal of Mr. Hastings', they divided eleven against eleven.[35] It fell to the Secretary to draw a deciding lot from the ballot glass – he pulled out Macartney's name. 'What a singular constitution is that of Leadenhall House,' commented the *Gazetteer*, 'that thus the fate of India should depend on a *toss-up*.'[36] Two weeks later those jesters at the same newspaper came up with an idea for a cartoon: 'A Contractor Refunding His Ill-gotten Wealth,' its caption would read. 'When a certain rum contractor had about a fortnight ago swallowed a dose of *vitriol* instead of a gentle purgative – Dr. Fordyce *hung him up by the heels*; a good hint for a caricature!'[37]

Richard next visited East India House on 28 February, in advance of a parliamentary debate about the Nawab of Arcot's debts and the ministry's recent recognition of their validity. That evening, in the House of Commons, Charles James Fox moved that correspondence on the subject from the Court of Directors be handed over for inspection; Philip Francis, seconding the motion, warned Pitt and Dundas that 'their personal characters were more endangered than they perhaps imagined' by rumours of a 'collusion between the board of control and the creditors of the nabob' – a declaration which Dundas, who spoke next, treated 'with some degree of ridicule'.[38] Just as the debate seemed to have run its natural course, Edmund Burke rose to his feet, showing signs of emotion; what followed would go down as one of this prodigious orator's most epic speeches.

If Burke's overarching theme that night was the damage caused by the greed of the East India Company, the chief villain of the piece was Paul Benfield – 'a criminal, who long since ought to have fattened the region's kites with his offal'.[39] Richard, as Benfield's 'agent and attorney', fared little better. 'Every one who hears me, is well acquainted with the sacred friendship, and the steady mutual attachment that subsists between him and the present minister,' Burke declared, before protesting at the manner in which Richard had been permitted to make Pitt's India Bill 'his own', and the 'authority with which he brought up clause after clause, to stuff and fatten the rankness of that corrupt Act'. Next, Burke turned his attention to the previous year's general election, observing that Richard had kept a 'sort of public office or counting-house' from which the business of securing Pitt's majority had been conducted:

> It was managed upon India principles, and for an Indian interest. This was the golden cup of abominations; this the chalice of the fornications of rapine, usury, and oppression, which was held out by the gorgeous eastern harlot; which so many of the people, so many of the nobles of this land had drained to the very dregs. Do you think that no reckoning was to follow this lewd debauch? That no payment was to be demanded for this riot of public drunkenness and national prostitution?[40]

The speech, brimming with high-flown imagery, was vintage Burke. He finally sat down at one in the morning, having hectored the chamber for five hours. 'So absurd, as well as unfounded, did the accusations appear,' recalled Nathaniel Wraxall, 'that the treasury bench remained silent' — but, then, he would say that, for he too was in Paul Benfield's pocket.[41]

LADY ANNE LINDSAY and Mrs Fitzherbert had arrived at Paris in December 1784. Lady Margaret Fordyce joined them there; the plan was that they would all take a tour of the Swiss glaciers, before returning to England in the summer. But Margaret brought worrying news of Richard's health; shortly before her departure he had suffered 'something resembling a paralytic attack', and his condition remained precarious. 'My heart,' wrote Anne, 'trembled at the sound of the Palsy.'[42] The sisters decided to stay in Paris to await further bulletins.

Richard returned to Brighton in early March, accompanied by his niece Dorothy. His letters to Paris were deceptively cheerful. 'All you have to do,' he told Anne, 'is to double the number of your letters while I am an invalid, as they will be my best medicine; amuse yourself well, and let me partake of it.'[43] And he expressly forbade the sisters from coming home on his account, insisting that their proximity to him would create a wish for more of their society 'than he ought to be indulged in'.[44]

With the arrival of spring, Richard seemed to rally. Bridget wrote to Dorothy on 19 April:

> I am glad your Uncle is better tho' ever so Little. Some people are even in this country very Long in recovering from a fever and yet Lives many many years which I hope in God may be the case with my good Brother and Freind, if I think ever so Little on the contrary I find it is one of the things I cannot bear to think on. I hope you will be gone to Brighthelmstone if you can be of Service to your Uncle do not mind forms but ask your Uncle and do not waite his asking you is he not in place of a Father and what is there out of Character in atending a Sick relation at any time or any place?[45]

Three days later, Richard felt well enough to sit up in bed and dictate a message for Francis Baring to deliver at East India House 'concerning the necessity of considerable and immediate Tea Purchases which opinion Mr. B is at liberty to make any use of he pleases'.[46]

But Richard's improvement turned out to be illusory, and his end was sudden. On 26 May a physician came from Lewes, who 'found his pulse to be that of a dying man'. At eleven that evening, Richard asked Dorothy to bring him a calf's foot jelly. While she was out of the room, and his servant was tidying up the bedclothes, he whispered *I shall faint*, and died 'without a groan or struggle'.[47]

PART II

The Torrid Zone

THIRTEEN

The Newcastle Attorney

I WISH I COULD describe Richard's final months in greater detail. Dorothy nursed him during this time, and she must have written to Bridget at Temple Sowerby with news of his decline – but no such letters have survived. As for what caused Richard's death, we cannot know for sure, but it seems likely to have been tuberculosis. (An explanation supported by Nathaniel Wraxall, whose memoirs – one of the livelier commentaries on the events of the period – refer to Richard being carried off 'in the vigour of his age' by a 'feverish and consumptive complaint'.)[1]

I was on the point of accepting that there was no more to know on the subject when I came upon the brief description of Richard's dying moments, including his last words, in a letter from Lady Elizabeth Yorke to her sisters in Paris. It was a wonderful archival discovery, as well as a vexing one; for while the first sheet of the letter had been preserved, the rest had gone astray. Elizabeth told how, on hearing news of Richard's death, and feeling it her 'duty to do all to *his* niece that I could have done for a *sister*', she had rushed to Dorothy at Fenchurch Street: 'Oh my dearest Sisters may you never enter that house again! for if I found it so melancholy, so chearless, what must it appear to you! I found her in the greatest affliction, the gloomy appearance of the House & the want of air, made me immediately consider that the best thing I could do would be to carry her' – and here the page ends . . .[2]

Many years later, Anne would recount the rest of this sad episode in her memoirs. Elizabeth had postponed a ball that she was about to give in London; instead she bundled Dorothy away to Hertfordshire in a well-intentioned attempt to 'restore her spirits', recruiting another guest to 'read Shakespeare to her from morning to night'. Evidently this treatment failed, however, for Dorothy had left the Yorkes earlier than planned, and hurried home to her mother in Westmorland – conduct which made her guilty, in Anne's opinion, of 'unpardonable' ingratitude.[3]

RICHARD'S DEATH left me bereft. He was such a dynamic personality, such an incurable optimist, and it seemed unthinkable that he would no longer be present in this story. (Although, as we shall see, his influence would reverberate down subsequent generations of the Atkinson family as they grappled with his complex legacy.) By chance he was the same age as me, almost to the month, when I came to write about his death – a coincidence that added a frisson to my emotional response. I certainly felt humbled by how much he had packed into his forty-six years.

Richard's character had embodied some startling contradictions. Indeed, the gulf between his private and public identities could hardly have seemed wider; on the one hand there was the rejected lover and saintly benefactor, as recalled by Lady Anne Lindsay, and on the other there was the shrewd businessman and political fixer, as portrayed by his critics. (He was also, lest we forget, a slave owner.) The more time I spent in the company of these multiple Richard Atkinsons, however, the easier I found it to see them as facets of the same man. I came to realize, too, that Anne's memoirs had been written with the rose-tinted nostalgia of thirty years' hindsight – but, equally, that the *ad hominem* attacks of the journalists often bore little relation to the target of their derision.

So now we reach what is, for me, the greatest mystery of this story – the discovery of a record so unsettling that it made me wonder whether I would ever know Richard at all. It consists of the copy of a legal deed, which I found within a crumbling volume in the archive of the Registrar-General's Office at Spanish Town, the old colonial capital of Jamaica. This document states that on 1 May 1785, Samuel Mure agreed to 'Grant Bargain Sell Transfer Assign and Deliver over unto the said Richard Atkinson his heirs and assigns the following Negro Slaves viz. Betty and her Three Children with the future Issue Offspring and Increase of the said Slaves', in exchange for £120 of the island's currency.[4] Betty's vendor, Samuel Mure, was one of Hutchison Mure's sons, and managed several of his family's sugar estates in Jamaica.

For what earthly reason could Richard have felt the need to purchase four 'Negro Slaves' less than a month before his death? I turned the question over and over in my mind, trying to imagine scenarios that might have led to so singular a transaction – but ultimately it seemed so domestic, so *private*, that I could only suppose Betty was Richard's mistress, and the three children were *his* children. Then I remembered the letter written by Richard in December 1782, sent to Anne along with the final draft of his will, in which he had expressed a desire to throw his 'whole Heart open to her' and to reveal 'its most secret Sensations'. As attentive readers may recall, he had continued in the same intimate vein: 'The Consciousness that her Eye must review it would be sufficient to keep out all the *black* Family, & as to human Frailties, the Heart knows much less than mine that does not know that under the Influence of a generous confidence they would become the very Cement of its best Happiness.'[5]

The first time I read that passage, I must confess, my eyes slid over it – I suppose I thought Richard's reference to 'the *black* Family' was an obscure figure of speech. It had not crossed my mind that he might mean a black family of his own, for I knew he had never visited Jamaica – the dense paper trail of his letters in all the archives left no gap long enough to allow for such an absence. But black servants could be found in many wealthy London households at this time, and it seems likely that the Mures brought Betty over to work for them; she must at some point have entered into a relationship with Richard. According to the laws of slavery, the offspring of an enslaved female automatically belonged to her owner; so presumably, through his deathbed purchase, Richard hoped to spare Betty and the children the fate of being returned to the West Indies. (If he had wished unambiguously to guarantee their liberty, he could have freed them in a codicil to his will – which would, however, have carried the drawback of declaring their existence to the world.)

The whole subject is deeply uncomfortable, especially as the scarcity of information has driven me so much further down the path of conjecture than I would like. A search of the parish records for the City of London yields nothing that I feel any confidence in passing on. There's the burial on 24 November 1792 at St Botolph, Bishopsgate of Elizabeth Atkinson, who died of the 'dropsy' aged fifty-six – but Atkinson is a fairly common surname, and we don't even know that Betty adopted it. I found nothing under 'Mure' or 'Muir'. The story of Betty and her family raises so many questions, none of which, I suspect, will ever be answered – there is too little evidence to go on. Where was she born? Where did she grow up? How did Richard treat her? What were the children called? Did Richard make provision for them after his death? Did they go on to have families? *Might any of their descendants be alive today?*

RICHARD'S BODY WAS INTERRED beneath the middle aisle of Brighton's ancient parish church of St Nicholas of Myra, patron saint of merchants, on a grassy hill high above the English Channel. His death automatically triggered several elections – within weeks a new MP for New Romney, a new alderman for Tower Ward and a new director of the East India Company had replaced him. As the economist Dr Richard Price wrote to the former Lord Shelburne, now Marquess of Lansdowne: 'Your Lordship has seen in the Newspapers that Alderman Atkinson is dead. He has made a great noise and bustle, and rose from a mean station to wealth and honours. But what does it all signify?'[6]

The *Morning Chronicle* ran an admiring obituary on 9 June, observing that Richard had arrived in London a 'mere adventurer,

Near this Place
in the Middle Iſle
Lies depoſited the
Remains of
RICHARD ATKINSON *Eſq.*
Member of Parliament for
New ROMNEY *and*
ALDERMAN *of the*
City *of* LONDON
Ob.^t 26.th May 1785
Ætatis 47

Richard Atkinson's tombstone in Brighton parish church.

unsustained by any inheritance, by few family friends of any power, and by no acquisitions, which education imparts, but common penmanship and arithmetick', and had managed through 'good sense and persevering industry' to rise from the 'bottom of society to the summit of affluence'.[7] Other newspapers ran less respectful pieces, which caused a few readers to leap to his defence. 'The fidelity with which the Alderman executed all his contracts with government is worthy of notice,' observed one correspondent to the *Public Advertiser*. 'Whatever mistakes or misconduct may be attributed to the commanders by sea or land employed by our then Ministry, no part of their ill success was ever attributed by them to any neglect of the late Alderman not fulfilling his contracts with punctuality.'[8]

Richard had planned his will to be the mechanism by which he would enrich his closest friends and elevate the next generation of the Atkinson family. As you might expect, it was highly detailed; it was also full of the windy repetitions and circumlocutions with which such documents abound. In essence, though, Richard expected the produce of his two Jamaican estates to fund annuities worth more than £5,000 a year. Lady Anne Lindsay, Lady Margaret Fordyce and John Robinson would each receive £700 a year; his brother Matthew Atkinson, sister Margaret Taylor and sister-in-law Bridget

Atkinson would each receive £200 a year, as would Captain John Bentinck's son William; while his nine nieces and George Fordyce's two daughters would each receive £200 a year as soon as they came of age. Richard also anticipated the estates generating surplus income, above what was needed to pay the annuities, which would accumulate into a substantial fund; lump sums of £3,000 would be paid from this fund to each of his eight nephews when they came of age, and any remaining money would be divided equally between his nine nieces and any daughters Lady Anne Lindsay might end up having. The Bogue estate would eventually pass to the sons of his brother George, while the Dean's Valley estate would go to the sons of his brother Matthew. It was soon to become all too clear that in attempting to spread his wealth so widely, Richard had disastrously overreached himself.

Anne and Margaret returned to London three weeks after Richard's death, filled with remorse at their failure to visit him before it was too late. Their family attempted to absolve them of their guilt. 'Do not, do not repine my dearest sisters that you were not at Brighthelmstone during the last moments of our much loved, much regretted Friend,' wrote Elizabeth. 'I feel your distresses & know how poignant your grief must be.'[9] Their brother, Lord Balcarres, insisted that their conduct had been perfectly correct: 'Whatever Regret you may have for not being present at his Dissolution, you have certainly no Room for reproach, and if you had come over I am certain it would have fretted him.'[10]

The size of Richard's fortune would be the cause of much gossip over the following weeks – £300,000 was a figure bandied about in the press – and the wax seal on his will had barely been broken before scurrilous rumours started circulating about the nature of his friendship with Anne, especially given the provision made for her non-existent daughters. '*The* WILL – *and the* AFFAIRS. What mistakes and pleasantry have Lady Anne Lindsay's *children* and Atkinson's *will* occasioned!' exclaimed the *Public Advertiser*.[11] As she would herself observe: 'Such generous conduct as Mr. Atkinson's is not made for the comprehension of the world.'[12]

Everywhere Anne went, people congratulated her on her inheritance – yet she felt 'bent down to the ground by private sorrow'.[13] Her memories of this time would remain raw for the rest of her life. 'Do I pretend to have a heart?' she would write years later. 'Am I not a stone that I should have hesitated and postponed my return when his health became a question? Would he not have gone to the end of the world to do good to mine? O! my kind friend! why had not you the shoulder of the person you loved to lay your poor head on?'[14]

FOR THE MURE FAMILY, Richard's death was a catastrophe. While their late partner had been building the reputation of their firm as one of the foremost merchant houses in the City of London, the younger Mures – Robert and William – led a bone-idle existence, shooting and fishing on their elderly father's estate in Suffolk. After the mansion at Great Saxham burnt down, in 1779, the family had moved into the stable block, on to which two wings had been added, giving it the air of an Italian villa. Apparently it was a dull household. 'Mr. Mure's daughter and sons didn't seem to me to be very fond of laughing,' recalled the Comte de La Rochefoucauld, who stayed at Great Saxham during the summer of 1784. 'The worst drawback there in going to dinner with Mr. Mure is the great length of time he stays at table, generally three and a half hours. I once sat there five hours, without leaving the table, just eating and drinking.'[15]

In Richard's absence, the Mures soon fell into financial difficulties, and they immediately set about talking down the size of his estate, a good deal of which would have to come out of the assets of the partnership. 'As very much depends upon the state of Mr. Atkinson's Personal Property we are busy in making up his accounts,' Robert Mure wrote to Lord Balcarres, a trustee of Richard's will, barely a week after his death. 'I have to observe that from the very large sums he had expended upon the Improvement of his Estates in Jamaica they will be very much increased in Value, his Personalty proportionately diminished.'[16] Two months later, the Mures would attribute their cash-flow problems to Richard having taken sums 'amounting to £78,000' out of the house between the time of writing his will and his death.[17] This was a foretaste of the wrangling that would consume the energies of an entire generation, and ultimately serve the interests of no one – save the lawyers.

BRIDGET ATKINSON had spent little time in her brother-in-law's company – the last occasion on which I can say they certainly met was in 1776 – yet his demise came as a heavy blow. Following the death of her husband, George, she had gratefully accepted Richard's offer to act as protector to her eight children: Dorothy, Michael, George, Richard, Matthew, John, Bridget and Jane. Already her two eldest sons had departed for the colonies. Michael had sailed for India in 1781; George, meanwhile, had gone out to Jamaica in the summer of 1784, and was now employed at the merchant house of Mures & Dunlop in Kingston, from where he could also keep an eye on his uncle's estates. (He took his hound out with him; Bridget's pocket account book records the purchase of a dog collar, engraved 'Jock – G. Atkinson – Deans Valley'.)[18] For the younger Atkinson boys, lacking their uncle's patronage, their futures were suddenly filled with uncertainty.

Bridget and her brother-in-law Matthew were both appalled when they learnt how much Lady Anne Lindsay stood to gain from Richard's will; they saw her as an undeserving heiress, and set out to frustrate her claim. Anne, not surprisingly, saw the matter in a rather different light: 'The family of Atkinson having seen their brother but once in the course of twenty years, were not in the habit of forming expectations from him, till his invitation of Dolly awakened them. They now affected to be mortified at the destination of his property.'[19]

The Mures started putting about rumours that their late partner's estate was too insubstantial to support his legacies. Matthew Atkinson and his brother-in-law George Taylor – who were both executors of Richard's will – travelled south for a potentially tense meeting at Fenchurch Street in March 1786. 'I am anxious to know upon what terms Messrs. Mures & my uncles parted I fear not well,' Dorothy wrote to Bridget, from Newcastle, on 31 March.[20] But the Mures evidently smoothed over the Atkinsons' concerns, for Dorothy wrote joyfully to her mother a few days later:

> I cannot let you remain a moment in ignorance of what I have learnt from my uncle. There is not the smallest doubt but every annuity and every legacy will be paid to a farthing – there are no chancery suits but *imaginary ones* – no difficulties but the *like* – and Mr. Taylor says that every one of the Mr. Mures have behaved with more kindness, attention and patience than he can describe. You may set your heart quite at rest – what needless vexation have we suffered.[21]

The Lindsay sisters would also soon experience the Mures' double dealings. In the eyes of the fashionable world, Anne was a wealthy heiress; wherever she went, she could sense once-indifferent bachelors sizing her up anew. (The *Morning Herald* commented with cheerful malice on her 'ostentatious' coach: 'It surely is a splendid compliment to Mr. Atkinson's *hearse!*')[22] But her true financial situation was far from clear, for she was yet to receive a penny of her legacy; and so she was aghast when John Smith, Richard's lawyer, informed her that the Mures were planning a raid on their late partner's estate to pay off 'old debts' of more than thirty years' standing. It might be necessary, Smith warned, for her to make 'some concessions'.[23]

Soon afterwards, Anne and Margaret had a bizarre meeting with Robert Mure. Anne later wrote:

> Never did I see so strange a wrestle amongst the good and bad qualities as appeared in his countenance. He entered covered with purple blushes, and a few tears, which the recollection of the benefactor of his House forced from his heart to his eyes, giving him the aspect of a red cabbage throwing off the dews of the morning; but the good emotion departed with the tears, and he became hard and collected like the said cabbage.[24]

Mure stammered that he and his brother William were planning, through the courts if necessary, to challenge Richard's estate for the stock he had acquired through floating the government loan of 1782, of which he had set aside £30,000 for Anne's benefit. The Mure brothers did concede that their father Hutchison, as senior partner, had told Richard that he could dispose of the stock as he pleased, but the permission had been granted verbally, not in writing, and therefore they considered it the property of the house.

AT TEMPLE SOWERBY, on 10 August 1786, Bridget locked and bolted her bedchamber door as usual before turning in for the night. She woke at about two in the morning to feel her bed shaking, 'as if somebody had got from under it', and the floorboards cracking, 'as if somebody was walking on them'. Were she to live in a land where earthquakes occurred, she wrote in her diary, she would suppose this to have been one – but instead she put it down to a 'nervous Simptom'.[25] The shock would be felt across the northern counties of England, but it is hardly surprising that Bridget blamed it on her nerves, for they were in an unusually jangled state.

A few months earlier, the Atkinson family had hired an ambitious young attorney-at-law, Nathaniel Clayton, to defend their interests against the Mures. Clayton came from a line of Newcastle upon Tyne worthies – his grandfather and uncle had both been mayor – and had started his legal practice in the Bigg Market back in 1778, when he was twenty-two. He was also town clerk of Newcastle, having paid £2,100 for the lease on that office in June 1785. The fees earned by the incumbent were quite nominal; its main advantage lay in the valuable inside knowledge to which the town clerk was privy through his dealings with the council.

Shortly after accepting the Atkinsons' brief, Clayton had fallen in love with Dorothy, who was staying with friends in Newcastle. His earliest letters to her still exist. The first starts: 'Madam, I cannot reconcile it to myself to delay a Declaration of my unalterable Regard, and that it has become absolutely essential to my Happiness to obtain your Confidence & good Opinion . . .'[26]

Dorothy's reply has not survived, but it seems to have caused him pain. 'Dear Madam,' began his second letter:

The Rapidity with which my favourable Opinion of you grew into Esteem, and that Esteem into Love, I have felt but cannot describe. I have urged on the Decision of my Fate with inconsiderate Rashness, & have now only to deplore how vain they are who teach that cruel Certainty is more tolerable than a state of anxious Doubt. *My* Heart has also undergone a solemn & a strict Examination. I find it unchangeably yours, and that it cannot be estranged, til it shall cease to beat.[27]

This time Dorothy must have given her admirer cause for hope, for his next letter is much more playful:

My most amiable Girl, I am much at a Loss to justify my giving you the Trouble of receiving my Letters, otherwise than by imputing it to that Propensity which Lovers have to *write* as well as *talk Nonsense* to their Mistresses, & to the hope that, as I have been pardoned for teazing my Angel with Declarations of my Love for her, I shall also experience her Lenity, when I more solemnly, in black & white, assure her that she is the dearest Creature upon Earth & that I am the most enamoured Swain.[28]

Bridget reacted badly to the news of her daughter's attachment – perhaps forgetting her own mother's opposition to her engagement nearly thirty years earlier – which in turn caused Dorothy to hesitate. 'I begin to think I have been too hasty with regard to Mr. Clayton,' she wrote to Bridget. 'I perceive an impropriety in marrying whilst our family affairs are in such an unsettled state. I shall be guided by your opinion, for I can with truth assure you my dear mother that I never will marry without your intire approbation.'[29] But Bridget did not stand in the way for long, offering Dorothy her acquiescence at the end of October 1786:

I have nothing to disapprove in Mr. Claytons conduct to you or to myself only I am very Sorry he ever distinguished you by his regard. If you continue in the same mind and wish for my consent you shall have it most certainly only pray do not Let Mr. Clayton write me any more it affects my Spirits more than you can imagen indeed the Loss of a companion and one I could at times consult upon every Occasion is hard to bear but – to part with a child is scarce supportable and yet a Match which all your Freinds think a very good one a man rising in the World I should not be able to bear my own reflections if I prevent it so God direct you for the best.[30]

Nathaniel Clayton rode over to Temple Sowerby on 22 November, a pouch full of gold rings in his pocket. 'The Goldsmith appearing to have but little faith in the Measure of thy *fourth* Finger you gave me I was much alarmed lest that mystical Instrument, which I am to give as an earnest of Happiness & Love, should prove a perpetual Source of Uneasiness by its not being of a proper Size,' he had written to Dorothy beforehand. 'From this Dilemma I have however been happily relieved by obtaining a Number of Rings of different Shapes & Sizes for thy Choice, & it will not be an unpleasant Duty on Wednesday Afternoon to try them all.'[31] The following day, they were married in the village church.

The newlyweds immediately set off for London, their purpose being to meet the various beneficiaries of the Atkinson estate and to prevent it from ending up in the Court of Chancery – for chancery suits were liable to drag on for generations, bleeding families dry. One night they dined with Anne Lindsay; Francis Baring was the only other guest. After they had finished eating, and Baring had left, Anne launched into a tirade about Robert Mure's 'iniquitous claims' upon Richard's estate, which she believed would prove 'equally ruinous' to the Atkinson family's interests as to her own.[32]

Back at Temple Sowerby, Bridget was furious when she found out who the Claytons had been fraternizing with. Dorothy wrote from lodgings in Charlotte Street:

You tell me you are 'angry very angry' that I should listen
to what Lady Anne had to say against Mr. Mure. Let me ask
you my dear mother how it is possible for me to judge of a
cause, without first hearing both sides, the truth of which
maxim cannot be more clearly evinced than by your violent
prepossession on behalf of Mr. Mure who is making claims
upon the fortune and casting reflections upon the memory of
my dear uncle, that are neither conscientious nor justifiable
– those are not the suggestions of Lady Anne but incontestible
facts.[33]

Dorothy and Nathaniel did not enjoy much of a honeymoon. It
rained almost the entire month they were in the capital, and their
business and social commitments left little time for shopping or
other gaieties. After Christmas in Westmorland, they returned to
Newcastle to take up residence at Nathaniel's house on Westgate
Street, next door to the Assembly Rooms. 'The business of today is
receiving cards of congratulation,' Dorothy wrote to her mother on
8 January 1787. 'Happily it is not the fashion to answer them.'[34] (She
was always a reluctant correspondent.) Within weeks, Dorothy had
fallen pregnant – a condition in which she would spend a large part
of the following two decades.

Nathaniel was called down to London in the late spring on
Atkinson family business. George Atkinson – Bridget's second
son – returned from Jamaica in early June, after three years away,
and struck up an immediate rapport with his new brother-in-law.
Together, Nathaniel and George tackled the legal representatives
of Paul Benfield – who of course owned half the Bogue estate in
Jamaica. They also dined with John Robinson at Sion Hill. During
his stay in the capital, Nathaniel found time to sit for a portrait.
'My Picture is finished,' he wrote to Dorothy on 30 June, 'and looks
so smart that I am in hopes beholders will cease to wonder how
I obtained the best woman upon Earth for my Wife.'[35]

By August, Dorothy had started to grow cumbersome in her
pregnancy. 'My Dorothy is vastly well,' Nathaniel told Bridget, 'but

does not move up & down Stairs quite so expeditiously as she has wont.'[36] A 'sweet little Boy' arrived in November, and was named after his father.[37] In the spring of 1788, after 'little Nat' had safely recovered from his smallpox inoculation, Nathaniel was yet again needed in London.[38] 'I confess I am not yet so fashionable a husband as to relish these unreasonable absences,' he told his mother-in-law. 'I have therefore endeavoured to prevail on Dorothy to accompany me on my next Trip which She has consented to do on Condition that you will take the Boy and be engaged under the penalty of forfeiting your whole Cabinet of Shells to return him on Demand.'[39]

THREE YEARS AFTER his death, Richard Atkinson's tangled affairs still attracted much prurient interest. In March 1788, James Boswell attended a dinner given by the Earl of Lonsdale at which 'much good wine' was taken.[40] One of the guests, Sir James Johnstone, insisted that 'Alderman Atkinson' had explicitly mentioned in his will a love correspondence between himself and Lady Anne Lindsay, 'his own letter consisting of twenty four pages and hers of twelve', and had left money to her three children, including one with whom she was secretly pregnant while in France.[41] Another guest, Sir Michael Le Fleming, disputed this account. The baronets made a wager, the forfeit being dinner at the London Tavern. Boswell, acting as referee, duly inspected Richard's will at Doctors' Commons the following Saturday; but his journal fails to record whether Johnstone was ever required to pay up.

By the summer of 1788, the negotiations around Richard's estate had stalled. What the various parties did agree was that he had owed his partners about £35,000 at the time of his death – a figure which had since risen to £50,000, including interest and bad debts. Richard had also owed Captain David Laird £16,500, secured as a mortgage on the Dean's Valley estate – this money was due for repayment in 1792. On the other hand, Richard's personal effects, including East India stock, his wharf and warehouses at Rotherhithe, and sizeable loans to the Nevill and North families, were valued at £22,000; additional holdings, including shares in the

Bessborough and loans to Lord Wentworth and the family of the late Captain John Bentinck, were worth £38,000. With the liabilities of Richard's estate greatly exceeding its liquid assets, the forced sale of the Jamaican plantations seemed inevitable. For his heirs, this would be the worst possible outcome, since the payment of their annuities depended upon the produce of those estates.

Richard had clearly stated in his will that he managed the business affairs of Lady Anne Lindsay, that he had borrowed almost £20,000 from her funds, and that this money remained hers. It was partly through Anne's own carelessness that her grip on the funds was less tight than it should have been, for Richard had repeatedly offered to buy her a bureau in which to lock up her financial certificates, reminding her that 'possession is eleven points of the law'.[42] But she had preferred him to look after them for her; she had also refused to let him reveal her identity when he used her money to fund loans to Lord Wentworth and the Bentinck family. Now she lacked the documentary evidence with which to stake her claims.

Anne was treated shabbily by almost all her fellow heirs; when John Robinson warned her against 'some intemperance' such as 'forcing the sale of the estates' in order to release the money that was owed to her, she described it as the 'speech of the Wolf to the Lamb whom he accuses of puddling the stream above, though she drinks below'.[43] Her own brothers offered little support against the bullies. Lord Balcarres, much of whose money was tied up in the Fenchurch Street house, was pressed by creditors from all sides. The next Lindsay brother, Robert, recently returned from India with a substantial fortune, was forced to choose between propping up his sister and his brother; he chose the latter. 'Whatever my intentions were formerly in your favor in case of a Law Suit I must now *retract them*,' he explained to Anne, 'for unless I step forward to assist Bal – with *my whole* he is ruined past redemption!'[44] The Atkinson family rejected a proposal devised by Anne's lawyer, which would have entailed 'considerable sacrifice' on her part but prevented the sale of the Jamaican estates.[45] Thus finding herself without a single 'friend to lean on', Anne felt she had no choice but to agree a 'miserable *Compromise*' with Richard's executors.[46] By a deed dated 10 June 1790, she signed away 'realities, claims, and expectations' worth by her reckoning around £48,000, so as to secure for herself and Margaret the £700 annuities left them by Richard.

Even once this distasteful business was concluded, Anne failed to find the serenity she craved. 'I had hoped to have been able to tell you that all our pecuniary plagues were settled,' she wrote to the politician William Windham, with whom she was in the throes of an intense but ultimately doomed romance. 'The Partners & Executors of my friend Atkinson, after beating me out of everything, are now quarrelling about the division of the spoils, and will not adhere to their own offers, or submit to arbitration. On this account I find myself most unwillingly obliged to pursue these gentlemen by law for redress. My hopes of ease are at an end, my prospects closed, and life will probably be consumed in the conflict.'[47] These words were more far-sighted than she could ever have imagined.

FOURTEEN

Taking Possession

TWELVE GENTLEMEN, united by their loathing of slavery, gathered for the first time at the offices of the publisher James Phillips at George Yard, in the City of London, on 22 May 1787. One of them was the civil servant-turned-campaigner Granville Sharp, who had been battling against the institution since 1767, when he managed to prevent Jonathan Strong from being bundled off to Jamaica on board one of Mure, Son & Atkinson's ships. Sharp had played an advisory role in the important Somerset case of 1772, when, the same week as the Fordyce financial scandal was unfolding, the Lord Chief Justice, Lord Mansfield, had ruled that slavery was unsupported by the common law in England and Wales. But Sharp's anti-slavery campaign remained a fringe cause, since so much of Britain's wealth derived from the West Indies.

Olaudah Equiano first visited Granville Sharp in March 1783. Equiano was a former slave who, as a boy, had been sent by his master to be educated in England; later, after returning to America, he had worked to buy his freedom. He had settled in London in about 1768, considering it safer than the colonies, where the danger of being kidnapped and returned to slavery was ever present. Equiano was moved to call on Sharp after spotting a newspaper report about a legal case then being heard at Guildhall, relating to some events during a transatlantic slave voyage, the facts of which 'seemed to make every person present shudder'.[1]

Originating in Liverpool, the *Zong* had set sail from the Gold Coast on 6 September 1781, headed for Jamaica with 440 enslaved Africans on board. The ocean crossing was beset by headwinds, contrary currents and navigational errors, and sixty of the captives had died from fever by the last week of November. As Captain Luke Collingwood observed his ship's supply of drinking water dwindling, and his valuable cargo perishing, he knew that the insurance policy taken out for the voyage contained a loophole; although those Africans who died from sickness counted as a 'dead loss', and were uninsured, compensation would be paid for any who succumbed to what was loosely termed the 'perils of the seas'. On 29 November, Collingwood ordered his crew to start throwing sick Africans overboard – 132 drowned over the following three days. On 28 December, the *Zong* anchored at Black River, Jamaica, disembarking just 208 slaves.[2] Back in London, when the underwriters refused to pay the £3,960 compensation that was claimed for the drowned Africans – £30 for each man, woman and child – the *Zong*'s owners took the dispute to court, arguing that rough seas had 'retarded' their ship and 'obliged' the crew to jettison its human cargo.[3] From a legal perspective, the case of *Gregson v Gilbert* was clear-cut – Lord Mansfield admitted that it was the 'same as if horses had been thrown overboard' – and the jury found for the shipowners.[4] Granville Sharp later unsuccessfully tried to have the crew prosecuted for murder.

The story of the *Zong* inspired many people to query the moral basis of slavery for the first time. Thomas Clarkson was a divinity student whose response to the question 'Is it lawful to enslave the unconsenting?' won the prestigious Latin essay prize at Cambridge University in 1785. His dissertation was published the following year as *An Essay on the Slavery and Commerce of the Human Species, particularly the African*. Clarkson's tract would prove highly influential – it was said that William Wilberforce, the earnest young MP for the county of Yorkshire, turned his attention 'seriously to the subject' after reading it.[5] Wilberforce's political stirring, however, would occur following a conversation that was said to have taken place under an ancient oak tree at William Pitt's estate in Kent.

The prime minister, witnessing the eloquence with which his friend spoke against the slave trade, urged him to take up the cause in the House of Commons.

Two weeks after first meeting, the twelve abolitionists gathered again, this time to decide what exactly they would be campaigning to abolish – the slave trade or, more all-embracingly, the institution of slavery. They soon agreed that the sheer weight of West Indian interests made the abolition of slavery too ambitious a goal. They also suspected they did not need to aim so high, for the enslaved population was in constant decline across the West Indies, with deaths outstripping births, and planters relied upon new arrivals to keep up their workforces; so were they to succeed in ending the slave trade, the abolitionists realized, they would be 'laying the axe at the very root' of slavery itself.[6] Thus the Committee for the Abolition of the Slave Trade was formed, with Granville Sharp in its chair, and William Wilberforce its parliamentary representative.

Thomas Clarkson would soon distinguish himself as the committee's most tireless campaigner. He immediately set out on a five-month investigation of the slave trade, with a focus on the ports of Bristol and Liverpool, where he interviewed hundreds of slave ship captains and sailors. In Liverpool, he spotted a sinister display of iron instruments in a shop window – handcuffs, shackles, thumb screws and a 'speculum oris', a surgical device used to force open the mouths of those on hunger strike – and purchased them as props for his public talks. While Clarkson was on the road, the committee launched the anti-slavery movement, sending out circular letters to a largely Quaker list of sympathizers. The pottery manufacturer Josiah Wedgwood was an influential early recruit to the cause; his jasperware cameos of a chained African, imploring 'Am I not a man and a brother?', which went into mass production during the autumn of 1787, proved wildly popular, and the 'kneeling slave' motif soon adorned bracelets, brooches, buckles, pendants and snuffboxes across the land.

Clarkson had experienced much hostility in Liverpool, so he was amazed by the warmth of his reception in Manchester; while

*The iconic image of the 'kneeling slave', believed to be
by the engraver Thomas Bewick.*

preaching a sermon to the packed collegiate church of this mill
town, he was startled to find a 'great crowd of black people standing round the pulpit'.[7] It was late October, and Clarkson had not
seen a newspaper in weeks – otherwise he would have known that
anti-slavery petitions were spontaneously breaking out around the
country. When Manchester's petition was delivered to the House of
Commons, on 11 February 1788, it was the heftiest yet, containing
the signatures of two-thirds of the town's adult male population. On
the same day, William Pitt ordered a committee of the Privy Council
headed by Lord Hawkesbury (as Charles Jenkinson was now known)
to carry out a thorough investigation of the slave trade.

Wilberforce was unwell for several months in early 1788, and
unable to put forward a parliamentary motion to abolish the slave
trade that year. But his friend Sir William Dolben, who was horrified by the cramped dimensions of a slave ship that he had visited on
the Thames, succeeded in pushing through legislation that limited
a vessel's human cargo to five heads for every three tons' capacity
up to 207 tons, then one head per ton. Some abolitionists felt that
Dolben's Act legitimized the viewpoint that the slave trade was not
fundamentally wrong, merely in need of tighter regulation; but to
those in the West Indies who depended upon a constant drip-feed

of slave labour, the measure signalled calamity. 'God knows what will be the consequence if the present Bill is passed,' wrote Stephen Fuller, the island agent and chief lobbyist for Jamaican interests. 'It may end in destruction of all the Whites in Jamaica.'[8]

Through the medium of Lord Hawkesbury's committee, the abolitionists could for the first time place on public record a mass of damning evidence against the slave trade. Clarkson rounded up witnesses, but found that many of those who had been happy to speak out in private were suddenly overcome by reserve, such as one previously garrulous man who explained that as the 'nearest relation of a rich person concerned in the traffic', he would 'ruin all his expectations from that quarter' if he testified.[9] Among those who did provide powerful statements were the slave captain-turned-clergyman John Newton, whose hymn about moral redemption, 'Amazing Grace', was little known at this point; and the ship's surgeon Alexander Falconbridge, whose *Account of the Slave Trade on the Coast of Africa* offered a first-hand report of its brutalities.

Stephen Fuller, meanwhile, assembled a heavyweight line-up to defend slavery, including five 'totally disinterested' admirals who had served in the West Indies.[10] Admiral Rodney claimed there was 'not a Slave but lives better than any poor honest day labourer in England', and especially so in Jamaica, where he had never known any planter 'using Cruelty to their Slaves'.[11] A Liverpool merchant, Robert Norris, likened the middle passage almost to a pleasure cruise, during which the African passengers were treated to delicious meals, entertained with music, dancing and games before dinner, and accommodated in pleasant quarters 'perfumed with frankincense and lime-juice'.[12] Clarkson and his allies exposed this particular lie by circulating a scale drawing of a Liverpool ship, the *Brookes*, tight-packed with captives laid out on bare boards. The cargo of 454 enslaved Africans depicted by the plan was in line with the new limit imposed by Sir William Dolben's recent legislation – but a caption revealed that the *Brookes* had at one time carried as many as 609 Africans, cramming them in by making them sit in lines between each other's knees, and lie on their sides instead of their backs.[13]

Hawkesbury's committee published its report on the slave trade in the spring of 1789. Pitt presented the weighty volume to the Commons on 25 April, which gave MPs less than three weeks to digest its contents before debating the subject. On 12 May, Wilberforce rose to address parliament on the subject of slavery for the first time. From the start, he maintained that questions of personal culpability were irrelevant. 'We are all guilty – we ought all to plead guilty, and not to exculpate ourselves by throwing the blame on others,' he advised his fellow members.[14] For the next three and a half hours, in his disarmingly melodious voice, he proceeded to discredit every aspect of the slave trade, ending his speech with twelve propositions in favour of its abolition. It was a mesmerizing performance, which achieved the rare feat of uniting both William Pitt and Charles James Fox in its praise.

Those speaking up for the slave trade based their arguments on cold, commercial logic. Lord Penrhyn, a prominent Jamaican absentee, claimed that £70 million of mortgages on West Indian property would become worthless if the trade were abolished. Alderman Nathaniel Newnham, a member for the City of London, said he could not consent to propositions 'which, if carried, would fill the city with men suffering as much as the poor Africans'.[15] Over the following weeks, the pro-slavery lobby worked on indecisive MPs, reasoning that the Hawkesbury report was too flimsy a body of evidence to inform so momentous a decision, and convincing them to place the issue before a select committee of the House of Commons. Through the use of such stalling tactics, the abolitionists would time and again be thwarted.

ELSEWHERE IN LONDON that summer, in the studio of the painter Lemuel Abbott just off Bedford Square, a young man sat for his picture. Curiously, Bridget Atkinson's third son was the first member of my eighteenth-century family of whom I was ever aware. In 1981, when I was thirteen, the portrait of a Richard Atkinson 'who lived at Temple Sowerby' came up for sale through Sotheby's. The black-and-white reproduction in the auction catalogue showed a handsome, serious young man wearing a powdered wig, plain cutaway coat and white shirt with a frilled stock; the vendor was identified as 'Mrs. Dixon Scott', who I now know to have been my dad's third cousin.[16] Although my mother gamely placed a bid, at a time when she could ill afford it, the price rose way beyond the estimate. I can still recall my disappointment on being told that my namesake's picture had been bought by a nameless collector.

Shortly after his portrait was finished, Dick sailed to Madeira to take up a position working for a British wine merchant. Four hundred miles off the coast of Africa, this Portuguese island was less remote than it might sound, for it was an important stopover on the shipping routes to both the East and West Indies. Bridget packed Dick off with various home comforts, including some cured meats. 'Your Hams were presented to Mr. Murdoch the only Partner at present resident in the Island & with whom I live,' he wrote on 6 September 1789, shortly after his arrival. 'I have a couple of rooms at a small distance from & on the opposite side of the street from the House; the one fronts to the street down which there is a fine cooling streem of water always runing, the other which is my bedroom looks into a small garden in which I employ some leisure moments.' Renowned though Madeira may have been for its grapes, Dick was less than impressed by its melons: 'Either from the little care that is taken in the raising them or from being chiefly of the large watery sorts, they are by no means superior nor indeed do I think them equal to many I have eat at T. Sowerby. I shall however send you some seed, especially of the Water Melon, which we have of an astonishing size.'[17]

On 4 November, the Atkinson family would be rocked by the death of Matthew, middle brother of George and Richard, the last male of the older generation. Bridget's diary entry for this day reads simply: 'My brother Matthew died at twelve minutes before nine in the morning.'[18] He left a widow and eight children, the eldest of whom was sixteen, the youngest less than a year old. Matthew's demise cut both his and Bridget's branches of the family adrift, for he had kept the Temple Sowerby banking business going since George's death eight years earlier.

Matthew's death was especially unsettling news for one of his nephews. Bridget had been nurturing hopes that her fourth son, Matt, would enter the family trade, which since 1778 had included responsibility for the collection of the land and excise taxes throughout Cumberland and Westmorland. But one of George and Matthew's former associates, John Jackson, had recently started 'Creeping into the Business', having applied for the 'Excise Money', and was openly boasting of his determination to unseat the Atkinson family.[19] Matt, who was an affable but directionless young man of twenty, stood no chance in the face of such blatant ambition.

Bridget laid bare her distress in an anguished letter that she wrote to her son-in-law, Nathaniel Clayton, a few days before Matthew's death. 'All is I fear lost to my poor Boys,' she lamented. 'George says there is an opening for them at Jamaica I do not Look upon the West Indies to be a place at present to make a fortune or Mend the Morals of a young man it kills me to think of all my Boys going to Jamaica and where else can they go.' Matt's health was a particular cause for concern: 'He has had a complaint in his Bowells for a Month past he is troubled with a Head ach which is at times very Bad and would render Jamaica dangerous and I think where he gos I will go for what comfort can I have when all my Sons are gone from me none here I am Sure my Heart is near Broke.'[20]

AS THE MURES' financial problems deepened, their relations with the Atkinson family deteriorated. By their reckoning, Paul Benfield and their late partner's estate jointly owed them at least £60,000 for the purchase of the Bogue estate – even though the property was worth £40,000 at most, as Robert Mure candidly admitted. During the autumn of 1789, the Mures spread the rumour that Benfield was on his way back from Madras to settle his debt with them, raising credit for their ailing house on the strength of this report; at the same time they threatened to have Benfield arrested for debt the moment he set foot on English soil.

By now, Benfield's legal team were starting to wonder whether the Bogue purchase had been deliberately dreamt up as a scheme to defraud their client. Robert Mure's multiple roles only thickened the fog that surrounded this 'entangled, perplexed, & complicated' business.[21] 'He is *one of the Persons who sold* the Bogue to you & Atkinson,' wrote Benfield's advisor, Nathaniel Wraxall. 'He is a *Partner* with Atkinson. He is an *Executor* to Atkinson's Will. He is a *Trustee* to Atkinson's Will; and He is, lastly, a *Demandant* for the Purchase Money due for the Bogue. How are we to negotiate with a Man in all these various, & discordant Capacities?'[22]

In March 1790, Benfield's lawyers applied for an injunction that would prevent the Mures from harassing their client. Although not granted – on a technicality, for Benfield's team were unable to subpoena Hutchison Mure, aged seventy-nine, on his sickbed in Suffolk – it was clear that the Mures could not afford to litigate, and would 'sooner or later' need to reach a compromise.[23] Now Benfield's lawyers went on the offensive against the Atkinson estate. Clutching a letter in which Richard had once offered their client the option of relinquishing his share of the Bogue, they threatened the estate with a lawsuit to force the payment of £36,000 – half the sale price, plus accumulated costs – to take Benfield's interest in the Jamaican property off his hands.

It was at this miserable juncture that Francis Baring, motivated by strong feelings of 'friendship & regard' for the Atkinson family, came to the rescue – negotiating with the Mures to buy out Benfield's half share of the Bogue estate for £22,000.[24] Baring advanced them £6,000 of the money and Nathaniel Clayton the rest, which is how both men came to be creditors to Richard Atkinson's estate.

THE SELECT COMMITTEE which had been set up after the first debates about the slave trade published its findings in early 1791, in three fat printed volumes. William Wilberforce planned to bring in a bill to 'prevent the farther importation of Slaves into the British West Indies' during the next session of parliament, but he realized that few MPs would care to wade through all 1,700 pages of the report, so he worked at full tilt to produce an abridged version that was ready just a few days ahead of the debate.[25]

Wilberforce opened the proceedings on 18 April, and spoke with supreme moral authority; the cross-party trinity of Pitt, Fox and Burke added their support. On the other hand, 'tun-bellied Tommy' Grosvenor, MP for Chester, conceded that the traffic in slaves 'was not an amiable trade', but pointed out that 'neither was the trade of a butcher an amiable trade, and yet a mutton chop was, nevertheless, a very good thing'.[26] Alderman Brook Watson, representing the City of London, argued that ending the slave trade would not only 'ruin the West Indies', it would also destroy the nation's Newfoundland fishery, 'which the slaves in the West Indies supported, by consuming that part of the fish that was fit for no other consumption'.[27] Past three in the morning, after two long nights of debate, the House divided. The abolitionists suspected they would lose, but were unprepared for the scale of their defeat – 163 votes to 88.

Vested interests had killed the slave trade bill. 'Commerce chinked its purse,' commented Horace Walpole, 'and that sound is generally prevalent with the majority.'[28] But other factors had contributed to its trouncing – most specifically, violent uprisings in France and the West Indies. On 14 July 1789, a mob had stormed the Bastille fortress, a symbol of royal authority in the middle of Paris. That autumn, Thomas Clarkson had travelled to the French capital in order to forge links with abolitionists; by the time he returned to London, six months later, the intoxicated mood of *liberté* had fermented into something more frightening. The revolutionary fervour soon spread to the West Indies. In October 1790, Vincent Ogé, a mixed-race coffee merchant who Clarkson had met in Paris, led a rebellion in the French colony of Saint Domingue, demanding civil rights for his fellow 'mulattoes' – it would end with his execution on the breaking wheel in the square at Cap-Français. Then, in February 1791, news arrived in London of a slave insurrection on the British sugar island of Dominica; although quickly suppressed, it gravely injured Wilberforce's embryonic bill.

The Comte de Mirabeau had memorably described the white population of Saint Domingue as sleeping 'at the foot of Vesuvius', and in August 1791 the volcano finally blew its top, as enslaved

Racial violence erupts in Saint Domingue in August 1791.

blacks from the Northern Province rose up in an orgy of arson and bloodshed. Soon, most of the plantations within fifty miles of Cap-Français had been reduced to ashes. Many of the *grands blancs* fled to nearby Jamaica, taking with them their most valued slaves and, as many British planters feared, the contagion of unrest. On 10 December, as rumours swirled round Jamaica of a secret society called 'the Cat Club', where enslaved men met to drink 'King Wilberforce's health out of a Cat's skull by way of a cup', General Williamson, the island's governor, declared martial law.[29]

Following the defeat of the 1791 bill, abolitionists hit upon a novel way to show their disapproval. William Fox's *Address to the People of Great Britain, on the Propriety of Abstaining from West India Sugar and Rum* suggested that all consumers of West Indian sugar had blood on their hands: 'A family that uses only 5lb. of sugar per week, with the proportion of rum, will, by abstaining from the consumption 21 months, prevent the slavery or murder of one fellow-creature.'[30] Fox's pamphlet ran to twenty-five editions, convincing thousands of 'anti-saccharite' families to boycott slave-produced sugar.

Ahead of the 1792 parliamentary session, the Committee for the Abolition of the Slave Trade set another petition campaign going. This time, unlike the spontaneous outbreak four years earlier, it would be a highly disciplined affair, with local committees receiving strict instructions to hold off from submitting their petitions until told to do so. ('By no means let the People of Brough add their Names to those of Appleby,' Clarkson cautioned his Penrith contact. 'The two Petitions must be perfectly distinct. It is on the number of Petitions that the H. of Commons will count.')[31] More than five hundred anti-slavery petitions, bearing half a million signatures, would arrive at Westminster that spring – at a time when the nation's population was about eight million, and perhaps half the adults were illiterate, this was an incontrovertible expression of public feeling.

Even so, with lurid tales circulating of the slaughter of French planters in their beds, and the rape of their wives, the insurgency in Saint Domingue greatly damaged the abolitionist cause. Many sympathizers urged Wilberforce to pause for a while, but he chose to plough on regardless. On 2 April 1792, after a passionate speech to a packed Commons, Wilberforce moved that the slave trade should be abolished, and the debate was opened up to the floor. Late in the evening Henry Dundas, now Home Secretary, rose to speak. He had long shared Wilberforce's views about the necessity of ending the slave trade, he declared – but he challenged the 'prudence' of an immediate abolition, instead proposing a 'middle way of proceeding' whereby the trade would be eliminated over the course of an unspecified number of years.[32] He then successfully moved for the word 'gradually' to be added to the original motion. At dawn the House of Commons overwhelmingly, by a margin of almost three to one, voted to 'gradually' abolish the slave trade.

This outcome left neither side satisfied. Wilberforce and his followers felt betrayed by Dundas. The pro-slavery lobby, suspecting that the motion would never have passed under its original wording, felt robbed of the chance to settle the question decisively. They need not have worried. The following month, the House of Lords rejected the bill, thereby stalling the abolitionist movement for fifteen years.

The Gradual Abolition of the Slave Trade, in which the royal family attempts to reduce its consumption of sugar 'by Degrees'.

AFTER BUYING OUT Benfield's interest in the Bogue estate, Francis Baring and Nathaniel Clayton settled with the Mures that Bridget's sons George and Dick would take possession of both their late uncle's West Indian properties; at least now they would be able to prevent their inheritance from falling into ruin. George sailed to Jamaica in the autumn of 1791, landing at the bustling port of Lucea shortly before Christmas; twelve miles along a winding, dusty road, he was reunited with Dick, who had been learning how to be a sugar planter at the Mures' Saxham estate. Samuel Mure (brother of Robert and William) relinquished his power of attorney over the Bogue and Dean's Valley estates without fuss. A few days later, the Atkinson brothers rode thirty miles along the north coast of the island to the Bogue, where Dick would remain.

Two miles south of Montego Bay, the Bogue estate encompassed 1,300 acres bordering the emerald lagoon from which it took its name; this was the deceptively Arcadian setting for a factory complex operated by about two hundred enslaved Africans. Its infrastructure comprised a sugar works, including a cattle-powered mill, boiling and curing houses, distillery, stores and trash houses; offices for the (white) overseer and his deputies; workshops for the (enslaved) blacksmiths, carpenters, coopers, stonemasons and wheelwrights; a hospital for the sick and injured; a 'great house' for the proprietor; and a village of palm-thatched huts. The enslaved families also had access to plots where they grew the beans, cassava, maize, pumpkins and yams, and raised the poultry, goats and pigs, with which they supplemented the basic salt provisions supplied by the estate.

Sugar estates ran according to the principle of divide and rule, with rivalries among the enslaved population actively promoted by their white overlords. Members of the same family were separated; and a class hierarchy was imposed, whereby workers with white fathers or lighter skin were privileged over those with darker skin, and domestic servants, artisans and drivers had higher status than field workers. One of the first 'skills' that Dick would be expected to acquire, as a newly arrived sugar planter, was that of asserting his authority. 'Men, from their first entrance into the West Indies, are taught to practice severities to the slaves,' wrote an old Jamaica hand, 'so that in time their hearts become callous to all tender feelings which soften and dignify our nature.'[33]

Grotesque evidence of this callousness is provided by Thomas Thistlewood's diary. Born in Lincolnshire in 1721, Thistlewood was for many years the overseer on the Egypt estate in Westmoreland Parish. A keen botanist who exchanged tree and shrub specimens with the Mures at Saxham, he was also a sexual predator who logged 3,852 acts of congress with 138 women, and a sadist who enacted the cruellest of penalties for the pettiest of crimes. Notoriously, he devised 'Derby's dose' to punish an enslaved boy who was caught eating sugar cane stalks; first the lad was flogged, then salt pickle, lime juice and chilli pepper were rubbed into his wounds, and finally another slave defecated into his mouth before he was gagged for several hours. Not surprisingly, the enslaved population continually showed signs of resistance, most frequently through minor acts of disobedience or running away, less often through assassination and violent rebellion; it was their fear of the latter, coupled with absolute impunity, that turned white men into despots.

At the end of each day, the tropical sun plunged into the sea on the horizon, and darkness fell within a few short minutes. While the fragrance of orange blossom drifted in the air, the tree frogs resumed their otherworldly nocturnal song and the fireflies shot 'electric meteors from their eyes', the white men amused themselves by drinking rum, playing cards, smoking cigars and raping the enslaved women.[34]

DICK'S ARRIVAL AT the Bogue coincided with the start of the harvest, or 'crop', as it was known. This was a noisy time of year, characterized by the 'beating of the coppers, the clanking of the iron, the driving of the cogs, the wedging of the gudgeons, the repetition of the hammers, and the hooping of the casks', as preparations were made for the intensive bout of sugar production ahead.[35] The cutting of the cane started after the Christmas holidays, when the enslaved workers were given three days off, and continued until the coming of the rains in April or May; for four months or so, the sugar works operated round the clock.

Cutting the cane – a tall reed with sharp, serrated leaves – was brutal work carried out by the physically toughest individuals, motivated by a driver cracking a whip. The moment the cane was cut, its juices started to ferment, and there was little time to lose; it was rapidly bundled on to waggons to be carted to the mill, which was positioned on a knoll above the rest of the sugar works. Here women pushed the canes, six or seven at a time, through three large hardwood rollers – forwards through the first and second, back through the second and third – to extract the cloudy, sweet liquor, which was channelled via a lead-lined gutter to the boiling house below. (A hatchet was kept close at hand, ready to amputate fingers caught in the rollers.) The cane trash was meanwhile collected up and kept as fuel. The women often sang while they worked. 'It appears somewhat singular,' observed one planter, 'that all their tunes, if tunes they can be called, are of a plaintive cast.'[36]

In the boiling house, the cane juice was funnelled into an enormous cauldron, a small amount of lime added, and a fierce fire lit beneath. As the liquid heated, a raft of scum rose up; the flames were then doused, and the cauldron was left for an hour or so to let further impurities float to the surface. The clarified juice was next siphoned into the largest of a tapering sequence of about six copper pans; once boiled to nearly the 'colour of Madeira wine', the liquor was transferred to a slightly smaller copper set over a slightly hotter fire.[37] The cycle was repeated through to the final, smallest copper. When the liquor was thick and tacky, it was conveyed to a shallow wooden container about a foot deep and six feet square – the same volume as a hogshead barrel – to cool into an oozing mass of coarse crystals. Workers assigned to the boiling house had to remain on their mettle for the duration of their twelve-hour shifts – the slightest lapse of concentration might cause, at the very least, a disfiguring burn.

Afterwards the treacly sludge was carried in pails to the curing house, a large, airy building next to the boiling house, and poured

A highly simplified illustration of the process of making sugar.

into upright hogsheads balanced on joists above a large cistern. Over about three weeks, the molasses dripped through holes bored in the bottom of the barrels into the cistern below, leaving behind dark muscovado sugar in the barrel. The molasses were then taken to the distillery, where they were mixed with water, the juice of tainted canes, the skimmings from the boiling house coppers and the yeasty sediment from previous batches known as dunder; once fermented, the liquor was drawn off to be twice distilled, ending up as puncheons of potent Jamaica rum.

AFTER DICK HAD SETTLED at the Bogue, George crossed the island to inspect their late uncle's other property, fifteen miles to the south in Westmoreland Parish. Located on a wide flood plain, and sheltered by densely wooded hills, the Dean's Valley Dry Works (to give the estate its full designation) was so called because it lacked access to the gushing spring that delivered power to the neighbouring Dean's Valley Water Works, instead relying on 'dry' cattle to drive its cane mill.

George was pleased to see the sugar crop at Dean's Valley looking 'very promising', but dismayed to learn that ten enslaved Africans had recently died there from fever; it seemed that the low-lying position of the estate hospital might be partly to blame. The great house, too, was so unhealthily situated, and in such a poor state of repair, that George wondered whether pulling it down and rebuilding it on the side of the hill might not be the best plan – for only then would he and Dick be able to stay for 'two or three weeks at a time, which at present it would be madness to venture'. It was necessary, George told Francis Baring, that these visits should be regular: 'The Negroes on both Estates are very deficient in that confidence and attachment which the residence of a Master alone inspires and which it will be our particular study to supply.'[38]

By February 1792, George was in Kingston, the commercial hub of the island. Worldly visitors, sailing into the town's magnificent harbour and viewing the 'sapphire haze' of the Blue Mountains for the first time, sometimes fancied a resemblance to the Bay of

*Kingston harbour, with Port Royal in the foreground,
the Blue Mountains behind.*

Naples.[39] But the spell was broken the moment they stepped ashore;
for Kingston's charms were notoriously coarse, and centred around
brothels, taverns and grog shops. In contrast the parish church,
which lay a few blocks back from the wharves, was conspicuously
neglected, moving one writer to comment: 'It is a pity that the
morals of the people are not corrected, so as to have it as much
frequented by the living as the dead.'[40]

Kingston's merchants mostly lived on the outskirts of town,
on higher ground, in residences with broad verandahs and shady
balconies; driving downtown to their offices at about seven in the
morning, they generally paused for a 'second breakfast' at noon,
shutting up shop in time for dinner at four. The Jamaican merchant
house of which Samuel Mure was a partner, Mures & Dunlop, was
by now so caught up in the disorderly finances of the Fenchurch
Street firm that George, sensing a trap, had wisely resisted the
Mures' attempts to have him join it; instead he would spend the next
few months sounding out potential business partners on the island.

George was a restless young man, with a volatile temper and a burning desire to make some money of his own; without his own establishment, however, his hands were tied. 'Opportunities have occurred since my arrival here by which had I been at liberty to have acted an ample fortune might have been realized without anything like comparative Risk,' he told Baring on 11 June.[41] So he boarded a ship home in July, somewhat reluctantly leaving Dick (who had not taken to the sugar planter's life) in charge of the family estates. 'He one day talks of taking a trip to America, the next he means to return to England,' George wrote about his brother. 'One day he is to go home to marry Miss Howard, another that she is to come out to him next year, in short I don't know what to make of him.'[42] As it happened, fate (arriving in a winged form) would soon swoop down and pluck the decision out of Dick's hands.

FIFTEEN

Fevered Isle

ON 1 FEBRUARY 1793, ten days after dispatching Louis XVI at the guillotine, the French Republic declared war upon Britain and the Netherlands. The Royal Navy immediately mobilized its press gangs – this being the only sure method of recruiting thousands of sailors at short notice. Locals often banded together to resist the navy's thugs; on 19 February the men of North Shields, a port at the mouth of the River Tyne in Northumberland, confronted a gang with 'their jackets reversed' (a mark of deep contempt), threatening to tear them 'limb from limb'.[1]

The following month, five hundred men marched on Newcastle to protest against another round of impressments, only turning round when they learnt that the army was preparing to use force against them. 'We had a little allarm in the afternoon yesterday, the Drums beat to arms, the Sailors at Shields are again in a state of Riot and confusion,' Dorothy Clayton wrote to her mother, Bridget, on 20 March. At the time Nathaniel was in London on business, leaving her at home with the children in Westgate Street: 'The three Boys are scampering round me little John is just as riotous and as entertaining as any of them he is surprizingly good humoured and at the same time extremely lively.'[2] After six years of marriage, Dorothy was in the early stages of her fifth pregnancy.

The war had an instantly stifling effect on the nation's trade. One day in early April, after a run of unexpected withdrawals, the

Commercial Bank of Newcastle stopped payment, and the rest of the town's banks soon followed. 'Mr. Clayton did not come home 'til four oClock this morning from a Committee of the principal Inhabitants of this Town,' Dorothy wrote to Bridget at Temple Sowerby. 'He bids me tell you that they have arranged a plan which will in a few days restore the public credit – I give you a *hint* at the begining of my Letter.' At the top of the first page, she had scribbled this urgent instruction: 'If you have any *Scotch Notes* get rid of them as fast as you can you may take any Newcastle ones with the greatest of Safety – *not a word* of this to any body for ye world.'[3] But the panic proved contagious; by mid-April more than a hundred small banks had failed. Meanwhile inflation was running rampant, and Bridget and Dorothy started comparing the cost of provisions in their respective neighbourhoods – '1 Bushel of Peas 12d., Cayenne Bottle 5d.', wrote the daughter in a letter dated 5 May.[4]

FOLLOWING HIS FRUSTRATINGLY brief stay in Jamaica, George Atkinson returned to London in September 1792, settling into lodgings at Gray's Inn. Over the winter, as one of his uncle's executors, he was obliged to attend regular meetings with the grasping Mures at Fenchurch Street. These were dispiriting affairs, for George realized not only that Robert and William Mure were utterly disinclined to promote his interests in Jamaica, but also that they had falsified their accounts in an attempt to cheat the Atkinson estate. As Nathaniel Clayton observed: 'There is something so bare-faced in the object, and the Measures to effect it are taken with such unblushing Effrontery that I am appalled at the Reflection that We have to do with such Men.'[5] For George, who had run up consider-able personal debt and could see no prospect of discharging it, this was a dark time – so much so that his sister Dorothy would later admit that his 'dispondency' had caused her to 'dread the worst of consequences'.[6]

One day in March 1793, Samuel Mure and William Dunlop, part-ners in the Jamaican merchant house, called on George to inform him that they planned to dissolve their concern and set up a new house to unite the London and Kingston branches of the Mures' affairs. They hoped he might agree to run the Kingston office; as the partner resident in Jamaica he would be entitled to one-third of the general profits. Moreover, William Dunlop had long held the post of Agent General of Jamaica, executing business on the governor's behalf – the position had netted him £10,000 a year during the American war – and he now promised to help George secure the office. This proposal must have been extremely tempting, for it was certain that the conflict with France would soon reach Jamaica. As the historian Bryan Edwards would explain in a book published that same year: 'Never were the West Indian colonies the cause of war; but whenever the two nations of France and England are engaged in any quarrel, from whatever cause it may arise, thither they repair to decide their differences.'[7]

But Nathaniel Clayton and Sir Francis Baring (who had recently been made a baronet) were both sceptical of the Mures' motives. 'I conceive the Mures to want Merchantile Credit, and the necessary energy to avail themselves of it if they possessed it,' wrote Nathaniel. 'I look at their Proposition as flowing from no wish to serve you, but founded on the Sole Views of securing a continuance of that prop to the declining Credit of the House, which the Funds of your Uncle, and the aid of your Friends afford.'[8] George replied: 'The Question appears to be whether something advantageous to myself and Family may not be made out of the proposal, at the same time steering clear of those dangers which threaten to accompany it.'[9]

His negotiations were a success. The Mures abandoned their plan that George should become a partner in the merged business, and George in turn persuaded Samuel Mure to return with him to Jamaica to form a different partnership – the two of them, plus George Bogle, formerly a clerk at Mures & Dunlop. (The Bogles were a prominent Glasgow merchant dynasty.) Although the new partnership – to be known as Atkinson, Mure & Bogle – would draw on the resources of the failing Fenchurch Street house, the Kingston partners were shielded from its liabilities. One early June morning,

George departed with Samuel Mure for Falmouth, where they boarded the packet boat to Jamaica. Nathaniel, who saw them leave Gray's Inn, afterwards sent his mother-in-law a comforting note: 'They both set off in high Spirits and I trust with very good reason. The Prospect is very comfortable, particularly to poor George, whose Time has hitherto been wasted with little advantage to himself or others. He has left some Things for you in my Charge which I will convey safe & soon – I will not say how valuable a Present the shells are that you may be the more delighted when they arrive.'[10]

Bridget was in need of some consolation, for the welfare of her boys had lately been causing her much anxiety. One event she had long dreaded had recently come to pass – her gentle fourth son, Matt, had gone out to Jamaica. He had left Temple Sowerby on 13 January 1793, boarding the *Hope* at Whitehaven; the ship had set sail, then put straight back into port. Rough seas had detained it there for three weeks, and during this time Matt had met Ann Littledale. The Littledales were a Whitehaven merchant family of considerable local standing; Ann's late father, Isaac, had captained his own ship, the *Hero*, which transported convicts out to the American colonies (this was before the revolution) and brought back Virginia tobacco. George Washington dealt with the partnership of Dixon & Littledale; the future first president hosted Isaac at Mount Vernon in February 1760, and attended the launch of the *Hero* in nearby Alexandria, an event that Washington recorded in his diary as going off 'extreamely well'.[11] Anyway – by the time of the *Hope*'s departure, on 7 February 1793, Britain was at war with France, and Matt and Ann were engaged to be married.

The rest of Matt's voyage was scarcely less eventful. The following week the *Hope* was caught in a storm, and nearly wrecked on rocks known as the Bishops and Clerks off the Pembrokeshire coast. On 16 February it put into Milford Haven, where its crew was pressed into the service of the navy. It sailed again for Cork on 24 March, pausing there another five weeks while waiting to join an armed convoy, as the seas were now swarming with French privateers. Matt disembarked at Jamaica on 24 June, and George arrived just a few weeks later. Wretched news awaited – their brother Dick had died at Saxham on 15 May.

Dick's death, at the age of twenty-five, was a reminder of the risks undertaken by young men who hoped to make a fortune in the 'torrid zone' – for one-third of them would be dead within three years of first landing in the West Indies. Malaria and yellow fever were the chief assassins. Malaria, spread by the *Anopheles* mosquito, was characterized by chills, fever and sweating, accompanied by nausea, vomiting and headaches. The most effective medicine was powdered 'Peruvian bark', or quinine, from the cinchona tree in the Andes, with which the patient was dosed in 'as great quantity, as his stomach will bear'; another common treatment was mercury 'rubbed on the legs and thighs'.[12] Yellow fever was carried by the *Aedes* mosquito, which had migrated from Africa on board slave ships. While most patients recovered from its early symptoms, a doomed minority entered a second phase. As their liver and kidneys disintegrated, they turned 'as deep a colour as the skin of an American savage' and began vomiting a 'matter resembling the grounds of coffee' – this was digested blood.[13] Their suffering was beyond endurance, and death came as a blessing.

BRIDGET ATKINSON had not seen her eldest son, Michael, in twelve years; the six-month voyage from India to England, and then back again, somewhat ruled out home leave. Since 1791, Michael had been based at Jangipur, an isolated spot a few days upriver from Calcutta, where he ran the 'greatest station for manufacturing silk in possession of the India company', employing three thousand people.[14] He had made it his purpose to improve the silk thread produced by the factory, finding the locally reared cocoons to be of inferior quality; it was through his vigorous lobbying that the directors at Leadenhall Street would order their servants at Canton to supply Chinese silkworms and mulberry saplings with which he initiated a breeding programme.

Only John, the youngest of Bridget's five sons, remained in England by the summer of 1793, and even he was two hundred miles away, at Cambridge University. John had been admitted to St John's College in June 1790, where he was lucky enough to secure some of the most desirable rooms in college: 'I have four of them, a *Gip* or Servants Room, a sitting Room, an excellent Bed room and a Study: my sitting Room measures 22 Feet by 24 and has *allowedly* the best *looks out*, and I am inclined to think the only pleasant one in Cambridge, it commands the Gardens of Trinity and the Library, the River Cam, and the Walks and Pleasure Grounds of both Trinity and St Johns, so far as the Trees in them will permit.'[15]

John was an affectionate son who always kept an eye out for fossilized shells for his mother during rambles through the chalky fields near Cambridge. 'I shall send some Auricula Plants,' he would write in a note that heralded a delivery to Temple Sowerby. 'I won't tell you what they cost me lest you should think me expensive. In the Box you'll also find the Seed of the Blue Flower which I gathered from different Stems, wherever I thought I saw a Difference of Shade & if I am not mistaken you'll find several Shades of Blue amongst them. I shall put in a Fossil or two rather to convince you of the Firmness of the Marl in which I found them – than for their own Value.'[16] John was also attentive to his younger sisters, Bridget and Jane, and took great pleasure in sending them parcels of books, along with advice on how to develop their literary tastes: 'I hope you will not think it is from giving you Books that I think myself entitled to dictate to you, but from a very different Reason, a Desire to see you possessed of what few Ladies are, a Capacity to write and judge of writing.' They might refine their handwriting, he suggested, by copying out articles from the *Spectator*: 'It has a wonderful Effect in making writing easy and elegant. I would not have you give more than half an Hour a Day to this Exercise; don't think it a *childish Exercise* for I assure you some of the most sensible Men I know do it.'[17]

Following his examinations at the end of May 1793, John travelled up to Temple Sowerby with a Cambridge friend, Christopher Wordsworth; they clubbed together with another local fellow to hire a post-chaise, which was 'very nearly as cheap' as the stage coach, and 'much more agreeable'.[18] John's plans for the long vacation encompassed reading, shooting, fishing and haymaking. 'We on Friday put 24 Cartloads of the Long Croft into the Stack and 11 out of the Moss field and intend today putting the Remainder of those Fields there, which will yield from 30 to 40 Load each,' John wrote to his mother on 29 July. (Bridget was holidaying with the Claytons at Newbiggin-by-the-Sea, in Northumberland.) 'There is a letter here from George Dixon who has arrived again in London, begging your Acceptance of some Shells which accompanied it they appear to be and he says they are very rare ones.'[19] I imagine Bridget finding this gift very acceptable indeed – since serving on Captain Cook's third voyage, Dixon had become famous as a circumnavigator, and in 1789 he had published *A Voyage Round the World; but More Particularly to the North-West Coast of America*, which included descriptions of wondrous shells he had found in the Sandwich and Falkland Islands.

Dorothy gave birth to her fifth child, yet another boy, on 10 October. 'He has shewn considerable Talents in sucking & sleeping,' Nathaniel wrote to Bridget two days later, 'and promises to be as strong & rompy as any of the rest.'[20] The first four Clayton offspring were said to be thrilled by the addition to their number: 'It has puzzled Nat much to find whence, how & when he came. Little John calls him "diddle" by which Name he goes til we have found out one for him, about which we are at a Loss. Can you help us to one?'[21] In the end, 'Michael' won the day, for reasons that Nathaniel would explain thus: 'Shawls – China – Pictures & everything desirable have corrupted Dorothy & nothing will serve her but that the Brat shall bear the Name of her Benefactor in the East Indies.'[22]

DURING THE SUMMER of 1793, while Matt was adjusting to his new life as a sugar planter, George was in Kingston, eyeing up business opportunities in the troubled French colony of Saint Domingue. The lawyer Léger Félicité Sonthonax had landed there the previous September, bearing orders from the republican government to implement equal rights for all free citizens, regardless of the colour of their skin. Meanwhile, in London, a delegation of royalist planters from Saint Domingue, terrified by the turn of events in their mother country, had initiated talks to transfer their colony's allegiances to George III.

Sonthonax realized that his best chance of preventing the British annexation of the 'Pearl of the Antilles' lay in a military alliance with the black population; therefore, on 29 August 1793, he proclaimed the abolition of slavery in the north of the colony. Ten days later the governor of Jamaica, General Adam Williamson, dispatched a small force to the coffee-growing region of the Grand'Anse, on Saint Domingue's southern peninsula; when the redcoats disembarked at Jérémie, the local planters were ready and waiting, welcoming the men with cheers of *Vivent les Anglais!* The Môle Saint Nicolas, a naval bastion commanding the strait between Saint Domingue and Cuba at the tip of the colony's northern peninsula, surrendered to another British force on 22 September.

The invasion of Saint Domingue could hardly have been better timed for the fledgling partnership of Atkinson, Mure & Bogle. General Williamson had already confirmed George Atkinson's appointment as his Agent General in Jamaica, and now George Bogle was invited to join the expeditionary force as Agent General in Saint Domingue, on the same package as his partner in Jamaica – a salary of a guinea per day, plus 5 per cent commission on all transactions passing through his books. Hugely to the partnership's advantage, the cost of occupying Saint Domingue would prove 'unavoidably great' right from the start.[23] Major engineering works were needed to restore the Môle Saint Nicolas to a 'proper state of defence'. Two camps of whites displaced by the turbulence in the north, each sheltering about eight hundred refugees, not only required basic provisions but also wine, candles, soap and clothes. The house of Atkinson, Mure & Bogle shipped everything over from Kingston, while increasing scarcity obliged George to pay ever more 'extravagant prices' for barrels of salt pork and beef, until there was 'none to be procured in Jamaica'. Soldiers, ships, weapons, fortifications, hospitals, prisons – with the expenditure on all these heads mounting uncontrollably, Bogle was hard pressed to show William-son accounts that were even 'tolerably accurate'.[24] Meanwhile, George felt rising panic about the solvency of the partnership, since many of its payments for the supplies were made with bills drawn upon the house at Fenchurch Street – and it was no secret that the Mures' finances were less well founded than they had once been.

Sir Francis Baring wrote to George in November, warning that the Mures were on the verge of bankruptcy; he also related a recent incident that summed up their incompetence. William Mure had written to Henry Dundas, Pitt's right-hand man, requesting the vacant Postmaster's office in Jamaica on behalf of the Kingston partnership: 'We think it not improper to state at the same time to Mr. Dundas that Mr. Atkinson, one of the Persons to be benefited by this appointment, is the Nephew of the late Mr. Richard Atkin-son and as such we trust may be considered as having some claim upon Mr. Pitt & Mr. Dundas's generosity from his Uncle's attach-ment & Services.'[25] Dundas had forwarded Mure's note to Baring: 'You may read it, put it on the fire, and tell your friends that if I had showed such a letter and made such a Proposition to Mr. Pitt, any further conversation on the subject would have been cut very short.'[26] George was livid when he heard about William Mure's bungling behaviour. 'This Man,' he fumed, 'seems born to perplex & ruin every Thing in which he is engaged.'[27]

The Fenchurch Street house finally stopped payments on 29 December, defeated by a court order to honour a debt of nearly £52,000 due to Mures & Dunlop. Hutchison Mure and two of his sons – Robert and William – were named bankrupts. Baring immedi-ately communicated the news to Nathaniel Clayton in Newcastle, who replied: 'I cannot look on any Event with much regret that will separate us from the house of Mures.'[28] On the same day, Nathaniel wrote to Bridget: 'I confess, my dear Mother, I am not surprised at what has happened. Their neglect of Business & enormous expences threatened the Storm which is now burst on the Mures. Though we may be Losers to a small Extent We shall get rid of them – an advantage more than overbalancing the Mischief.'[29]

Richard Atkinson's former residence at 32 Fenchurch Street, and its contents, were sold off in March 1794, in hundreds of lots including 'Window Curtains, Mahogany and Japaned Chairs, Pier Glasses, Turkey and Wilton Carpets, capital large Dining and Counting-house Tables of fine Mahogany, Wardrobes, Drawers, Bureaus and Bookcases, Sideboards, Kitchen Utensils, &c. &c.'.[30] Nathaniel, who attended the first day of the auction, sent Bridget a copy of the catalogue. 'There is no such Thing to be found there as the Collection of Hogarth's Prints,' he wrote. 'As soon as the Bustle which the Sale must occasion is over I will endeavour to learn what has become of it.'[31] Hutchison Mure would die a few months later, aged eighty-three, reportedly from a 'broken heart, in consequence of the unfortunate state of his affairs'.[32]

The Mures' bankruptcy might easily have brought down the house of Atkinson, Mure & Bogle – but Sir Francis Baring saved the day, and agreed to honour all the Jamaican firm's outstanding bills drawn on the Fenchurch Street house, worth some £36,000. Through his intervention, the partners emerged from the crisis with creditworthiness that was not only unimpaired, but improved; from this time onwards, they enjoyed the privilege of drawing on Barings in London, and they could not have wished for a more prestigious connection. As Baring himself would later write: 'By these means the house at Kingston was saved, secured, & when it was found that our support could be relied on, their credit rose in such a manner, that the premium on their bills which was only 5 per cent at the commencement was soon 10, 12 & finally 15 per Cent.'[33]

I WOULD NEVER have found out the half of my family's business dealings in Jamaica had it not been for a stroke of tremendous luck. I discovered early on in my research that Richard Atkinson and Francis Baring were friends, for family papers mentioned the connection between the two men. Later, when I started looking into Richard's rum contracts, and then his role at the East India Company, I learnt that Baring had also been involved. Even so, a certain mystery surrounded their friendship, for no correspondence between them seemed to exist. I suspected that since they were neighbours – Baring lived at Mincing Lane, just round the corner from Fenchurch Street – there was little need to write down what could quite as easily be spoken.

By the mid-1790s, Baring had established one of the most revered merchant banks in the City of London – a status it would retain for two centuries, until catastrophic losses caused by a Singapore-based derivatives broker called Nick Leeson brought the house down in spectacular style. On 26 February 1995, the Dutch bank ING purchased Barings for the nominal sum of £1; among the assets it acquired was a collection of papers spanning the firm's 230-year global history, including thousands of letterbooks, deal prospectuses, ledgers and maps. The Baring Archive is now kept at ING's Moorgate offices.

Archival research can feel a bit like old-fashioned mineral prospecting – it is a highly speculative business, where you turn up for work motivated by the possibility that you might unearth a seam of documentary ore, suitable for conversion into polished narrative. Before I visited the Baring Archive for the first time, in April 2011, I had told the librarian that I wished to see anything connected with the Atkinson family's activities in London or Jamaica – not the most focused of requests, I must admit. On arrival, I was ushered into a small, windowless reading room and shown a pile of folders containing papers mostly dating from the 1820s onwards. They all had an Atkinson connection – but they were too tangential and impersonal to add much to the story I was researching.

Four years later, my family research hobby had evolved into a full-blown book project. I was halfway through a draft manuscript, and had started fretting about how I would account for the great gaps in my knowledge about the Atkinsons' business affairs in Jamaica – a subject on which the family correspondence had proved remarkably unforthcoming. One day, I was exploring the Baring Archive's website, reading a guide to the earliest part of the collection, when a sentence leapt out from the screen: 'Of particular note are some boxes of papers relating to the business of Atkinson,

Mure & Bogle of Jamaica and elsewhere, following the failure of their London agent in 1793.'[34]

This threw me off balance, for I was convinced I'd never seen any material that matched this description. I made another appointment to visit the archive. A few days later, to my utter astonishment, the librarian produced five volumes containing twenty years of correspondence between the houses of Atkinson and Baring in both directions of travel – more than a thousand pages. This was the motherlode I had been dreaming of.

DURING THE EIGHTEENTH CENTURY, most of the senior administrative positions in the West Indies were 'patent offices', granted to their holders as marks of favour by the Crown. These sinecurists almost invariably lived in Britain, delegating their official obligations to deputies on the spot. The system was every bit as rotten as it sounds; quite how much so can be shown through one example. During the dying hours of Lord Bute's ministry in 1763, Charles Wyndham, the three-year-old third son of the Earl of Egremont, a crony of the outgoing prime minister, was granted the office of Island Secretary of Jamaica for the duration of his lifetime. When, in 1781, Wyndham reached his majority, he leased the office to Hutchison Mure and Richard Atkinson for twenty-one years, in exchange for £2,500 a year – useful pocket money for a young libertine about town.[35] Since William Dunlop's retirement, George Atkinson had been acting as Island Secretary, performing its duties and raking in the appropriate fees.

The Island Secretariat occupied a large brick building on Spanish Town's main square, close by the King's House, the residence of the governor. This was the colony's bureaucratic hub; it was here that Jamaica's laws and proclamations were published, its property titles registered and its business transactions recorded. (It was in one of its volumes that I found the deed relating to Richard Atkinson's purchase of Betty and the three children.) Edward Long, the eighteenth-century historian of Jamaica, described the Island Secretary as a 'great pluralist', listing nine posts that fell within his compass: 'He is secretary of the island, clerk of the enrollments and records, clerk of the council, clerk of the court of errors, clerk of the court of ordinary, clerk of the committee of correspondence, associate-judge on trials *per* commission for piracy, commissary-general of the island, and notary-public, besides some other duties relative to trade, persons leaving the island, &c.'[36] In peacetime, only the governorship of Jamaica was considered more valuable than the Island Secretary's office. 'The fees attached to it are very considerable,' observed one critic. 'Every patent commission, and other instrument, has its stated price, and even the records of office can only be opened with a *golden key*.'[37] In time of war, however, its greatest value lay in the overlap with the duties of the Agent General (a far more potentially lucrative post in the gift of the governor), which made it practical that the two offices should be held by the same person.

One of Sir Francis Baring's first actions on behalf of Atkinson, Mure & Bogle, following the collapse of the Fenchurch Street house, was to secure the Island Secretary's office for them. In February 1794, when Charles Wyndham's rent for the lease fell due, the Mures' assignees in bankruptcy (the court officials with responsibility for distributing their assets to their creditors) refused to pay up. Instead Baring shouldered the expense, and subsequently renewed the lease on George Atkinson's behalf for the same annual rent, plus a lump sum of £6,000. Nathaniel passed on the news: 'With such a Friend all must go well.'[38]

OVER THE SUMMER of 1793, William Pitt and Henry Dundas were planning a major campaign to dislodge the French from their most prized West Indian possessions. 'Success in those quarters I consider of infinite moment,' Dundas wrote, 'both in the view of humbling the power of France, and with the view of enlarging our national wealth and security.'[39] General Sir Charles Grey accepted the military command, and Admiral Sir John Jervis that of the navy. The original scheme was for the fleet to leave Portsmouth on 20 September, reaching the Caribbean at the end of the rainy season;

this would allow six relatively disease-free months for the conquest of Martinique, Guadeloupe and Saint Lucia. In fact, the expedition sailed two months late and at half its planned strength.

Before its departure, Sir Francis Baring wrote to his friend Admiral Jervis, warmly recommending the services of Atkinson, Mure & Bogle should mercantile assistance be required. In Jamaica, towards the end of January 1794, George received the 'kindest possible Letter' from the admiral, whose fleet was then at anchor off Barbados, with an invitation to act as agent to the expeditionary force; the commanders would consider no other candidate until they had heard back from him. 'I am using every Exertion to be able to embrace the earliest Opportunity of joining Sir John Jervis & Sir Charles Grey,' George wrote to Baring on 8 February. 'Whatever Commercial Business occurs whilst I am there, of course will be thrown into the Channel of your House; and in Case the Expedition against Martinique is attended with success I am inclined to think it may prove considerable.'[40] George wrote in a similarly buoyant mood to Nathaniel, who offered this prediction to Bridget: 'The Continuance of the war even a year will make his Fortune unquestionably.'[41]

As George boarded the schooner *Berbice* to make his rendezvous with the fleet, the British forces started picking off the French sugar islands one by one. Martinique, where the most important French naval base in the region was located, fell on 25 March, after a siege lasting forty-seven days. Grey immediately appointed the officials necessary for the 'purpose of carrying on some regulation & collecting the Port duties, &ca at Martinico'.[42] George missed out on these spoils, however, for he was still five hundred miles away. After a rough passage from Jamaica, the *Berbice* had put in 'for the second time in great Distress' at Puerto Rico, whereupon its captain had dropped dead from a fever, leaving insufficient hands to sail the ship. 'The unforeseen Delays I have met with in this Voyage have been peculiarly irksome,' George wrote from San Juan on 4 April. 'My Stay with Sir John Jervis must now necessarily be very short.'[43]

Saint Lucia fell without the loss of a single man on 4 April, and Guadeloupe gave way soon afterwards. On 28 April, five days after General Grey declared the campaign 'successfully closed', George caught up with the fleet.[44] The last three months had been a complete waste of his time, as he wrote to tell Baring from a cabin on board Jervis's 98-gun flagship, the *Boyne*:

> I now am only anxious to get down by the quickest possible Conveyance to Jamaica. If the Jamaica Packet does not put in here in a Day or two, Sir John is so obliging as to promise to dispatch a 74 the Instant we get to Martinique for which place we expect to sail in a day or two. Sir Chas & he are as you readily will believe in high Spirits at the Termination of so glorious a Campaign – I could for more Reasons than one regret my not having been a Witness & Companion through it, but having escaped my late Dangers with Life I think I should be culpable of complaining.[45]

SIXTEEN

Maroon War

RETURNING TO JAMAICA on 12 May 1794, George Atkinson had barely been on dry land an hour before being served with a writ, arising from one of the Mures' creditors, which threatened the seizure of the Dean's Valley estate. The following week, having worked his way through a great stack of correspondence, George wrote to Sir Francis Baring: 'No Words can express the Sense I entertain of your Friendship in rescuing our Establishment from the Ruin which threatened to overwhelm it.'[1] A month later, as he was preparing to go to court over the estate, George learnt that his patron Baring and brother-in-law Nathaniel Clayton had jointly paid off Captain Laird's mortgage on the property, thereby forestalling the legal proceedings.

The British occupation of Saint Domingue had hitherto remained confined to Jérémie and the Môle Saint Nicolas, pending the arrival of reinforcements; but at last, on 30 May, a naval squadron dropped anchor near the colony's capital, Port-au-Prince. Two nights later, under cover of a thunderstorm that muffled the noise of their approach, sixty bayonet-wielding redcoats captured Fort Bizoton, which commanded the harbour; and on 4 June the British took control of the town, having sustained just thirteen fatalities.

The French royalist inhabitants of Port-au-Prince offered the invaders a guarded welcome. The British commander, Brigadier John Whyte, responded by seizing forty-five merchant vessels, many of them heavily laden with sugar, coffee, cotton and indigo destined for France – an undiplomatic way to start the occupation. The house of Atkinson, Mure & Bogle was well placed to handle the sale of the ships and their cargoes, conservatively valued at £400,000. 'Mr. Bogle is at Port au Prince as Commissary and is appointed one of the three Prize Agents for the Army; which as the Booty taken is considerable will throw some Emolument in the way of our House,' George told Baring on 15 June. 'The Competition in Purchases will I imagine be considerable and Speculators will crowd from this & other Islands.'[2]

George married Susan Dunkley, the seventeen-year-old heiress to sugar estates in Clarendon Parish, on 30 July. (The previous year, in London, he had proposed to Dorothy Baring, Sir Francis' second daughter – it would have been a shrewd alliance – but she had 'positively refused to go out with him to Jamaica'.)[3] Due to the vagaries of the postal service, it was several months before the rest of the Atkinson family, back in England, heard George's scintillating news. 'A letter from George talks of his Wife but evidently refers to a former Letter announcing his Marriage which has not yet come to hand,' Nathaniel told Bridget on 18 November.[4] John, who was then studying law in London, managed to obtain a little more information about this mysterious new sister-in-law: 'I have been enquiring of different West India People and find that she is a very beautiful young Lady of the first connections, was educated at Queen Square but not remarkable for the Largeness of her Fortune which on the whole I was rather glad to find for I was apprehensive he might have married to free himself from his account with the Mures &c. but I now see clearly that he has shot ahead of all his Difficulties.'[5]

WHILE THE REDCOATS garrisoned at Port-au-Prince dug fortifications against the French republican forces camped in the nearby mountains, the harsh tropical sun and rain beat down upon them, and yellow fever scythed through them. By November 1794, more than a thousand British soldiers were dead from the disease.

'They dropt,' wrote the historian Bryan Edwards, 'like the leaves in autumn.'[6] In neighbouring Jamaica, too, this would prove a sickly year. George wrote to Baring on 17 November apologizing for the lateness of the partnership's quarterly accounts, due to the recent deaths of two of his clerks; soon afterwards he suffered a 'violent attack' of his own, which he was lucky to survive.[7] George would remain too feeble to tackle anything but the simplest correspondence for several months.

The cost of occupying Saint Domingue escalated rapidly following the capture of Port-au-Prince. For the three months ending 30 September 1794, George's account with General Williamson of 'money paid and advanced by him for carrying on His Majesty's Service' totalled £124,216 – about the same amount as for the first nine months of the occupation.[8] George Bogle and George Atkinson, as the agents for Saint Domingue and Jamaica respectively, were each entitled to charge a 5 per cent commission on their official transactions; and since the whole of this expenditure passed first through Bogle's books, and then through George's, the partnership benefited twice over.

A few months later, after General Williamson warned the Treasury Board that he had drawn bills totalling £152,324 for the final quarter of 1794, Henry Dundas demanded the 'most regular and minute Investigation' into the accounts.[9] 'The Rate of the Commission to the Agent General, for Business done by him, a Part of which is merely the negociating Bills, appears to be much too high,' reported George Rose, Secretary to the Treasury, 'but the double Commission to one Agent in St. Domingo, and another in Jamaica, for the same Sums, is utterly inadmissible.'[10]

Williamson would draw more than £230,000 during the first quarter of 1795, and the Treasury's foot-dragging over the payment of these sums only added to George's worries. 'I am very sincerely sorry for the Difficulties you have met with,' he wrote to Baring in July 1795. 'My Mind is the more harrassed from the Rapid Increase of Expenditure on account of the new Corps raising in St. Domingo, all of whom we must pay & feed; and the least Hesitation or Check on our part would occasion the immediate Loss of that Island.'[11] The Lords of the Treasury did eventually agree to honour Williamson's bills in full, even as they registered their distaste at the 'exorbitancy' of the commission paid to Atkinson, Mure & Bogle.[12]

After a strong start for Britain and her allies, the momentum of the war had soon switched. In the West Indies, the French took back Guadeloupe in October 1794 and Saint Lucia four months later. In northern Europe, where a coalition of British, Hanoverian, Dutch, Austrian and Prussian forces had been struggling to hold back a massive French army, the following winter would prove one of the bleakest ever recorded. In December the great rivers froze over, enabling French troops to advance deep into Dutch territory; the following month, a revolutionary committee in Amsterdam proclaimed the birth of the Batavian Republic, and welcomed the French into their city. The ragtag remnants of the British army were forced to beat an urgent retreat. Thousands of men perished in the cold; a hardy minority reached the port of Bremen, from where they were shipped home.

One day in April 1795, while John Atkinson was on his way to a trial at Westminster Hall, he met some survivors of the Flanders campaign who had only that morning disembarked at Greenwich. He was deeply moved by their stories, and the same evening described the encounter in a letter to his mother:

I addressed myself to one of them who assured me that he was the only one remaining of his Company and that 14 were all that remained of the first Detachment, which originally amounted to upwards of 3000 Men. The Hardships they endured were he said inconceivable, that he himself in their Retreat from Holland counted one afternoon on a Common 86 Men frozen to death and that the whole Loss in that Retreat amounted at least to 5000 Men. Whilst I was talking with him a Man came up to inquire for a Friend of the Grenadiers Company of the same Detachment, his answer was 'I did not know him, but I believe I saw the last of them lay down in a field one Day'. To 8 or 10 other Inquiries he was more clear in his answers but they were invariably the same, that *they were dead*. Upon the whole I cannot say that I ever have been more affected with what so little concerned myself.[13]

THE EARL OF BALCARRES – Lady Anne Lindsay's brother – landed at Jamaica on 21 April 1795 to replace General Williamson. He had long sought a lucrative military posting overseas, and the Jamaican governorship – said to be worth some £9,000 a year – was the plum for which he had been waiting. George welcomed Lord Balcarres' arrival, in spite of tensions between the Atkinson and Lindsay families. 'I cannot think he would act hostilely towards me,' he told Sir Francis Baring. 'By making himself thoroughly Master of the real Situation of my late Uncle's Estates here, he may be enabled effectually to remove all Expectation still existing in the Minds of his Sisters that they are to receive Emolument therefrom.'[14]

The new governor found Jamaica in a tense state; within weeks of his arrival, a mysterious fire consumed much of Montego Bay. Balcarres was convinced that the French government – the National Convention – lay behind this mischief. 'Although there is every

Alexander Lindsay, sixth Earl of Balcarres.

appearance of Happiness & Contentment among the slaves in Jamaica that has not deterred the Agents of the Convention from introducing persons of various descriptions into the interior of the Country, & particularly Mullatoes & Negroes from St. Domingo,' he told the Duke of Portland, the cabinet minister to whom he reported. 'I think the Gentlemen of the Country shew a Supineness & a Carelessness upon this Point.'[15]

Perhaps this was true – but threats from within were a fact of life to which the planters were wearily habituated. Surprisingly, given their occupation of the island since 1655, the British had never fully completed the conquest of Jamaica; the descendants of Africans enslaved by the original Spanish colonists continued to live free in its rugged interior. During the early decades of British rule, these 'Maroons' had regularly plundered and burned plantations that they perceived to be encroaching on their territory. By a peace treaty signed in 1739, the colonists had acknowledged the existence of five Maroon strongholds dotted along the island's mountainous spine, and had permitted the inhabitants to exist on their own terms, albeit under the supervision of a resident British officer. The Maroons, in return, had agreed to hunt down and hand back runaway slaves.

The treaty had held for more than fifty years – during which time large expanses of Jamaica's western parishes had been cleared and planted with sugar cane – but on increasingly frayed terms. At Montego Bay, shortly after the fire, a couple of Maroon lads were caught stealing pigs and sentenced to be flogged; a runaway slave who had recently been returned to his owner by the Maroons was assigned to administer the punishment. The Maroons retaliated against this unforgiveable affront with the expulsion of Captain Craskell, the British superintendent of Trelawny Town, the most populous of their settlements. On 18 July the magistrates at Montego Bay wrote to Lord Balcarres, warning that a 'very serious disturbance' was imminent at Trelawny Town: 'All the people belonging to the town have been called in; the women are sent into the woods; and, between this and Monday, they propose to kill their cattle and their children, who may be an incumbrance.'[16]

The Maroon settlement at Trelawny Town.

In Spanish Town, on 2 August, Lord Balcarres called a council of war. 'My opinion is, strike at the Maroons of Trelawney Town,' he argued. 'Strike at that source of rebellion, and its fibres will be cut off.'[17] The council voted unanimously for martial law to be imposed and the island militia to be mobilized. Balcarres appointed George Atkinson to serve as one of his aides-de-camp, conferring upon him the militia rank of lieutenant-colonel. (This explains why several of the governor's private dispatches to his superiors in London, now held at the National Archives, are in George's handwriting.) It is hard not to form the impression that Lord Balcarres and his advisors were spoiling for a fight.

Two weeks earlier, due to a mix-up at the War Office in London, a convoy of merchant ships transporting the 83rd Regiment of Foot to Saint Domingue had landed by mistake in Jamaica, which caused their charter-parties to expire; it had fallen to George, as Agent General, to hire new vessels to carry the troops onwards. Now Lord Balcarres ordered the regiment back to Jamaica; the men disembarked at Montego Bay on 4 August to join the light dragoons already mustered there, as well as the massed ranks of the militia. Matt Atkinson, an ensign in the St James Parish corps, must have been among them; but I know nothing more about his military exploits than this. (The only reference I have found to Matt from around this time is in a letter written by one of his mother's neighbours at Temple Sowerby, which refers to him having been 'called off to carry a musket' due to the 'insurrection of the Maroons', and thus failing to send home some cinnamon trees with the last sugar fleet of the year.)[18]

The opposing forces were ludicrously mismatched. On the one side were the Maroons, few in number but skilled in disguise, light on their feet and familiar with the complex terrain. On the other side were the British, ten times more numerous, but stupidly conspicuous in their bright woollen uniforms and hopelessly attired for scrambling through bush.

Lord Balcarres arrived at Montego Bay on 8 August and at once issued a stern proclamation. The Trelawny Maroons had four days to submit to 'his Majesty's Mercy', or they would bear the consequences. 'You have entered into a most unprovoked, ungrateful, and a most dangerous Rebellion,' he thundered. 'You have forced the Country which has long cherished and fostered you as its Children to consider you as an Enemy.'[19] The Maroons marked the passing of the governor's deadline, on 12 August, by burning Trelawny Town and retreating into the hills; they also ambushed and shot dead the colonel of the light dragoons, along with fourteen of his regiment and thirteen militiamen. At headquarters that evening, Lord Balcarres slipped on a wet plank and banged his head; but George was on hand to provide 'able assistance' while he recovered from his concussion.[20] The next day, a sizeable bounty was announced for each Maroon brought in as prisoner – £20 for men capable of bearing arms, £10 for women or children.

The British soon learnt that ousting the Maroons from the densely wooded limestone terrain of the 'cockpit' country would be harder than they had anticipated. In mid-September, Balcarres returned to Spanish Town to address the House of Assembly, leaving General George Walpole in command. It was Walpole who suggested a way of breaking the deadlock. 'I was Informed at Black River by a very Old Gentleman that in the last Maroon Rebellion they had a Sort of Dog which was of great Use in detecting Ambuscades,' he wrote to Balcarres on 20 September.[21] The Assembly embraced the plan, nominating one of its members to travel to Cuba, where bloodhounds were routinely used to hunt down runaway slaves, and bring back a pack of the animals. A ship belonging to Atkinson, Mure & Bogle was taken into government service – this was the *Mercury*, a copper-bottomed schooner manned by a crew of thirty-five, armed with twelve guns to fend off privateers – and on 17 October it sailed for Batabanó, on Cuba's southern coast.

George Atkinson returned to the cockpit country in November, where he observed the redcoats bombarding the Maroons with howitzers – to little effect. 'The Country they possess is so strong; so perfectly known to *them*; so much the reverse to *us*; that this will be tedious,' he commented.[22] As the seasonal rains eased off, and the island's sugar crop approached ripeness, a resolution became an urgent necessity, since most of the men serving in the militia would be required on their estates in time for the start of the harvest soon after Christmas. There was also the terrifying possibility of the cane fields being set on fire, for they would soon be so parched that a single spark might cause the destruction of dozens of plantations. 'It is equally in the power of a few Maroons, as of the whole Body of them, to burn down the Cane-Pieces,' Balcarres told Henry Dundas on 16 November. 'I have a Month still to act in, before that dry and dreaded moment arrives.'[23]

The *Mercury* returned from Cuba on 16 December, landing one hundred bloodhounds, with forty handlers, at Montego Bay. The dogs soon showed their teeth. 'A Negroe Woman having struck one of them was instantly killed by the animal. A Soldier of the 83d having teized one of them was torn very much in the arm & with difficulty saved,' wrote Balcarres in his dispatches. 'Should these Dogs have the full Effect of reducing those Rebel Maroons I shall

Two bloodhounds and their Cuban handler.

certainly endeavour to preserve the Breed.'[24] General Walpole hoped the mere threat of unleashing the fearsome beasts would be enough to end the conflict. On 21 December, at a meeting with the Maroon chiefs in the woods, he gave them his solemn word that they would not be banished from Jamaica on condition they surrendered within ten days, and begged the king's pardon 'on their knees'.[25]

At Spanish Town, Balcarres was appalled when he heard about Walpole's pledge – for he knew that many planters wished to be rid of the Maroons for ever. Nonetheless, the governor returned to the scene of the conflict, where he grudgingly ratified the treaty on 28 December. When only a handful of Maroons had handed themselves in after ten days, Walpole argued for giving them more time; but patience was not one of the governor's strong suits. On 13 January 1796, Balcarres ordered the first outing of his 'Bloody Ambassadors'.[26] Even in their muzzled state, the dogs would prove all too effective; by the end of the month, more than three-quarters of the Maroons had yielded.

A rift developed between Lord Balcarres and General Walpole over how the Maroons should be punished. Balcarres insisted the Maroons had flouted the treaty, and he therefore saw it 'absolutely as nothing'.[27] Walpole, who favoured clemency, having staked his honour upon his pledge to the Maroons, reckoned himself 'scandalously traduced' by the governor.[28] On 11 March, when martial law was finally lifted, Walpole sent Balcarres the following message, along with his resignation: 'Content yourself, my lord, with this reflection: That the island, by firmness and humanity together, has been saved, without a *single cane destroyed*; and at a time when the *slaves were set agog by Mr. Wilberforce.*'[29]

The prisoners were brought round to Port Royal in the *Mercury* and other vessels. A secret committee of the House of Assembly concurred with Balcarres' view that the Maroons' failure to respect the ten-day deadline had invalidated Walpole's promise not to deport them; only the few who had surrendered in time would be spared this fate. The cold, dark colony of Nova Scotia, two thousand miles to the north, was chosen as the place of the Maroons' exile. George assisted with the arrangements, liaising on the governor's behalf with the naval commander, Sir Hyde Parker, who offered to convey them there on board two large transport ships, the *Mary* and the *Ann*, together with a frigate, the *Dover*, as part of a sugar convoy bound for England. 'The Admiral appears most ready to forward your Lordship's wishes to the utmost of his Power,' George told Balcarres on 17 April.[30]

Late in the day, however, Lord Balcarres was beset by doubts, and decided to await instructions from London before making his final judgement on the Maroons' fate. 'Lieut. Wilson commanding the Dover has just mentioned to me that he has learned from Mr. Atkinson that it is intended for the Maroons to be continued here & remain on Board the Dover & transports a considerable time,' wrote Sir Hyde Parker, irritably, on 3 May.[31] While the ships remained at anchor off Port Royal, it was Atkinson, Mure & Bogle's responsibility to keep the soldiers guarding the Maroons provisioned with 'Vegetables and Roots of various kinds, and new baked bread', as well as rum, sugar, coffee, candles and soap.[32] (The prisoners, one can safely assume, had rougher fare.) Finally, at the end of June, Lord Balcarres received the confirmation for which he had been waiting, and 568 Maroon men, women and children departed the shores of Jamaica for ever. (They did not thrive in Nova Scotia; four years later, in 1800, they would be taken onwards to the colony of Freetown, on the Sierra Leone River in West Africa.)

The governor's uncharacteristic hesitancy had arisen after he learnt that his tactics against the Maroons were the cause of controversy back home. On 21 March, General Macleod had tabled a motion in the House of Commons denouncing in the most gory terms the use of the bloodhounds; in Cuba, he said, it was customary for the Spanish to 'feast their dogs' upon the flesh of children, 'that they might be unnaturally bloody and fierce'.[33] Although the motion was subsequently withdrawn, many MPs were dismayed by such claims. Henry Dundas had already written to Balcarres conveying the king's misgivings on this subject: 'However great the disadvantages under which Military operations must be carried on, His Majesty cannot think these, or any possible motives, sufficient to justify the mode of warfare proposed to be carried on against them by the Dogs procured from Cuba.'[34]

Balcarres angrily defended his conduct, and his reputation, in a letter published in the *Royal Gazette*. The dogs, he maintained, had been deployed as protection against ambush: 'Why do the laws and customs of war authorize a fort to fire red-hot shot and deny it to a ship of war? The reason is obvious; the one is defence, and the other aggression. It is upon that principle that I used the instrument in question in Jamaica.'³⁵ To the Duke of Portland, his superior, he sent a defiant response: 'I have very shortly to observe that what I have done admits of no Medium. I have either deserved the Thanks of my Country, or I merit to be branded with Infamy and separated from Society as a Monster of Cruelty and Barbarity.'³⁶

ALL THIS TIME, the cost of occupying Saint Domingue, in terms of hard currency as well as human life, continued to rise to an almost overwhelming degree. Bills worth £2,232,177 would be drawn upon the Treasury in favour of George Atkinson, Agent General in Jamaica, between January 1794 and March 1796 – terrifying sums which stretched the resources of the Kingston house to such an extent that George wondered whether he and his partners had laid themselves too much 'at the Mercy of Ministers'. So when, in October 1795, he heard that John Wigglesworth had been seconded from Pitt's Committee for Auditing the Public Accounts, and would take over from Bogle at Port-au-Prince, George's reaction was profound relief – this, he felt, was the 'most fortunate Circumstance' that could have befallen Atkinson, Mure & Bogle.³⁷ Meanwhile, in London, Baring heard whispers that the ministry was 'disposed to abandon' Saint Domingue, or at least its 'hopes of acquiring it' from the French, and he wrote to the partners on 4 December, urging them to extricate themselves from all business there as soon as possible: 'I need not observe to you that your measures cannot be taken too quietly nor too secretly.'³⁸

During 1796, the balance of power in Saint Domingue tipped decisively towards Toussaint Louverture, the black general of an army of ten thousand former slaves. A devout Catholic who had himself been born into slavery, Toussaint had three years earlier made a bold proclamation: 'Brothers and Friends, I am Toussaint Louverture, my name is perhaps known to you. I have undertaken vengeance. I want liberty and equality to reign in Saint Domingue. I work to bring them into existence.' Now that Toussaint held that sway in the mountainous north of the colony, any lingering British ambitions of completing the conquest withered away. In June 1796,

Lord Balcarres expressed the view that Saint Domingue was 'lost to Europe'.[39]

By the start of 1797, after four years of a conflict fought on multiple fronts, Britain was lurching towards insolvency. Due to the overprinting of banknotes since the start of the war, the face value of all the paper money in circulation was now twice that of the gold bullion held in the Bank of England's reserves. On 18 February, the townsfolk of Newcastle flocked to local banks to exchange their notes for gold coin, and the panic quickly spread from there. As Sir Francis Baring would observe: 'Persons of almost every description caught the alarm: tradesmen, mechanics, and particularly women and farmers (to whom I am ashamed to add many of a superior class and rank) all wanted guineas, for the sole purpose of hoarding.'[40]

Rumours of a French invasion had been rife for a while. Atrocious weather frustrated attacks on Ireland's Bantry Bay in December 1796, and on Newcastle in January 1797, but a third expedition achieved landfall. On 22 February, 1,400 French troops came ashore near Fishguard in Pembrokeshire; they surrendered two days later, following clashes with local militia. The Welsh landings brought the financial crisis to a head. On 26 February, following an emergency meeting of the Privy Council, the king declared that the Bank of England would no longer be legally required to convert paper money into gold. Through this unprecedented measure of suspending payments in coin, the nation's bullion reserves were preserved, the Treasury continued to pay its bills, and the public credit remained alive.

THE OCCUPATION OF Saint Domingue would prove a calamitous waste of life and money; it was also, due to the astronomical sums that passed through their books, the means by which the partners of Atkinson, Mure & Bogle made their fortunes. Early in 1797, Samuel Mure and George Bogle both announced their plans to retire at the end of the year. While George Atkinson, at thirty-two, did not feel ready for such a move, it was necessary that he should spend more time in England, focusing on his duties as his uncle's executor. He did not, however, relish the thought of his unreliable brother Matt running the Kingston office; and so he resolved to hand over to his youngest brother, John, who arrived at Jamaica in December 1797.

George, Susan and their three-year-old son sailed for England in June 1798. Shortly before leaving, George accounted for his departure to Lord Balcarres. 'My Constitution is so much impaired by repeated Indisposition during the last two years that I really apprehend a Return of Fever in the Autumn might be serious,' he explained. 'Under these Circumstances added to the Private Affairs in England which press for my immediate Attention, I trust you will not attribute my Determination to visit England at this Period to any other than the real Causes.'[41] But there was in fact another, secret reason for George's voyage home – he had seriously displeased Sir Francis Baring.

It was one of Baring's articles of faith that a merchant should, as much as possible, resist the distractions of public life; so he had viewed George's military and political activities with mounting concern, especially since his election to the House of Assembly. While George's attentions were diverted elsewhere, the Saint Domingue business had expanded so massively, and communications from Jamaica had become so erratic, that Baring grew alarmed at the risk posed to his own merchant house. As he later admitted in a memorandum to his partners: 'Our fortunes, & even our existence, was in real danger, in consequence of our unbounded confidence & devotion to the house at Kingston.'[42]

George wrote to Baring from Temple Sowerby on 28 August – not exactly a grovelling letter, but with a note of contrition. 'I trust my Gratitude for your unlimited Friendship will cease but with my Life,' he started, before going on to list some of the challenges he had faced over the previous five years, including seven bouts of malaria which had taken him 'to the Brink of the Grave'. He explained that motives of loyalty had led him to follow Lord Balcarres into the field during the Maroon war, but he also denied being too close to the governor: 'That I have been in his Confidence and have used private

Influence to forward his measures, is undoubtedly true; but I am safe in saying I never made an Enemy by the manner of doing it, and as to attendance upon him I am positively certain I did not during the last 18 Months of my Stay in the Island, breakfast or dine six times in the Government House.'[43]

Nathaniel Clayton offered a dispassionate view of his brother-in-law's transgressions, writing to Baring:

The Excess of George's Misconduct may be learnt from your Displeasure, which, I know, is not easily excited. I own his military Expedition appeared to me little less than an act of Insanity, and you convince me that his parliamentary measure was nearly as absurd. His entangling himself in *new* Engagements in Jamaica was in the face of my repeated Exhortations & his own solemn Promises. I more than ever deprecate his Return to Jamaica. His Temper will not suffer itself to be controlled by a younger Brother, and he has such an unconquerable Propensity to act on the Spur of the Moment that Remonstrances from a distance are unavailing, for they come too late. It is my Consolation that you will find John the very reverse of his Brother. His Talents are not brilliant but I hope they are solid, & they are certainly accompanied with an excellent Temper & uncommon Industry.[44]

Meanwhile, the British withdrawal from Saint Domingue was well under way. Brigadier Thomas Maitland signed an armistice with Toussaint Louverture on 30 April; the evacuation from Port-au-Prince took place on 8 May, at two in the morning. Maitland wrote to Lord Balcarres on 25 June, requesting permission to evacuate the garrison at Jérémie, which he believed to be vulnerable to attack, but Balcarres refused to take responsibility for 'deciding on a point, where the consequences are so immense'.[45] In late July, following the arrival of definite orders from Henry Dundas, the Secretary of State for War, Maitland announced his intention to remove all troops from the French colony.

The British slipped out of Jérémie harbour after dark on 20 August, once 'all the Stores of every description' had been loaded on to a motley assortment of transport ships.[46] On 1 September, John Atkinson wrote to Lord Balcarres hurriedly requesting clearance to land 'from one thousand to twelve hundred Barrels of Gunpowder, the Number of Barrels could not be exactly ascertained from the Circumstance of their having been embarked in the Night'.[47] The governor did not hide his exasperation: 'I scarcely do not know in what capacity you address me – whether as Commissary for Jamaica or for St. Domingo? I have no Place to store 1000 Barrels of Gun Powder nor Artillery Stores. Fort Augusta is now entirely full.'[48]

At daybreak on 3 October the last of the British fleet, packed with troops, refugees, ordnance and other stores, sailed from the Môle Saint Nicolas, bound for Jamaica. But John was not present to supervise the landing. Four weeks earlier, a fever had suddenly struck him down, and he had died on 11 September, aged twenty-seven. His mortal remains were added with little ceremony to the overflowing churchyard at Kingston.

SEVENTEEN

Black Pioneers

NATHANIEL CLAYTON purchased the Chesters estate in 1796 – his legal practice was flourishing. Some twenty miles west of Newcastle, as the crow flies, the mansion was a rather dour stone box of a building, but it commanded delightful views across open fields down to the banks of the North Tyne. Scattered round these meadows were the remnants of Cilurnum, a Roman cavalry station which had once guarded an important river crossing. Nathaniel immediately got started on improvements to the property, first diverting the public road running through the middle of its park, then tidying up the Roman rubble. 'Large masses of ruins rising in heaps over a spacious field speak of former greatness,' wrote a visitor in 1801. 'The mutilated figure of a woman standing on the back of some animal has lately been dug up and is at present put in a wall enclosing a plantation; I should think it deserved a better situation.'[1]

Nathaniel soon proved himself a capable farmer. New field drains, dug at considerable expense, paid swift dividends. 'My Neighbours begin to think that I am not such a Ninnyhammer as they first took me for,' he told his youngest sister-in-law, Jane. 'I am greatly bent on making two Blades of Grass grow where one only grew before.'[2] Across the country, a disastrous harvest in the summer of 1799 caused many poor families to go hungry the following winter; in Newcastle, a large soup kitchen was erected in the Poultry Market to feed those who were 'ready to perish'.[3] Even that most basic of staples, peas, were hard to come by. 'I imagine they must be very scarse,' wrote Jane, who was staying with the Claytons at Westgate Street, 'for at the Soup Kitchen they substitute Potatoes, which at present bear a very high price in proportion with every other kind of grain.'[4] With vegetables at such a premium, Nathaniel felt justifiably proud of his yield at Chesters. 'My farming Skill has become notorious,' he told his mother-in-law in February 1800, 'for I had the best Crop of Turnips within 20 Miles of me, and Turnips were this year but another Name for Gold.'[5]

Ever since 1786, when he was hired by the Atkinson family to protect their inheritance, Nathaniel had worked tirelessly to promote the interests of his wife's relatives. To give one minor example: in the spring of 1798, after reading in the *Gentleman's Magazine* that a second cousin of the Atkinsons, a Miss Addison (daughter of Joseph Addison, the celebrated essayist and founder of the *Spectator*), had died intestate, Nathaniel made it his business to find out the value of her estate. 'If I find the play worth the Candle,' he told Jane, 'I see a reasonable Ground to hope that I shall prove our Brother Michael entitled to the Property.'[6] But Nathaniel's efforts to establish his brother-in-law's claim as the old lady's 'laughing heir' must have come to naught, for the subject was soon dropped.

The Clayton children often stayed with their grandmother and unmarried aunts at Temple Sowerby, and saw it as a second home; during the light summer months, it was possible to ride across the moors from Chesters in a single day. When they were seven, the boys were each in turn sent to board at the Rev. John Fisher's school at Kirkoswald, ten miles from Temple Sowerby; having acquired groundings in Greek and Latin, as well as 'broad Cumberland' accents, they would go on to public schools in the south.[7]

Nat, the eldest, went to Harrow, and his letters to Bridget show him to have been a clever, amusing boy. During the Easter holidays of 1799, when he was eleven, he visited Parkinson's Museum, which was housed in a rotunda on the south side of the Thames by Blackfriars Bridge. He reported back to his grandmother:

Among other curious things, we saw a piece of beef, which had gone round the world with Commodore Anson; also a great many Indian clubs, and a goat of Angora stuffed, all kinds of Butterflies and insects, and what amused Nurse most of all, a pair of Chinese woman's shoes. In the second Gallery we saw a Chinese Pheasant, a blue bellied creeper, a Parrot, a swallow's nest which was built in the wing of an owl, a bat, and a stuffed shark. As I know that you like long letters, and as I have nothing else to write about, I will proceed. I saw also a sea Hawk, a stuffed lap dog, a Tyger, a lion, a Buck, a Toucan, a scarlet humming Bird, a blue humming bird, a green humming bird, a Pelican, also silver and Iron ore, a stuffed ostrich, and a Cougar, a common hen and chickens with which Nurse was remarkably well pleased, a large collection of Shells, which she thought were Superior even to yours, the only specimen of the bread Fruit, which Captain Cook brought with him from the Island of Otaheite, a stuffed Cormorant, and a Crane.[8]

Little Bridget and John Clayton, aged nine and seven, spent the autumn months of 1799 at Temple Sowerby. They were engaging children, and their grandmother relished having them nearby as she knitted heroic quantities of woollen stockings for them and their siblings. 'I am very glad that Mr. Clayton and you consent to Bridget and John's staying a Little Longer with me who at present are in perfect good Health and are growing Stout and Strong for which I have to thank John Ching it has made such an alteration for the better,' Bridget wrote to Dorothy on 27 October. ('John Ching' was a proprietary brand of worm lozenges – its principal ingredient being mercury.) 'Bridget is fond of Patching and sits close by me and John plays at Cards by himself with the greatest good hummor and Dummy and he never disagrees.'[9]

FOLLOWING HIS RETURN to England, George Atkinson had spent a good deal of the autumn of 1798 on turnpikes, shuttling between family in the north and various 'intricate unpleasant' concerns demanding his attention down south.[10] The winding up of the house of Atkinson, Mure & Bogle was his first priority, with funds of almost £250,000 to be shared out between the three Kingston partners, as well as Sir Francis Baring, who had financed their business from London. Inevitably, some frank exchanges of opinion ensued. The Jamaican contingent argued that they deserved the lion's share, since their possession of the Agent General's office, through which the vast majority of the spoils had flowed, predated Baring's formal connection with their business. Baring, on the other hand, reminded them that the Island Secretary was placed by virtue of his position in 'so important, confidential a situation with the Governor' that it almost always led to his appointment as Agent General – which was why, following the Mures' bankruptcy, he had gone to the great trouble of renegotiating the lease on the Island Secretary's office with its aristocratic owner, Charles Wyndham.[11]

George was unusually subdued during these discussions, perhaps on account of the dressing-down he had received from his patron that summer; certainly Baring noticed that he seemed 'disposed to acquiesce with any terms we should propose'.[12] Once the Kingston partners had conceded the point over the Island Secretary's office, Baring was generous in his settlement, accepting a lump sum of £70,000. His primary motive, he reminded his own partners, had always been to 'reestablish & thereby serve the Atkinson family'.[13] Both sides signed the letter of agreement on 1 December 1798; and thus the books of the house of Atkinson, Mure & Bogle were closed.

The news of John's death in Jamaica reached his mother and sisters at Temple Sowerby in late November. Although it must have caused them great anguish, their letters are entirely silent on the subject. Maybe the family gathered to mark John's passing; George certainly travelled up to Westmorland in early December. As was the custom of the time, Bridget would wear black for the first year after her son's death, moving on to muted colours for the second year. (On the first anniversary of Dick's death, back in May 1794, Dorothy had written from Newcastle to tell Bridget that she had just dispatched a 'french Grey callico gown for you of a sort much in use here for second mourning – also a very dark purple one for visiting the Hotbeds &c'.[14] I love the thought of Bridget pottering about the kitchen garden at Temple Sowerby, honouring her son's memory as she tended her melon pit.)

Later that winter, in February 1799, George returned to London to make preparations for what he anticipated would be a 'Hot Campaign' at the Court of Chancery, where various of the Mures' creditors were lining up to 'commence Hostilities' against his uncle's estate.[15] 'Their Claims are immoderate and very extraordinary,' George wrote to Lord Balcarres. 'Upon the whole I apprehend I shall have very ample Employment in the Liquidation of these Concerns for many months. I have abandoned all Hopes of returning to Jamaica this Season.'[16]

WITHIN DAYS OF his brother John's death, Matt Atkinson was sworn in as Island Secretary of Jamaica; the family's affairs in the colony now rested on the shoulders of its laziest member. Shortly after Christmas, Matt slipped away from Kingston to inspect the estates at the west end of the island. 'The Bogue is coming round fast I expect 200 Hhds this Crop,' he told Baring on 10 February 1799. 'There wants a great deal to be done at Deans Valley, both as to establishing Guinea Grass, draining Land, and putting on Negroes, before the Estate can be brought to what it ought to make, which is 280 to 300 Hhds.'[17] Following years of underinvestment, parts of Dean's Valley were on the point of collapse, with urgent repairs needed to the sugar works, overseer's house and other buildings – a local surveyor estimated that 'it would require 40,000 Shingles and 10,000 feet of Boards to do what is Absolutely necessary'.[18] On both estates, the workforces were 'much upon the decline'.[19] Over three years – from the beginning of 1797 to the end of 1799 – the enslaved population at the Bogue would fall by fifteen, to 215 (seven births, minus twenty-two deaths), while at Dean's Valley it would fall by thirteen, to 208 (twelve births, minus twenty-five deaths).[20]

In London, George set up a new merchant house, to be known as G. & M. Atkinson. He would look after its interests in England, while three partners – brother Matt, John Hanbury and Hugh Cathcart – would manage its operations in Jamaica. 'I think it is time that we should begin a private correspondence,' Baring wrote to Matt on 12 August – by which he meant a frank correspondence, transcending the platitudes of the monthly letters between the two houses. Baring had been speaking to John Wigglesworth, the former commissary in Saint Domingue, who had told him that Matt could not decide whether to focus on the sugar plantations or on the mercantile branch of the business. Baring strongly urged Matt in the latter direction: 'In my opinion there can be no doubt under the present circumstances, for you cannot make your Counting house too strong whilst such various & important commercial objects are passing before you.'[21]

During the autumn of 1799, a transaction took place concerning the ownership of the two Jamaican estates; insignificant though it might seem, it would subsequently cause a great rupture in the Atkinson family. Now that he was rich in his own right, George agreed to buy out the interests in the Bogue and Dean's Valley estates which Nathaniel had some years earlier acquired from Paul Benfield and Captain Laird. On 6 December, Nathaniel and George visited Baring at his mansion near Lewisham. 'I have the Satisfaction to tell thee that we yesterday closed our accounts; visiting Sir Francis at Lee for that Purpose,' Nathaniel later wrote to Dorothy. 'They met with his entire approbation & after they were examined & closed he turned to George & thus expressed himself (forgive, my dear Girl, my Vanity) "George I want Power to express how much the Atkinson family & you in particular, are indebted to Mr. Clayton: It is impossible that they or you can ever forget it." This as thou wilt readily believe was very grateful to thine ever, N.C.'[22]

SUCH WAS THE mortality rate that military service in the West Indies was seen as more or less a death sentence for white rank and file; and yet, whenever the British authorities proposed drafting enslaved Africans, the planters made clear their aversion to the idea of 'slaves in red coats'. But the mobilization of a large black army in Saint Domingue had increased pressure to boost the sugar islands' defences; which is why, in 1795, Henry Dundas ordered the formation of eight regiments made up of Africans discreetly purchased by the government. (The discretion being necessary to avoid embarrassing ministers who publicly backed abolition.) The First West India Regiment, which assembled in the Windward Islands, acquitted itself with great credit; but when Lord Balcarres attempted to raise a West India Regiment to serve in Jamaica, the House of Assembly blocked him from doing so.

If the idea of placing weapons in the hands of black men made these powerful white men shudder, they unquestioningly accepted the use of black 'pioneers'. These were the labourers who performed the drudgework of military life; armed with pickaxes, saws and shovels, they built fortifications, dug trenches, hauled ordnance and provisions, and generally carried out the most backbreaking tasks. Two pioneers were attached to each of the fifty-six companies garrisoned in Jamaica, although Balcarres hoped to increase this number to six. For the past fifteen years, the island's pioneers had been largely composed of free blacks who had emigrated from Georgia following the American revolution; but most of them were now either exhausted or dead. To fill the gaps, the army had been hiring enslaved men for up to 5s each per day, saddling the island with an annual bill of more than £20,000 currency. In November 1797, the House of Assembly passed a resolution approving the governor's proposal to place the pioneers on a cheaper footing.

Lord Balcarres' plan involved putting the contract to supply pioneers out to public tender. The government would offer to pay £15 currency for the annual hire of each enslaved pioneer, plus an annual clothing allowance of 46s, and a day rate of 8½d – such terms, Balcarres assured the Duke of Portland, would not only prove less expensive for the island, but would furnish a 'very good Return indeed to any Contractor who may chuse to speculate' – and yet, a year after the Assembly passed its resolution, not one merchant in Jamaica had expressed interest in taking on the business.[23] Baffled by the failure of his scheme, Balcarres consulted 'some of the first

Merchants in Kingston', who told him they believed that military service would make enslaved men unfit for other forms of work.[24] At last, though, a willing merchant was found. On 24 August 1799, the contract with Balcarres, who was acting 'on behalf of the British government' – at least, that is how the official paperwork defines his role in the transaction – was signed by Matt Atkinson. The house of G. & M. Atkinson would supply 'so many able negro men as Pioneers for the several white Regiments of Cavalry or Infantry' stationed on the island, 'at the rate of 6 Pioneers per Troop or Company'; a year's notice was needed to terminate the agreement, following which such pioneers 'as shall not be dead or runaway' would be returned to the contractors in Kingston.[25]

This was a corrupt, self-serving business, and not just for the obvious reasons – for, secretly, in collusion with Matt Atkinson's firm, Balcarres had taken a one-third stake in the pioneer deal, which made him a party to both sides of the negotiations. At the beginning of 1801, eighteen months into the contract, the Kingston house (and their silent partner) would have 357 pioneers on hire to the British army.

From the very start of my investigations into my ancestors, I knew that I was bound to unearth some unpalatable details of their slave-owning activities, and as the grim revelations piled up, my sorrow and regret about this aspect of their lives increased. By the time I came upon the pioneer contract, in the archive of the National Army Museum, I was quite far along with my research, and thought I had seen it all. But this discovery exposed a new dimension to my ancestors' participation in slavery, one I hadn't anticipated. Not only had they possessed hundreds of enslaved Africans on their estates; they had also acted, to a perhaps unique extent, as suppliers of slave labour to the British armed forces.

IN JULY 1798, the United States suspended trade with France and its colonies in retaliation for privateer attacks on American merchant shipping; the embargo caused great hardship in Saint Domingue, which relied on the mainland for much of its food. However, both

General Toussaint Louverture.

Britain and the US wished to maintain a friendly dialogue with the black general Toussaint Louverture, so as to deter the 'dissemination of dangerous principles among the slaves of their respective countries'.[26] In May 1799, Brigadier Thomas Maitland, who had overseen the British withdrawal from Saint Domingue the previous year, returned there with a mandate to make a treaty with Toussaint on behalf of both nations; the ports of Port-au-Prince and Cap-Français, it was agreed, would be opened up to trade. Subsequently, Lord Balcarres prevailed on Hugh Cathcart and Charles Douglas 'of Mr. Atkinson's Office' to act as resident agents in the two towns.[27]

Toussaint had hoped to keep the treaty a secret, but his arch-rival, the 'mulatto' general André Rigaud, soon came to hear of it. The feud between the men had been simmering for a while, but Toussaint's Anglo-American convention provided Rigaud with the *casus belli* for the vicious power struggle that would become known as the War of Knives. 'Rigaud is already in motion, and has put to death a very considerable number of the White Inhabitants both at Jeremie and aux Cayes,' Maitland briefed Balcarres on 20 June. 'I find Toussaint is in very great want indeed of Provisions so much so that his Troops are at a stand for want of them.'[28] Matt Atkinson duly arranged for 'two thousand Barrels of Flour, fifty Barrels of Salt Fish, two hundred Barrels of herrings, one hundred Barrels of salt Beef, fifty Barrels of salt Pork, three hundred Barrels of Biscuit' and 'ten Hogsheads of Tobacco', along with arms, ammunition and gunpowder, to be loaded on to three ships that sailed to Port-au-Prince three weeks later.[29]

Meanwhile the French Republic's agent on Saint Domingue, Philippe Roume, was working on a plan to undermine its British neighbour. The merchants Isaac Sasportas and Barthélémy Dubuisson arrived in Jamaica in early November 1799, with orders to spy on the island's defences and incite rebellion among the enslaved population; General Toussaint's army would then mount an invasion during the Christmas holidays. But Sasportas and Dubuisson were arrested soon after reaching Kingston – and their betrayer was none other than Toussaint, who had detected in Roume's plot the motive of driving a wedge between him and his British backers. Shortly afterwards, Lord Balcarres received a shopping list of armaments urgently required by Toussaint, which included 6,000 muskets, 2,000 pairs of pistols, 30,000 pounds of lead and 100,000 pounds of gunpowder. The British agent in Port-au-Prince, Hugh Cathcart – a partner of the house of G. & M. Atkinson – was summoned for regular meetings with Toussaint about these supplies. 'I have been with him almost daily for these last three weeks (& have become an immense favourite),' Cathcart wrote on 26 November. 'He has pressed me very hard, lately, to buy him a Frigate, and seemed rather dissatisfied, at my not complying with his request – altho' I assured him that it was totally out of my power. He then asked me, if that I thought Lord Balcarres, would procure him one.'[30]

After the discovery of the French plot, the conspirator Dubuisson escaped the noose by confessing to everything; but Sasportas was hanged from gallows thirty feet above Kingston parade ground, wearing a label that spelled out the word 'SPY' in large letters.[31] Lord Balcarres – whose fate was to have been poisoning 'by an infusion' into his coffee on the morning of 26 December – declared martial law, and ordered 'every French male Person of Color above the age of 12' to be shipped off the island.[32] The house of G. & M. Atkinson made the necessary arrangements for the deportation of nearly one thousand men to Martinique and Trinidad.

Toussaint's relations with the British cooled in December 1799, however, when four of his armed ships were seized mistakenly by the Royal Navy and condemned as prizes by the Court of Admiralty. Despite warnings that Toussaint would become a 'most implacable enemy', Sir Hyde Parker, the naval commander in Jamaica, stood firm in his opposition to the vessels' return.[33] Following the theft of his ships, Toussaint was in no hurry to honour debts to British merchants, and so Cathcart – who had sold supplies to the general on credit, and invested £80,000 of his partners' silver in coffee and other produce on Saint Domingue – was forced to linger at Port-au-Prince, pressing for payment and praying that the partnership's goods would not be impounded. Finally, after an impasse lasting several tense months, Cathcart could return to Kingston with good news. 'I feel well pleased to have it in my power to be able to say to you that I have received full payment from the Black General,' he wrote to George Atkinson on 12 June. 'We are now fairly out of the scrape and I trust we shall never again get ourselves into such another. Every thing is brought off excepting about Forty Bales of Cotton, for which I could not find freight, but I look for them in a Vessel that is daily expected.'[34]

SAINT DOMINGUE HAD ENTERED the 1790s as the richest colony in the West Indies, but its productivity plummeted as it was engulfed by conflict. In marked contrast, this was a buoyant decade for Jamaica. The wholesale price of sugar almost doubled on the back of Saint Domingue's misfortunes, and the proprietors of estates returned to cultivation land previously given up as exhausted. During this decade, most Jamaican planters abandoned the old 'Creole' sugar cane, brought to Hispaniola by Columbus in 1493, in favour of the 'Otaheite' variety, introduced from the South Seas by Captain Bligh in 1793. This succulent newcomer was taller than its predecessor, tolerated poor soil, and yielded up to a third more sugar. Jamaican sugar, long regarded as overpriced, enjoyed strong demand in continental Europe.

But it all came to a juddering halt in 1799. The collapse started in the German port of Hamburg, home to more than three hundred sugar refineries, the highest concentration in Europe. The Jamaican merchant fleet arrived there later than usual that spring and was unable to offload its cargo; an American fleet carrying Cuban sugar had docked first and flooded the market. 'The total Stagnation in the sale of West India produce has occasioned such distress as cannot be described,' Baring wrote to the Kingston partners on 5 October 1799. 'Above forty houses, some of these considerable, have failed at Hamburg & we expect to hear of more on the arrival of every mail; about Ten houses have failed here.'[35] By the end of the year, the warehouses along the River Thames were clogged up with tens of thousands of unsold hogsheads of muscovado.

During the boom years of the 1790s, the Jamaican planters' hunger for fresh supplies of slave labour had reached frenzied levels, building to a peak at the end of the century. In 1800, more than 22,000 African men, women and children would land at Jamaica on board sixty-five slave ships – this would be the second highest year of arrivals on the island. The house of G. & M. Atkinson handled the sale of six of these human cargoes, comprising 2,350 people; so while it might be observed that the Kingston partners were late-comers to this line of trade, they nevertheless embraced it fully.

Usually, a slave shipowner made arrangements with a Jamaican merchant house for the sale of its human cargo at the start of a tri-angular voyage; but sometimes the ship's captain would complete the middle passage, then assign the business on the spot. Either way, the Kingston merchant handled the money side of the sale, advancing bills drawn on its corresponding London merchant house (Barings, in the case of G. & M. Atkinson) to pay the shipowner for the cargo, extending credit to planters buying the enslaved Africans, and securing guarantees from those planters to sell their produce through the London house. This despicable business was replete with financial hazard from beginning to end – especially so for the London merchant house, which depended upon the planters sending back produce of sufficient value to pay for the slaves they had recently purchased. At a time when the price of sugar was in freefall, the speculations of G. & M. Atkinson placed Barings in a dangerously exposed position.

The Kingston partners were preparing to sell off their first cargo – 275 Africans who had arrived on board the *Mary* – when they received Sir Francis Baring's gloomy letter about the collapse of the sugar market.[36] Clearly it didn't faze them too much. 'We have been induced to take up another Guineaman called the Will with 405 Eboe Negroes, the sales of which we have effected without even the expence of advertising, at an average of £75 Stg principally to people of this Town,' wrote John Hanbury, the partner driving the business, on 23 March 1800.[37] Baring's reply, warning that planters who purchased Africans on long credit might not be able to pay for them, given the current 'low prices of produce', crossed with Hanbury's subsequent letter, which notified him that G. & M. Atkinson had taken up ships called the *Sarah* and the *Young William*, and also, by prior agreement, guaranteed two cargoes from the Liverpool slave traders J. & H. Clarke.[38]

In his next letter to Jamaica, dated 8 August, Baring made plain his displeasure: 'If you carry on every branch of your business on a presumption that I am able to answer such boundless demands I must inform you very distinctly that my capacity nor my disposition are not equal to your expectations.'[39] George Atkinson further warned his partners: 'On your Guinea Concerns I have only to repeat my former Caution, that you carefully avoid any Connection which can involve you deeply with the Soil of the Island. Credits to Planters are at all Times dangerous; but just now most eminently so – for be assured a Storm hangs over our Island, the bursting of which we must guard against by every possible Precaution.'[40]

So great was Baring's alarm that he urgently called George down from Newcastle for a meeting with himself and George Bogle, who had held on to a stake in the Kingston house since retiring.

G. & M. Atkinson's advertisement for two human cargoes,
placed in the Jamaica Gazette of December 1800.

Despite his poor health (three years earlier, a lead ball had lodged in his thigh during a naval engagement off Martinique, causing him constant pain), Bogle agreed to go out to Jamaica to apply some discipline to the operation. He wrote to Baring on 2 January 1801, four days after landing at Kingston; although he was not yet able to judge the conduct of the individual partners, it seemed that 'from an apprehension of the War not lasting long', they had thrown themselves headlong into the slave factorage business, 'tempted by the appearance of great profit but without recollecting that they were thereby leading you into tremendous advances'. So as to disguise the real reason for his 'sudden appearance' in Jamaica, he had ordered a notice to be placed in the local newspapers, announcing the firm's name 'being changed to Atkinsons Hanbury & Co'.[41]

Three weeks later, Bogle was ready to offer a fuller analysis. It seemed that the late John Atkinson, during his brief stint at the helm, had 'constantly resisted' more hazardous lines of business. The problems had started after his death, with the establishment of G. & M. Atkinson. Instead of setting up a system by which each partner took responsibility for a branch of the business, everything had fallen upon the most experienced partner, John Hanbury – and thus, while it would be fair to say that Matt Atkinson had 'cordially acquiesced' in these speculations, Hanbury had been the 'principal mover' behind them.[42] Matt wrote privately to Baring on 28 January, expressing his 'astonishment and shagrin' at what had gone on; he had been quite genuinely under the impression that all was going swimmingly.[43]

LORD BALCARRES' devil-may-care style of governance earned him the gratitude of the island plantocracy – 'perhaps the assembly of Jamaica never agreed more perfectly and uniformly with any governor than it did with the Earl of Balcarras', a contemporary would write – but he was viewed by his ministerial superiors as a maverick and a liability.[44] In the autumn of 1800, General John Knox was appointed to replace him as governor, but drowned during a hurricane on his way out to Jamaica.

When Balcarres learnt that he was about to be recalled, he set aside his public duties and focused on putting his personal affairs in order. During the six years of his governorship he had made plenty of money – much of it through negotiating government bills for the subsistence of émigrés from Saint Domingue – and had ploughed it into coffee estates in the parishes of St George and St Elizabeth that were said to be worth 'not less than £60 or £70,000'.[45] As the time of his departure neared, Balcarres' neglect of his official workload increased. 'Our Governor is a strange Man,' George Bogle wrote on 20 June 1801. 'He has been living secluded at his Mountain in St. Georges for a Month past and although the Packet has been arrived these three weeks, he only returned to the Kings House yesterday to open his Letters.'[46]

Before Bogle returned to England, he composed a memorandum assigning clear duties to each of the Kingston partners:

The Business of the Agent General, and Settlement of
accounts with the Governor, to be under the immediate
management of Mr. Hanbury, also the correspondence with
the House in London . . . Mr. Atkinson will conduct the Island
Correspondence, with that concerning the Consignments
from Ireland &c. – also the Correspondence with Head
Quarters . . . Mr. Atkinson will likewise take upon himself
the superintendance of the Sales of produce; and I particularly
recommend to him to peruse in the Day Book every morning,
the Transactions that have taken place in the preceding day.
The Partners should be in the Office from Eight in the
morning until Four in the afternoon. Indeed in this climate
going out of Doors should as much as possible be avoided,
for a person cannot again that day set down to business in
a collected manner.[47]

On 23 July, Bogle boarded the *Lowestoffe*; strong currents, however, drove the ship aground soon afterwards in the Caicos Passage.
Bogle returned to Jamaica, and there he would remain for the rest of
the year, until the risk from hurricanes had abated.

The arrival at Port Royal on 29 July of the new governor of
Jamaica, General George Nugent, was marked with gunfire 'so
stunning' that his wife hid in her cabin on board the *Ambuscade*,
holding a pillow over her ears.[48] Maria Nugent would cut a glamor-
ous figure in Jamaica, for ladies of rank were a rarity out there – and
Mrs Nugent was a small, neat woman, with a reputation as an
'amazing dresser' who never appeared 'twice in the same gown'.[49]
More significantly, she was a sharp-eyed diarist, who left behind
easily the most vivid account of life on the island during the first
decade of the nineteenth century.

Some of her first observations relate to the filthy state in which
she found the King's House, and the poor personal hygiene of the
outgoing governor. 'I wish Lord B. would wash his hands, and use a
nail-brush, for the black edges of his nails really make me sick,' she
wrote after breakfast on her second morning. 'He has, besides, an

extraordinary propensity to dip his fingers into every dish. Yesterday he absolutely helped himself to some fricassée with his dirty finger and thumb.' She was grudgingly amused, however, by an 'extraordinary pet' that patrolled the dining room — a 'little black pig, that goes grunting about to every one for a tit-bit'.[50]

Before Lord Balcarres' departure from the island, in November, he signed the power of attorney that passed responsibility for his estates to Matt Atkinson. Martin's Hill, Balcarres' coffee estate and cattle ranch in St Elizabeth Parish, became a favourite staging post for Matt during his journeys to the west of the island. 'I have built a room off the North end of the House at Martins Hill and have sent a Bed there for myself,' he would tell Balcarres.[51] Matt particularly appreciated the hospitality laid on by Robert White, the estate's overseer: 'I had as good corned Pork, and poultry, as any man would wish, and he has now got into a stock of good Old Rum. I call this very excellent plantation fare.'[52]

Lord Balcarres had gone out to Jamaica with a view to replenishing his family's coffers, and his governorship had certainly served the purpose – even if most of his newly acquired fortune was tied up in West Indian property. The Countess of Balcarres, who had not seen her husband in nearly seven years, wrote to him from Edinburgh on 4 January 1802, ahead of his ship's return: 'I hope this will greet you on your arrival in perfect health & spirits, after all the toils & dangers you have so long encountered. No man can shew his face to the world with a better grace, or a sounder mind, than you can, & I am much prouder to congratulate you on *that*, with the very moderate sum you bring home – than what you *might* have made, with the smallest reflection on your conduct.'[53]

EIGHTEEN

The Nabob's Return

THE LAST TIME we met Lady Anne Lindsay, in June 1790, she had been boxed into the 'miserable compromise' with Richard Atkinson's executors that was supposed, at least, to protect the £700 a year left to her and her sister Margaret – but the estate had been plagued by difficulties ever since, and their annuities had not once been paid. Later that same summer, Anne had purchased 21 Berkeley Square, paying £2,600 for the house in (then, as now) one of London's most expensive neighbourhoods. Shortly afterwards, she had broken off her romance with the vacillating politician William Windham – known as the 'Weathercock' – once it became apparent that he had no plans to marry.

Finally, in October 1793, Anne had wedded Andrew Barnard, the son of the Bishop of Limerick, at St George's, Hanover Square. Fashionable folk sneered, because she was forty-two, while he was a penniless army officer twelve years her junior – but she had always held out for a love match, and the marriage would bring them both great happiness.

The Mures' bankruptcy had dealt a further blow to the Lindsay sisters' hopes of gaining anything more from the Atkinson estate. 'I now see it probable that knavery or confusion may still trick us out of our property,' Margaret wrote in January 1794, before reminding Anne about a dream she had had nearly four years earlier, the night after she signed the 'compromise' papers:

You dreamt that Atkinson opened your curtains, and with a
grave but benign countenance told you that he had liberty
to give you, as the person he loved best on earth, *one advice*,
which was to marry the first kind-hearted man who proposed
to you, as you would never get *one shilling* of what he had
destined for you. I think in the literal sense you have complied
with this, for Barnard was the first man who after the date of
this dream made direct proposals, such as required a positive
Yes or No.[1]

It was through the patronage of Anne's old friend Henry Dundas
that Andrew Barnard was in 1797 posted to the Cape Colony, after its
capture from the Dutch, as First Secretary under Lord Macartney.
The Barnards sailed out to Africa together, a fairly unconventional
arrangement for the time. Every so often, a passing British fleet
would drop off a 'parcell of delightfull letters' at Paradise, the
thatched cottage at the foot of Table Mountain where they made
their home, and Anne would momentarily immerse herself in the
latest news and gossip from London. Margaret attempted to keep
her abreast of the Atkinson business, but every advance in the Court
of Chancery seemed to be matched by a setback. In one letter, she
congratulated Anne that the drawn-out 'Cause of the Omnium', concerning the government loan stock to which the Mures had latterly
staked their claim, had gone in their favour; in her next letter she
reported, 'having been misinformed', that it had gone against them.
As Anne confided to her diary: 'For, against, it makes little difference to me, as I know that I shall never receive any advantage from
my share of West Indian property unfairly administered as it is, and
wilfully as well as accidentally intangled.'[2]

Wilfully entangled or otherwise, the Atkinson estate was certainly a mess, for which much of the blame lay with the deceased.
From the moment of Richard's death, his two sugar plantations had
proved unequal to the task of generating the income needed to cover
his legacies. 'His talents & imagination are so rapid that they always
run away with judgment,' Baring had once observed of his friend

– and nothing would expose this delusional side of Richard's character more starkly than the terms of his will.[3]

And so the lawsuits rumbled on. George Atkinson and Nathaniel Clayton went down to London together in April 1801, taking rooms at a hotel just off the Haymarket. Nathaniel was occupied by Newcastle-related parliamentary bills, while George attended to Jamaican business, but they also found time to meet some claimants to the Atkinson estate. (Though they did not see two of the main legatees – Lady Anne Barnard was in Africa, while a dinner with John Robinson at Sion Hill was repeatedly postponed.) In early June, the brothers-in-law headed north again. 'I was very much surprised to learn this Morning, that Mr. Atkinson and Mr. Clayton had left London,' William Duncan, the lawyer representing the Mures' creditors, told Robinson. 'I am told that they have for several years past (*when in London*) made professions of wishing for an Amicable Adjustment of these Concerns, but, have always gone off, as they have now done without coming to any decision.'[4]

'I am very sorry that you have not considered my letters of the 8th July & 26th October sufficiently explicit of my sentiments,' George would write to Robinson in January 1802, as he yet again defended his and the Atkinson family's position. The Mures' claim that their late partner had deliberately deprived them of the government loan stock to which they were entitled, and had instead shared it out among his friends, was particularly offensive, given its innuendo of fraud; while their attempts to claw back losses sustained by their own Jamaican plantations in the sixteen years since Richard's death were quite intolerable. 'Let the account between my uncle and his surviving Partners be divested of those charges which have been created long subsequent to the Period when his interest in the Business terminated,' George insisted. 'Unless that is done, however painful to my feelings, I own I cannot see a Probability of the Affairs being settled elsewhere than in the Court of Chancery.'[5] The Atkinsons' strategy was to play for time; whereas for John Robinson, time was running out. He would die at his constituency of Harwich on 23 December 1802, aged seventy-five.

IN JAMAICA, the first weeks of General Nugent's governorship were marked by parades and parties in his honour. Before dawn on 2 October 1801, the Nugents rose and dressed by candlelight; the fireflies covered the walls of their chamber at the King's House with 'gold spangles'. At 4 a.m. they set out for Kingston, where Maria Nugent alighted at Matt Atkinson's house on North Street; here she would spend an awkward couple of hours while her husband reviewed the 69th Regiment. 'Mr. A. made grand efforts to amuse me,' she told her diary. 'The mountain wind, the sea breeze, slaves, plantations, and the prices of different articles, were the edifying topics, till a little after 7, when breakfast made its appearance, and Mr. A.'s spirits were relieved by the appearance of Mrs. Pye, who came to offer her services, hearing that I was in Kingston. Poor man, he seemed very happy, so was I.' That evening, Matt hosted a reception attended by 'half Kingston and Port Royal' – aside from the eye-catching Mrs Nugent, no ladies were present.[6]

William Pitt had resigned as prime minister in March 1801 after seventeen years in office. Henry Addington's ministry made peace with France its first priority, and signed a preliminary treaty on 1 October. Napoleon Bonaparte decided to take this opportunity to reassert control over the wayward colony of Saint Domingue, notifying the British of his intention to send out a large army commanded by his brother-in-law, General Charles Leclerc. In defiance of Napoleon's orders, Toussaint Louverture had recently invaded the neighbouring Spanish colony of Santo Domingo and drawn up a constitution that guaranteed equal treatment for all races. In Jamaica, where the 'Black General' had once provoked derision, he now commanded a good deal of respect. On 21 October, the Nugents attended a dinner for Edward Corbet, the British agent in Saint Domingue, at which Matt Atkinson was also a guest. Toussaint was the subject of much conversation around the table. 'He must be a wonderful man,' Maria Nugent wrote afterwards, 'and I really do believe intended for very good purposes.'[7]

Following the peace treaty with France, General Nugent received instructions to behave with strict neutrality towards Saint

Domingue. 'Toussaint's Black Empire is one, amongst many evils, that has grown out of the War, and it is by no means our Interest to prevent its Annihilation,' wrote Lord Hobart, the Secretary of State for War and the Colonies.[8] French troops began landing in Saint Domingue in January 1802; soon General Leclerc had gained control of the south of the colony. On 6 May, Toussaint rode into the northern port of Cap-Français, where he negotiated an amnesty. What he did not know, however, was that Leclerc had secret orders to deport all black officers from Saint Domingue.

Within weeks, Toussaint had been tricked into arrest, and exiled to a fortress in the remote Jura mountains of eastern France. Toussaint's inglorious fate unleashed a fresh wave of violent resistance against the French by the black rebels – but mosquitoes would prove a still deadlier enemy. 'The French troops are dying very fast,' Matt Atkinson wrote on 28 June. 'It is supposed they have not more than 5,000 Men fit for service at this time.'[9]

General Leclerc now fixed upon a strategy of genocide. 'We must destroy all of the blacks in the mountains – men and women – and spare only the children under 12 years of age,' he wrote to Napoleon on 7 October. 'We must destroy half of those in the plains and must not leave a single coloured person in the colony who has worn an épaulette.'[10] But Leclerc would not see through this murderous plan, as he died from yellow fever three weeks later. Napoleon continued to send reinforcements to Saint Domingue until May 1803, by which time France and Britain were once again at war. The French army finally capitulated to the rebels six months later, and on 1 January 1804, General Jean-Jacques Dessalines proclaimed Saint Domingue the independent Republic of Haiti. One of the new president's first acts was to order the extermination of all remaining Frenchmen and women. His death squads went from house to house, killing entire families with knives and bayonets. 'Dessalines arrived here on Friday afternoon last and turned loose 400 to 500 blood thirsty villains on the poor defenceless Inhabitants,' wrote one Englishman in Port-au-Prince. 'I had five in my house & it gives me great pain to think I was not able to save a single one of them.'[11]

The bloodshed in Saint Domingue would have momentous consequences for the United States. In 1802, in a secret treaty with Spain, Napoleon had acquired the Louisiana Territory, a vast tract stretching from New Orleans into present-day Canada – approximately 827,000 square miles. But as the French army lost its sway in Saint Domingue, Napoleon realized that this American landholding might prove a liability during a future war with Britain – so instead he decided to sell it to the US for $15 million, or three cents per acre. The deal was concluded on 30 April 1803; at a stroke, the US had doubled in size.

To finance the transaction, the US Treasury turned to Barings, their banking agents in London; and Sir Francis Baring enlisted the assistance of Hope & Co. of Amsterdam. It was these businessmen who would actually purchase the Louisiana Territory from Napoleon; they would then transfer the land to the US in return for bonds, to be repaid over fifteen years. 'We *all* tremble about the magnitude of the American account,' Baring wrote to one of his sons-in-law, a partner at Hope & Co.[12] Henry Addington subsequently asked Baring to desist from 'being party to any remittances to France' on account of the Louisiana Purchase; but it seems the prime minister's plea was in vain, for the French government would receive its final tranche of gold coin, as scheduled, in April 1804.[13]

MATT ATKINSON, who would be thirty-five in 1804, was a reluctant pen-pusher. 'My Health thank God is very good, but I have at present a good deal of extra work on hand which will occupy me during every spare hour I have till the end of the Year, this consists in examining three large transcribed deed Books with the Mutilated Records from the Secretary's Office,' he wrote to brother George on 11 March. 'I assure you while I do not care for labour I have been pretty well used to it for some years past.'[14] The *Jamaica Almanac* for 1802 lists nine public offices under Matt's name – Island Secretary, Agent General, Commissary General, Notary Public, Clerk of the Council, Clerk of the Court of Ordinary, Assistant Judge for Hanover, Magistrate for Surrey and Collector of Customs at

Kingston – and they kept him disagreeably desk-bound. Although Matt remained Governor Nugent's Agent General, there was no warmth between the two men. The value of the government business, while still substantial, had fallen off since the turbulent 1790s; the largest contract was to provision the troops stationed on the island, which steadily turned over around £100,000 a year for the Kingston house.

Since the establishment of the West India Regiments in 1795, the British government had come to rely upon slave labour for the defence of the sugar islands to such an extent that it had become the largest single buyer of Africans; more than thirteen thousand enslaved men would be drafted over twelve years, often straight off slave ships. Many of these dealings were carried out by the governor of Jamaica through his Agent General – to give one example, in order to finance the purchase of 180 men for the 5th West India Regiment at £90 and £95 per capita in January 1804, the Kingston house was obliged to draw 'very largely' on Barings in London.[15]

Matt's disenchantment with his life as a colonial bureaucrat was deepened by the unnerving conduct of his partners. The main mercantile priority of the Kingston house had shifted to the collection of debts, and Hugh Cathcart's favoured approach was to pursue everything through the courts. 'There are several debts which I am sure he is making worse, but I cannot help myself,' Matt wrote to George. 'I am sorry to trouble you on this but if you could by any means prevail on him to go home, it would be of service to us all, if it cannot be accomplished I will do the best I can, but my nerves are not so strong as they once were, to enable me to meet his arguments, which God knows are curious.'[16] Matt would soon conclude that Cathcart was 'not perfect in his upper storey', after his partner ordered the senior clerk of the house to concentrate on transcribing articles about the execution of the French spy, Isaac Sasportas, even though the Barings accounts were three months overdue. 'If there was any good to be attained by what he is doing I am sure I would support it with all my power,' wrote Matt, 'but what he has done and is doing is not of the value of an old Newspaper.'[17]

In February 1804, Matt was suddenly called to the Dean's Valley estate after the death of its overseer by poisoning. While their partner was busy in Westmoreland, John Hanbury and Hugh Cathcart quietly purchased a cargo of two hundred enslaved Africans and had them shipped onwards to South Carolina. 'I rather think they will burn their fingers,' Matt wrote to George when he heard about this venture. 'They took care not to write me on this subject, or indeed any other when I was absent which was three weeks.'[18] When George received Matt's letter, in Newcastle, seven weeks later, he immediately forwarded it to Sir Francis Baring. 'It appears,' he wrote in his covering note, 'that the Spirit of Speculation is reviving.'[19]

MICHAEL ATKINSON, the eldest of Bridget's three living sons, would sail back to England in the spring of 1804, after twenty-two years in Bengal. Nabobs, as returning East India Company servants were labelled, were expected to bring back tidy fortunes with them, and Michael would prove no exception. Even so, his homecoming would turn out to be a sad business – a world away from the joyful reunion of which his 71-year-old mother had dreamed.

Towards the end of May, Bridget spotted a newspaper announcement that the *Earl Howe* Indiaman had docked in London with a 'Mr. and Mrs. Atkinson' on board – this was the first she had heard not only of Michael's return, but also of his having a wife.[20] She immediately wrote, warmly welcoming him home – and heard not a word in reply. Meanwhile, rumours of Michael's domestic arrangements soon reached Temple Sowerby. Mary Hasell of nearby Dalemain had heard that Michael had a 'Large Family of Black Children' – news which 'very much shocked' his mother. ('I told her if it was so I hoped he would leave them all in the country and provide for them there.') Another neighbour, Edward Lamb, an East India Company captain, revealed that Michael had a longstanding white consort, Sophia Mackereth, who was thought originally to have gone out to India 'as a Mistress to Lord Cornwallis'.[21]

The reason for Michael's bizarre behaviour soon came to light. It seemed that some opportunistic lawyer – no doubt anticipating

The Torrid Zone. Yellow fever, depicted as a flame-snorting demon, reigns in hell. Above the ground (represented by a scythe blade), white Jamaicans go about their daily business; looking down, a bilious angel swigs from a bottle marked 'opium'.

A sugar boiling house. The cane juice was reduced in a tapering sequence of copper pans; it was then transferred to cool in a shallow container before being cured in hogshead barrels. This was a dangerous environment, where enslaved workers often suffered disfiguring burns.

Three of Bridget Atkinson's five sons. Dick, above, succumbed to fever soon after arriving in Jamaica. George, below left, made a fortune by financing the British occupation of St Domingue during the 1790s. Matt, below right, left debts and illegitimate children in his wake.

Mount Mascal, near Bexley in Kent. Michael Atkinson purchased the estate in 1808 but signally failed to 'disgavel' it in his will – much to the glee of the vengeful Claytons. The house fell derelict after the Second World War, and was demolished in 1959.

The Tyne Iron Company's works at Lemington, near Newcastle. Nathaniel Clayton and his brothers-in-law George and Matt Atkinson were partners in the enterprise; by the mid-1830s, when this engraving was made, the next generation had taken over.

George Atkinson, above, the disreputable head of the Kingston merchant house from 1825 to 1846; and my great-great-grandfather Dick Atkinson, right, who was the last of the family resident in Jamaica, returning to live at Temple Sowerby in 1856.

Montego Bay in the 1820s, from James Hakewill's *A Picturesque Tour of the Island of Jamaica*. The uncultivated islands dotting the bay belonged to the Bogue estate. This engraving was probably coloured by someone who had never seen the dazzling azure waters of the Caribbean.

Kingston in the early nineteenth century. Above, the intersection of Harbour Street and King Street, a block back from the wharves. Below, the view from the parish church, overlooking the parade ground – the gravestone of John Atkinson, who died in 1798, is likely among those shown. Nowadays the parade is a public park, while the churchyard is a parking lot.

John Clayton in 1862. His black clothes, and documents tied with pink ribbon, indicate his legal profession. The backdrop of Grey Street alludes to the transformation of Newcastle while he was town clerk. The photograph of the garden front of Chesters, below, dates from around this time.

The hall at Chesters, following its makeover by Norman Shaw, photographed for *Country Life* in 1912. The portraits on either side of the fireplace show Nathaniel and Dorothy Clayton – I wish I knew where they are now.

My great-grandparents Jock and Connie Atkinson on leave from India in 1896. By this time their three children – George, Jack and Biddy – were at boarding schools in England, and saw little of their parents.

My grandfather Jack Atkinson, right, with his second cousin Dick Atkinson at Bamburgh, Northumberland, in about 1912. Dick would many years later send Jack the cardboard box full of old family letters that kick-started my research for this book.

The King's House in Spanish Town, Jamaica. This grand building was gutted by fire in 1925; its brick façade and portico are all that is left.

The remains of Richard 'Rum' Atkinson's sugar estates. The Bogue, right, is now an affluent suburb of Montego Bay, with clipped bushes and manicured lawns. The sugar works at Dean's Valley, below, has been much plundered for its dressed stone, and is fast being overtaken by bush; a cast-iron boiler nestles in the rampant vegetation.

years of litigation ahead – had managed to persuade him that brother George had stolen the Jamaican estates which Michael believed, as his uncle Richard's eldest nephew and heir-at-law, to be rightfully his. 'Now nothing can be further from the truth but he is gone to Law with George about your Uncle's effects,' Bridget wrote to Matt in Jamaica. 'However he has not taken the smallest notice of any of our Letters and to think how many sleepless nights his Long absence has caused me it is almost too hard to bear.' Most hurtful of all, for Bridget, was the discovery that she had a fifteen-year-old granddaughter who for the past five years had been resident at an establishment for young ladies near London: 'If Michael had thought proper to have acquainted me with his sending over a Daughter I really would have seen after her but I knew nothing about her till this year.'[22]

Dorothy Clayton travelled down to London in June, hopeful of making her brother see sense, but was repeatedly refused entry to his residence in Welbeck Street. Following the failure of Dorothy's mission, Bridget decided to make a rare visit to the capital. 'I will see the worthless woman if I can will see his unfortunate Daughter for what must she be brought up under such a Mother,' she told Matt. 'I will endeavour to purchase his Estate at Temple Sowerby and get him to change his name and go out to India again. In short he has disappointed all my hopes and made me very unhappy.'[23] But Bridget's intervention also miscarried – for Michael had given his servants strict instructions to turn his elderly mother away from the door.

Michael was not the only one of Bridget's sons with a shadowy private life. Around this time, in Jamaica, Matt received a letter from youngest sister Jane about a secret matter concerning the precious memory of their brother John. 'George gave me a piece of Intelligence,' she wrote, 'that poor John had left a Child in Jamaica to whom he requested one Thousand Pounds might be given; will you my dear Matt inform me what became of the Child.'[24] She asked Matt not to address his reply to Temple Sowerby, but instead to the house of their sister Bridget, who had lately married Henry Tulip, a 'very rich' Northumberland squire whose Fallowfield estate ran alongside Nathaniel Clayton's at Chesters.[25] Such intrigue was necessary since letters from Jamaica were considered family property and passed widely around – which perhaps explains why so relatively few of them have survived.

Matt was able to confirm the existence of a child – a boy – who had been born on 8 April 1799, seven months after John's death, and christened in the parish church at Kingston. His mother was a free woman of colour called Emilie Peychiera, identified on the child's baptism records as a 'mestee' – but where she came from, and whether she was even alive by this stage, is an enigma.[26] Her name suggests that she may have been an émigrée from Saint Domingue.

What Matt did not care to reveal – and one assumes his mother and sisters never found out – was that he had several children of his own scattered around Jamaica. There was Sarah Atkinson, the daughter of Charlotte Wright, who was four when she was baptized at Kingston on 19 December 1802.[27] Matt had already released Charlotte from slavery three years earlier, along with 'her two female Quadroon Children named Betsey and Sally'; he must have been fond of them, for it cost rather more to free an enslaved person than it did to purchase one.[28] (Under Jamaican law, a former slave received an annual allowance of £5 currency, paid out by the authorities on behalf of the former owner; so it was only once Matt had deposited £300 currency with the Kingston churchwardens that the manumission of Charlotte, Betsey and Sally was complete.) Then there was William Atkinson, a 'Mulatto child' born to an unnamed enslaved woman, and christened at Kingston on 12 March 1801.[29] But Matt's most enduring relationship in Jamaica was with Janet Bogle, a freeborn 'quadroon' woman who lived with him in Kingston.[30] Janet turned sixteen a few weeks before the birth of their first child, Bridget Atkinson, on 2 October 1800.[31] (One can only wonder what the child's grandmother would have made of her namesake.) A second daughter, Janet, was born on 18 March 1803.[32] Although it is impossible to verify – some parish records do not display the names of white fathers alongside those of black mothers, while it is also probable that these offspring would never have been baptized – it seems likely that Matt had still more children on estates in the west of the island.

Reprehensible though it may sound, Matt's conduct was quite ordinary on an island where white men viewed enslaved women as sexual prey, and openly kept free women of colour as mistresses. 'Almost every householder, for few of them are married, keeps his *miss*, without being at all thought guilty of any breach of morality or decorum,' wrote an observer of Jamaican life. These 'housekeepers', as they were euphemistically known, were expected to perform 'all the duties of a wife, except that of presiding at table'.[33] The colony's richest planter, Simon Taylor, never married, but was reputed to have large families on each of his various estates. Maria Nugent described a visit to the Taylor residence at Liguanea where, as was often the case, she found herself the only woman at dinner. 'When I left the gentlemen,' she wrote, 'I took tea in my own room, surrounded by the black, brown and yellow ladies of the house, and heard a great deal of its private history.'[34]

The Anglican church abetted such racial prejudice through the precision with which it logged the heritage of non-white mothers. The status of a black or mixed-race child born in Jamaica, whether free or enslaved, was inherited from its mother, which explains why the labels 'mulatto', 'quadroon' and 'mestee' are littered throughout the island's baptismal records. The word 'mulatto' was used to describe the child of a white man and a woman of pure African blood; 'quadroon' the child of a white man and a 'mulatto' woman; 'mestee' the child of a white man and a 'quadroon' woman. Beyond this point lay what the historian Bryan Edwards, writing in 1793, described as the 'boundary which the Law has drawn between the perfect white and the Man of Colour'.[35] The child of a white man and a 'mestee' woman, separated by three generations from the pure African blood of his or her maternal great-great-grandmother, was deemed 'competent' to enjoy the full range of civic privileges.[36] Since Emilie Peychiera was a 'mestee', this meant that her son – John Atkinson's son – was, legally speaking, white.

MICHAEL'S HOSTILITY towards the rest of the Atkinson family only grew during the months following his return from India. He began especially to fixate on his brother-in-law Nathaniel Clayton's role in the 'theft' of his late uncle's Jamaican property, nicknaming him 'Murphy', after a crooked lawyer in Henry Fielding's novel *Amelia* who was hanged for the forgery of a will.

In September 1804, Matt received not one, but *three* copies of a seemingly deranged letter from his eldest brother; it had been sent to Jamaica in triplicate to ensure that no mishap would prevent its arrival. Michael had written:

> I shall not at present enter into a most disgusting, but true
> detail to deprive me of the fair course of the service in India,
> and to prevent me from ever having it in my power to return
> to England. I shall not state this to you, but I do purge myself
> for ever from the family, and I might lay before you, a train of
> circumstances, fully proving the wish of my nearest relations
> for my death, which, horrible as the reflection is, it is
> nevertheless true. My great bane has been the connection with
> that unparalleled villain, Murphy the Newcastle Attorney. This
> detestable miscreant has long ago placed himself at the head of
> my family; and, literally, converted my father's house into a den
> of thieves. Now, Matthew, I put you to the test: I admit of no
> medium between you and this miscreant attorney, whose name
> is infamy, and whose touch is pollution. You must either adhere
> to him, or to me; I leave you to chuse; and, unless I hear from
> you by the first opportunity after receiving this, I shall consider
> you as Murphy's man.[37]

Mild-mannered Matt answered the letter in neutral language; he also forwarded a copy to his hot-tempered brother George.

By now, Matt was preparing to return to England. Bridget wrote to him at Christmas – she was on remarkably cheerful form, given that Michael had recently threatened to sue her for a larger share of his father's estate than he had already received. Bridget's letters tend to flit between topics, which makes them somewhat hard to edit, but here's an extract:

> I am exceeding anxious about you if you come home the
> dangers of the seas and the desire of seeing you will make me
> equally uneasy. I beg you will if you can Let me know how
> much you have made to come home with I wish to know and
> if you do I will not say a word about your affairs to any one.
> I have settled my own so far as that none of you can be plagued
> with Michael I also beg you will send me his Letter to you or
> a coppy of it. You must if you come away consider poor Black
> Thomas Leave him as happy as you possibly can. I disire you
> will my Dear Matthew Look over John's papers and Letters
> and see if there be any Letters from Michael or any coppies of
> Letters from John: to him he hinges a great deal of his Mallice
> on a Letter John wrote him from Jamaica. If John ever did write
> any such Letter it is Strainge but I hope it is only an excuse
> in Michael to cover with some degree of plausibility his
> wonderfull behaviour to us all. It certainly was not John who
> has influenced his mind to this excessive degree no it was some
> Serpent in England that has wrote to him who it is most Likely
> I shall never know but you may & whoever it may be mark
> them as Long as you Live, however it has not had a very bad
> effect on me for I have had the best Health I have had for some
> years past.[38]

Bridget's reference to 'poor Black Thomas' is particularly tantalizing, since there are so few mentions of enslaved individuals in the family correspondence – but who Thomas was, and what became of him, must remain a mystery. Her letter would have reached Matt only just before he left Jamaica, for he arrived at Temple Sowerby on 30 April 1805, suffering from a chill after three days and two nights spent in the mail coach from Falmouth.

We know that another, much younger member of the Atkinson family made the same voyage from the West Indies to Westmorland that spring, for within Bridget's household accounts is listed a payment of £1 16s 4d, made to a Miss Monkhouse for 'bringing the Boy'.[39] John Atkinson's six-year-old son would be raised by his grandmother and aunt at Temple Sowerby. Although the child's baptismal name was John, the family always called him James.

MICHAEL ATKINSON had for so long believed himself to be the chief beneficiary of his rich uncle's bounty that he could only assume skulduggery when he found this not to be the case. However, he failed to follow through his threats to have his uncle's will exposed as the forgery of 'Murphy the Newcastle Attorney', muttering darkly that he was unable to find a lawyer who was prepared to act against another member of the profession.[40] After a year of putting up with this nonsense, Nathaniel would tolerate his brother-in-law's slurs no more, and he sued for libel, basing his lawsuit on Michael's infamous letter to Matt.

The case of *Clayton v Atkinson* came before the Lord Chief Justice, Lord Ellenborough, at Guildhall on 6 March 1806; each brother-in-law was represented by one of the most famous silks of the day. Nathaniel's barrister, William Garrow, opened by stating that his client had been forced with great reluctance to bring the action, because by neglecting to do so he would have surrendered his character for life. 'A more malignant diabolical composition the arch-fiend of hell could never have prepared,' he observed of Michael's letter. 'I charge on the Defendant, black, poisonous, destructive malice. The libel now complained of was not uttered in the heat of conversation; it was gravely prepared in the form of a letter, and not the irritation of a moment.' Matt was present in court, and he confirmed the letter to be in his eldest brother's handwriting. Sir Francis Baring next took the stand, and gave warm testimony of Nathaniel's 'great propriety as a lawyer', and of the affection he had shown towards the Atkinson family.[41]

Robert Dallas, defending Michael, conceded that the letter had been defamatory, but described it as the natural expression of his client's disappointment on finding the estates of his uncle, from which he had expected to derive a 'princely fortune', so tied up in litigation. Dallas ridiculed Nathaniel for having brought this family argument before a court of law, and chastised Matt for having circulated what ought to have remained a private communication: 'He should either have committed the letter itself to the flames, or should have concealed it for ever from observation.' But Lord Ellenborough dismissed Dallas's suggestion that Michael's conduct had been a 'sort of temporary insanity'; he judged that a libel had taken place, and instructed the men of the jury, in assessing the damages, to weigh up the 'insult' and 'vexation' suffered by the plaintiff.[42] In a very public blow to Michael's standing, they ordered him to pay the considerable sum of £1,000.

MATT HAD BEEN ENGAGED to Ann Littledale for the whole of the twelve years that he had spent in Jamaica. 'Marry in haste, repent at leisure' was not a proverb that would apply to this particular couple. Poor Ann – with every year that Matt failed to return from the West Indies, her fear of abandonment increased. During the summer of 1804, when Ann was thirty-two years old, she and her mother Mary had chosen, in what appears to have been a desperate attempt to forge a stronger alliance between their families, to visit the Derbyshire spa town of Buxton while they knew that Bridget and Jane Atkinson would also be there. At the time, Jane had written with characteristic bluntness to Matt:

I must say that I think Ann is too expecting. Every Assurance has been given to her that the moment you come to this Country & make her your Wife that every kind of respect shall be shown her, in the mean while it is uncomfortable to all parties, we cannot acknowledge the engagement & Ann does not seem satisfied with my Mother treating her as kindly as she would any other young Lady. But my Mother cannot consider her as one of the family till your return, the rest is all Romance & making difficulties where none exist, you need not be under any apprehension of loosing the Lady, there is no probability

of her having any offer at all equal to Yourself. Therefore treat
the Matter coolly, it will make you of far more Consequence
& the Lady less expecting.[43]

But before he could make good on his pledge to marry Ann, Matt
would have to draw his Jamaican affairs to a conclusion. The winding
up of Atkinsons, Hanbury & Co., which followed his departure from
the island in the spring of 1805, was marred by disputes between
the partners. George eventually agreed to buy out his younger
brother's share of the Kingston house for £20,000, for Matt had
left behind large personal debts, and had no intention of returning
there. Shortly afterwards, George entered into a new partnership
with George Bogle. They would advance the capital for a merchant
house – to be called Atkinson, Bogle & Co. – while Robert Robertson and Edward Adams, two clerks of the former house, would run
the office in Kingston.

Bridget had always cherished hopes that Matt would settle down
at Temple Sowerby, but instead he chose to move to Newcastle,
where family business connections meant his prospects were considerably brighter. One day in November 1806, he set out from the
Claytons' townhouse for the Cumberland coast, with the purpose of
fulfilling a promise 'too long delayed'.[44] On 1 December, he and Ann
were married at the church of St Nicholas in Whitehaven.

A brief postscript – and it may seem churlish to mention this,
so soon after the happy nuptials – but Robert Robertson wrote
to Matt from Jamaica a few weeks later with news of his former
'housekeeper'. Following Matt's departure from the island, Janet
Bogle had given birth to another girl, whom she called Bridget –
one can only assume that her firstborn Bridget had died in infancy.[45]
Now Robertson informed Matt that Janet had 'lost another of her
little ones' – which one, he did not say – and that he had recently
stopped her allowance, on account of her having gone 'to live with
Dr. Crosbie'. Janet had since returned various items of furniture
and plate to the Atkinson residence in Kingston's North Street, and
Robertson had decided 'upon maturer consideration' not to give her

money to buy replacements. 'I now think that you have done already quite enough for her,' he told Matt, 'and shall therefore not say a word more on the subject.'[46]

DURING THE 1790s, while the British sugar islands prospered and Saint Domingue was torn apart by racial violence, the movement to abolish the slave trade had lost impetus; even to many sympathizers, the introduction of a measure that would risk the safety of these fruitful imperial possessions seemed ill-advised. Since the turn of the century, however, with the price of sugar in free fall, the campaigners had felt the argument shift again in their favour; for the planters' strategy of maximum cane production enabled by bottomless imports of enslaved Africans no longer made commercial sense.

William Pitt returned to Downing Street in May 1804 after three years out of office. A Wilberforce-sponsored bill for the abolition of the slave trade sailed through the Commons the following month, but arrived at the upper house too late in the parliamentary session to complete its legislative passage. Unfortunately, when Wilberforce brought back the same bill in February 1805, the pro-slavery lobby was this time fully primed, and it failed to pass even the lower house.

Pitt's second ministry would be short-lived, for he died on 23 January 1806, aged forty-six, probably from a stomach ulcer aggravated by his fondness for port. His cousin Lord Grenville, a determined abolitionist, immediately formed the government that would be known as the 'Ministry of All the Talents', which embraced figures from across the political spectrum. Wilberforce's brother-in-law, the lawyer James Stephen, came up with an ingenious new plan for the abolition campaign. Stephen, who had lived in Barbados, knew that French planters in the West Indies relied almost exclusively on British slave ships for their labour supply, such was the national domination of the trade. His scheme was to introduce legislation that would prevent British subjects from trafficking slaves to the colonies of France and its allies. Dressed up as a patriotic blow against the interests of a detested enemy, the bill proved uncontentious. On 23 May 1806 it passed into law, at a stroke criminalizing more than half the British slave trade.

Now it was time to finish the job. At the start of the next parliamentary session, Grenville decided to invert the usual procedure by placing Wilberforce's bill first before the House of Lords, where it passed easily; next it went before the Commons. The bill came up for its second reading on 23 February 1807. After ten hours of debate, the House divided; it passed by 283 votes against sixteen. Wilberforce received a rare standing ovation, but was too overwhelmed to take it all in. Four weeks later, Grenville wrapped up the committee stage of the bill by congratulating his colleagues on the completion of 'one of the most glorious acts' ever performed by 'any assembly of any nation in the world'.[47]

The Abolition of the Slave Trade Act, which came into force on 1 January 1808, would outlaw the transatlantic trade, but not slavery itself. No slave would be set free as a result of the legislation; around 750,000 men, women and children would remain enslaved in the British West Indies, more than 300,000 of them in Jamaica alone. Even so, the planters saw themselves as wronged parties, and resigned themselves to ruin. 'I do now consider that all property is now annihilated in the Islands and that every person who has lent his Money or Creditt to them must look upon it to be lost,' wrote Simon Taylor, as news of the bill arrived in Jamaica. 'For my part after this Year I never mean to plant a Cane.'[48]

NINETEEN

End of an Era

NEWCASTLE'S PRE-EMINENCE as a coal town dated back hundreds of years, for the exposed seams of the combustible rock that were found along the River Tyne could be extracted and shipped with far greater ease than deposits deeper inland. The local abundance of coal in turn caused manufactories, foundries, breweries and refineries to proliferate along the lower reaches of the river. The works of the Tyne Iron Company was situated on its north bank, four miles upstream from Newcastle; Nathaniel Clayton and George Atkinson had between them purchased nine of the company's twenty shares in 1803, following a bank failure that ruined its founding proprietors, and they had since ploughed much capital into developing the 'very extensive' eleven-acre site.[1] But George soon bemoaned his investment, blaming Nathaniel for some alarmingly large outgoings. 'The very heavy Debt of Obligation which I must ever owe to Mr. Clayton, will I trust plead my Apology for engaging therein at his Suggestion and Request,' he told Sir Francis Baring in February 1805.[2]

To the company's broad quays at Lemington, the ebb and flow of each tide brought fresh supplies of ironstone, arriving by sloop from nearby coastal beds, and carried away the 'ships anchors, chains, spades, shovels, nails, steel, edge tools, files, and all kinds of domestic utensils' produced at the ironworks.[3] The coal came by waggon from Wylam Colliery, five miles away, dragged by horses along

Coal is loaded into ships on the banks of the Tyne.

iron rails – but these four-legged beasts would soon be usurped by
locomotives, for 'Puffing Billy', the world's first commercial steam
engine to move along 'simply by its friction against the rail road',
would be built in 1813 specifically for the purpose of hauling coal
from Wylam to the docks at Lemington.[4]

The Tyne Iron Company's two blast furnaces, blown by vast
bellows coupled to Boulton & Watt Double Power 32 Horse steam
engines, disgorged around sixty tons of red-hot pig iron each week,
ready for moulding and beating into shape. The buildings at the
works also included a casting house; a forge with seven puddling
furnaces and a relentless engine-driven hammer and anvil; a rolling
mill for making plate iron, bars and rods; a boring and turning mill
for the manufacture of cannon and cylinders; joiners' and smiths'
shops; twenty-eight ovens for baking coke; eleven kilns for roasting
ironstone; a manager's residence and forty-three workers' dwellings. The ironworks presented an infernal sight at night, when the
'curling flames' that darted upwards from the 'numerous furnaces'
were said to give the 'appearance of a city on fire'.[5]

Matt Atkinson had returned from the West Indies with insufficient wealth to slip into the leisured mode of existence that would
no doubt have suited him best; and so it was decided (primarily by
his brother George and brother-in-law Nathaniel) that he would run

the head office of the Tyne Iron Company on Newcastle's Quay-side. Thus Matt and Ann settled down to their new life in the town, lodging with the Claytons for the time being. 'It is a great Satis-faction to me, if I have any way contributed to your Son Matthew's Happiness,' Nathaniel would tell Bridget on 6 January 1807. 'I derive also much Satisfaction from the strong hope I entertain that he has married a sensible, well informed & well disposed woman.'[6] Later that spring, Matt agreed to buy three of his brothers' shares in the company for £18,000, a bargain which, while consuming nearly his entire capital, put his holding on an equal footing to theirs. So sin-cere were Matt's feelings of gratitude towards both men that when Ann gave birth to a first child at Westgate Street, in April 1808, they named him George Clayton Atkinson.

SOON AFTER HIS public humiliation in the law courts at the hands of his brother-in-law, Michael Atkinson had taken the lease on 67 Portland Place, an imposing townhouse in Marylebone. Michael was also looking to buy a fine country residence; a newspaper advertisement for the Mount Mascal estate near Bexley, thirteen miles south-east of London, caught his eye in April 1808. The prop-erty comprised a 'capital' Jacobean mansion 'suitable for a family of the first distinction', positioned on a 'bold but gentle ascent' within a landscaped park of fifty acres, surrounded by nearly five hundred acres of woods, meadow, pasture and arable.[7] With fifteen bedrooms, the house was perhaps slightly larger than necessary – any smaller, however, and it might not have been able to accommodate Michael's bruised dignity.

Various members of the family had reason to gravitate towards London during the spring of 1809. Nathaniel, who was called there on legal business – 'a ship cause of considerable Importance' – went down with Dorothy, who renewed old friendships and fulfilled shop-ping commissions while he attended court.[8] Jane's trip to the capital was precipitated by a love affair – not one of her own, it should be said, but involving her nineteen-year-old niece Sophia, Michael's daughter, who had passed much of the previous winter at Temple

Sowerby. Sophia was a beautiful, nervous young woman, and viewed by her close relatives with a good deal of pity. ('The tempers of both her Parents were so remarkably bad & Mrs. A never by any accident a day sober,' Jane later recalled, 'that any human being would have felt for a Girl so situated.')[9] The details are obscure, but it seems that while she was up north, Sophia formed an intense attachment to an unidentified suitor. Her father, however, flatly prohibited the match. Jane came south with Sophia in March, hoping to promote her niece's cause. Three months later she returned to Temple Sowerby, her hopes frustrated; Michael remained as 'bitterly averse' to his daughter's marriage as ever.[10]

George continued to make frequent visits to London, where the Mures and their creditors still held the Atkinson estate under siege; as one of his late uncle's executors, he was often needed at the Inns of Court. The Lords of the Treasury, meanwhile, having belatedly discovered the degree to which the merchant house of Atkinson, Mure & Bogle had enriched itself through the occupation of Haiti in the 1790s, were intent on clawing back the 'double Commission' which had arisen from the army's expenses first passing through George Bogle's books in Port-au-Prince, then George Atkinson's in Kingston, before being settled with Sir Francis Baring in London.[11] When the West India Commissioners investigated, they found insufficient grounds to support the Treasury's case, but their Lordships would not let the matter rest.

Baring was by now an old man, and very deaf, but his mind remained perfectly agile. He had officially retired from business in 1803, leaving the great merchant house which he had built from scratch in the hands of his sons Thomas, Alexander and Henry. Baring's favourite recreation during his dotage was making improvements to Stratton, the Hampshire estate he had purchased from the Duke of Bedford in 1801, and filling the mansion with old master paintings. His standards were high and his pockets deep; only the works of Rembrandt, Rubens and Van Dyck tempted him, he would tell his son-in-law, 'and the first must not be too dark, nor the second indecent'.[12] He rarely passed up the opportunity to acquire local landed property. As one wit remarked: 'Sir Francis Baring is extending his purchases so largely in Hampshire, that he soon expects to be able to inclose the county within his own park paling.'[13]

When business brought him to town, Baring lived at the Manor House at Lee, near Lewisham, and it was here that he died, in September 1810, aged seventy. 'Few men understood the real interests of trade better,' wrote his obituarist in the *Gentleman's Magazine.* 'He was unquestionably the first merchant in Europe; first in knowledge and talents, and first in character and opulence.'[14] Sir Thomas Baring, who inherited the Lee residence, rented it out following his father's death. George and Susan Atkinson, who had been searching for a house close to the capital, were the first tenants; their ninth child, Harriet, was born there in February 1811.

AFTER TWO YEARS living at Westgate Street, Matt and Ann finally bought a home of their own in 1809. Carr Hill House, built in the 1760s, had originally operated as an asylum 'for the reception of *lunaticks*, in easy, genteel or opulent circumstances'; it was located two miles south of Newcastle, on the edge of Gateshead Fell, a dark, wild moor pockmarked with pits and quarries, and notorious for its highwaymen, cutpurses and ruffians.[15] Carr Hill village, on a breezy summit nearly five hundred feet above sea level, commanded views in all directions. The area was studded with windmills, including one in Matt and Ann's fifteen-acre grounds. They shared a love of the outdoors, and their large garden would prove a 'great source of amusement to them both'.[16]

This was an unpretentious district; the Atkinsons' new neighbours included corn millers, nurserymen, quarrymen, earthenware manufacturers, a flint glass maker and a fire brick maker. Matt would forge an especially close friendship with John Hodgson, the vicar of the next village, who was primarily a writer – indeed, some years earlier he had turned down a job at the Tyne Iron Company since he wished 'to pursue a literary, rather than a mercantile life'.[17] On 29 April 1811, shortly after the publisher of the popular 'Beauties of England and Wales' series commissioned Hodgson to compile the volume devoted to the county of Westmorland, he and Matt set out from Carr Hill on a brisk, sodden tramp across the Pennines for the purposes of researching the book. Two days later, groping at times through 'thick dark mist', they reached the top of Dun Fell, where they rewarded themselves with their first glimpse of Westmorland and a late breakfast. 'In a miner's shop we had our beef and bread and some excellent rum and water – rum made in Jamaica by Mr. A. nine years since,' wrote Hodgson.[18]

That afternoon they strode into Temple Sowerby, where they found spring several weeks ahead of the east side of the Pennines, and Bridget's garden in a flourishing state: 'Mrs. Atkinson has apricots against a common stone wall as large as pigeon eggs, and the foliage of the trees is nearly in perfection, except on the oaks and ashes.' Hodgson greatly admired Bridget's library, her collections of Roman and Saxon coins, and her shells gathered from around the globe. He was equally impressed by her continuing stamina. 'Mrs. Atkinson, although 78 years old, is up every morning at six o'clock, a practice that she and her children have always pursued, as recommended as the very best preservative of health,' he told his wife. 'Never, she says, let any person, on any consideration whatever, take a second sleep.'[19]

Now that she was in her late seventies, Bridget might have put her feet up and passed the day-to-day running of the house over to Jane, but she remained cheerfully hands-on. The book of 'receipts' which she had started compiling for Dorothy in January 1806 suggests that her knowledge of cookery was based upon a lifetime of practical experience; it also demonstrates her attachment to her eldest daughter, and the love of good food they shared. Bridget and Dorothy often exchanged parcels of provisions – in February 1809, for example, a crate of honey and rose water from Temple Sowerby made the return journey filled with oranges purchased in Newcastle – but neither mother nor daughter was ever quite as diligent a correspondent as the other wished her to be. Dorothy, in particular, expressed displeasure at her mother's shortcomings in this area. 'My Dear Dorothy,' Bridget wrote on 28 June 1812, 'I find by your writing to Jane that you were quite angry and thought I ought to have wrote to you at the time I wrote to Bridget' – this was Bridget's middle daughter, Bridget Tulip – 'but realy I was so busy with the Stairs Carpet I could not affoard time for any one else so do not impute it to slight or neglesence for it was neighter and when I am done you will see what a punctual correspondent I will be. I Long to see you here and then you will Judge what I have been doing but I am afraid you will give Jane all the credit.'[20]

While not engaged in carpet-cleaning or other domestic chores, much of Bridget's time must have been absorbed by her antiquarian hobbies. Here in front of me, on my desk, is Bridget's handwritten copy of the annals of the Clifford family, contained within two leatherbound volumes. They consist of an account of the sea voyages of the Earl of Cumberland, an Elizabethan courtier, and the diaries of his daughter Lady Anne Clifford, who spent forty years in litigation before winning the right to inherit her father's estates, which included Pendragon, Brough, Appleby and Brougham castles in Westmorland. It seems most likely that Bridget took her copy from a version held at Dalemain – the mansion had once been owned by Sir Edward Hasell, Lady Anne Clifford's steward. The cyclical appearance of Bridget's handwriting – each session starting neatly, deteriorating as she tires – hints at how long it must have taken her to transcribe this work.

Bridget's collections were well known in the neighbourhood, and her coins, shells and books a draw for passing enthusiasts. They had certainly made a strong impression on Matt's friend, John Hodgson, who was now working with the Newcastle bookseller John Bell towards the launch of an organization dedicated to the history of the northern counties – the first provincial counterpart to the Society of Antiquaries of London. The inaugural meeting of the Antiquarian Society of Newcastle upon Tyne took place on 6 February 1813, at Loftus's Long Room on Newgate Street, with the election of twenty-nine founder members, including Matt Atkinson and Nathaniel Clayton. The Duke of Northumberland graciously accepted the 'honourable Situation of Patron' – but the most striking

Bridget in old age, an engraving taken from
a miniature now lost.

mark of distinction to be conferred that day was the first honorary membership, upon 'Mrs. Atkinson' of Temple Sowerby.[21]

Among the original artefacts to enter the society's collection were a 'Celtic Hammer of very hard granular stone, found near Kirkoswald Castle, in Cumberland; a silver Penny of Henry the Second, found with a great quantity of the same kind of coin, at Cutherston, near Bowes, in Yorkshire, about the year 1782; a Silver Penny of Edward the First, coined at London; a Silver Penny of Edward the Second, coined at Canterbury' and a 'Swedish Copper Dollar, of Charles the Twelfth, dated 1716' – all donated by Bridget.[22] She, in turn, received a diploma, printed on parchment, enclosed in a neat wooden box. In coming years, great men would have honorary membership of the society bestowed upon them – Sir Joseph Banks, Sir Humphry Davy, Sir Walter Scott – but no other woman would be permitted to join its ranks until the 1870s.

GEORGE ATKINSON had been bracing himself for the forfeiture of much of his fortune, but finally, after pondering the subject for five years, the Treasury Board gave way on the matter of the 'double

Commission'. On 26 February 1813, the Law Officers declared that while George had not, strictly speaking, been entitled as Agent General of Jamaica to charge an additional 5 per cent on the bills drawn upon him by his partner in Port-au-Prince, he would have been permitted to apply the same charge – which they acknowledged as the 'proper and usual Commission' – had he been acting in his capacity as a private merchant.[23]

The decision must have been a tremendous relief for George, coming at a time when he was weighed down by ill health and an excessive workload; too much of his energy was still being absorbed by the lawsuits which were gradually devouring his late uncle's estate, and he felt increasingly aggrieved that his siblings expected him to shoulder the burden. As he complained to brother Matt: 'Altogether my Executorship has been a ruinous Concern as well as attended with incalculable Vexation, and has been an obstruction instead of an aid in my commercial Pursuits.'[24] It was about time, he resolved, that the wider family carried some responsibility – most pressingly, in making a decision about the Bogue estate.

Back in 1791, when Nathaniel Clayton and Sir Francis Baring bought out Paul Benfield's interest in the Bogue, they had declared by deed of trust that any profits from the estate's future sale would be 'divided Share & Share alike' among Bridget's children.[25] George had acquired Nathaniel's (but not Baring's) interest in the property eight years later, following his return from Jamaica. Two decades of under-investment had since taken their toll on the Bogue, and recently the crop had fallen badly short. In 1812 the plantation had consigned a mere forty hogsheads of sugar to Barings in London, which was scarcely enough to pay the overseer's salary, let alone the interest on huge debts of more than £40,000.

Nathaniel laid out the problem in a lengthy memorandum, dated 28 June 1813, which he circulated around the family (to everyone, that is, apart from Michael, with whom he could 'hold no correspondence'). While expressing hope that they would all profit from the future sale of their late uncle's property, Nathaniel pointed out that they might also lose money on it – and here lay the crux of the matter. Surely it was unfair that any of this risk should fall upon the estate of Sir Francis Baring, who had 'acted merely for the Benefit of Mr. Atkinson's Family'? Which invited the next question – if not Baring's heirs, who would be prepared to assume the risk? On this point Nathaniel asked each family member to 'judge for themselves'; they could either buy further into 'this Adventure', or opt out from it entirely.[26] The eventual gains, or losses, would be shared out accordingly.

Matt, indecisive as ever, declared himself 'perplexed' by the question. He told Nathaniel:

> You both know perfectly well how I am situated as to
> income. At the same time you will recollect I owe you nearly
> £500, and my Mill will run me in debt £200 more which
> must take me some time to Liquidate, and if you deem this
> undertaking hazardous, I really think I ought in prudence to
> relinquish all hopes of advantage rather than run much risk
> of involving myself further – but however I shall in this be
> entirely governed by whatever you & my Brother George
> agree I should do.[27]

NATHANIEL AND DOROTHY would be blessed with eleven children, with just sixteen years separating them, every one of whom reached adulthood. As they grew up and left home to fulfil their various callings, each Clayton family gathering became an increasingly rare and precious moment. 'The Children are all well & happy & I was a proud Man indeed, when I saw them all assembled at the Table on the first Day of this year,' Nathaniel had written to Bridget on one such occasion. 'God only knows whether this joyful Circumstance will again happen to us.'[28] The boys, of course, needed careers, and their father earmarked Nat, John and Michael for the legal profession; Nat would practise at Lincoln's Inn in London, while John and Michael were articled to the family firm in Newcastle. George Clayton came second in the brotherly pecking order, between Nat and John, but was insufficiently studious to pursue a legal career. In December 1813, after graduating from Oriel College, Oxford with a third-class degree, he sailed for Jamaica to join his uncle's merchant house – the first of the next generation of the family to do so.

Another of Bridget's grandsons, James Atkinson – John's orphan son – turned fourteen in 1813. Since his arrival at Temple Sowerby from Jamaica, eight years earlier, his grandmother and Aunt Jane had discreetly raised the boy – so discreetly, in fact, that family letters contain scant clues about his upbringing. Bridget's household accounts, however, reveal that several bills were paid to a 'Mr. Robinson' between 1807 and 1811. This John Robinson, not to be confused with the late Secretary to the Treasury, was headmaster of the grammar school at Ravenstonedale, about twenty miles south of Temple Sowerby; the fees for 1808 came to just over £30.[29] More evidence of James's education can be found on the shelf beside me; within a copy of *Corderius's Colloquies*, a textbook 'designed for the Use of Beginners in the Latin Tongue', can be found both his neat signature and the date, 24 February 1808, inscribed on its front endpaper.

I had hoped to learn so much more about James's life; but the trail seemed to peter out after 1811, and I started worrying that I would never find out what happened to him. One day, however, while leafing through John Hodgson's papers at the Northumberland Archives, and trying not to be too diverted by his fascinating, but for my purposes entirely tangential correspondence with Sir Humphry Davy about ways of 'preventing explosions from fire damp' – ninety-two men and boys having perished in a blast at Felling Colliery, a mile down the road from Carr Hill, in May 1812 – I was surprised to come across a document in a familiar hand.[30] This was one of Bridget's chatty letters, addressed to Matt at the Tyne Iron Company; and it enclosed the formula for a 'Thorn-Apple Burn Ointment which is by far the best I ever saw'.[31] It also offered an ending, of sorts, to the story of James Atkinson.

Bridget was writing to Matt on 25 October 1813, the day after James had sailed for . . . she does not give his final destination, but

I would guess it to be Jamaica. The week before, Jane and James had apparently hurried to Whitehaven in the post-chaise, not stopping 'on the road to eat or drink', but they discovered when they arrived that the ship for which they were rushing had already left. They then headed without delay to Liverpool in hopes of catching a vessel to take James to Cork, where the West India merchant fleet was gathering in readiness for a naval convoy. At Liverpool, Jane had called on Thomas Littledale – Ann's brother, a cotton broker – who had offered 'every assistance and got James every thing he wanted as a Mattrass Blanket Blue woolling trousers &c', and had also helped find him a passage to Cork. 'Never one could behave better than James did – but I will tell you all when you come over and you shall shoot me a Little game for Mr. Littledale.'[32] *I will tell you all when you come over* – rarely have the confines of the written word been more teasingly articulated. Beyond this point, I have no idea how James's life panned out – for his name never crops up again in a family letter.

BRIDGET HAD LONG SUFFERED from rheumatism and poor circulation, and she spent part of the autumn of 1813 at the resort of Allonby, on the Solway coast, where she derived a 'great deal of Benniﬁtt' from warm indoor baths. ('I thought I had lost the use of my Fingers in writing,' she told Matt, 'but I hope I shall recover all again.')[33] The following winter would prove exceptionally harsh. In January 1814, blizzards swept the land, depositing a blanket of snow several feet deep. In the capital, for a few dreamlike days in February, the ice between Blackfriars and London bridges was thick enough to support crowds of revellers, roasting oxen and even an elephant – this would be the last Frost Fair ever to be held on the River Thames. Up north, the Tyne and Solway Firth both froze hard.

By the beginning of March, Bridget was dangerously ill. Dorothy went over to Temple Sowerby to help Jane nurse their mother, while Nathaniel consulted the family physician, William Ingham, about her condition. 'He thinks it probable that there may be some Disease about the Vessels of the Heart, but that all the Symptoms detailed to him might proceed from Debility alone,' reported Nathaniel on 13 March. 'The only Remedy is sustaining the Patient and recruiting her Strength. To this End all your united Endeavours should be directed, and he thinks that as the Strength is recruited, the Quantity of Laudanum administered may be abated.'[34] While Bridget lay in bed, the family was filled with foreboding; they would not have long to wait, though, for she died on 28 March.

Bridget left her house, land and money to her youngest daughter Jane – all her property apart from Skygarth, the tiny farm acquired through the enclosures forty years earlier, which she left to Michael. Ten years earlier, at the height of the family row, Bridget had rewritten her will with the express purpose of disinheriting him: 'I declare it to be my intention totally to Exclude my eldest son Michael Atkinson from any share or interest in any of my Estates or effects real or personal.'[35] It is not clear what caused her change of heart, but in April 1811 she had written him back into her will. However, Bridget's bequest came with a condition; if he caused Jane, her executrix, 'any trouble molestation or disturbance' by demanding more than had been left to him, then the property would be forfeit.[36] Michael was apoplectic when he discovered this stipulation, perceiving it to be Nathaniel Clayton's work. 'I am sure there is *something* in the business which will not bear the light,' he fulminated, 'and to that *something* I ascribe the Disgusting Clause in my Mother's Will.'[37]

Six weeks after Bridget's death, on 11 May, George died suddenly at Lee, aged forty-nine, leaving behind a widow and nine children. It was a great shock to the entire family; although they knew that George's years in Jamaica had 'decayed' his constitution, they had not suspected him to be in mortal danger.[38] Michael attended the reading of his brother's will. 'I am as much in the Dark as possible as to what he possessed of property, for he *specified nothing*,' he told cousin Matthew Atkinson. 'The Will appeared to me a Complete Attorney's Puzzle.' George's executors were named as the Nathaniel Claytons, father and son; 'Matt the Blacksmith' (Michael's jeering name for his brother at Carr Hill); and nineteen-year-old George Atkinson, who had inherited his father's share of the merchant house in Kingston.[39]

Matt told Lord Balcarres that he believed his brother's family would 'be reasonably well provided for', once his partnerships had been wound up.[40] This would prove an understatement. George's estate was valued for probate at £140,000, which placed him among the ten richest men to die in Great Britain that year.[41]

TWENTY

Settling Scores

FOR THIRTY YEARS, Richard Atkinson's executors had ridden roughshod over the claims of Lady Anne Barnard; so when the last of them, Robert Mure, died in January 1815, her lawyers saw a chance to step into the breach. Michael Atkinson, motivated by his deep sense of grievance against Nathaniel Clayton, decided to join Anne's cause, and together this unlikely pair filed a petition for the Letters of Administration that would grant them control of the estate's assets.

But they had not reckoned on the opposition of Richard's nine nieces. Like Anne, these middle-aged women had been left annuities of which they had not received a penny; more significantly, though, they were the 'residuary legatees' of their uncle's estate. While planning his will, Richard had been so wildly optimistic in his financial projections that he had envisaged the profits from his Jamaican plantations accumulating into a fund from which all the annuity payments would be paid, and from the *residue* of which his nieces would each receive a lump sum of £4,000. This placed them next in line to take over the administration of the estate; Jane volunteered to represent her sisters and cousins in court, and Nathaniel dealt with the necessary paperwork.

When Michael learnt that his female relatives had shown the temerity to place their own interests ahead of his, he fired off a letter to Jane – '*short* and *very very tart*' – conveying his ill feelings. She was in Newcastle at the time, and she instantly warned cousin Matthew Atkinson, who lived across the village from her at Temple Sowerby, about some petty ways in which her brother's displeasure might soon make itself manifest: 'I expect Michael will be writing to you probably to take immediate possession of the Moss field.' (This was part of the small farm left him by their mother.) 'There is a large Compost Heap which at all events I would be obliged by your telling Isaac to remove immediately & any thing that you may observe that might be claimed.'[1]

The Prerogative Court of Canterbury sat in June 1815 to weigh up the rival petitions for the administration of the Atkinson estate. As Jane predicted, the 'spirit to pursue Mr. Clayton' gripped Michael in the courtroom, and his evidence spewed forth as a litany of bitter accusations.[2] Whether Michael's animosity influenced the judgement is not clear, but Sir John Nicholl brushed aside both Lady Anne Barnard's claim as an annuitant and Michael's as a legatee. 'It is objected that Mrs. Jane Atkinson resides at a distance, and is a spinster: but really these objections are ludicrous,' he pronounced.[3] As a residuary legatee – even when there was no prospect of inheriting any residue – the youngest sister's claim took legal precedence over that of the eldest brother.

BY ANY STANDARDS, Lady Anne Barnard had lived an eventful life – from mixing with royalty and statesmen to clambering up Table Mountain – but these days she barely left her house in Berkeley Square. Her late husband, who had remained in the Cape Colony after she returned to England in 1802, had posthumously sprung a surprise upon her – for no sooner had she received word of his death out there in 1807, than another letter arrived informing her that he had fathered a daughter by an enslaved woman. Anne saw it as her duty, a 'debt of honour' even, to care for the child, as the 'accident of an unguarded moment' after she had left her 'poor husband a lonely widower'.[4] Christina Douglas, this 'dear little girl of colour', went to live with her adoptive mother in London during the summer of 1809, when she was six.[5]

The other great love of Anne's life, her sister Margaret, died in December 1814. Following Alexander Fordyce's death in 1789, when she was thirty-six, Margaret had lived on and off with Anne in Berkeley Square, before ultimately enjoying two blissful years of marriage to Sir James Burges, a longstanding admirer. Anne had spent much of 1815 mourning the loss of her sister; but the first day of the following year found her in resolute frame of mind, as she sat down to draft an eighteen-page memorandum addressed to her heirs: 'A Hasty Sketch of Particulars respecting my Acquaintance with Richard Atkinson Esq. and his management of my affairs – For the Information of those who may one day have an Interest in them'. She meant by this a *financial* interest – for she was considering how best to pass her claims on the Atkinson estate down to the next generation, having accepted that she was 'too old' to pursue further litigation.[6] 'With a nest of young Attorneys, Claytons & Atkinsons on the Estates, living like princes, war is better than peace, at least to the Clayton folks,' she observed to her brother, Lord Balcarres, on 24 March 1816.[7]

By now, Anne was immersed in a major literary project – she was writing her autobiography. For several years she would labour away on this magnum opus in her forty-foot drawing room at Berkeley Square, under the watchful eyes of her beloved sister, as portrayed by Thomas Gainsborough, surrounded by ghosts and papers from her past. Inevitably, what she had once envisaged as a 'sketch' of her life expanded into a sprawling narrative.[8] As her health and her handwriting deteriorated, she increasingly relied upon Christina, her 'young amanuensis', whose careful script would end up filling the pages of six volumes.[9]

Anne's lively, candid memoirs caused a good deal of disquiet within the Lindsay family. Her siblings – particularly the decorous Countess of Hardwicke – feared she would unburden herself of secrets that would bring discredit upon them all. Anne calmed their nerves by giving 'feigned names' to her 'real characters', including herself, and thus the manuscript acquired the title *The History of the Family of St Aubin and the Memoirs of Louisa Melford*. (Richard

Atkinson became 'Robert Williamson'.)[10] She also decreed that the work could never, ever be published: 'I utterly debar it.'[11]

FOLLOWING THE ABDICATION of Napoleon Bonaparte from the French imperial throne in April 1814, the triumphant allies – Britain, Austria, Prussia and Russia – assembled in Paris to negotiate a treaty to restore peace to the ravaged continent. Ever since Admiral Nelson's victory off Cape Trafalgar in October 1805, which had secured Britain's maritime supremacy, the Royal Navy had kept French trade in check; but now, at the peace talks, it was suggested that France might be allowed a five-year revival of the slave trade, so its planters could put their West Indian possessions back in order. There was no mistaking the reaction of the British public to this regressive proposal. Thomas Clarkson, the veteran activist and chairman of the African Institution, called for petitions to be fired at Westminster from every corner of the country; by the time parliament rose for the summer recess, on 30 July 1814, more than eight hundred petitions had already been delivered.

In the British West Indies, as abolitionists had always predicted, the enslaved workforce dwindled without regular cargoes from Africa. In March 1810, two years after the Abolition of the Slave Trade Act came into force, the Kingston house of Atkinson, Bogle & Co. had told Lord Balcarres that they were finding it 'exceedingly difficult to obtain singly, prime Negroes of either Sex', and the supply had shrunk further since then.[12] 'The Sum of my Inclination as to my Jamaica Properties is this,' Balcarres had written to the house, in clear frustration, three years later: 'I do not want Money – I want Negroes.'[13] But a proportion of the slave trade still carried on underground, and it was to smother this business that William Wilberforce tabled a parliamentary motion, in June 1815, to make the registration of slaves compulsory. Not only would the name, age and sex of every enslaved person be recorded; any changes to their status due to their sale, escape, manumission, or death, would also be logged. By keeping much stricter tabs on the numbers and movements of the enslaved population, it would be far harder for slave owners to conceal instances of illegal trafficking.

So outraged were West Indian planters at this attempt by Wilberforce's 'party of fanatical bigots' to meddle in their internal affairs, however, that the Westminster bill was withdrawn; instead the separate island assemblies were persuaded to enact the legislation at a local level.[14] The House of Assembly in Jamaica would pass its registration bill in December 1816. Prior to registration, most anti-slavery campaigners had known little about the people in whose welfare they took such interest; but the new law meant that slave owners could no longer treat their human property as an abstract mass. From now on, the enslaved population would be composed of counted, named individuals.

During this time the Kingston house was in a state of flux. After George Atkinson's death, Edward Adams and Robert Robertson had returned to England to wind up their late partner's affairs, bringing (it was said) some £300,000 with them. Subsequently, in an alliance which raised eyebrows within the wider family – certainly it was 'not impeded by any antediluvian Notions of Coyness & Reserve', remarked Nathaniel Clayton – Robertson, who was thirty-eight, had married Bridget Atkinson, George's sixteen-year-old daughter.[15] Meanwhile out in Jamaica, George Clayton, second son of Dorothy and Nathaniel, had died of a fever in April 1816 at the age of twenty-six.

It was the responsibility of the Kingston house, as Lord Balcarres' attorneys on the island, to file his first slave return. But there was a catch – for the registration process threatened to expose, after eighteen years' concealment, the corruption that lay at the heart of the pioneer contract, whereby the former governor had secretly signed up for a one-third share of the business of supplying 'black pioneers' to the army. 'I do not perceive any Means of omitting your Lordship's name in the Return,' warned Edward Adams in February 1817.[16]

Adams wrote to Balcarres again in August, this time to tell him about a letter written by a junior minister which suggested that the pioneer contract should be ended immediately: 'It also mentions

Lord Balcarres' Interest, and insinuates the Contract to have been a *Job*.'[17] The degree to which Balcarres was spooked by this message is plain from the many scrawled sheets of foolscap, scarred with crossings-out, in which he fabricated a story that would clear him of wrongdoing. 'I think I have made out a strong case,' he told Adams. 'I deny the Job & deny that I am the holder of the share.'[18] Adams counselled Balcarres to keep quiet. 'The Paragraph I quoted to your Lordship is information collected quite privately,' he wrote. 'We could give no reason for imputing to ministers, therefore, a suspicion of the Contract being underhanded. Consequently, an attempt to justify it would appear like being betrayed by a guilty conscience.'[19] This was sound advice, for neither was the pioneer contract terminated, and nor did any investigation come about. By November, moreover, Adams was able to pass Balcarres some 'satisfactory Intelligence' from Jamaica.[20] The pioneers had been registered by the commanding officers of the regiments they served, and not by the Kingston house; and thus his Lordship's good name remained unsullied.

THE ANTI-SLAVERY MOVEMENT had deep roots within Nonconformist Christianity; the majority of the founder members of the Committee for the Abolition of the Slave Trade had been Quakers. Meanwhile some of the most vocal abolitionists, notably William Wilberforce, were evangelical Anglicans who worshipped at Holy Trinity Church on Clapham Common; they came to be known as the 'Clapham Sect' or, not entirely respectfully, the 'Saints'.

In the West Indies, the planter class had long tried to keep the enslaved population as ignorant of Christianity as possible. Recently, however, a battle for their souls had broken out in Jamaica, stirred up by Wesleyan missionaries preaching the creed that all men were equal in the eyes of God. The House of Assembly, observing how the 'dark and dangerous fanaticism' of the Methodists seemed to resonate among the black population, resolved to spread 'genuine Christianity' among them.[21] The Rev. George Wilson Bridges came to Jamaica in 1816, at the invitation of the governor, and was installed as rector of St Mark's Church in Mandeville, the capital of the newly formed parish of Manchester. Bridges was almost certainly the most active of the Anglican clergymen who were recruited by the authorities to tend to the spiritual needs of the enslaved population; he would later claim to have baptized 9,413 slaves.[22] These ceremonies involved the candidates gathering 'either at the churches, or on the estates, sometimes from fifty to a hundred or more'. No religious instruction was given beforehand; they were merely asked what their Christian names and surnames were to be, and then 'baptized *en masse*, the rector receiving half a crown currency for each person'.[23]

Two estates belonging to Lord Balcarres – Martin's Hill and Marshall's Pen – were in the parish of Manchester, and Bridges baptized 220 of the enslaved population there in December 1818 and January 1819. Further west, in Westmoreland Parish, the Rev. James Dawn baptized 121 'Negroes belonging to Dean's Valley Dry Works', as the church records describe them, on 17 November 1820. One-third of the inhabitants of this estate took one of two surnames – of course, we will never know to what extent these were their own choice, or foisted upon them. Two Amelias, Eliza, Elizabeth, George, James, Mary Ann, Robert, Thomas and William – they would be known as Clayton. Alexander, Amelia, Andrew, Catherine, Diana, Eleanor, Eliza, Elizabeth, George, Henry, three Jameses, Jannett, John, Lucea, Margaret, Mary, Mary Ann, Matthew, Rebecca, Richard, Robert, Romeo, two Susans, Thomas and three Williams – they were all now Atkinsons.[24]

By this time, the long-term decline of the enslaved population at Dean's Valley had reduced the estate to near paralysis. Back in 1797, there had been 221 slaves on the property; now just 134 were left. 'Unless the strength is increased,' wrote the Kingston house, 'we contemplate not a falling off in the Crop but the utter impossibility of carrying on.'[25] As the debts on both the Bogue and Dean's Valley estates escalated, and the value of sugar plantations slumped, the Claytons attempted to clear the legal path to their sale. Michael Clayton – Nathaniel and Dorothy's fourth son – managed

Alphabetical List and valuation of Negroes on the 'Bogue' Estate, with their age, occupation, & condition September 26th 1818.

No.	Names	Males above 12 years	Females above 12 years	Males under 12 years	Males under 6 years	Females under 6 years	Total of Males	Females total	Ground total	Condition	Occupation	Valuation
	Adam	1				1		1		Able	Field	160
	Asa	1				1		1		Weakly	Watchman	130
	Adam	1				1		1		Ditto	Ditto	20
	Anthony	1				1		1		Able	Att.J Stock	150
5.	Apollo			1		1		1		Healthy	under age	40
	Affie		1				1	1		Able	Fields	140
	Abigail		1				1	1		Ditto	Ditto	120
	Ann			1			1	1		Healthy	House	130
	Amelia					1	1	1		ditto	under age	30
10.	Belinda		1				1	1		Weakly	Field	
	Bella		1				1	1		Able	Ditto	140
	Betty	1				1		1		ditto	Ditto	140
	Bogady	1				1		1		Weakly	Carpenter	160
	Bottle Rum	1				1		1		Able	Att.J Stock	140
15.	Bessy					1	1	1		Healthy	Under age	20
	Brutus	1				1		1		Able	Watchman	40
	Bacchus	1				1		1		Weakly	Cook	80
	Belinda		1				1	1		ditto	Att.J Nancy Stewart	
	Betsey		1				1	1		Able	Field	160
20.	Bacchus	1				1		1		Old & Weak	Invalid	
	Chelsea	1				1		1		Weakly	Att.J Sheep	
	Charles	1				1		1		Sickly	In flat house the last 12 months	
	Charles	1				1		1		Able	Field	140
	Cuthbert	1				1		1		Weakly	Watchman	30
25.	Chloe		1				1	1		Able	Field	120
	Cumba		1				1	1		ditto	ditto	80
	Chloe		1				1	1		ditto	ditto	50
	Christie		1				1	1		Old & weak	Invalid	
	Celinda		1				1	1		Able	Field	170
30.	Chance		1				1	1		Yaws	Ditto	150
	Clarinda		1				1	1		Old & weak	Invalid	
	Diamond	1				1		1		Able	Field	200
	Daniel	1				1		1		ditto	Carpenter	200
	Damsel		1				1	1		ditto	Field	170
35.	Doll	1				1		1		Weakly	ditto	
		16	16	..	1	1	2	17	18	35		£ 3130

A valuation of the enslaved population on the Bogue estate in September 1818.

the business from the London chambers of the family firm at 6 New Square, Lincoln's Inn.

But Michael Atkinson's refusal to go along with his relatives' wishes presented an obstacle to the properties' disposal, causing Nathaniel to file two chancery bills against his brother-in-law. Michael wrote to Lord Balcarres in October 1818, complaining of not having received 'one Shilling' from the estates while they were managed by those who would now sell them 'in Liquidation of Debts due to themselves', and seeking to form an alliance against the lawsuits.[26] But Balcarres brushed him off: 'Your Uncle Richard Atkinson left his affairs in that State of Confusion & perplexity as to convince me that I could be of no manner of use.'[27]

One day around this time, while he was poring over his uncle's will at Doctors' Commons, Michael noticed that it no longer bore its original seal; and so, in January 1819, he filed a 'voluminous' bill to have the document set aside as defective.[28] Although Lady Anne Barnard felt a degree of sympathy for Michael, she realized he was entirely the puppet of lawyers who saw a 'good suit for *them* out of it', and declined his invitation to join the legal action.[29] It would prove a wise decision.

The case finally came before the Lord Chief Justice, Sir Charles Abbott, on 1 August 1821. The Solicitor General started by informing the jury that it was their duty to decide upon the legitimacy of a will which had been 'in operation' for more than thirty years; the seal it had once borne had 'by time or accident' been lost, and now the testator's nephew had chosen 'for the first time' to suggest that his late uncle had deliberately torn it off 'as a mode of cancelment'. Two employees of the Prerogative Office suggested that the damage might easily have taken place at Doctors' Commons, given that the 'practice was to carry the will into the great room, where as many as 200 persons were frequently collected at the same time, and where, of course, to attend to the conduct of every one was impracticable'.[30] Michael could offer no evidence to support his argument – and thus, unsurprisingly, the jury pronounced Richard Atkinson's will to be completely valid.

SINCE HIS RETURN from India some seventeen years earlier, Michael had expended much of his remaining energy on pointlessly feuding with his relations over their Jamaican inheritance; but this would be the final lawsuit to go against him, for he died six weeks later at his Portland Place residence. Michael's daughter Sophia had five years earlier married Bertie Cator, a good-natured naval captain, and the Cators now stood to inherit a considerable fortune. But Michael's obstinacy had exacted a heavy toll on the rest of the family, and the Claytons, being lawyers, now came up with a legalistic way to settle the score.

The inheritance of landed property in Kent had, since Anglo-Saxon times, followed the laws of tenure known as 'gavelkind', which determined that in cases of intestacy without legitimate issue, it should be divided among male next of kin – all land in the county was included, unless specifically 'disgavelled'. Michael had made his will in 1807, naming his daughter Sophia as his lawful heir. He had purchased the Mount Mascal estate the following year, but had failed to update his will in order to disgavel the property. And, furthermore, the family had always strongly suspected that Michael had never married his 'wife'.

Nat Clayton spelled out the potential implications in a letter to his uncle Matt at Carr Hill. 'Supposing the Illegitimacy of Mrs. Cator,' he explained, 'it would follow, that you as surviving Brother take one half of the Mount Mascal Estate and that the five sons of your deceased Brother George take the other half amongst them in equal Shares.'[31] Nat made some enquiries, and found three highly respectable gentlemen – a director of the East India Company, an East Indiaman captain and an army general – who were prepared to swear affidavits. 'We have been hitherto very fortunate in obtaining Information relative to Michael Atkinson's Affairs; & a curious History it will turn out,' Nat told his mother, Dorothy, on 21 November 1821. 'In the course of our Inquiries one thing has led to another in an extraordinary Manner; & we have met with ample Information in Quarters where we had the least reason to expect it. The Begum's Life in point of singularity & variety looks more like a novel than a reality.'[32]

The word 'begum' was a term of respect on the Indian sub-continent. Nat was using it ironically, of course – for it appeared that Michael's 'wife' had lived a dissolute youth, to say the least. The story of Miss Sophia Mackereth had begun in London during the 1780s, where as a 'girl of the Town' she had been entangled with John Manship, an East India Company director; he had 'got rid of her by sending her off to Madras'. As soon as she landed in India, in July 1785, she had apparently 'made a great outcry' that a trunk containing her jewels and letters of recommendation had been stolen. 'The whole story was a fabrication,' recalled Joseph Dorin, captain of the *Duke of Montrose*. 'The people of Madras were imposed upon by it & treated her with great kindness.' Soon afterwards she took up with a Mr Woolley, with whom she stayed for a few months before they fell out; he later died in a duel. She then sailed up the coast to Calcutta, where she was invited 'from motives of compassion' to live in the residence of the governor, Sir John Macpherson; finally, in May 1786, she had run off with Michael Atkinson. General Mackenzie, commanding the 78th Highlanders, remembered spending several days with Michael at Jangipur in 1797: 'He had at that time a Lady living with him who took his name. In the course of conversation I asked him if he was married to her to which he replied without hesitation *that he was not.*'[33]

Although Matt stood to benefit most, the rest of the family deliberately excluded him from these discussions. 'Brother Matt must not be trusted with any one thing,' Jane reminded Dorothy, 'for the Weakest of Creatures may impose upon him.' Both sides showed a readiness to fight their corner; Sophia Cator declared herself prepared 'to go through fire & water' to prove her legitimacy.[34] 'My Father would tell you that the Begum or rather Capt. Cator is determined not to give up Mount Mascall without a hard struggle,' Michael Clayton told his mother on 13 July 1822. 'I met the Captain a few days ago accidentally and what will surprize you the introduction on his side was attended with the most cordial & hearty shake of the hand notwithstanding the exertions he knows I am making against his Interests. The subject was only slightly adverted to and Capt. Cator said it gave him of course great pain but he knew that we were only doing our duty – there is no difference of opinion as to *his* worth.'[35]

By this point, the parties were hammering out a compromise. Bertie Cator ultimately agreed to pay £14,500 – which was how much the Claytons calculated that Michael's refusal to agree to the sale of the Jamaican estates 'when implored to do so' had cost the rest of the family – to his late father-in-law's male next of kin.[36] Matt received a memorandum relating to his half-share of the proceeds, in his nephew John Clayton's handwriting: 'By the agreement now executed, Mr. Matthew Atkinson agrees to relinquish all claim to the Mount Mascall Estate on having the sum of £7250 secured to him upon it to be paid on the 5th day of August 1834 unless Mrs. Michael Atkinson shall die before that time in which case the principal money is to be paid within 12 months after her decease.'[37]

The episode must have been excruciating for Sophia Cator, the Begum's daughter, but soon afterwards she appears to have written in conciliatory language to her uncle Matt. This letter has not survived, although Matt's reply hints at his great relief that the matter was closed:

> I know very few things that would have added so much to the
> very satisfactory & amiable compromise that has recently been
> made, as the receipt of your affectionate letter today. I think
> you know me well enough, my dear Sophia, to doubt a moment
> of my embracing in the most lively manner the kind & friendly
> terms proposed & burying all that has past in oblivion, you
> little know how anxiously I have always hoped some fortuitous
> circumstance might restore the lost affection of my deceased
> brother, but Providence ordered it otherwise.[38]

IN MAY 1823, aged seventy-two, Lady Anne Barnard composed a letter to her brother Lord Balcarres, to be opened after her death: 'You will not receive these few lines till I am no more – they are only to bid you adieu in the anxious hope of meeting you again in a world of everlasting Happiness and love. I wish my funds were as ample as they *ought to be*, but I will still hope that something may be gained to your family by my means.'[39] Anne was in a leave-taking frame of mind, putting her papers in order and making them fit for the prying eyes of the next generation. Much of her correspondence ended up on the drawing room fire; happily, she spared a bundle of Richard Atkinson's old letters. 'Most interesting & noble man', Anne pencilled at the top of the letter in which he had proposed marriage to her.[40] 'A strong & solemn testimony of the motives which governed the conduct of this Excellent man', she wrote on the letter he had sent her alongside the final draft of his will.[41] 'May we not call him the prince of English merchants?'[42]

Meanwhile, with Michael no longer around to block the business, the Atkinson estate was crawling towards a final settlement. By the close of 1822, terms had been agreed for the sale of Dean's Valley – the land, buildings, enslaved workers and livestock fetching just over £16,000 – and a prospective buyer had also been found for the Bogue. ('I hope we shall soon be able to submit to the Trustees for Sale a proposal for getting rid of this disastrous Property,' Michael Clayton told Lord Balcarres on 18 November 1823.)[43] Meanwhile, Richard Atkinson's heirs had mostly learnt to manage their expectations. 'I quite despair of Receiving a Shilling from our uncle's Effects,' wrote Joseph Taylor, the son of Richard's sister Margaret, on 10 March 1824. 'Indeed I dismiss the Subject from my Mind, and almost wish that no Part of my Family or myself had been mentioned in the Will.'[44]

The Master in Chancery finally made his report on the Atkinson estate at the beginning of 1825. A notice in *The Times* called on the Mures' remaining creditors to gather on 29 March at the Court of Commissioners of Bankrupts in the City of London, 'to assent to or dissent from a compromise of all matters depending between the estate of Richard Atkinson, and the estate of the said Hutchison, Robert and William Mure'.[45] Here the terms of the settlement were agreed 'to the satisfaction of all parties'.[46] Richard's estate was in the end valued at £88,000. (Forty years earlier, it had been reckoned worth £300,000.) More than three-quarters of this sum went to the heirs of George Atkinson and Sir Francis Baring, to pay off their loans to the two Jamaican estates, leaving about £20,000 to be shared out among the extended family. As for Lady Anne Barnard's inheritance – had there been anything for her, it would have been too late, for she died on 6 May 1825.

TWENTY-ONE

Human Relics

THE CLASSIC NARRATIVE ARC of a family's fortune spans three generations – the enterprising first generation amasses it, the complacent second generation sits on it, the feckless third generation squanders it. (Although my family doesn't entirely fit this template – not least because, for some truly world-class feckless-ness, it would have to wait till the sixth generation.) At this point in the saga, as the second generation withers and the third generation emerges, the family splinters into branches of cousins, too numerous to follow individually.

A little confusingly, two George Atkinsons inhabit this next part of the story. (As I've already mentioned, my forebears were unimaginative where first names were concerned.) The more prom-inent of these Georges is George and Susan's eldest son, a Kingston merchant; I'll sometimes refer to him as cousin George. The other George is Matt and Ann's eldest son, a Newcastle naturalist; he's either George or, more formally, George Clayton Atkinson. In case you're wondering, I'm descended from his youngest brother, Dick – and it's down this branch of the family that I will be increasingly drawn. (At this point, you may be forgiven for sneaking a glance at the family tree near the front of the book.)

It's somewhat hard to reconcile Matt the careless progenitor of many illegitimate children in Jamaica with Matt the devoted pater-familias at Carr Hill; but it would appear that he and Ann enjoyed a tranquil domestic life. George Clayton Atkinson, in a halcyon recollection of childhood, described mornings starting with his father – who was always first to rise – sneezing twice 'with much vigour' as he went downstairs, tapping the barometer as he passed through the hall, and heading outdoors with one or more children in tow. 'How delicious the remembrance of walking about the garden with him, now is,' wrote George. 'He was six feet high, & stooped a little in later years; he used moreover to roll rather in his walk; & I can just fancy him walking along the front walk with his pruning knife in one hand, & Jane or Dick holding the other: stopping now & then to trim a straggling carnation, or stepping over the border to eradicate an unsightly shoot from the far extending root of one of the peach trees.'[1]

Matt and Ann were unshowy people, and their home was simply furnished – as George remembered it, there was just one oil painting in the house, a smoky scene of Tynemouth Castle, which hung over the chimneypiece in the school room. The five children – George, Isaac, Mary Ann, Dick and Jane – were an unruly gaggle with only seven years between them, and it fell to Ann to keep their 'more fervid schemes' in check, for Matt was an indulgent parent. 'My poor father, he certainly had the kindest heart, best temper I ever knew,' recalled George. 'Nothing went wrong with him, everything pleased him: whatever happened it was all right, & he gives me in recollection, a finer personification of entire contentment than I remember to have met with.' On dark winter evenings, Matt would read aloud to the family beside the fire, with a 'very favourite grey cat' on his knee, while Ann stitched and the young ones quietly amused themselves.[2] The girls were educated at home by a governess, while the boys went off to board at St Bees School near Whitehaven, and then, to tame their 'Northern Manners & Dialect', at the Charterhouse School in London.[3]

If there was one trait that pervaded Matt's working life, it was an unfortunate allergy to paperwork – this would trigger a short but painful dispute with his brother-in-law Nathaniel, conducted via half a dozen letters in March 1816. A fraud had been uncovered at the Tyne Iron Company; the loss to the firm was nearly £100. The partners, believing Matt to be in daily attendance, were shocked to find that he had not once, during the nine years he had managed its head office, bothered to bestow 'five minutes on the cashing up of a single page of the Cash Book of the Concern'. Nathaniel was furious, and berated him for his neglect: 'Your Attendance at the Office, applied as it must have been, was at once a Snare to your Partners, and a Temptation to the unhappy Man, who is now expiating his Crimes.'[4] In reply, Matt complained of having been 'led into the concern' in the first place, and of his capital having been 'locked up so long without any return'.[5] But it was Nathaniel's suggestion that Ann was partly to blame for his inattention, by insisting that he left the office at midday to be back at Carr Hill in time for dinner, which wounded Matt most of all. 'It was no arrangement of my Wife's that obliged me to it,' he wrote, 'but my own taste for early hours as I can with Truth affirm that she has devoted herself entirely to my wishes since we married, and I may add her utmost pride has been in doing so, you may easily imagine how much we were both hurt at the insinuation of her not entering into the interest of her husband.'[6] Nathaniel terminated the exchange with a wish to 'bury the Subject in oblivion'.[7]

Matt was most in his element when out rambling with his friend John Hodgson, the local parson. Hodgson took a close interest in the Roman wall; indeed, through the study of inscriptions on excavated rocks, he would reach what was, for the time, the unorthodox conclusion that the emperor Hadrian had been its builder. During one of their long walks, Matt had been delighted to show Hodgson the words PETRA FLAVI CARANTINI – 'the rock of Flavius Carantinus' – carved on to a ridge of hard sandstone on his brother-in-law Henry Tulip's Fallowfield estate.

The two men set out on another trip to Westmorland in May 1817. This was a period of great geological discovery – William Smith's first map of England and Wales, delineating their different rock strata, had been published two years earlier – and Hodgson, the son of a Shap stonemason, had always been fascinated by the

The view across Ullswater.

diverse geology of his native county. Over several days, they would together examine the 'limestone, schist, and sandstone' in the bed of the River Lowther near Askham, the 'thin laminae and lumps of fibrous white gypsum' by the River Eden at Winderwath, and a 'bed of peat-coal' by the River Eamont.[8]

This time, incidentally, Matt and Hodgson did not sleep at Temple Sowerby; instead they put up twelve miles away, beside Ullswater, as the guests of Matt's sister-in-law Elizabeth Little-dale and her husband Captain John Wordsworth, a cousin of the celebrated poet. The Wordsworths' residence, Eusemere, had been built by the great abolitionist Thomas Clarkson, after repeated set-backs had driven him to seek peace in the Lake District during the late 1790s. The house was built of rough stone and roofed in local slate; its casement windows framed magnificent views. William and Dorothy Wordsworth had often visited the Clarksons there; it was while they were walking along the lake shore, on their way home to Dove Cottage, that they had observed the 'long belt' of daffodils, 'about the breadth of a country turnpike road', which had inspired Wordsworth to write his most famous verse.[9]

Matt and Ann would pass on their great love of nature to their children; while he issued them with 'grave injunctions' not to touch birds' nests during the breeding season, she encouraged them to press wildflowers between the pages of books.[10] During the summer holidays of 1825, while thirteen-year-old Dick was staying with Aunt Jane at Temple Sowerby, he came across the nest and eggs of a bird that he did not recognize. Back home at Carr Hill, he consulted the well-thumbed family copy of Thomas Bewick's *Birds* and identified them as belonging to a pied flycatcher, although he did notice that the author seemed unclear about certain aspects of the species.

Bewick was one of the Atkinsons' neighbours, and something of a Tyneside celebrity. He had stayed with Matt and Ann at Carr Hill in August 1812, while recovering from pleurisy, and afterwards moved to a house at Gateshead, on the road into Newcastle. During his long career as a wood engraver, Bewick had illustrated many subjects; but rural scenes were his forte, often including minuscule details that revealed a wicked sense of humour. His enduring masterpiece, however, would be his two-volume *History of British Birds*, which first appeared in 1797. (Fifty years later, Charlotte Brontë would start *Jane Eyre* with her beleaguered heroine finding refuge within its pages: 'With Bewick on my knee, I was then happy: happy at least in my way.')[11] Bewick's artistic medium was dense boxwood, which accounted for the fine detail of his cuts; indeed, 'so incredulous' had George III been that 'such beautiful impressions could be procured from wooden blocks' that he had commanded his bookseller to call in the blocks for royal inspection.[12]

Dick and his eldest brother George decided to call on the old man to 'give him the benefit of Dick's observations' on the pied flycatcher.[13] Bewick expressed himself delighted to see them and questioned the boy closely on the habits of the bird, 'taking memoranda on the margin' of a copy of his book that he used for gathering corrections.[14] Seventeen-year-old George subsequently struck up a firm friendship with Bewick, and would go and sit with him two or three times a week. During one memorable discussion, the old man

Thomas Bewick's engraving of the pied flycatcher.

claimed that if George threw some eels into the pond opposite Carr
Hill House, they would soon multiply to ten thousand. 'I took the
hint,' wrote George, 'and shortly afterwards, put in two or three
buckets full, none of which I have since had the pleasure of seeing.'[15]
Another day, Bewick asked: 'Are you a collector of relics, Mr. Atkinson?' Barely knowing how to answer such a strange question,
George replied in the affirmative, to which the old man responded:
'Should you like to possess one of me?'[16] He then fumbled in his desk
drawer, before handing George a tiny packet. On the paper wrapping was written the following: 'I departed from the Place – from
the place I held in the Service of Thomas Bewick after being there
upwards of 74 Years, on the 20 of November 1827.' Folded within,
George found a tooth.[17]

THE SUDDEN DEATH of uncle George Atkinson in May 1814
had led to the winding up of the Jamaican merchant house of Atkinson & Bogle; the partnership which had replaced it disbanded in
December 1824, following Edward Adams' retirement, to be succeeded by Robertson, Brother & Co. The new firm took over the
wharves and warehouses in Little Port Royal Street, the butchery
where the beef for provisioning the navy was prepared, the running of several absentee proprietors' estates, the contract to supply
enslaved pioneers to the army, and sundry other concerns on the

island. The Kingston office would be run by Robert Robertson's 29-year-old brother-in-law, George Atkinson, who had inherited his late father's share of the firm. Cousin George, who was the only one of his siblings to have been born in Jamaica, and who had been educated at Harrow, was by all accounts an unpleasant individual, with a 'very great idea of his own importance' as well as a 'great lack of common sense & discretion'.[18]

Soon George's next brother, nineteen-year-old Frank, came out to join him on the island. Frank did not care much for Jamaica – a 'Dog hole', he called it – and was particularly struck by the locals' lack of enterprise, writing home:

It would astonish you to know how science is neglected here, and to see the indolence of the people, whites & all, on that score. There is no doubt that we could obtain the finest vegetable oils in the world, not only from cocoa nuts but from mango and innumerable plants here. And in the streets of Kingston & Spanish Town the Gamboge Thistle grows in abundance, one of the strongest narcotics known, and from which many maintain opium is made and not from the poppy; this is put to no use, commercial or otherwise, and all oil is imported. Bees of various species abound. Notwithstanding the excellent market for wax in the Catholic countries round us, only one man during the last 30 years ever kept them as a source of profit, near Kingston, and he has not had any since the Storm of 1815 which blew them all away.[19]

Frank had anticipated returning to England many years later, with 'spectacles, a stomach, and the gout', but he quarrelled badly with George and left the island after just a year.[20] Another brother, William, came and went under similar circumstances; and when Matt Atkinson, in 1827, wrote to his abrasive nephew enquiring whether a clerical position might be available for his seventeen-year-old son Isaac, the reply was a decided negative. Robert Robertson found George's treatment of his younger siblings unfathomable, and wondered whether it arose from some kind of unfounded terror that they would bring ruin upon him. 'He certainly makes out his own situation as one of *great destitution*; and if we were to give full credence to his case, as he has described it, you would suppose him to be on the high road to the *Poor House*,' Robertson remarked to Matt. 'But having been one of his father's Executors, you will as far as his father's Estate is concerned, know, that in the distribution which was lately made, he received *his due proportion*: and for his situation in the house, you would hardly believe, after all he has said, that he cannot for his share be deriving much less than £4000 a year – he may try many parts of the world before he will find the means of doing better.'[21]

IT WAS ESPECIALLY HARD on Nathaniel Clayton, as an un-flagging writer of letters, that the use of his right hand would be badly hampered in his later years by gout. Nathaniel's poor health was a constant source of anxiety to Dorothy; but it was she who would die first, on 3 August 1827, after a combination of medicine and leeches failed to ease a bowel complaint from which she had been suffering.

I found myself moved quite unexpectedly by Dorothy's death. Early on during my family research, I went up to Northumberland to explore the Atkinson–Clayton correspondence in the county archives; over three exhilarating days, I read my way through six boxes filled with hundreds of letters, and met many family members for the first time. On the afternoon of my last day at the archives, as closing time approached, I had almost finished going through the final box. Right at the bottom, I found a small roll of paper, the size of a cigar, on which I noticed that Nathaniel had inscribed, in the shaky handwriting of his old age, these words: 'A lock of my beloved wife's hair.'[22] I unrolled it, taking care to disturb the contents as little as possible. The hair was mousy brown, very fine, with just a glint of silver. I fought to hold back the tears when I realized what was happening. I was reaching across five generations and touching – yes, actually *touching* – my great-great-great-great-aunt.

Dorothy's death was the first of a run of family bereavements over the next few years. I feel bad that Ann hasn't been a more conspicuous presence in these pages, especially given that she is my direct ancestor, but this is due to none of her letters having survived. One morning in October 1828 she was pacing up and down the breakfast room at Carr Hill, talking with her son George, when suddenly she grabbed the chimneypiece, murmuring, 'I feel very queer almost as if I was tipsy.'[23] Matt was called in from the garden, and he took her up to her room. She had suffered a massive stroke; soon she was unable to speak, and paralysed down her left side. Aunt Wordsworth rushed across country from Cheshire and found her sister 'still living tho' totally insensible to every thing'.[24] Within three days, Ann was dead.

At the time the younger Atkinson boys, Isaac and Dick, were in Liverpool, where they were apprenticed to the merchant house of J. & A. Gilfillan (an arrangement made through their well-connected Littledale uncles). George, in the meantime, was being groomed for a managing role at the Tyne Iron Company, while also acquiring a local reputation as an upstanding young man. On 24 January 1829, the *Newcastle Courant* ran the story of a boy who was skating on the pond at Carr Hill late one afternoon when he fell through the ice; he would have drowned but for George, who 'threw himself in, and by great personal exertion, and at the greatest risk of his own life, succeeded in rescuing his friend'.[25] In the summer of that year, aged twenty-one, George was elected to the committee of the newly founded Natural History Society of Northumberland, his first gift to its collection a 'very beautiful specimen of the Stormy Petrel' which he had shot over the Tyne.[26] As the society's curator for ornithology, George was responsible for soliciting donations from far and wide. The celebrated naturalist John James Audubon contributed the 'Skins of thirty Birds' in August 1830; he had visited Thomas Bewick at Gateshead three years earlier, while raising money for his own magnum opus, *The Birds of America*.[27]

Following Ann's death, Matt cut a shadowy, shambling figure, and his failing eyesight meant that he could barely read or write;

he died on 24 December 1830. I couldn't locate a copy of his will in the usual public archives, and it took me a while to track one down to Durham University Library.[28] I was curious to find out whether Matt had in the slightest way acknowledged his 'other' family – but this would prove wishful thinking on my part. Whatever happened in Jamaica, stayed there.

'WHO KNOWS BUT that emancipation, like a beautiful plant, may, in its due season, rise out of the ashes of the abolition of the Slave-trade,' Thomas Clarkson had written in 1808, the year the landmark act came into force.[29] His optimism had not been entirely misplaced, for the institution of slavery showed signs of crumbling; in the early 1820s, though, its collapse still seemed some way off. The inaugural meeting of the Society for the Mitigation and Gradual Abolition of Slavery took place on 31 January 1823; abolitionists now set out to present themselves as pragmatists, not seeking immediate emancipation, instead hoping to 'improve, gradually' the lives of the enslaved population by giving them greater protection under the law, and conferring upon them 'one civil privilege after another', until one day they would rise 'insensibly to the rank of free peasantry'.[30] William Wilberforce, who was too infirm to lead the parliamentary campaign, passed the baton to Thomas Fowell Buxton, the MP for Weymouth.

On 15 May, in the House of Commons, Buxton moved a resolution that slavery was 'repugnant' to both the British constitution and the Christian religion, and 'ought to be gradually abolished'.[31] Alexander Baring – Sir Francis' second son – warned that should abolition take place, the sugar islands would be of no further value to Britain. He also insisted that the hardships endured by the enslaved population had been much exaggerated: 'The name of slave is a harsh one; but their real condition is undoubtedly, in many respects, superior to that of most of the peasantry of Europe.'[32]

This mischievous argument – that the enslaved people of the West Indies were 'as well, or perhaps even better' off than European labourers – was one to which pro-slavery lobbyists resorted with such frequency that Thomas Clarkson set out to debunk it in a polemic using adverts drawn from the *Jamaica Gazette*.[33] The first example he gave was as follows: 'Kingston, June 14th, 1823. For Sale: Darliston-Pen, in Westmoreland (Parish), with 112 *prime Negroes*, and 448 *head of stock*.' (Darliston was a cattle ranch owned by the Kingston house – thirty-eight of its enslaved population had taken the surname Atkinson when they were baptized three years earlier.)[34] 'I stop now to make a few remarks,' Clarkson wrote. 'First, it appears that the slaves in the British colonies *can be sold*. Can any *man, woman,* or *child* be sold in *Britain*? It appears, secondly, that these slaves are considered in no other light than *as cattle*, or as *inanimate property*. Now, do *we think or speak of our British labourers or servants in the same way*?'[35]

Over the next few years, the government attempted to straddle two diametrically opposed viewpoints through the policy known as 'amelioration', by which the enslaved population would be gradually prepared for their liberty. The Colonial Secretary Lord Bathurst, in consultation with the Society of West India Planters and Merchants,

The lot of 'the happy free labourers of England' is contrasted with that of 'the wretched slaves in the West Indies'.

THE HAPPY FREE LABOURERS OF ENGLAND.   THE WRETCHED SLAVES IN THE WEST INDIES.

drew up a programme of measures that the legislative bodies on the individual islands were then pressed to adopt. Religious instruction would be given to enslaved people, and marriages between them would be encouraged; families could not be separated by sale; enslaved women could no longer be punished by flogging; enslaved men could receive no more than twenty-five lashes.

Cousin George Atkinson was elected to the Jamaican House of Assembly in 1826 as one of Kingston's three representatives. The members for the town were seen as radicals: 'They are strenuous opponents to the Saints and Lord Bathurst, and all attempts at *legislating* for the Island.'[36] The Assembly saw Bathurst's 'ameliorative' measures as outrageously meddlesome, of course, but nodded them through nonetheless; believing emancipation to be inevitable, they were now focusing their energies on capitulating to the will of Westminster under the best possible financial terms. 'Compensation' had become the planters' watchword.

By the start of the 1830s, however, many abolitionists had lost patience with the government's softly-softly approach to their cause. On 15 May 1830, at a rowdy meeting of more than two thousand activists at the Freemasons' Hall in London, a resolution passed to demand that parliament set a date after which all newborn babies would automatically be free. 'They ought to aim at the extinction of slavery, by taking off the supply of children,' declared Thomas Fowell Buxton.[37]

But first, before it was ready to liberate the enslaved population of the colonies, parliament would need to put its own house in order. The system by which the British electorate picked their representatives was indefensibly archaic, with most of the swelling middle classes still excluded from the franchise. The constituency map portrayed a bygone age, where tiny rotten and pocket boroughs such as Old Sarum and New Romney continued to return two MPs, while the booming northern industrial city of Manchester – an abolitionist heartland – lacked even one representative.

The summer of 1830 saw the eruption of the 'Swing riots', as disaffected agricultural labourers rallied under the battle cry 'Bread or Blood' and set about torching haystacks, barns and farms. The unrest soon spread from Kent, where it had started, across much of England. Many among the ruling class accepted that electoral reform was overdue. 'The state of England is truly grievous but there is no remedy except by the aristocracy holding together to preserve the Peace,' Bertie Cator, who was close to the action at Mount Mascal, wrote to Jane Atkinson at Temple Sowerby. 'Tho I speak of Aristocracy holding together I don't mean we ought not to yield to public opinion. I am anxious for Reform because it appears requisite. I mean that people who enjoy wealth should exert themselves to preserve Peace and good order.'[38] (In spite of all the unpleasantness which had gone before, cordial relations now existed between the Cators and the rest of the family.)

On 22 November, following the defeat of the hidebound Duke of Wellington in a motion of no confidence, Earl Grey pledged his new Whig ministry to pushing through the necessary legislation. Three months later, Lord John Russell placed a reform bill before the House of Commons; it scraped through its second reading by one vote, but was sabotaged by a wrecking amendment during the committee stage. Grey immediately took the risk of forcing another general election, and in July 1831 he won the thumping landslide that would pave the way for change.

JAMES LINDSAY, the seventh Earl of Balcarres, viewed the management of his recently inherited Jamaican plantations with considerable distrust. Following his father's death in 1825, he had gone through the old estate accounts, as submitted by the Kingston house, and was shocked to find that they had barely turned a profit in seven years. It was true that the coffee estate in St George Parish, plagued as it was by frequent landslides and a 'turbulent' workforce, had been failing for a long time; but the poor perform- ance of the adjoining Martin's Hill and Marshall's Pen properties, in Manchester Parish, was harder to swallow.[39] For here, under George Atkinson's direction, and at vast cost, 140 acres of wood- land had been felled and planted with coffee; a works had been built, a pulper installed and extensive patios laid on which to dry the beans; and three hundred acres of guinea grass pasture had been added, enclosed by three miles of dry-stone walls.

The new Lord Balcarres was far from reassured by a private letter from Edward Adams, who, as a former partner of the Kingston house, knew the estates well. With startling candour, Adams warned that he had never known West India properties to be 'ultimately profitable' to absentee proprietors. 'Subject to Hurricanes, Rebellion, Emancipation, Contagion among Slaves, at best their returns are precarious,' he wrote. 'You always are at the mercy of your local Agent, and each of them in turn, speciously and with glittering anticipations may undo the act of his Predecessor by an idle Expense of Thousands. You cannot sell it but on credit, and to recover the amount, you must wade thro' Chancery; and on selling, if you get the value of the Slaves and Cattle, your Land and Works you are well contented to sacrifice!!'[40]

George's letters to Lord Balcarres brimmed with his high hopes for the estates, but less rosy reports reached their owner by other channels. The overseer at Martin's Hill disclosed that the Kingston house, which held the contract to supply the navy's beef, regularly used the pasture there to fatten up 'their own Cattle'.[41] On one occasion, only a small proportion of a cattle shipment from Puerto Rico had been safely delivered to Martin's Hill; and George's explanation that the rest had died in transit had failed to satisfy their purchaser. 'The whole transaction about these Spanish Cattle is most disgraceful, & almost dishonest,' wrote Balcarres. 'I have no doubt he has made a pretty penny of the transaction, & pandered upon me what is not worth any thing like the value charged.'[42]

Jamaican attorneys were notorious for their chicanery, and it is not hard to reach the conclusion that George was plotting to seize these estates for himself, by saddling them with so much debt that their owner would consider it almost an act of mercy to be relieved of them. Lord Balcarres certainly believed this to be the case, but he faced a 'very delicate' predicament – for were he to appoint a new attorney to manage the estates, George would no doubt do his damnedest to cut him out of his one-third stake in the lucrative pioneer business.[43]

On 1 January 1830, cousin George wrote to inform Lord Balcarres that his partner Robert Robertson would soon be retiring. He would continue to run the house in Jamaica, while James Hosier, who had previously managed the dry goods branch of the business, would now represent its interests in England; and he trusted that his Lordship would show the partnership of Atkinson & Hosier the same 'confidence' that he and his father had been pleased to confer upon its predecessors.[44] At this point, Balcarres contemplated cutting loose, but Edward Adams offered one clear nugget of advice – on no account should the earl jeopardize his interest in the pioneer business. 'Consider the immense returns on the amount of their Investment that they *regularly* yield,' Adams wrote. 'What would you get for them, if sold? Depend on it, not a Fraction more than the intrinsic worth of the men, and nothing in consideration of the productiveness of the Contract.'[45]

And so, for the time being, Lord Balcarres' estates languished under the management of the Kingston house. 'They hope that I shall be satisfied with the improved state of Martins Pen, having 95 head of Cattle more than the last year, but they here omit to state, that most of these Cattle have been purchased and a debt incurred,' Balcarres observed to his London agent on 6 February 1831. 'It is like congratulating me that my servants have not robbed my house a second time.'[46] But on 16 May, his mind made up, Balcarres wrote to George Atkinson: 'It is now upwards of six years since I succeeded to my West India property. It is unnecessary for me to state how much I have been disappointed in the expectations held out to me.' Having read some recent comments by George about the 'dreadful state of Jamaica property', he explained, he no longer believed his own plantations could prosper under the care of an attorney who so evidently thought they 'must shortly and inevitably be reduced to actual Ruin'; and thus, 'as Drowning Men will catch at straws', he had recently dispatched a new power of attorney to a gentleman living close by the Manchester estates.[47]

George reacted with predictable fury to his discharge, firing off a letter listing the great strides taken at Martin's Hill and Marshall's Pen under his command: 'The unprofitable drudgery of getting the property into condition to be profitable has been performed by us, and your new Attorney only reaps the fruit of our exertions.'[48] Afterwards he submitted the estates' final accounts, of which Balcarres would observe: 'A more Rascally set of Closing Accounts were never delivered in.'[49]

Meanwhile, the two parties were locked in a bitter dispute over the pioneers. In March 1830, Lord Balcarres had demanded that an 'absolute conveyance be made out in *my own name* without loss of time, of my undivided third of the contract, & of the whole of the Pioneers, each Pioneer to be named therein'.[50] But George refused to comply, arguing that since Atkinson & Hosier held the majority stake in the business, they needed shielding against anyone representing the minority interest who might choose to withdraw a proportion of the pioneers, or even terminate the contract: 'Our object is merely to protect from all possibility of prejudice our own larger interest.'[51] Edward Adams, when shown George's letter, dismissed these grounds as 'utter sophistry'.[52]

POLITICAL TENSIONS had long been simmering in Jamaica, where the planter class continued to cling on to every scrap of power; although free people of colour now outnumbered whites by two to one, they were still disbarred from voting in elections or giving evidence in criminal cases, and disqualified from serving in the House of Assembly or holding a commission in the island militia. But finally, in December 1830, the Assembly passed an act declaring that 'all the free brown and black population' would be 'entitled to have and enjoy all the rights, privileges, immunities and advantages whatsoever to which they would have been entitled if born of and descended from white ancestors' – a milestone in the social and political evolution of the colony.[53]

The island elite had always tried to shield their enslaved workforce from news of outside events. 'So completely has all intercourse with Hayti been heretofore guarded against,' wrote one planter in the 1820s, 'that the slaves of Jamaica know no more of the events which have been passing there for the last thirty years than the inhabitants of China.'[54] But it was impossible to prevent whispers of abolition from circulating round the island. In late 1831, the rumour arose that parliament had voted to end slavery, and that the king had sent papers ordering the liberation of the slaves – but that the masters were conspiring to keep them in chains.

As the story spread, Samuel Sharpe, an enslaved man who was also the charismatic deacon of a Baptist chapel at Montego Bay, convinced his brethren to mount a show of resistance; they would refuse to cut the ripe sugar cane on their estates unless granted their liberty and paid for their labour. Local white missionaries soon heard about the planned strike. 'I learn that some wicked persons have persuaded you that the king has made you free,' preached the Baptist minister William Knibb in his sermon on 27 December. 'What you have been told is false – false as hell can make it.'[55] Kensington Pen in St James Parish was the first of dozens of estates to be set on fire that night, turning the dark sky a sinister shade of orange. The insurrection quickly gathered pace, with perhaps sixty thousand enslaved men and women coming out in support.

By the time the armed forces had restored peace, two weeks later, nearly three hundred properties in the west of the island had been put to the torch. (Not that they belonged to the Atkinson family any more, but both the Bogue and Dean's Valley estates were damaged.) At least two hundred blacks and fourteen whites died in the conflict, which would become known as the Baptist War. In the reprisals that followed, more than three hundred men were executed in the main square at Montego Bay. 'Generally four, seldom less than three, were hung at once,' recalled the Wesleyan missionary Henry Bleby. 'The bodies remained, stiffening in the breeze, till the court martial had provided another batch of victims.'[56] Meanwhile, vigilante groups adhering to the Colonial Church Union, an organization set up by the pro-slavery Anglican clergyman George Wilson Bridges, destroyed fifteen Nonconformist chapels. Samuel Sharpe was the last of the rebels to be executed, on 23 May 1832. 'I would rather die upon yonder gallows than live in slavery,' he told Bleby shortly before his end.[57]

THE REJECTION of a second reform bill by the House of Lords sparked serious disturbances across England during the autumn of 1831; and fears that the violence would continue for as long as the political establishment resisted change were only stoked by the shocking news from Jamaica.

At the start of the next session of parliament, in December 1831, Grey's ministry tabled yet another reform bill; it easily cleared the Commons in March 1832. However, the recalcitrance of the upper house left the government with little choice but to propose the creation of enough new Whig peers to outvote the reactionaries – a measure which William IV would not consent to. As a result, Grey resigned on 9 May. The monarch invited Wellington to form a new ministry; but the duke failed to build sufficient parliamentary support, and Grey took office again on 15 May. The Representation of the People Act – commonly known as the Reform Act – passed into law on 7 June. It swept away those swamps of vested interest, the rotten boroughs, in their place creating 130 new seats; and it almost doubled the size of the electorate, extending the franchise to small landowners, tenant farmers, shopkeepers and householders paying annual rent of £10 or more.

The general election that followed, under the new franchise, brought in a fresh generation of free-thinking MPs – some representing previously ignored manufacturing towns – who were impervious to the blandishments of the West India lobby. From the start, Grey's new ministry faced sustained pressure to abolish slavery, with dozens of petitions arriving at Westminster every day. In the House of Commons, on 14 May 1833, the Colonial Secretary Edward Stanley unveiled the principles upon which the government planned to base its abolition bill – but not before Thomas Fowell Buxton and three other MPs had manhandled a 'huge feather-bed of a petition' on to the table of the chamber.[58]

Stanley's proposals fully satisfied no one. To the abolitionists, the suggestion that former slaves should undergo a twelve-year period of 'apprenticeship', when they would be obliged to give their former owners three-quarters of their labour in return for food and shelter, smacked of slavery in all but name. To the West India interest, the £15 million loan that would assist the planters' recovery from this hammer blow seemed derisory. But the House did agree to Stanley's first resolution, which was that immediate measures should be taken 'for the entire abolition of slavery throughout the colonies'.[59]

Behind the scenes, the West Indians lobbied strenuously. On 10 June, Stanley informed the House that he believed the proposed £15 million loan was too hard on slave owners. The government now planned to offer them £20 million in outright compensation for the loss of their human property; he had received assurances that this figure would be sufficient to secure 'their full concurrence and co-operation'.[60] Twenty million pounds was such a vast sum – about 40 per cent of the annual national budget – that it exceeded the comprehension of most MPs, even those accustomed to dealing with enormous amounts of money. 'The magnitude of the sum almost passes the powers of conception,' Alexander Baring commented. 'In the present distressed state of the country, and in the still greater state of distress to which it will be reduced by the failure of this experiment, you might as well talk of £200,000,000.'[61]

By 25 June, the abolition bill was ready to receive its first reading. The debates that followed were largely passionless, and focused on practicalities; at times it seemed that MPs had forgotten who the bill was intended to benefit. 'I cannot help observing, that, in discussing this question, we do not enough bear in mind that there are such persons as a large black population,' the veteran reformer Sir Francis Burdett scolded his fellow members. 'Everybody seems to think that either the commerce of this country, or the property, as it is called, of the West India proprietors, is the only matter of importance.'[62]

The abolitionists' final objections to the bill concerned the number of years for which the so-called 'apprentices' would be expected to continue working for their former masters. They had already accepted that 'praedial' slaves – those who were connected to the cultivation of the land – would have to endure longer apprenticeships than 'non-praedial' slaves. During the bill's committee stage, Stanley proposed fixing these terms at six and four years respectively, which was enough of a concession to satisfy the abolitionists. William Wilberforce, who had recently said that he felt 'like a clock which is almost run down', heard the news of the breakthrough three days before his death on 29 July 1833.[63] The bill passed the House of Commons on 7 August. Three weeks later, and despite the Duke of Wellington's last-ditch efforts to hobble it with amendments, the Slavery Abolition Act was signed into law.

TWENTY-TWO

A Spice of the Devil

NATHANIEL CLAYTON died in March 1832, aged seventy-five, leaving the Chesters estate to his three eldest surviving sons, Nat, John and Michael, and sizeable lump sums to the rest of his children – largesse that he could well afford. He had already secured his legacy in the corporation of Newcastle, having seamlessly handed over the town clerk's office to John in December 1822.

Nat's story would be one of potential unfulfilled. As a schoolboy, he had shown vast promise, coming top of the Harrow sixth form exam above Robert Peel, the future prime minister, and Lord Byron, the future literary titan. (Byron later recalled: 'Clayton was another school-monster of learning, and talent, and hope; but what has become of him I do not know. He was certainly a genius.')[1] Nat had gone on to practise law in London, where he was appointed a Commissioner in Bankruptcy under the patronage of his father's childhood friend, Lord Chancellor Eldon. But during his thirties he had been afflicted by a nervous disorder, with symptoms that included involuntary laughter and a difficulty swallowing; and after his recovery, he found that he had no further appetite for business. He would justify his retirement to Northumberland, aged forty-three, in a melancholy letter to his disapproving father:

> I should have retired from a lucrative Practice most unwillingly,
> & certainly not without a struggle. But recollecting that

previous to my Illness my professional Prospects frequently
induced a Despondency that was very difficult to combat, I felt
afterwards that I had neither Health nor Spirits to play what is
called the whole game of the Law; & after so long an Interval,
I was willing to spare myself the mortification, not to say
Humiliation, of pursuing it otherwise.[2]

John, on the other hand, would prove a worthy heir to the
Clayton dynasty. After the passing of the Reform Act, it was local
government's turn to face scrutiny, and when royal commissioners
turned up to investigate Newcastle in October 1833, John was the
first man called to give evidence. George Clayton Atkinson would
write admiringly of his cousin's performance: 'He seemed to know
everything connected with the corporation – understand all the
little complicated byelaws, & remembered every circumstance in
such an extraordinary way, that he completely astonished the Commissioners, & has done himself immense credit.'[3]

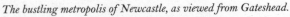

The bustling metropolis of Newcastle, as viewed from Gateshead.

The Municipal Corporations Act of 1835, which came out of the royal commission, overhauled the local government of 178 towns and cities in England and Wales – and John Clayton emerged unscathed from the upheaval. In 1836, an anonymous Newcastle journalist described him as follows:

Has all the craft and subtlety of the devil. Great talents, indefatigable industry, immense wealth, and wonderful tact and facility in conducting business, give him an influence in society rarely possessed by one individual. Was unanimously re-elected Town Clerk, because the Clique had not a man equal to supply his place. Can do things with impunity that would damn an ordinary man. A good voice, speaks well, and never wastes a word.[4]

Everywhere, the spirit of reform was in the ascendant, and the patronage from which the aristocracy derived so much of its wealth and influence was under attack. William Cobbett was a particular adversary of this 'old corruption' through the pages of his newspaper, the *Weekly Register*. 'These blades are brothers, I believe, of the Earl of Egremont,' Cobbett had written about Charles and Percy Wyndham, who reportedly received £11,000 a year between them for an assortment of Jamaican offices. 'They have had these places since 1763. So that they have received *Six hundred and forty-nine thousand pounds*, principal money from these places, without, I believe, ever having even *seen* poor Jamaica.'[5] In the wake of the Reform Act, an investigation into West Indian sinecures was launched; and it was perhaps a tad ironic, given the late Sir Francis Baring's dealings with Charles Wyndham on behalf of the Atkinson family, that the committee was chaired by one of his grandsons, another Francis Baring, who was an unyielding critic of the patent offices.

CARR HILL NO LONGER felt much like a family home after Matt and Ann's deaths, and over the next few years their five children would scatter round the globe. But first, in May 1831, two of the boys – George and Dick – embarked on a tour of the western isles of Scotland. George was the driving force, being keen to visit some of the 'great breeding places of the sea fowl' and gather specimens for Newcastle's new natural history museum – a mission into which he threw himself with energy, on one occasion stripping off and swimming out to a rocky island in the middle of a loch on the isle of Harris, dragging behind him with his teeth a 'water proof bag' designed for conveying eggs to shore.[6] (Dick, meanwhile, 'insinuated himself into the good graces' of the villagers. 'The old crones,' recalled George, 'used to clap him on the back and in their lack of more appropriate English, call him *pretty boy*.')[7]

The Atkinson brothers' final destination was the remote archipelago of St Kilda. To make the sixty-mile crossing from Harris they hired an eighteen-foot yawl crewed by three local men, containing a sack of oatmeal, a peat fire in an iron pot, and half a dozen bottles of whisky. Their first impression of the St Kildans who hauled the boat on to the wide beach was of good health; they had the 'most beautiful teeth imaginable'.[8] The islanders, the brothers discovered, depended upon birds for their every need: 'Except from the rocks, fishing is not pursued, for they have only one very clumsy boat, and manage it miserably; so in fact, fowling is their only occupation.'[9] Dick's terrier, Crab, soon became expert at extracting puffins from their burrows, 'for he is so small, that the larger holes easily admitted him, and the bites he at first received only made him more determined'.[10] On their third and last morning at St Kilda, some boys presented them with a pair of young peregrine falcons that they had plucked from a nest on a precipitous cliff; George took the hawks back to Carr Hill, hoping to observe 'their progressive changes of plumage' as they grew into maturity.[11] But it was not to be, for both birds would fly off.

Mary Ann was the first of Matt and Ann's children to be married, to John Dobson, a Gateshead solicitor. Not long afterwards, in 1833, the couple emigrated to Van Diemen's Land, in the far-off penal colony of New South Wales. (The territory would be renamed Tasmania in 1856.) By the time of their departure, there was no love lost between John Dobson and his Atkinson brothers-in-law, who were furious that he had drained all the ready money from their late father's estate, and grief-stricken at the permanent loss of their beloved sister.

Isaac, the middle Atkinson boy, had left for Jamaica in late 1831 – cousin George having agreed to employ him at the Kingston house – but illness forced his return after barely a year away. Soon he was placed under the supervision of a physician at Kirkby Lonsdale in Westmorland, within visiting distance of Aunt Jane from Temple Sowerby. Dick, meanwhile, sailed out to Jamaica to fill Isaac's shoes. On 10 December 1833, George would write to Dick with news of their brother's declining health: 'Poor Isaac – your forbodings that you should never see him again – I fear are too true.'[12] On 24 January 1834, in a feverish state of mind, and haunted by past sins, imaginary or otherwise, Isaac started writing what he clearly knew would be his last letter to Dick in Jamaica: 'I was as you well know sunk in Every kind of wickedness & set my God at defiance, & mocked him Continually, yet his goodness never tires & when hell was gaping for me he stretched out his arm to me, & has by prayer thro' Christ so opened my Eyes to a sense of my own insufficiency.'[13] He died on 11 May, aged twenty-four, and was laid to rest in the churchyard at Temple Sowerby.

DURING THE TWILIGHT days of slavery, the Kingston house was one of the few active participants in the market for slave labour in Jamaica; in a sense it was bound to be, for it remained subject to a £10,000 bond that guaranteed its performance of the pioneer contract. In November 1832, cousin George Atkinson agreed to supply forty-eight pioneers to the 37th Regiment; as a result, he would purchase forty-one men over the following twelve months. As it happens, the last pioneer he bought, for £45 currency on 23 October 1833, was an individual called Richard; this was during the slender gap between the passing of the Westminster abolition act, on 28 August, and the corresponding local law, on 3 December.[14] The House of Assembly in Jamaica was the first colonial legislature to ratify its own abolition act; to stall would merely have delayed the distribution of the £20 million compensation money, a process that could not commence until all nineteen slave colonies had enacted legislation deemed adequate by Westminster.

One of the first deeds of the Slave Compensation Commissioners, operating out of Whitehall, was to order a full census and valuation of the enslaved population throughout the empire; the governor of each colony appointed men to manage the process locally. George Atkinson was named one of Jamaica's eight assistant commissioners in February 1834, but he did not hold the post for long. That same month, the local Court of Chancery awarded him the receivership of Norwich estate in Portland Parish, prising the property out of the hands of James Colthirst, its indebted owner. Colthirst, who had served as a clerk at the Kingston house for fifteen years, soon took revenge by revealing to the partner of a competing merchant house that George had knowingly embezzled $5,000 which had been mistakenly overpaid while settling a transaction back in 1819. The rival merchant sued for the return of the funds, the case coming to trial in July 1834. In the face of some damning evidence, the judgement went against George, and although this was only a civil case, not a criminal one, it left a stain on his character. George was discreetly advised to retire from the compensation board, and took the hint. 'I have just received from him a tender of his resignation on the grounds of ill health,' the governor, the Marquess of Sligo, wrote to Thomas Spring Rice, the Colonial Secretary. 'I have accepted, and trust that you will approve of my adopting this mild course in preference to one more painful to his feelings.'[15]

The start of the 'apprenticeship' – the period during which it was envisaged that former slaves would learn to live freely – passed without incident on 1 August 1834, which surprised many whites who had prophesied bloodshed. 'I for one certainly expected a much more serious difficulty to have followed on a change so entire & so sudden,' wrote George. 'I augur well for the Colony even after the Apprenticeship ceases. The embarrassed Mortgagor must go and the overforced cultivation of sugar must decline but another & in my opinion a healthier state of cultivation will ensue.'[16]

The enmity between Lord Balcarres and the Kingston house would erupt again during the compensation process. According to rules published in the *London Gazette*, all claims for a slice of the £20 million compensation money needed to be filed within three months of the start of the 'apprenticeship'. By this date, 31 October 1834, cousin George had submitted nine claim forms for the pioneers – encompassing 255 men based in seven parishes – under his own name as 'joint owner with James Hosier'. Balcarres' one-third interest was not mentioned on the paperwork, since the rules specified that claims should be made by those whose names had appeared on the 'latest returns made in the office of the Registrar of Slaves' – and the earl's share of the pioneers remained unregistered.[17]

Since his dismissal by Lord Balcarres three years earlier, George had made a point of providing the earl with only vague accounts of the pioneer business, of withholding his income for as long as possible, and of using his properties without permission as places of retirement for old and infirm pioneers. 'With respect to the House of Atkinson I really do not know what is to be done with them,' Balcarres wrote to his London agent. 'Their undoubted intention is to cheat us in the winding up of the Pioneers if they can, & of course our policy is to prevent them if we can, & it is clear that they will furnish no information unless they are forced to it by Law.'[18]

Although George had shown himself to be devious, it may be that Lord Balcarres was here being unnecessarily suspicious. While it was perfectly true that George and his partner James Hosier had refused to place Balcarres' name alongside theirs on the slave register, they had never disputed his one-third share in the pioneers. Indeed, they had admitted it 'unequivocally', and in countless letters; they had also offered him a letter from Barings, their agent in London, guaranteeing his share of any compensation money.[19] Nonetheless, Balcarres chose to file a counterclaim against each of George's nine claims, a hostile act he defended on grounds of Hosier's insolent tone towards him: 'The few letters that he addressed to me personally, were of a description & language, that in this Country no Gentleman makes use of to another.'[20]

In August 1835, the Treasury awarded the contract to supply the majority of the compensation money to a syndicate led by the financier N.M. Rothschild. Meanwhile, in London, the commissioners began the process of adjudicating – colony by colony, and in Jamaica's case parish by parish – the 46,000 claims they had received to compensate for the loss of 668,000 slaves. By Christmas, the first payments had been made; over the ensuing months, snaking queues of former slave owners and their agents, waiting to pick up cheques from the National Debt Office at 19 Old Jewry, would become a familiar sight in the City of London.

Shortly after his first payment for the pioneers came through, Lord Balcarres wrote to George Atkinson: 'Perhaps this may be a proper opportunity for me to assure you that it has been a subject of great regret to me, that there has been a considerable degree of irritation in our Correspondence for some time past, and which I submit during the very short time that our connection will now subsist had better be discontinued.'[21] The final cheque for the pioneers was released in April 1836, bringing the total payout for 255 men to £6,577, or £25 per capita.

I spent the best part of a week trawling through Lord Balcarres' correspondence about the pioneers at the National Library of Scotland. He had kept every letter on the subject, later annotating some with pithy comments. 'From the House of Atkinson respecting the Compensation Claim for the Pioneers – a Bullying Letter which I answered in his own style,' he had written on the back of one of George's notes.[22] 'A most intemperate ungentlemanlike letter,' he had scrawled on another.[23] Not for the first time during my investigations, I felt bruised by the ugliness of what I was finding. Lord Balcarres' distrust of the 'House of Atkinson' was completely understandable, but even so I disliked his haughty tone and his assumption of the moral high ground, for neither party had emerged covered in glory. Following this research trip, I wrote to the current earl, who had allowed me access to these papers, mentioning my disappointment that our families should have ended up at loggerheads. I was grateful for the kindness of his reply. 'My experience of family archives,' he said, 'is that each family invariably regard their correspondents as rogues and themselves as innocent gentlemen.'

On top of his portion of the pioneer money, George Atkinson shared in payments for a further 511 enslaved men and women, most of whom were based on three properties where he was acting as receiver – Norwich and Whydah estates in the parish of Portland, and Stanmore Hill in the parish of St Elizabeth. Incidentally, claimants were not required to give the *names* of their former slaves on the official paperwork, except under exceptional circumstances; the only individual named by George, on account of his having been 'born in Gt. Britain' – which meant that compensation could not be paid out for him – was a certain William Robertson.[24]

So who *was* this William Robertson? Yet again, when it came to matters of mixed blood, the family letters offered minimal clues. All I could find was this: in the 1817 slave register for Kingston, William was identified as the eighteen-year-old 'mulatto' son of Flora, a forty-year-old 'negro' woman attached to George's household.[25] So William was born in about 1799, and had a white father. But who might this parent have been? Was it George's brother-in-law and former business partner, Robert Robertson? Or could it have been George's own father, George, who had returned to England in 1798, perhaps taking Flora with him as a servant? In this scenario, George and William would be half-brothers – which may sound quite unlikely, but I really wouldn't be surprised. Having spent so much time poking around in my family's past, it now takes a great deal to surprise me.

IN APRIL 1835, when Dick Atkinson had been in Jamaica about eighteen months, a violent strain of yellow fever swept the island. George, who was lodging with his young cousin while his own house was being renovated, had the presence of mind to send for a doctor as soon as Dick's symptoms surfaced. Mercifully, Dick managed to throw off the fever on the third day, after being 'severely bled & blistered', a swift recovery that George attributed to his 'prudent sober manner of living'.[26]

His careful temperament may, perhaps, have saved his life; but Dick was too diffident to flourish as a merchant. 'All he wants is confidence in himself, & activity – what in the world is termed a Spice of the Devil,' George (who possessed Spice of the Devil aplenty) told Aunt Jane.[27] 'His only chance of getting on is to become a clever salesman & good man of business which with the opportunities he has got depends entirely on himself. In temper & steadiness he is all I can wish.'[28]

George and Dick were regular correspondents with their aunt at Temple Sowerby. Jane continued to add to her mother's collection of shells and other natural wonders, and they were always on the lookout for specimens. 'My dear Aunt,' wrote George on 11 July 1836:

I heard from Richard that you were desirous of getting an Alligator and having been fortunate enough to procure one about 5 feet long I have had it stuffed and send it to you by Capt. Hughes of the *Laidmans*. It is in excellent preservation & I hope will reach you so. In the same package I have sent a small Box containing 37 Jamaica Land Shells many of which I believe are unknown in England & all of which may be new in your Cabinet as I understand that the collecting of them has commenced within very few years past. Another Box contains a snake skin of a large size. This was the fruit of Richard's skill & prowess & he would have it sent. I doubt whether it will shew well by that hanging on the little Parlour.[29]

Dick's fascination with nature had stayed with him since childhood, and he was sometimes assisted in his explorations by a 'faithful & good servant' called William. 'I have collected a pretty good lot of Insects chiefly Butterflies which will be forwarded by the *Laidmans* next trip,' Dick wrote to Aunt Jane on another occasion. 'It was William's proposition to collect them & send them as he was very anxious to make some humble return for your great kindness to him after poor Isaac's death.'[30] To return to an earlier line of speculation, I wondered whether this 'William' to whom Jane had shown such kindness was the same 'William Robertson' who was named on George's compensation form?

FROM HOBART TOWN in Van Diemen's Land, John Dobson sat down to write to Dick, his brother-in-law, on 30 March 1837. His letter opened with the joyful news that Mary Ann had just given birth to their fourth child: 'They are both doing well, & I suppose we have a good chance of having at *least* a dozen, the more the merrier say I, especially in a land where they are wanted. I trust you are rapidly making your fortune, if not, pray come here, & turn Wool Grower, instead of a Sugar Planter.'

Here John paused, picking up his pen again three days later: 'I had written thus far, the happiest of men, & now alas I am the most miserable.' That morning, John had visited Mary Ann in her bedroom before going down for breakfast; moments later he heard a loud thump on the floor above. Mary Ann had climbed out of bed, the footstool on to which she stepped had slipped, and she had banged her head, dying instantly. 'I don't know what to think or what to say,' John continued. 'Who now can ever bring up our dear children with the same gentleness & affection as their sainted Mother, surrounded too by convict Servants I cannot bear to think of it. I write in a hurry dearest Richard to save the next ship, the last for some weeks. I must write – yet I feel stupefied with horror, & with amazement, & with Grief – I wish I was dead too.'[31]

John's letter reached Dick in Jamaica, via England, six months after the sad event it describes. A letter from Aunt Jane arrived by the same ship. Dick's reply to her reveals his distress. Not only had he been extremely close to his sister Mary Ann, but his brother George recently seemed to have forgotten about his existence: 'It is two years since I have received a line from him, & during that time I have written him repeatedly; however I suppose the Balls and gaities of Newcastle entirely drive from him the recollection of a Brother so far removed from him. My Dear Aunt if this rambling letter appear to be written peevishly or in an illnatured strain you must excuse it as my spirits are not of the most buoyant description.'[32]

WITH FLAWED OPTIMISM, the British government had imagined the 'apprenticeship' as a time when former slaves might acquire the industrious habits of free citizens, and former slave owners might adapt their businesses to the demands of a wage economy. But many planters – perceiving this to be their last chance to exploit their former human property – refused to let apprentices take days off to which they were entitled, withdrew their supplies of food and medicine, and packed wayward individuals off to 'dance' the treadmill at the local house of correction.

Cousin George Atkinson had been the sponsor of the legislation to introduce the treadmill, also known as the 'everlasting staircase', which the Jamaican House of Assembly in 1827 approved for use 'in lieu of imprisonment in the workhouse, committal to hard labour, or flagellation'.[33] A treadmill might keep 'upwards of 20 prisoners' occupied in the 'grinding of Corn, pumping of Water, or any other purpose where power is required'; it comprised a large, horizontal wooden cylinder attached to an iron frame, with shallow steps and a handrail to which wrists were strapped.[34] Stepping on to the cylinder caused it to rotate; as it gained momentum, the prisoners were forced to 'dance' ever more nimbly, while an overseer lashed them

The treadmill, or everlasting staircase.

from behind. The ground below the treadmill was invariably sodden with blood.

Eighteen months into the 'apprenticeship', a parliamentary committee was set up to look into allegations of the excessive use of corporal punishment by the Jamaican magistracy. Towards the end of 1836, the Quaker philanthropist Joseph Sturge embarked with three colleagues on a tour of the West Indies. In Jamaica, they came across a boy who had recently suffered seven continuous days on the treadmill at Half Way Tree workhouse. 'His clothes had been flogged to pieces there. His chest was sore from rubbing against the mill, and he is still scarcely able to walk from the effects of an injury in the knee, inflicted by the revolving wheel, when he lost the step,' Sturge wrote in his bestselling account of the expedition.[35] The first-hand testimony of James Williams, a young man brought back by Sturge from Jamaica, would also generate a great deal of publicity. Williams' description of the brutalities to which he and his fellow apprentices had been subjected was another reminder that the task of abolition was not yet completed.

The committee was to prove a toothless body; but soon the government could no longer ignore the clamour of the British public against the 'apprenticeship'. On 11 April 1838, less than four months before the first, 'non-praedial' category of former slaves was due to be emancipated, parliament passed a bill to amend the Slavery Abolition Act of 1833. Henceforth, the travel time to and from the apprentices' places of work would be included within the forty hours and thirty minutes of free labour they were compelled to give their former owners each week; the punishment of female apprentices through the treadmill, flogging, or 'cutting off her Hair', was prohibited; and apprentices who were cruelly treated could be freed early.[36] But ultimately it was a ruling by the Law Officers that brought the matter to a head. They directed that apprentices employed as mechanics on estates should be reclassified as 'non-praedial', even if they performed occasional field labour; this would qualify them for liberty two years earlier than their 'praedial' co-workers. Without these skilled men, the manufacture of sugar would

Beneficent Britannia bestows liberty upon an African family.

be practically impossible. Left with little choice, the Jamaican House of Assembly voted to end the 'apprenticeship' in its entirety from 1 August 1838.

On 31 July, as midnight approached, many men, women and children climbed to the hilltops in anticipation of the most richly symbolic sunrise of their lives. The following morning, on the steps under the portico of the King's House in Spanish Town, the governor Sir Lionel Smith declared the end of slavery to a rapturous crowd. All those who had grimly predicted rivers of blood were yet again proved wrong; the day passed peacefully, marked by services of thanksgiving and scenes of joyous feasting.

TWENTY-THREE

Farewell to Jamaica

AT THIS POINT, I hope you won't mind briefly visiting Temple Sowerby with me, in order to tie up an important loose end. Cousin Matthew Atkinson, whose father Matthew had died in 1789, has played a peripheral role in this saga; for while they were beneficiaries of their uncle Richard's will, he and his younger brothers wisely stayed away from Jamaica, and kept out of the feud which divided their aunt Bridget's branch of the family. Even so, I owe Matthew a debt of gratitude, since it was through him that I stumbled upon this story in the first place – for it was a cardboard box of *his* letters that my sister and I inherited, and which I spent many weeks deciphering, all the while believing them to be addressed to my direct ancestor Matt.

Although these first cousins shared a name, and enjoyed fishing together, they were cut from very different cloth. Industrious Matthew (as opposed to indolent Matt) had followed his father into the business of banking; he was a stalwart of the local magistrates' bench, three times Mayor of Appleby, and High Sheriff of Westmorland. The fortunes of Matthew's Penrith Bank had started to sink following the stock market crash of 1825, when optimistic speculation in the wake of the Napoleonic Wars peaked, then collapsed; and in February 1826 he was forced to go cap in hand to Lord Lonsdale, the local grandee, who agreed to guarantee him 'to the extent of £10,000'.[1]

By 1837, after a turbulent decade during which he was never far from the abyss, Matthew had decided to retire. 'I rejoice to hear that you have determined to wind up your Banking concerns,' John Clayton wrote to his older cousin. 'I always thought that you carried them on more for the Benefit of others, than of Yourself.'[2] But all Matthew's efforts over the next few years to merge his business with another more stable operation would come to nothing; more than thirty privately owned banks toppled during the 'dark and heavy period' which began in mid-1840, and the Penrith Bank was one of the first to fall.[3] Matthew was declared bankrupt on 15 September. 'Death would be more welcome to me a thousand times than a forfeiture of honor & Integrity,' he had once written, and in those days there were few things more discreditable than financial ruin.[4]

On 25 March 1841, Matthew's Temple Sowerby residence – The Grange – and his farms were sold by auction at the Crown Hotel in Penrith, raising £26,200 towards his debts.[5] (Cousin George Atkinson, with a view to retiring there from Jamaica, made an unsuccessful bid on the house.) Matthew was meanwhile in France, evading arrest; his accomplice in planning his escape had been his cousin Jane Atkinson. She was now in her mid-sixties, her eyesight was poor, and she rarely left the village; during that winter, however, she started sending her coach out regularly, so that it became a familiar sight around the neighbourhood. Then, one night, Matthew took flight in it. Jane also arranged for his private papers to be taken to her house for safe keeping – which is how they came, circuitously, to be in my possession.

VARIOUS FACTORS WOULD conspire to drive the planters of Jamaica to the brink of collapse during the 1840s, the most obvious being the rupture to the labour supply that occurred at the stroke of midnight on 1 August 1838. Sugar cane was a demanding crop, requiring a large, disciplined workforce, and most newly liberated men and women chose no longer to toil in the fields of their former masters. Many planters tried to hold on to their workforce by imposing coercive contracts that linked the continued occupation of huts and provision grounds to compulsory labour, and when their former slaves refused to submit to such terms, some landowners responded by demolishing settlements, slaughtering livestock and chopping down breadfruit trees. These clashes caused an exodus from estates throughout the island.

Many evicted families squatted on vacant land, of which there was plenty; the more enterprising saved money to purchase small-holdings, often from debt-ridden planters selling off plots for as little as £2 per acre. Within a few years of abolition, however, the standard charge of a day's wages as weekly rent for housing, and the same for the use of provision grounds, had been established around the island. The principle that no planter could force his tenants to work for him was also widely accepted; they were free to work for whomsoever they wished.

Cousin George Atkinson sailed back to Jamaica in January 1840 after spending nearly a year in England, much of it with Aunt Jane at Temple Sowerby, recovering from an accident that would cause him to 'hobble sadly' for the rest of his life.[6] On his return, he was relieved to find March's Pen, his property near Spanish Town, in good order. 'My Farm here has suffered some what by my absence though not more perhaps than from so great a change as the Emancipation might be expected,' he told Jane. 'I found my house here as if I had been absent only for one of my usual three weeks planter rounds – and that not one of my people had left me for Freedom or any other cause which is very gratifying. In fact I must say I doubt whether any body of people would on the whole have behaved themselves so well under such a change as my dingy Country folks have done.'[7]

A visitor to Jamaica, the Quaker minister Joseph John Gurney, attended a dinner hosted by George in March 1840, and observed the optimism of his fellow guests: 'These men of business take a hopeful view of the improved condition of affairs within the last few months, and appear to look forward, on substantial grounds, to the future prosperity of the colony.'[8] Many planters embraced agricul-tural machinery for the first time, having previously shown little interest in it. (The enslaved workers who were needed in large numbers to process the cane during the intensive crop period had always been relatively under-employed during the quieter months, when planting and weeding took place; the plough and harrow would only have made them even less busy.) The planters also looked to new fertilizers to revitalize their exhausted cane fields. 'You should try the Guano on your light Temple Sowerby soil,' George advised Aunt Jane. 'I am satisfied you would find it answer.'[9]

In the end, it was not the labour shortage, but a radical change of economic policy, that sounded the death knell for the Jamaican plantation system. The old imperial model of trade dating back to the Navigation Acts of the 1650s, which through preferential tariffs protected British goods and produce against foreign imports, and restricted the traffic between the mother country and her colonies to British-owned ships, now felt insular and outmoded; meanwhile British consumers were fed up with the prohibitively high prices that arose from stifled competition. For many manufacturers, merchants and shipowners, the adoption of free trade had become a burning cause.

In their shared opposition to the principles of free trade being applied to sugar, the West Indian and anti-slavery lobbies enjoyed the strange sensation of being on the same side, for perhaps the first and last time. Certainly, Joseph John Gurney shuddered at the thought of cutting import duties on foreign sugar. He told his brother-in-law, the abolitionist Thomas Fowell Buxton:

> A market of immense magnitude would immediately be
> opened for the produce of the slave labor of the Brazils, Cuba,
> and Porto Rico. The consequence would be, that ruin would
> soon overtake the planters of our West Indian colonies, and
> our free negroes would be deprived of their principal means
> of obtaining an honorable and comfortable livelihood; but far
> more extensive, far more deplorable, would be the effect of such
> a change, on the millions of Africa. A vast new impulse would
> be given to slave labor, and therefore to the slave trade.[10]

Dick Atkinson became a partner in the Kingston house from 1 January 1844, despite his older cousin's reservations about his temperament. 'I do wish he had more activity of mind and really would give himself more to Business,' George wrote to Aunt Jane. 'I know he thinks me very savage in my attacks on him but my only motive has been to rouse him and to prevent his falling into that apathy and careless fashion which in my Uncle Matthew caused such serious injury to my Father's House.'[11] While advocates of free trade made political headway at Westminster, commercial confidence ebbed away in the West Indies. 'Business is extremely dull here and I think if War was declared, it would do us good, at all events in these dull times we should have something to talk about,' Dick wrote home in October 1844.[12]

During the early 1840s, the Conservative prime minister Sir Robert Peel would abolish or cut more than a thousand tariffs, including those on cotton, linen and wool, replacing lost revenues with a new 3 per cent income tax. 'There hardly remains any raw material imported from other countries, on which the duty has not been reduced,' he declared in January 1846.[13] Peel made an exception for sugar, though, arguing that it should be 'wholly exempt' from the principle of free trade, since to give slave-grown sugar unfettered access to the British marketplace would mean 'tarnishing for ever' the national achievement in abolishing slavery.[14] He also wavered about grain. The Corn Laws had been passed in 1815, to prevent cheap continental grain from undercutting the homegrown product; but they also propped up the landed gentry at the expense of both the urban poor, who endured the high cost of bread, and industrial magnates, who needed the rural peasantry to be freed from the fields to provide labour for their factories and mills. Peel had repeatedly voted against repealing the Corn Laws, but the poor harvest of 1845 and the devastating famine in Ireland made him change his mind. In June 1846, Peel won the repeal of the statutes in the teeth of fierce opposition from protectionists within his own party. They would punish him for this victory, however, by instantly forcing his resignation.

Lord John Russell, a Liberal, followed Peel into office; by August 1846, he had carried the Sugar Duties Act through parliament. The duty on all foreign sugar would drop with immediate effect to 21s per hundredweight and fall incrementally each year for the following five years, until all sugar entering British ports was taxed equally. The effect of this legislation upon the Jamaican economy was cataclysmic. West India merchants in London suddenly stopped offering credit, to the distress of their clients who purchased estate necessaries every autumn with money advanced against the forthcoming sugar crop. A programme to ease the labour deficit in Jamaica by bringing indentured 'hill coolies' from India – the first ship had arrived from Calcutta in May 1845 – was instantly suspended. The planters saw the Sugar Duties Act as a profound betrayal, an act of heedless vandalism.

GEORGE ATKINSON RETIRED from the Kingston house at the end of 1846 – he was fifty-one – leaving Dick and another partner, Charles MacGregor, to take over the business. After twelve years under the thumb of his domineering cousin, Dick found the new set-up infinitely more congenial. As he told Aunt Jane, in a sentence that speaks volumes about his opinion of George: 'Let times be ever so bad, and our work ever so laborious, I have the satisfaction of being joined in Copartnership with an honest, good man, and who places the same confidence in me, as I should always do in him, allowing us, altho' not making money as former Firms did, to enjoy happiness, free from all suspicion of one another, and living on good terms with all our neighbours.'[15]

After the Sugar Duties Act passed into law, mercantile business more or less dried up in Jamaica. Atkinson & MacGregor's most flourishing concern was their flour mill and bakery, which produced 'excellent Bread' and hard, dry 'Sea Biscuits' for the navy – '100 puncheons of 346 lbs. each, per week' – but this barely kept one of the partners busy, let alone both of them.[16] With estates everywhere being sold off cheap, often for one-twentieth of the price they might once have commanded, Dick turned to property speculation. John

Clayton's law firm handled his purchase of the Lloyds, Coldstream and Mount Sinai estates in the parish of St David, subdividing the properties so that they might be sold off as small 'parcels of Land'.[17]

A bumper sugar crop in 1847 caused an oversupply that wiped more than a third off the London wholesale price of sugar, and bankrupted thirteen merchant houses dealing with the West Indies. Not only was British free-grown sugar more expensive to produce than the foreign slave-grown variety; it also cost twice as much to carry it across the Atlantic, on account of the Navigation Acts. Dick wrote to brother George on 7 September:

> The Colonies have been, and continue to be most unjustly treated. Why did not they grant the same free trade to us, as the Slave colony of Cuba enjoys. Why not let us get an American, German, Prussian, or Sardinian vessel to take our Produce to market at the rate of 2s. to 2s. 6d. per ½ ton – instead of paying a British vessel 5s. & 6s. per ½ ton – if the Tories have been unable to stop the very sweeping free Trade views of the Rads, they should fully & fairly for better or worse carry out the meaning of free trade – attack the navigation laws, and let us, and all the British Possessions look to the cheapest market they can find for their shipping.[18]

The Navigation Acts would finally be repealed in 1849, opening up the imperial trade to the vessels of any country.

The plunging price of sugar soon finished off many plantations. 'A great number of Estates are entirely abandoned – and others are following from the necessary supplies of money being stopped,' Dick wrote in November 1847. 'I am continuing the cultivation of Lloyds & Mt Sinai in the hopes of better times – but I must say I often think I am wrong in so doing.'[19]

Dick would hold his nerve a few more years; in October 1849 he paid £800 for the 1,400-acre Norris estate, located a few miles from his other properties in St David Parish.[20] Often, when he wished to escape the suffocating heat of Kingston, he would ride out to his 'pretty little House' at Mount Sinai in the 'certainty of enjoying a cool Bed'; the cottage nestled on the banks of the mighty Yallahs River, with views across to the Judgement Cliff, the site of a massive landslide during the fabled earthquake of 1692. 'A few days there, bathing regularly, set me up wonderfully,' Dick wrote.[21]

These days, in contrast to its past reputation as a tropical grave-yard, Jamaica was considered a salubrious place to visit. Dick's younger sister, Jane, spent the winter of 1848 on the island; he had urged her to come out for the benefit of her delicate constitution. The physician Robert Scoresby-Jackson – an expert on the effects of climate upon health – stayed with Dick around this time, and was much struck by the range in temperatures to be found in Jamaica:

> In the middle of May I left the hospitable mansion of Mr. Atkinson at 6 a.m., after a restless and feverish night on the plain of Liguanea, and at noon, under the guidance of a kind friend, reached Pleasant Hill, part of the journey having been performed in a carriage, and the remainder on mules, over narrow mountain roads, down steep declivities, across the rapid Yallahs River, and amid grand, picturesque, and ever varying scenery. The change of climate was delicious, the air cool, fragrant with the white and red rose, and perfumed with the orange blossom. On the Liguanea Plain, during the previous night, the lightest covering had been scarcely bearable, yet at Pleasant Hill a couple of blankets were agreeable.[22]

Dick must have made this trip countless times, for Pleasant Hill, in the Port Royal Mountains, was a property he managed. But I'm not sure he would have described it quite so evocatively – by his own admission, he was notorious for 'writing stupid letters'.[23]

ABOUT DICK'S COURTSHIP of Elizabeth Pitter, I know noth-ing – on matters of the heart his letters are silent – but they married in May 1849, when he was thirty-six and she was twenty-one. It is possible that they met through Dick's planter friend William

Georges, who was married to Eliza's older sister Julia. The Pitter sisters were sixth-generation Jamaicans, descended through their paternal grandmother from Richard James, an officer on the buccaneering Penn and Venables expedition which had seized the colony from the Spanish in 1655; their three-times great-grandfather was said to have been the first white man born of English parentage on the island.

In July 1851, Dick, Eliza and their two infant children boarded the *Medway*, one of the speedy new Royal Mail steam vessels which had cut the passage time between England and the West Indies to just three weeks. Its captain, William Symons, was Dick's brother-in-law. Jane Atkinson had married Symons within months of her return from overwintering in Jamaica three years earlier – I imagine she must have met her husband on board his ship.

The *Medway* arrived at Southampton on 20 August; Jane and her baby son were waiting to greet the party. Before heading north, Dick and Eliza were delayed a week while they recruited a new nurse-maid. 'I brought one from Jamaica, a colored Woman, but she will not do for this Country, I must send her back,' Dick told Aunt Jane. On their way through London, he and Eliza visited that triumphalist celebration of global free trade, the Great Exhibition in Hyde Park. Out of thousands of goods representing every permutation of human ingenuity – from the electric telegraph and an unpickable lock to papier-mâché furniture and a bust of Queen Victoria carved from soap – Jamaica had offered one meagre contribution, a display of artificial flowers made from the fibre of the yucca plant.

Dick planned to spend a year in England, but was not yet sure where to base his family: 'This is a puzzle that often perplexes me, I do not like Newcastle or the neighbourhood, the Lake district, or the vicinity of Liverpool might suit me, the former I am so fond of, and in the latter there are so many Friends.'[24] At his aunt Wordsworth's house near Liverpool, Dick met up with brother George and their cousin Bolton Littledale, and the three men immediately set out on a fishing expedition. Surrounded by close relatives, with a rod in his hand, Dick was reminded of all that he had missed during nearly twenty years' absence from England; next time he brought the family home, he resolved, it would be for good. 'The recollection of the few unhappy years, of constant craving after wealth, that both my cousin George & Mr. Hozier exhibited – is quite sufficient reason for me to drop Business – while I yet have constitution & strength of mind to do so,' he told Aunt Jane. 'Neither the Wife or self have extravagant tastes, and as to the children we must just bring them up to suit my *Fortune*.'[25]

When Dick and Eliza returned to Jamaica, at the end of 1852, it felt more like a backwater than ever. Everywhere, bush scrambled across the neglected fields of once-flourishing plantations – a total of 316 properties, or nearly half the island's sugar estates, would be abandoned between 1834 and 1854.[26] Kingston was in large parts a slum, with 'lean, mangy hogs' and 'half-starved dogs' scavenging its unpaved, rubbish-strewn streets.[27] 'Jamaica, the oldest colony of the British crown, presents the most extraordinary spectacle of desolation and decay the world ever witnessed,' commented one former resident. 'It now lies helpless and ruined by the policy of the mother-country, that should have fostered its resources, and smoothed its difficulties, during a transition of no ordinary nature.'[28]

Kingston in the 1850s, looking up King Street towards the parish church.

Meanwhile, the island's northern neighbour continued to welcome slave ships into its ports: 'Cuba is prosperous, and red with the blood of the African, she has splendid cities, quays, and wharfs, long lines of railroads, an unexceptionable opera, costly equipages, and every luxury worthy of the first capitals in Europe, and instead of borrowing money from the mother country she sends home a princely revenue.'[29]

It was Aunt Jane's death in March 1855, a week after she turned eighty, that ultimately prompted Dick's decision to quit Jamaica. In her will, Jane divided her possessions unequally among her nieces and nephews. To Dick, for example, she left £1,000; to her brother George's children, whom she considered quite wealthy enough, she gave nineteen guineas apiece. To Sarah and Anne Clayton, she left her furniture, plate, linen, china, books, prints, pictures and wine, and to Sarah alone she gave her shells and coins. Temple Sowerby House, her farms and portfolio of property in the village passed to her executor, John Clayton; the gossip on the Atkinson side of the family was that Aunt Jane had borrowed so much money from her rich nephew that it would all have gone in his direction, whether she had bequeathed it to him or not.

To cut a long story short, John Clayton agreed to let Temple Sowerby House to Dick for the cousinly rate of £45 a year. On 27 April 1856, as heavy rains turned the streets of Kingston into 'formidable rivers', Dick, Eliza and their three young children climbed aboard the *Parana*, and waved farewell to Jamaica for the very last time.[30]

DICK AND ELIZA moved into the ancestral home in July 1856. They found it emptier than it had been in Aunt Jane's day; only the largest, shabbiest pieces of furniture remained, unclaimed by the Clayton sisters to whom they had been left. My great-grandfather John Nathaniel (known as Jock) was born in May 1857, and four more babies would follow, bringing the final tally of children to eight; with a governess and six servants also living under the same roof, it was a busy household.

Although he was just forty-three when he returned to England, Dick would trouble himself no further with business; henceforth the family would live off the income from his investments, mostly in American railroad stocks floated by Barings. He cut the last of his financial ties to Jamaica in 1861, with the sale of the Norris estate to his brother-in-law William Georges for just £500. Apart from Lizzy, their eldest daughter, none of Dick and Eliza's offspring grew up with memories of the colony; it must have seemed a fabled place, represented by their mother's lilting accent, the wooden cases of crystallized tropical fruits their parents sometimes had shipped over as a treat, and the stuffed crocodiles on the gallery.

From now on, the flow of family correspondence declines to a trickle, which means that I must rely upon the pocket diaries in which Dick diligently recorded the events of his uneventful rural existence. Nineteen of these slim volumes, one accounting for each of his remaining years, are stacked up on the desk before me. Snowdrops in January, pruning fruit trees in February, potting geraniums in March, the first cuckoo in April, swarming bees in May, haymaking in July, the first snow settling on Cross Fell in October, the slaughter of the pig in November – the seasons beat the same rhythm every year. Most days, except Sundays, Dick devoted at least an hour or two to field sports; he kept a note of his bag, and if you were to tot up all the hares, rabbits, grouse, partridges, pheasants, pigeons, snipe, woodcock, chub, salmon and trout that perished at his hands, the number would run into tens of thousands. Apart from twice-yearly fishing and shooting expeditions to Loch Awe in the Scottish Highlands, where cousin Bolton Littledale owned a hunting lodge, Dick and Eliza rarely strayed from hearth and home; dinner with neighbours at Acorn Bank or Newbiggin Hall, barely a mile away, was almost as far as their social lives took them.

AFTER THREE DECADES as town clerk, John Clayton remained the most powerful man in Newcastle – 'like the Sphynx in the desert,' wrote a journalist, 'while the sands of time sweep round his feet.'[31] Under his watch, the town had been transformed

*Grey's Monument, at the heart of Newcastle's magnificent
new town centre.*

from an old-fashioned place, criss-crossed by winding alleys and
tightly enclosed within medieval walls, into a modern metropolis,
the clanking heart of the industrial revolution. On a twelve-acre
greenfield site, formerly the grounds of an ancient manor house, an
elegant new town centre had been built from scratch, masterminded
by the developer Richard Grainger; its principal thoroughfares were
named Clayton Street, Grainger Street and (in honour of the great
Northumbrian architect of parliamentary reform) Grey Street.

But for John Clayton's support, the scheme might easily have collapsed. Grainger was a visionary, but he was also an incorrigible speculator, who financed his developments through a complex web of mortgages and remortgages. John's involvement undoubtedly calmed investors' nerves; he not only acted as Grainger's solicitor, but also lent him large sums of money. Clayton Street would be the most 'chastely ornamented' of the three main roads, in keeping with the sombre dignity of the legal gentleman for whom it was named; it was left to Grey Street, with its descending curve and Corinthian façades, to project the town's swaggering confidence.[32] (John would later claim that the bend in Grey Street had been his idea, inspired by Oxford's High Street.) By 1840, six years after the building works began, nine new streets had been completed, boasting amenities that included a new market, a grand theatre, a music hall, a lecture room, a dispensary, two chapels, two auction markets, ten inns, twelve public houses, 325 combined shops and residences, and forty private houses. 'You walk into what has been long termed the *Coal Hole of the North*, and find yourself at once in a city of palaces; a fairyland of newness, brightness, and modern elegance,' wrote one visitor, a touch breathlessly.[33]

John's vast personal wealth, in part generated through his fees as solicitor not only to Richard Grainger, but also to the Corporation of Newcastle and the Newcastle & Carlisle Railway Company – a pile-up of interests that would be unthinkable today – did not go unnoticed by his fellow citizens. An anonymous observer wrote in 1855:

A pendulum of sovereigns – steady, round, and bright – appears always to regulate the internal machinery of the Town Clerk. It is difficult to discover more diligent success in acquiring money over a space of thirty years by the humblest, and meekest, and most common-place drudgery. Mr. John Clayton never speculated. He never threw dice. He never sunk a pit. He never founded a bank. Slow, sure, regular, and passionless – like a Laplander trudging and toiling over a waste of snow

– Mr. John Clayton has pursued the even tenor of his way; but instead of his feet being clogged, like the Laplander's with snow, they are clogged with yellow dust, unalloyed gold, of sure and most indubitable accumulation.[34]

During the week, John shared the old Clayton mansion on West-gate Street with his younger brother Matthew, his partner in the family firm, which had grown into the largest legal practice in the north of England. Both men were bachelors; indeed, only three of Nathaniel and Dorothy Clayton's eleven children would marry, and just one, their youngest son Richard, would perpetuate the family name. Beyond his official and professional duties, John's main recreation was the preservation of the Roman wall that stretched between the Solway Firth and the River Tyne. Locals had freely plundered the wall for its 'well-shaped, handy-sized stones' for as long as anyone could remember, and a passing antiquarian had been dismayed in 1801 to find John's uncle, Henry Tulip, in the process of dismantling ninety-five yards in order to 'erect a farm-house with the materials'.[35] John purchased his first section of the wall in 1834;

Hadrian's Wall to the west of Housesteads, prior to its restoration by John Clayton.

he would end up owning eighteen miles, from Carvoran in the west
to Planetrees in the east.

John started restoring the wall in 1848, and the project would
continue for more than twenty-five years. The techniques adopted
by the labourers working under his supervision – he set aside Mon-
days for site visits – were surprisingly sensitive for the times. First
they cleared the loose rubble along the sides of the wall; next they
used these stones, without mortar, to build a protective skin around
the exposed Roman masonry, thus preserving the original core; and
finally they capped it off with turf. John also ordered the demolition
of a number of farm buildings that were encroaching on the wall,
and he put an end to arable farming along its path, instead introducing hardy breeds of cattle and sheep to complement the upland
scenery. When people think of Hadrian's Wall these days, they are
most likely to picture the rugged scenery to the west of Housesteads,
where the sturdy structure hugs the craggy Whin Sill – this is the
section known to cognoscenti as the 'Clayton Wall'.

DICK BEGAN CASTING around for occupations for his sons as
they approached manhood; his pocket diary for 1872 contains several pages of closely written notes about the admissions criteria for
'Indian Civil Engineering College', and the salary, in rupees, that its
graduates might earn. It seems likely that Dick mentioned this as
a possible career for fifteen-year-old Jock when cousin Annie Clayton came to stay at Temple Sowerby in April 1873, as a few weeks
later her sister Sarah, the boy's godmother, sent a cheque for £100
to cover the cost of tutoring him for the fiercely competitive public
exam to enter the Indian Civil Service.

Dick's health began to fail shortly after his sixtieth birthday. On
5 April 1875 he went fishing, pulled two trout from the river, walked
home 'not feeling very well', sent for the doctor, and took to his bed.
His diary is almost blank from then on – a break that feels shockingly abrupt after nineteen years of assiduous record-keeping – and
the few remaining examples of his handwriting are visibly feeble.
During the autumn, after a moment when the family believed him

to be gaining strength, Dick went into a steep decline. 'We had him downstairs in the fishing room for an hour or two on Thursday, but he did not recognise the room and kept talking about leaving this house and going home,' reported 21-year-old Jane on 4 December.[36] A week later Jock, who had been cramming for the India exam in London, arrived at Temple Sowerby for Christmas. 'It is a great comfort to have him,' wrote Jane. 'Daddy recognised him as he does everybody at first sight, but the remembrance of people passes from him directly the first flush of recognition is over.'[37] Dick died, nine months after the onset of his illness, on 18 January 1876.

JOHN CLAYTON RETIRED from the Newcastle town clerk's office in 1867, when he was seventy-five – he and his father having served eighty-two years between them – and subsequently devoted himself to his Roman studies. As the objects unearthed by his excavations along the wall grew into a large collection, finding space for them became an increasing challenge. A stone colonnade was built along the front of Chesters mansion to provide shelter for some of the bigger sculptural and inscribed pieces; a wooden summerhouse in the garden was also pressed into service.

John would remain active into his nineties; under his direction, a significant hoard of sculptures and altars dedicated to the war-god Mars Thincsus was found at Housesteads fort in 1883. He kept open house at Chesters, and archaeological enthusiasts often dropped by. Treadwell Walden, a visitor from Boston, called in 1886:

The servant who answered our ring took our cards and ushered us into the library – a large room, filled with books, and whose walls were covered with paintings. When Mr. Clayton was ready to receive us we found him reclining on a couch in the middle of the great room. He at once greeted us with cordial courtesy, and remarked smilingly that he had been troubled with an old enemy, the gout, and that 'he was somewhat older than was convenient,' but it would give him great pleasure to show us the Roman remains on his grounds, as well as those collected in the house. He then conducted us out into the broad hall, and took us from one to another of the fine figures in bas-relief that stood there, repeating to us in full the somewhat illegible and frequently missing parts of the inscriptions. We were shown, also, the smaller articles in another room. Of these there was the richest variety. There were coins, literally by the peck, enclosed in many bags, heaped upon a box.[38]

These must have been the spoils of the famous dig at Carrawburgh, ten years earlier, when John's men had discovered the remains of a chapel dedicated to the goddess Coventina, and found a large, square well containing twenty-four altars and at least 16,000 copper coins, as well as 'sculptures, pottery, glass, bones, rings, fibulae, dice, beads, sand, gravel, stones, wood, deers' horns, iron implements, shoe-soles, and a due proportion of mud'.[39]

But mortality caught up with John Clayton in the end; he died on 14 July 1890, aged ninety-eight, and was buried on a stormy day in the churchyard at Warden, alongside his parents and siblings. Apart from some minor legacies – including money for the upkeep of a terrier, Marcus Aurelius – John's fortune passed to his nephew, Nathaniel George Clayton, the eldest son of his youngest brother Richard, who inherited personal estate valued at £728,746, more than 26,000 acres in Northumberland, and twenty-two properties at Temple Sowerby, including the Atkinson house occupied by Dick's widow Eliza and her unmarried daughter Katie.

MY GREAT-GRANDFATHER JOCK married Constance Banks in a whitewashed church in the Indian coastal town of Cocanada on 8 July 1885; at twenty-eight, he was assistant collector of Kistna district in the Madras Presidency. They had met out there, for Connie, the fifth daughter of the vicar of Doncaster, was one of those spirited young women of gentle birth – known collectively as the 'fishing fleet' – who had travelled to the subcontinent with the intention of catching a husband.

Connie brought their three children back to England in April 1893, settling seven-year-old George and five-year-old Jack into boarding school before taking two-year-old Biddy back to India. The following spring, in May 1894, Jock, Connie and Biddy came home again for a short vacation; the passage from Bombay, via the Suez Canal, took seventeen days. (A century earlier, the same voyage by sailing ship, round the Cape, would have lasted the best part of six months.) The whole family spent an idyllic month at Temple Sowerby. One beautiful day, Jock initiated the boys into the art of minnow fishing; by teatime Jack had cast his line all the way across the stream, a feat which earned him half a crown. Another day, Jock took the train over to Northumberland to see a second cousin, John Ridley, who lived at Walwick Hall, half a mile from Chesters; the two men strolled out to view the recent changes to the Clayton property. Since Jock's last visit to Chesters, its new owner had commissioned the architect Norman Shaw to add wings to either side of the Georgian house, more than doubling its size. This was pure *folie de grandeur*, for Nathaniel and Isabel Clayton surely had no need for forty bedroooms. 'Enormous & very ugly,' wrote Jock in his diary. 'Family all away.'

While old John Clayton was alive, Eliza Atkinson had enquired through his land agent whether he might sell her Temple Sowerby House; but word had come back that 'Mr. Clayton regarded that property as the apple of his eye & wouldn't part with it'.[40] Now Eliza and her daughter Katie found themselves in the awkward position of being poor relations to a landlord they barely knew. This must have been preying on their minds, for while Jock was passing through London, he called on Nathaniel Clayton at home in Belgrave Square in order to ascertain the status of their tenancy. The conversation lasted barely three minutes – he arrived just as his second cousin was about to go out – but the outcome was satisfactory enough. 'N.G. Clayton assured me that he would not let the T.S. property pass from himself & the Atkinson family to outsiders,' Jock noted.

This time, when Jock and Connie returned to India, they left all three children behind under the care of their maternal aunts.

George, Jack and Biddy waved their parents goodbye at the railway station on 20 July. 'Fortunately,' recorded Jock, 'their thoughts were distracted at the time: & they seemed hardly to realise it.' The couple's reasoning may have been sound enough – India was reckoned a dangerously unhealthy place to raise a family – but it meant they would barely know their children. In due course, the boys would follow Jock to his alma mater, Marlborough College, while Biddy attended Hendon Hall, a girls' boarding school just north of London.

Jack, my grandfather, was called to the bar after graduating from Cambridge; but he never practised law, instead falling in with a set of rich, spoilt young men. Jack was an engaging and decorative fellow, but he lacked the funds to make a proper career of loafing around, and his father's threats to cut off his allowance eventually took effect. In May 1914, aged twenty-six, he emigrated to Halifax, Nova Scotia, where he found work as a stockbroker.

Three months after Jack's departure, his parents came home to England, settling near Alton in Hampshire. Jock's loyal service to the empire had ultimately been rewarded with a knighthood. The *Madras Times* marked his retirement with a lengthy tribute that was lavish in its faint praise: 'You naturally look back upon the landmarks of Sir John's service when the time comes for parting with him, and you don't find any. And this means that he has been content with simply doing his duty. He has worked well with his equals, his superiors, and his subordinates. And this, after all is said and done, is the highest achievement possible to an Indian Civil Servant.'[41]

The Great War offered Jock and Connie a chance to rekindle their relationship with their younger son. Jack enlisted in the Canadian Expeditionary Force in December 1915; six months later, his parents bade him farewell at Folkestone as he departed for the front with the 13th Battalion Royal Highlanders of Canada. Within days, the battalion had been posted to Sanctuary Wood, a hellhole of waterlogged ditches, tree stumps and barbed wire, where it would experience the horrors of intense bombardment for the first time. Jack had the good fortune to contract trench fever in August 1916;

while he was recuperating at army hospitals in Saint-Omer and Boulogne, and then with his parents in Hampshire, hundreds of his fellow men from the 13th Battalion would lose their lives in the Battle of the Somme.

Nor was Jack to be found in the main assault on Vimy Ridge in April 1917 – an action noteworthy as the first time that all four divisions of the Canadian Corps fought together. Instead, it was his responsibility to deal with the corpses. 'Lieut. J.L. Atkinson is detailed to supervise the clearing of the battlefield,' ordered the adjutant prior to the offensive. 'He will report at Battalion Headquarters before dawn and will work in conjunction with, and under the orders of, the Divisional Burial Officer.'[42] The capture of the ridge came at enormous cost, with 3,598 dead out of 10,602 Canadian casualties. No medals for gallantry would be pinned to Jack's chest, but the mere fact that he survived the war more than suffices for me. He would remain in France until February 1919. On the afternoon of 5 April, as the 13th Battalion was in the process of being disbanded, Jack walked up the hill behind his parents' house and fired off the last rounds of his automatic pistol, thus concluding his military career. Four months later, he sailed back to Canada.

DURING HIS RETIREMENT YEARS in the 1920s, Jock would be struck down by what he described as a 'violent attack of pedigree mania' – a seemingly hereditary condition, only treatable by visits to the Public Record Office and the British Museum's Reading Room.[43] Genealogical research became Jock's obsession, and he poured his findings into a short 'history of Temple Sowerby and of the Atkinson family' in which, surprisingly, he did not once mention Jamaica – the family's activities there being a subject about which he was curiously ignorant. ('Have you among your papers got any information about Matthew?' he would ask a cousin about their common ancestor, Matthew Atkinson, who had died in 1756. 'I wonder did he ever go to Jamaica? His son Richard made a large fortune there, & at least one of his nephews went out.')[44] At Jock's request, Isabel Clayton, his second cousin's widow, trawled the library at Chesters, hunting for heraldic clues in volumes which had once been shelved at Temple Sowerby: 'The schoolmaster who dusts the books for me at present was here yesterday evening & we had a good search for a Crest, or arms, in a book plate of Bridget Atkinson – a great Number of books with Bridget Atkinson written at the beginning but never a sign of there ever having been a Crest.'[45]

Isabel Clayton died in April 1928, and the Chesters estate skipped a generation, passing to her 26-year-old grandson. Jack Clayton had been raised at Newmarket, where his late father kept racehorses, and he mixed with a fast, careless crowd; he soon resolved, having run up vast gambling debts, to liquidate his entire inheritance. First to go under the hammer, in a lively auction held at Newcastle's Assembly Rooms in June 1929, were 20,000 acres of agricultural land, broken up into 112 lots, including 'many capital hill farms' straddling Hadrian's Wall.[46] Housesteads Farm was one of the few lots that failed to reach its reserve; potential buyers were put off by the burden of maintaining the Roman fort that came with it. The eminent historian George Trevelyan, whose family owned nearby Wallington Hall, shortly afterwards agreed to purchase the farm minus the fort, on condition that Jack donated this, plus a stretch of adjoining Roman wall, to the National Trust. *The Times* reported 'Mr. J.M. Clayton's Gift' of Housesteads Fort in glowing terms – but the evidence suggests that Jack was a reluctant donor, and was more or less shamed into this act of philanthropy.[47]

The disposal of the mansion at Chesters was immediately followed by the dispersal of its contents – 'one of the great displenishing sales that has been held on the Borders in living memory', said the *Hexham Courant*.[48] The auction began on 6 January 1930; the eighth and final day saw the clearance of the library and the scattering of more than six thousand books, among them Moxon's *English Housewifery* (1764), Johnson's *Journey to the Western Islands of Scotland* (1775), Gibbon's *Decline and Fall of the Roman Empire* (1781), Cook's *Voyages* (1784), Dixon's *North-West Coast of America* (1789), Bligh's *Voyage to the South Sea* (1792), Edwards' *Survey of Saint Domingo* (1801) and Perry's *Conchology, or the Natural History of Shells* (1811).

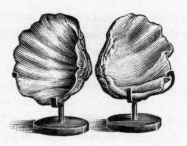

*A giant clam shell, all that remains of Bridget's shell collection,
now in the museum attached to the Roman fort at Chesters.*

These titles are so redolent of the life and times of Bridget Atkinson that I can only imagine they must once have belonged to her. I wonder where they are now.

THE LAST DECADE of Jock's life was blighted by problems with his heart, and chest pains often followed the most trivial exertion, as per this diary entry: 'Chastised dog for getting on drawing room sofa, & in consequence suffered much discomfort for a short time.'[49] He died at home in Hampshire in March 1931, aged seventy-three. Jock's unmarried youngest sister, Katie, died ten months later; she had lived at Temple Sowerby all her life. Following her funeral, Katie's executors spent two days sorting through heaps of old papers, many of which ended up on a bonfire in the garden.

The ancestral house was sold by auction at the Tufton Arms in Appleby on 27 August 1932. Everyone had expected it to leave the family for ever, but one of Dick and Eliza's grandsons – Kenneth Kay, the son of their daughter Jane – bought the property in anticipation of his retirement from the textiles business in Madras. The proceeds of the sale, of course, lined the pockets of Jack Clayton, whose 'bold betting' had recently been generating what the *Sunday Times* described as a 'good deal of animation in the rings'.[50]

Meanwhile my grandfather, Jack Atkinson, was working as a journalist on the *Montreal Star*. He married my Canadian grandmother, Evelyn Hay de Castañeda, in Quebec on 30 April 1930.

(A musical, cosmopolitan woman, she had already been widowed twice; her second husband was Secretary of the Spanish Legation in Tangier.) Jack's inheritance prospects improved markedly after the sudden death of his elder brother George, a railway engineer in India, in September 1932. He returned with Evelyn to England the following year and they set up home in London; John, their only child, was born in March 1934. When Jack's mother Connie died, in June 1947, he inherited a life interest in the small farm that his father had purchased at Temple Sowerby. At the invitation of Kenneth Kay's widow, Dorothy, who was living alone in the old house, Jack, Evelyn and John moved up to Westmorland that same year. When Dorothy died, in April 1955, she left the property to Jack.

In January 1957, Jack took delivery of a parcel from a second cousin, Dick Atkinson, containing bundles of papers spared the bonfire by Aunt Katie's executors twenty-five years earlier. 'I had hoped that I might have brought them over to you, but the petrol position forbids doing this,' Dick wrote from his home near Newcastle. (Fuel rationing was then in place, following the Suez Crisis.) 'I don't envy you your job of going over all these letters, I have looked through some of them & I wonder why they were preserved, there are very few that are of much interest.'[51]

This was the box full of old correspondence that my sister and I would inherit nearly twenty years later, and which would remain untouched for a further thirty years, until I was ready to embark on my long journey into the past.

TWENTY-FOUR

Distant Cousins

THE BUNDLES OF LETTERS tied up in pink ribbon may have seemed worthless to cousin Dick – but they were gold dust to me, for they introduced me to my eighteenth-century family at a time when I was grieving for the family I would never have. Over the next few years, not only would I enjoy getting to know a whole host of dead relatives, but also, to my delight, many living ones. Phillipa was the first of the long-lost cousins I would meet, and I felt a special kinship with her from the off. (It was her grandfather, Dick, who had seen so little value in the old family papers.) I often stayed at Phillipa's house during my research trips to Cumbria, and came to see it as a kind of northern home from home.

About a year after my stay at Temple Sowerby House, when I had been in pursuit of Bridget's 'receipt book', Julie Evans emailed me out of the blue. Another guest claiming Atkinson ancestry had recently visited the hotel – would I mind if she put them in touch? This was how I found out about the Scandinavian branch of the family. Renira Müller, its matriarch, would have been my dad's second cousin, which made her my closest living Atkinson relative, apart from my sister and her children. Shortly afterwards I called Renira and said I hoped we might meet; she warned me not to 'dilly-dally', for she would soon be ninety. A few weeks later, one freezing day in December 2011, I stood on the threshold of her apartment in the Norwegian port city of Haugesund.

The moment Renira welcomed me into her cosy home, full of books and mementoes from an evidently full life, we started a conversation that would last the best part of three days. Although her eyesight was no longer what it had once been – a source of obvious frustration – her powers of recall remained undimmed. She had never met my father, but she did have a clear memory of staying with his grandparents, her great-uncle Jock and great-aunt Connie, when she was about four, and of being harassed by their small, yappy dog – this must have been the same pet that Jock would not tolerate jumping up on the sofa. Renira's father, Geoffrey Atkinson – one of Dick and Eliza's grandsons – had worked in the oil business in Morocco, and she had lived there as a child until the outbreak of the Second World War. Back in Britain, she had served as a wireless telegraphist in the WRNS, listening out for enemy Morse code signals; meanwhile she had married a Norwegian resistance fighter who was stationed in London. Their children were brought up in Norway but instilled with a strong sense of their English heritage; it was one of Renira's daughters who had lately been a guest at Temple Sowerby House.

Fast-forward five years, to April 2017, and I was still grappling with the first draft of my manuscript when an email arrived from Renira's son, Jon Müller. Not unreasonably, he was wondering whether I'd finished writing yet: 'My mother will be 95 years in May, and I would like to give her the book for a birthday present if it is done.' (No pressure, then.) Jon, who is a retired optician, added that he had started looking into his own ancestry, and had recently taken a DNA test; an American woman whose father was born in Westmoreland Parish, Jamaica, had since been in touch, identifying herself as a DNA match, and wondering how they might be related. Did I have any thoughts?

To be perfectly honest, I'm not sure why it hadn't occurred to me until that moment to have my own DNA tested, for I suddenly realized – and I feel slightly ashamed to confess that it took me so long to work this out – that the process might reveal hidden branches of the family tree. It might even lead me to descendants of Betsey, Bridget, Janet, Sally, William and any other children who my male ancestors might have left behind in Jamaica. It was too tantalizing a prospect to ignore.

Even so, I had mixed feelings about sending off my DNA for analysis – because the implications of this technology for one's privacy are quite mind-bending. (Not to mention all those stories one hears about people finding out that their parents aren't actually their parents . . .) The test involves taking genetic material, provided in the form of saliva or a mouth swab, converting it into machine-readable code, then comparing it with other samples captured on a massive database. Each of the companies offering this service has a slightly different sales pitch; which one (or ones) you choose will depend on whether you wish to build a family tree, discover where in the world your ancestors lived thousands of years ago, or find out whether you carry certain genes that might affect your health. I signed up with Ancestry DNA; with a customer database into the tens of millions, it seemed best positioned for tracking down long-lost relatives. A few days later, a small cardboard box containing a clear plastic tube dropped through my letterbox; I spat into the tube, then posted it off to a laboratory in Utah.

Our connection to our closest relatives – parents, siblings, first cousins – is always manifest through the sheer abundance of DNA we have in common with them. With distant relatives, however, we might share too little DNA to register a match, or such a small amount that it could just as easily be a mismatch, a snippet of genetic code shared by chance with an unrelated stranger. I was staggered to find, when my results came through, that Ancestry had conjured nearly 30,000 potential cousins from its database. (I say 'potential', because Ancestry's confidence in these matches ranged from 'extremely high' to 'moderate'; it expressed 'extremely high' or 'high' confidence in my connection to seventeen individuals, and 'good' confidence for 550 more, but only 'moderate' confidence that I was related to the remaining 29,000.) Anyhow – now that I had enough matches (or mismatches) to fill a football stadium, my next challenge was finding out which ones were related to me through the Atkinson line. The only way of doing this, I realized, would be to triangulate my results against those of members of other branches of the family, and see who we had in common. Luckily for me, Renira Müller and David Atkinson both gamely agreed to send their saliva off for analysis.

I felt such a strong family bond with David; not only had he encouraged my research into our ancestors, he had also entrusted me with many of their letters. Still, I wasn't too surprised when his DNA sample didn't match mine – I had read enough to know that there is only about a two-thirds probability of detecting a relationship with a fourth cousin. (If you think of two identical decks of cards, each time they are shuffled, the number and length of sequences they have in common will be reduced. This is also true with DNA, where with each 'shuffle' of the generations, the number and length of common sequences is diminished.)

Renira's test results, on the other hand, revealed that we shared 77 centimorgans of DNA across six segments. I set about compiling a list of our mutual relatives from the matches in which Ancestry had expressed 'extremely high', 'high' or 'good' confidence; this added up to about six hundred people for each of us. Within this data set, Renira and I had seven people in common, including one young woman whose surname was Pitter, the maiden name of our ancestor Eliza, who was born in Jamaica in 1829. The most startling revelation? All seven of these distant cousins of ours were of West African ancestry.

At this point I felt torn. I could easily have been in touch with my new-found relatives there and then – for Ancestry enables you to contact DNA matches through its message board – and part of me was keen to do just this. But a more cautious part of me resisted the urge, for fear of treading where I was not wanted or welcome. I understood that this kind of genealogical research was especially meaningful for the descendants of those who were deprived of their names and families when they were enslaved; so it was very possible that the last person they would hope to hear from was me, the white, male descendant of a slave owner who had likely raped their female ancestor. Nor did I quite know how I would introduce myself under such circumstances. I pondered the predicament for several months before consulting a wise friend, who counselled against crossing this line. Maybe I should have reached out to my black cousins – I'm still not sure – but this felt like the right call. It was not that I had no interest in them; it was that I believed their stories were personal, and not mine to explore.

MY FIRST GLIMPSE of Jamaica is from the plane; I spy the Blue Mountains swaddled in cloud, and tiny cars beetling along the coast road. BA2263 is a boisterous flight, and cheering erupts when the wheels hit the tarmac. We left London that morning wrapped up against the icy grip of winter; ten hours later, we have reached Kingston in the warm glow of late afternoon. By the time I emerge from the airport terminal, having shed several layers of clothes, darkness has fallen. Next morning, on a verandah high up in the hills, I breakfast on saltfish and ackee, locally grown coffee, and a fruit salad known as 'matrimony' – a combination of orange, grapefruit and star apple, spiced with nutmeg and sweetened with condensed milk. Nearby, a lizard basks on a banana leaf, while hummingbirds flit between brightly coloured flowers.

Idyllic this scene may be, but I am here with a purpose – for I have come to visit some of my ancestors' old haunts, not that they would recognize them today. A great fire in 1882, then an earthquake in 1907, reduced much of Kingston's historic business and warehouse district to rubble. Later, during the politically turbulent 1970s, the *rat-tat-tat-tat* sound of gunfire became familiar as gang warfare engulfed parts of the city, hastening the exodus of the middle class to the suburbs. These days only fairly adventurous tourists are drawn to downtown Kingston, as the crucible of the music for which Jamaica has become world-famous. Although the city is largely safe, and Jamaicans can be some of the most easy-going people you'll meet, its violent reputation lingers.

The streets around the Parade – a park since the 1870s – form the commercial heart of downtown. Here under shady colonnades, against a backing track of dancehall music blaring out from tinny speakers, market traders offer wares ranging from goldfish to gold hotpants. Kingston Parish Church faces the Parade, on the corner with King Street, and it's here that I hope to locate the burial place of John Atkinson, my four-times great-uncle who died in 1798. But I soon realize that my guide, *Monumental Inscriptions of the British West Indies*, which was published in 1875, is hopelessly out of date – for the old graveyard now serves as the church's parking lot.[1] Only a few tombstones remain, embedded in the concrete surface and smeared with engine oil – and John's monument is not among them.

Another day I drive out to Spanish Town, the seat of colonial government until 1872. It ought to be a tourist mecca, given the fine collection of Georgian buildings clustered around its centre, but visitors are a rare species – I think I may have spotted a pair of back-packers roaming in the distance, but I couldn't swear to it. I stand on the broad, wooden verandah of the former House of Assembly, the present-day headquarters of St Catherine Parish Council, looking down on the main square, and try to picture the air thick with the cigar smoke of the slave-owning plantocracy. This requires a certain leap of imagination, since the verandah is now a dumping ground for old filing cabinets and other bureaucratic detritus.

The exquisite marble statue of Admiral Rodney, who in 1782 prevented Jamaica from being invaded by the French, still dominates the north side of the square under its octagonal cupola. The Island Secretary's Office, once the lucrative domain of the Atkinson family, remains an administrative building, although it hardly seems busy; its faded green hurricane shutters are tightly closed despite the stormy season ending two months ago. The King's House, occupying the west side of the square, was gutted by fire in 1925; only its brick façade is left. Likewise the old court house on the south side, which burnt down in 1986.

It is hardly surprising that the prevailing attitude of Jamaicans towards their built heritage is one of fatalistic neglect, especially given how little money can be spared for conservation works. It's not as though the British cared greatly about these structures in the first place, since they saw Jamaica as a colony to be exploited in the short term, not settled for the long term; for that reason they tended to build meanly, prioritizing utility over beauty. So it seems certain that Spanish Town, and countless great houses and sugar factories dotted around the island, will continue to decay – many of them discreetly, hidden beneath vegetation, others in plain view. And why, you might wonder, should modern Jamaicans give a damn about these relics of a time when their ancestors were transported there in chains, deprived of their human dignity and subjected to conditions of almost unthinkable cruelty? Why would any of this be worthy of preservation?

UNFAMILIAR AS I AM with the byways of rural Jamaica, and unversed in the local *patois*, I would be hard pressed to track down the remains of my ancestors' sugar estates without a guide; so I'm lucky that Peter Espeut has agreed to accompany me on a short road trip into the island's interior. Peter is well known for his weekly column in *The Gleaner* newspaper, has a distinct Father Christmas-meets-Fidel Castro look about him, and is recognized wherever he goes. He is also a clergyman, environmentalist and sociologist, as well as the author of a historical gazetteer of the island's estates – in short, I couldn't wish for a more ideal travel companion.

We set out from Kingston, breaking our drive to the west end of the island at Marshall's Pen, near Mandeville. This coffee and cattle estate in Manchester Parish once belonged to the Earls of Balcarres, and was managed by the Atkinsons until the falling-out of the 1830s. The great house, built for the overseer in about 1817, lies at the end of a bumpy track edged with dry-stone walls – were it not for the lushness of the vegetation, one might almost be in the Cotswolds. Its current owner, Ann Sutton, shows us round; the property was purchased by her late husband's family in 1939, and its wood-panelled rooms, chintz furnishings and mildewed pictures evoke an English country house of that period.

Ann manages the Marshall's Pen estate as a private nature reserve – the glossy brown cattle that graze its rolling pastures are part of a breed conservation programme – and also, as one of Jamaica's leading ornithologists, conducts birding expeditions all over the island. Her expertise in this field offers me an opportunity that is too good to resist. On the screen of my laptop, I show her photos of the colourful stuffed birds that used to be in the gallery at Temple Sowerby House, and are now in my sitting room in London. I assume they were my great-great-grandfather Dick's handiwork, dating from his time on the island, but it turns out that I am wrong. Ann tells me that these species are unknown in Jamaica, and probably native to Central and South America – regions which, so far as I am aware, none of my ancestors ever visited.

The following day Peter and I are in Hanover Parish, hunting for traces of Saxham estate, the property of Richard 'Rum' Atkinson's partner, Hutchison Mure. Peter has worked out its rough location from James Robertson's 1804 map of Jamaica, where a dot marked 'H. Mure's' can be found at the end of a road – although this road doesn't seem to match one that exists today. We turn off the coastal highway at Green Island and head into the hills; after several false leads, we reach the bottom of a steep track.

A farmer, Albert Miller, soon appears and offers to show us some ruins which, he says, are at the top. Ordinarily I might have qualms about letting a machete-wielding stranger into my car, but he seems friendly enough, and we invite him to climb in. We follow the track for a mile or so, rising all the way; scrubby vegetation eventually gives way to open grass, and I park under a shady tree. We scramble under a barbed-wire fence, then tramp through undergrowth to a place near the crest of the hill.

Albert points towards the ground with his blade; ankle-height stones trace the outline of an old building. Peter and I have been expecting to find Saxham's sugar works – but this lofty spot, with its panoramic view of hills and sea, seems more likely to have been the site of a great house. One of Bridget Atkinson's sons, Dick, died at Saxham in 1793, and Peter speculates that he may have been interred on the property, given the distance from the nearest church – but we see no signs of a burial place.

It is about an hour's drive to our next destination, Montego Bay, via the coast road, passing through what used to be rich sugar terrain; only the conical towers of a few windmills remain to bear witness to that era. Leaving the parish of Hanover and entering St James, we cross a police checkpoint – in a drive to reduce the number of murders and other gang-related crimes around Montego Bay, a state of emergency is currently in place. The Bogue estate, which once upon a time belonged to Richard 'Rum' Atkinson, is these days a suburb of Jamaica's second city. During the 1960s, a land reclamation scheme merged some of the bay's mangrove islands, formerly uncultivated areas of the Bogue, into a cruise terminal and duty-free shopping area; a gleaming white ship is currently in port. We turn off the dual carriageway that cuts through what used to be cane fields into Bogue Heights, a neighbourhood of upscale villas shielded behind electric gates. Apart from a few breadfruit and ackee trees, which often hint at the past site of a slave village, there are no obvious signs of the sugar plantation that once occupied this land.

Much of the following morning is spent fixing a puncture, and it is almost midday by the time we reach Galloway village, which lies within the boundary of what used to be the Dean's Valley Dry Works estate. We pause outside the small stone Methodist church to admire the view before dropping down to the flood plain below. Despite our best efforts at map reading, we still end up going round in circles, and I start to despair of ever locating the remains of this particular property. Then we turn on to a stony track, drive round a corner, and there, ahead of us, we see a crumbling pillar of cut limestone emerging from a backdrop of rampant vegetation, over-shadowed by a towering African tulip tree with bright red flowers. Unmistakably the ruins of an old sugar works.

We pull over. A man emerges from a nearby house, curious to know our business, and we in turn ask him questions. His name is Rawle Davis; he tells us that his family has lived here for more than thirty years, and offers to show us round. We tread carefully through dense foliage growing out of uneven heaps of rubble. It seems there are three ruined buildings – presumably a boiling house, curing house and distillery – although it's hard to discern them as separate units. In a few places, thick stone walls more than twice our height rear up out of the bush; elsewhere an enormous cylindrical cast-iron boiler languishes in the undergrowth.

I feel almost overwhelmed to find myself in this place where hundreds of enslaved Africans were once forced to manufacture sugar; and appalled to think that these people had been the *lawful property* of my family. I can't help but wonder, did my ancestors ever pause to reflect how posterity might judge them?

BEFORE I FLY HOME, the Jamaican Historical Society has invited me to give a lecture about my project. Writing a family memoir is not an undertaking to be entered into lightly; so far it has taken me eight years, but this will be the first time I have spoken about it in public. On a rainy evening, about twenty-five people turn up to hear my talk at a school in the Kingston suburb of Papine; they are a sympathetic crowd, and it feels surprisingly liberating to tell them what I've been up to all this time.

Afterwards, refreshments are served – spicy beef patties and slices of watermelon. A woman approaches me, smiling genially; she introduces herself as Suzanne Francis-Brown, before delivering the quite startling news that she has two ancestors called Richard Atkinson, a great-grandfather and a great-great-grandfather, on different sides of her maternal line. Suzanne goes on to tell me that her mother's family, the Atkinsons, were a tall, light-skinned clan from Catadupa in St James Parish, about twelve miles from both the Bogue and Dean's Valley estates. Her late uncle, a keen family historian, had always said that three Atkinson brothers came to Jamaica from the north of England in the late eighteenth century . . .

Clearly, the resonances between Suzanne's family story and mine are too great to be discounted. We meet the following day at the museum she curates on the University of the West Indies campus at Mona, and spend a couple of highly enjoyable hours indulging in wild speculation about whether we might be related – and if so, how. But there's only one way to find out for sure. Suzanne has already had her DNA tested through 23andMe, not a company I've used, and I volunteer to do the same. It's a long shot, of course – for even if we *are* distant cousins, the odds are stacked against her DNA matching mine.

Back in London, I post my saliva sample to the laboratory. Three weeks later the results come through; they connect me to more than one thousand 'DNA Relatives'. I scan the list of names, but Suzanne's isn't among them. I email to say how disappointed I am, and she comes right back with a message that is typically Jamaican in its warmth. 'Hush,' she writes, 'we'll be honorary cousins.'

APPENDIX I

Richard Atkinson wrote this 'heart-breaking letter' to Anne Lindsay one evening during the summer of 1781, mindful that his future happiness depended on it.[1]

Sunday 7 o'Clock.

I was not disappointed in my expectation of seeing so far yesterday into the business I mentioned, as to satisfy my Mind of the propriety & safety of trusting to a *general* View of the present State of Affairs, without waiting for that more particular one which can only result from considerable time employed in Settlements which various intervening accidents may delay. The Night & the forenoon have afforded an opportunity of making this general Review, and I firmly believe that the anxiety of my Heart has not imposed upon my Judgement, nor prematurely broke loose from the Restraint so long imposed upon it, in flying as it does to the *Counsel* of that gentle Friend who has condescendingly promised advice, on a subject where she is *eminently* qualified to give it. The important question it wishes to submit is, whether under the circumstances to be described, its hopes are too presumptuous to be encouraged, or whether they ought to be submitted to the Object of them. To enable *my kind Counsellor* to judge of this, it becomes necessary to lay every part of the subject, & of my History as far as it relates thereto, before her without disguise, which shall be done in the very simplicity of Truth.

Introduced into Life a mere Schoolboy without fortune & without connections in this part of the Country my very early Years were unavoidably spent in the pursuit of an establishment in Life, which was not attained till the year 1766 when I entered into Partnership with Mr. Mure upon that footing of Inferiority in point of share which was not under such beginnings unjust or oppressive. Those dispositions which have ever predominated in my mind, had in the mean time at the age of twenty led to an attachment, very sincere at the time on my part, to a Lady who (perhaps from our being almost the only humanized Minds that were within the reach of each others Conversation) was not insensible to it. The Family proved in a high degree adverse. Her obedience carried her to break off a forbidden Correspondence, and when at the end of about five years I found myself in a situation by means of my connection with Mr. Mure to expect better Treatment from her Friends, I found that she had not possessed the Stability of Character I had supposed, and that my renewed overtures were received with warm professions of Esteem & Friendship, but *nothing more*; and there ended our Intercourse. Whether some new attachment or what other Bizarrerie of the human character had led to this change, whilst nothing like blame was imputed to *me*, I could not at the time discover, and I will confess that a spice of Indignation helped me soon to give up the least desire to enquire farther about it.

A few Years after this disappointment, other Connections led me into an Acquaintance with *one* whose Attractions I will not attempt to describe because my *gentle* Counsellor shall not accuse me of a prolixity which would be very extensive could I do Justice to my own Conceptions of the subject, but it shall for the present suffice to observe that if they were not in my Eye superior to those of all the rest of the world, the asking the Advice I do would be an act of worthless Folly. Whilst I was taking measures for securing a larger Share in our Partnership, which would have been essential to the success of my Hopes as it would have been vain to indulge them till such addition was secured, the Horrors of the Year 1772 at once swept away the whole foundation & fruit of my labours, and threw the mild Firmness of her Virtues so forcibly on my Mind as to be absolutely irresistible. From that Moment a tender regard for her Welfare took the lead of every other Sentiment, and if I could think I had pretensions to the praise of Heroism for any Act of my Life, I would other Connections led me into an Acquaintance with one whose Attractions I will not attempt to describe because my gentle Counsellor shall not accuse me of a prolixity which would be very extensive could I do Justice to my own Conceptions of the subject, but it shall for the present suffice to observe that if they were not in my Eye superior to those of all the rest of the world, the asking the Advice I do would be an Act of worthless Folly. Whilst I was taking measures for securing a larger Share in our Partnership, which would have been essential to the success of my Hopes as it would have been vain to indulge them till such addition was secured, the Horrors of the Year 1772 at once swept away the whole foundation & fruit of my Labours, and threw the mild Firmness of her Virtues so forcibly on my Mind as to be absolutely irresistible. From that Moment a tender regard for her Welfare took the lead of every other Sentiment, and if I could think I had pretensions to the praise of Heroism for any Act of my Life, I would ground my Claim upon having controuled the strong Impulse of my Soul in neglecting to improve Moments when Compassion & Friendship left openings to try to bring them to a softer appellation, and upon having stood out even the apparent Risque of losing her for ever, whilst I often shunned

Page three (of fifteen).

ground my Claim upon having controuled the strong Impulse of
my Soul in neglecting to improve moments when Compassion &
Friendship left openings to try to bring them to a softer appellation,
and upon having stood out even the apparent Risque of losing her for
ever, whilst I often shunned an Intercourse attended with Effects too
powerful for my peace, rather than hazard the entangling her in
Scenes of Distress which for many Years appeared hopeless.

Useful as the School of Adversity is to the Heart, its long
continuance however wastes the powers of the body. And whilst like
the Traveller upon the Alps, straining over one Hill, I have till lately
still found a higher one behind it, altho' I have persevered from the
Consciousness of right Intentions, and have overcome successive
difficulties which would have appalled me had they made their
appearance all at once, yet the Conflict has impaired the best powers
of Life, and my nervous System has never recovered the Shock it
received from the consequences of Mr. Wedderburn's conduct in the
Rum business. At that moment I stood in a situation to have made *such*
Use of a decision as would have enabled me to have entered upon an
immediate explanation of my affairs similar to the present, and the
delay which ensued with all its Train of consequences, envelopped *all*
in new Obscurity and gave an adverse Turn to everything. I say this
without Resentment, because he knew not what he was doing, but the
consequences have been all that I describe. I confess that my Mind
sunk under them, and that till very lately my Hopes were narrowed
(even in contemplating a happy Event of my Engagements) to a
solitary endeavour to pass worthily through the Administration of
what providence had placed in my hands, but without almost an
expectation of enjoyment to myself from any thing but trying (by
means not easy soon to bring to bear) to be permitted to *take care* of
a very humble part of the concerns of *one*, whose *highest* I had aspired
to be united with.

But insensible Circumstances have led to a Revival of Hope. The
Clouds which threatened the want of Tranquility in the Enjoyment of
a Fortune in my Judgement more than sufficient, have in a wonderful
way, within a very short time cleared up; indeed to such a degree as

to render it perhaps a criminal Distrust any longer to stand in fear of the Event.

I cannot learn that the various applications to which I have been obliged to leave the Object of my Affection exposed, have led to any deep Impression upon her Heart, else be assured, *my best Counsellor*, I would not disturb her Peace by any explanation of my deep attachment; for it *is not* profession, but reality, *that I prefer her Happiness to my own.* Thus circumstanced I have been led to ask myself, is it *impossible* that at the age of just 42, a Nervous System debilitated by too long and too anxious an attention, might be restored in the Enjoyment of *that Union*, the eager pursuit of which has exhausted it? Should this even fail, which cannot beforehand be known, *may* it not happen that there are *unknown to herself*, in the Friendship which she undoubtedly bears me, the Seeds of a mutual affection which would lead her to more happiness with me even under the worst of my fears than in any other Connection? And *should* this be the case, am I not at once unfaithful to her Happiness and my own if I do not seize the first moment in which I can to the satisfaction of my own Conscience say that my Solicitation is not likely to draw her into Scenes of difficulty?

To enable *My Friend*, to judge how far an able Architect may with the materials before us erect the Castle of Reason, of Affection & Honour, it seems proper not only to state as I *have* done the deep rooted Attachment on one side, which if it can excite reciprocal Sentiments, would perhaps be sufficient to cement *any* Materials, but also to enter into some Detail of what may affect domestick Life, and my way of thinking upon many particulars.

My Fortune, engaged as it is, cannot be estimated within a few thousand Pounds more or less, but according to my best Judgement it is as follows – I have the half of two Estates in Jamaica, my own separate Property out of Trade which my Partners have no Concern with. The one is called *the Bogue* of which Mr. Benfield has half, the other is called *Dean's Valley* of which Capt. Laird has half. My half of the Bogue has cost me £18,000 Sterling which is by agreement to accumulate upon the Estate for three Crops after the present one, and

I am confident that the Produce afterwards may safely be relied upon to keep up at least from £3500 to 4000 Sterling a Year, which will give from £1750 to £2000 Sterling a Year for my half. In good Years it *must* bring *more* but I have not a Conception of its *ever* bringing less.

My half of Dean's Valley is nearer a state of perfect Cultivation than the Bogue and will come a Year or two sooner into its greatest produce, but will hardly ever produce so much as the Bogue. I think however it may justly be depended upon as far as £1200 to 1500 a Year for my half, so that the two together may be relied upon to produce from £3000 to 3500 a Year free of all deductions, which is a greater Sum of *Spendable Money* than most landed Estates in England of a nominal £5000 a Year would produce.

Besides these Estates, my Capital in Trade, after taking out all bad Debts that I know of, cannot, upon the Close of the existing Engagements in my opinion stand at *less* than fifty thousand Pounds. I think a prosperous ending of what is now in hand would raise it *considerably* above sixty, and the future Profits of the House upon its present Establishment, whether we have War or Peace, cannot but be very considerable over and above the Interest of the Capital invested in it. It is therefore I think clear, that in point of Property we have Elbow Room enough for every rational purpose as well in possession as in prospect, and in the confidence which becomes this Intercourse I may be allowed without the Imputation of boasting to add, that I am not conscious of possessing a single Shilling that upon my Death bed I would wish I had not acquired.

I am of opinion that a Settlement for a Lady's Life to her separate Use independent of her Husband is exceedingly proper where it can (as here) be done without crippling the Capital that might often be more profitably employed. Not that I think they should have *separate Interests*, but that Independency cannot be too securely guarded. If I become the happy Object of Approbation in other respects I know I shall not be distrusted in *this*, and I should certainly embrace any explanation of her Wishes on this head. What I should myself make a point of her permitting me to do, would be to settle upon her my half of the Bogue together with *all* her *own present Property* which

I would wish to leave at her disposal in any way and at any time she pleases, not only as to this last in point of the annual Interest but of the *Principal*.

I say nothing of Dean's Valley in this View, because it is no way unlikely that it may hereafter appear proper to part with it and try to get Benfield's half of the Bogue, which, unless Circumstances vary greatly, I should wish to add to the Settlement so as to give her the whole Produce of that Estate for Life. To talk beforehand of what destination it might further be right to make of Property by Will, would be absurd. The Event of having a Family or not, and many other Circumstances ought to render it dependent on future Events, but the Principle of *bare Justice* in my opinion is, that a Widow should be enabled to maintain the same way of Life as in her Husband's Life time. How much farther her power should be extended must depend on Circumstances. Abhorring as I do all Attempts at judging for others after we are dead, I should reprobate the Idea of restraining a second marriage. But whilst I strongly approve of a Settlement on a Wife, I greatly object to extending it to Children, as tending to weaken the Parental Authority provided by God & Nature for their Guidance in Youth, and which I hold to be of much more Importance to them than property.

With respect to Modes of Life, I have no settled Plans or opinions, but conceive they must arise out of a few simple Principles applied to Connections and circumstances as they occur. Those Principles appear to me to be solid, but like everything else dependent on Judgement, they would be liable to alteration from the effect of that intimate Communication of every Thought & every Wish which I aspire to. I hold that the true Spring of all human Happiness rests upon an humble Reliance on Providence, upon conscious Rectitude of Intention, and a constant endeavour as far as human Frailty admits to do what appears right under every Circumstance. That where two Minds unite in this disposition and in an unbounded Confidence, they deserve infinite Support & Strength from each other; that every ignoble Passion, every false Shame, and every trifling Vanity, flies before them. That if a certain degree of knowledge of the World has unmasked the warm expectations formed in early Youth of a degree of felicity not compatible with the State of Humanity, no Inequalities of Temper, no unkind Sentiments will in *such* Minds arise from disappointment to such a Height as to sour or estrange them from each other, but that mutual Love will make them abundantly indulgent to each others failings and watchful to prevent Inroads from any turbulent Passion upon their Felicity.

I conceive that *such* a Pair enjoying the Power, will endeavour to pursue what is really agreeable to themselves, rather than merely what is fashionable, and will not affect an over ostentatious Parade. In short they will *use* their fortune in the amplest Sense of the Word, but will not disgrace themselves by abusing it, nor sacrifice their time and attention (beyond what a common Compliance with the Habits of the World they live among renders necessary) to the frivolous, but rather bend their attention to cultivate the Society of the amiable the cheerful & the worthy in a domestick way, which they can never do too much.

I conceive that their *mutual* Honour in the World can only be supported by the respect in which the Husband is held in the Line in which he moves, and consequently that their Way of Life in many respects will be governed by his Avocations. The Mercantile Line is by no means divested of either Power or Distinction without affecting to mix in Politicks which together with the characters of nearly all the Ministers I have ever known, are by no means Objects of my Admiration. I have no wish to be in Parliament, but rather the contrary (unless I am doomed by the failure of my Hopes to seek Amusement instead of Happiness) because the Evening attendance would interfere with the domestick Enjoyments my Soul thirsts after. To dispose of my Avocations so as to have ample time for this purpose, cannot in the nature of things be done on the Instant, but I think that in a few Weeks I can bring up every thing that is in arrear, and that afterwards, even during the War (getting into the Habit of Hours moderately early) I can very rarely have occasion to do any business taking up much time after dinner; and in time of Peace the business of a West India Merchant of all others requires the least personal attention. If his affairs are well regulated, he may with facility spend two or three days in the Week in the Country or make any excursions he pleases.

I am conscious that from the Scene I have been confined to, I am grown quite a Rustick, and that in the presence of that Person before whom alone I am anxious to cut the best figure I uniformly cut the worst. But these appearances against me will soon wear off; my disposition to social Life is as warm as ever. I love some of the nearest Friends of the Object of my Pursuit not only for *her* sake but their own & flatter myself that I stand well in their esteem. In short I am not aware of a single Circumstance except the fear of Health &ca as above stated, that should lead me to doubt my power of doing Justice to the Partiality I seek to excite. But I love her too sincerely to hazard from false Delicacy or any other Motive the Concealment of anything that could have the remotest Tendency to mislead her Judgement.

And now, by what *tenderest* Epithet, shall I adjure *My Counsellor* to tell me whether my Desires ought to be laid at my fair Friend's Feet or not! I tremble from the fear of diminishing the Share I at present hold in her Esteem, but the Knowledge I have of the Generosity of her Heart supports me in the Hope that she will not put an unkind Construction upon any part of my Conduct. And altho' I suspect her in one particular to be *an Economist* yet I am sure she is *no Niggard*, but that her Heart will feel the *inestimable* Value of a frank Avowal – and that if *your happy* Counsel at eleven tomorrow (if not forbid) is to embolden me to submit my Passion – *she* will with *one* Look of Kindness at our *first* Interview extend to me the Golden Sceptre and tranquilize my Spirits by *that* assurance that there exists no absolute & insurmountable Bar to my Happiness; beyond which meaning I will not attempt to interpret her Goodness till she gives me leave. How many Blessings does my Heart wish to pour upon her!

APPENDIX II

Richard Atkinson's will was the mechanism by which he hoped to spread his wealth among his family and closest friends; this is how he envisioned it would work.[1]

An Abstract of the Will of Richard Atkinson, Esq., of Fenchurch Street in the City of London, made on 23 December 1782.

The remainder of the purchase money for the Bogue & Dean's Valley Estate to be paid out of the Personal Estate. The said Estates given to Trustees for the following purposes, vizt.

1st. To carry on the Cultivation & Improvement thereof.

2nd. To pay the following Annuities, vizt.
£700 per annum to Lady Anne Lindsay – To commence at my decease
£700 per annum to Lady Margaret Fordyce – ditto
with £300 continued after her death to Mr. Fordyce – ditto
£700 per annum to John Robinson – ditto
£50 per annum to Thomas Hogg – ditto
£1,800 per annum to nine Nieces – To commence as they come of age
£200 per annum to Geo. Fordyce's 2 Daughters – ditto

And for the five first years during which the Estates may hardly come to their full yielding, the Personal Estate to make good all deficiencies.

3rd & 4th & 5th. To raise a fund out of the overplus of the produce of the Real Estates, which is to stand as a security against accidents to the Estates and to make good all such, and to accumulate till the year 1803 when my youngest nephew will come of age. And at that time if the Fund does not amount to £15,000, it is to be continued till it does.

If it amounts to more, then £15,000 is to be reserved for the purpose herein after mentioned, and the overplus to be added to the balance of the Personal Estate, and if both shall be sufficient to give £4,000 a piece or more to each of my nieces & each of Lady Anne Lindsay's Daughters (after paying the Legacies of £3,000 a piece to my nephews out of such balance) then the whole is to be so divided; but if the Fund is not sufficient it is to be continued till it becomes sufficient.

6th. If the Savings & Personal Estate added together shall have raised the Fund of £15,000 and paid the Nephews & Nieces as in the last article, before the annuities are reduced to £2,500 per annum the further savings till such Reduction happens to be added to the £15,000.

7th & 8th. When the annuities shall be so reduced to £2,500 per annum, to pay Lady Anne Lindsay £5,000, and all the savings above £15,000, or in case of her death as she shall by Will appoint, and to convey my half of the Bogue Estate to my Brother George's Male Heirs.

9th. Thence forward to pay the annuities out of Dean's Valley and the £10,000 remaining in the Fund, & pay the future Savings to my Brother Matthew's Male Heirs.

10th. When the annuities are reduced to £2,000 per annum, to pay Lady Anne Lindsay out of the Fund £5,000 more.

11th. When reduced to £1,500 per annum, to pay her the remaining £5,000.

And lastly, when all the annuities cease, to convey Dean's Valley Estate to my Brother Matthew's Male Heirs.

All Estates the property of the Partnership of which the legal Title may happen to be vested in me given to the Partnership.

The Sums of £4,500 lent to Lord Wentworth & £15,653 to the Bentinck Estate declared to be Lady Anne Lindsay's property, and all accounts settled with her to the time of my death.

All Sums advanced to Mr. Nevill given to John Robinson.

All Sums due by Mr. Fordyce given to Lord Balcarres.

House in Fenchurch Street and all loose scattered Effects left to the Partnership and the Balance directed to be settled at £75,000.

Out of the Personal Estate the future payments for the purchase money of the Bogue and Dean's Valley to be made.

Also £10,000 to be laid out on those Estates.

And £5,000 set apart for Lady Margaret Fordyce.

And to pay £200 per annum annuity to my Brother Matthew & his wife
    £200 per annum to Mr. & Mrs. Taylor
    £200 per annum to my Brother George's widow
    £200 per annum to Wm. Bentinck till his mother dies

And to pay £3,000 a piece to my nephews as they come of age. And at the Division of the Personal Estate in the year 1803 as above mentioned to pay them £3,000 a piece more and then divide the remainder as before mentioned.

APPENDIX III

This is a small selection from the compendious book of 'receipts' which Bridget Atkinson wrote out for her daughter Dorothy Clayton, a labour of love that she started on 8 January 1806.

Minced Pyes – Wolsingham – 1758
Take a pound of Apples a pound of Beef Suet, shred small a pound of Currants, clean picked and washed, and rubbed, three quarters of a pound of Sugar, a small Nutmeg, a Little Cloves, Cinamon, and Mace, one Large Lemon or Seville orange pared, as thin as posible and shred very fine, then squeeze in the Juice of the Lemon, and Orange, two or three spoonfulls of Sweet Mountain, or Sack, if not Sharp enough put in a Little more Lemon Juice or Verjuice, put in Candied Orange Lemon or Cittron as you think proper and besure bake them in fine puff Paste – Note – I think these will be near as good as the Lemon Minced Pyes.

Bread and Butter Pudding with a Crust
Choose a penny Loaf of a day old, and cut it into Bread and Butter as for Tea, make a rich puff Crust and cover with it the bottem and sides of a Dish, Butter the Crust, and Lay the slices handsomly in the Dish wash and pick some Currants very well and strew them over the Slices of Bread and Butter, then some more Bread & Butter then more currants till your Dish is half full and no more, beat four eggs with a Pint of Cream dust in a Little Salt grate in a Little Nutmeg, sweeten it to your taste, and Last of all add two teaspoonfulls of Rose water and one of Orange Flower water, pour the whole into the Dish upon the Bread & Butter & send it to the Oven half an Hour will bake it.

Snow and Custard

Make a rich boiled custard, and put it in a China or Glass Bason, take the whites of eight Eggs and beat them up with water and triple refined sugar, put some milk and water into a stew pan, and when it boils, take the froth and Lay it on the milk & water and just give a boil Lay it on the custard to serve it up.

A Syllabub under a Cow

You may make your Syllabub of wine, or Cyder, sweeten it and grate nutmeg into it milk the milk into it or you may make it at home by heating milk as hott as from the Cow pour it out of a Tea pot only holding it very high while you pour it and pour over the top half a Pint of Cream.

Mackroons

Take a pound of Sweet Almonds and blanch, and beat them in a Marble morter, and whilst you are beating them moisten them with the whites of eggs, or with Orange Flower water or Rose water, Least they oil, then take a pound of fine Sugar, and beat and sift it; and four whites of eggs, and a Little musk, beat all well together and shape them round on Wafer paper and bake them carefully in a Slow Oven or at Least a gentle one.

Pepper Cake – Miss Lambert – Newbrough

Take three pound of Treacle, set it before the fire to warm a Little, three pound and a quarter of Flour, two Ounces of beat Ginger, two Ounces of Carraway Seeds, and one Ounce of Jamaica pepper, all grownd in the same mill, and Sifted, six Ounces of Sugar, and five eggs. Beat them and run them thorough a Seive or Strainer three quarters of a pound of Butter disolved in the Oven, the rind of a Lemon cut small, half a Pint of Brandy mix the Treacle, and Butter, together then add the Other ingredeints, beat it well for half an Hour, with a wooden spoon, put in Candied Lemon or Orange as much as you please; Butter and paper your Cake pan, and bake it in a Soaking Oven, it will take three Hours to bake it – NB – I think it must mean the twenty ounce pound.

To Pickle Mackrell call'd Caveach

Cut your Mackrell into round peices, divide one into five or six peices, to five or six Mackrell, you may take an ounce of beaten pepper, three Large Nutmegs, a Little Mace, and a Little Salt, mix your Salt and beaten Spice, together, make three or four holes in each peice, and put some seasoning in each hole, and rub the peices over with the Seasoning fry them brown in Oil, and Let them stand till they are cold, then put them into Vinegar and cover them with oil they will keep a Long time if well cured and are dilicious – Black pepper and Jamaica pepper do extreemly well soals or trouts are extreemly proper to Caveach but the vinegar must be boiled before you put in your Fish.

To Pickle Colliflowers – yellow

Take the whitest and hardest Cauliflowers you can get and cut them in Little peices, and throw a handfull of salt amongst them cover them with a cloth, and Let them Lay in the brine for two or three days, then drain them in a Culender, and spread them seperatly on Stone Dishes, and set them in a cool Oven and Let them stand till they are as dry as a chip, then boil some vinegar and pour upon them to take out the salt in some degree boil some more vinegar with Black Pepper and Jamaica and Long Pepper and a Capsicum if you have any if not put in some Sliced Onion but first pour on the boiling Vinegar and Spices on the Cauliflowers slice in Onions Horse radish and a good deal of white mustard seed and fine Turmeric – to colour it yellow.

To preserve Strawberrys – Miss Hasell, Dalemain

Take three pound of Loaf Sugar, to four pound of Strawberrys, you must be carefull not to boil them too much but when they Look clear they are enough, try them by taking a Little up in a Spoon, when they frett boil them up again at the end of a few days, and then you may put a paper close over them dip'd in Brandy, it is best to put them in small Jarrs, so as to use one at a time it will not keep open but will Lose their Colour.

To Make Currie Powder – Mrs Scott

Take a quarter of a pound of Turmeric, one ounce of white cummin Seed, half an Ounce of Corriander Seed, one Ounce of Powdered Ginger, a quarter of an Ounce of black pepper I rather think Cayen pepper, is meant instead of Black, three Ounces of the small black mustard seed, parched & beaten to Powder, these will cost Little more than a shilling and will make a Dozen or two of Curries, when you have used the first quantity you will know how to moderate the ingredients to your pallate if there should be any too predominating only observe it should taste of Cayen pretty hott.

To Make Portable Soup for travellers

Take three Large Logs of Veal, and one of Beef, the Lean part of half a Ham, cut them in Small peices, put a quarter of a pound of Butter at the Bottem of a Cauldron then Lay in the meat and Bones with four ounces of Anchovies, two ounces of Mace the white of six heads of Cellery, wash them quite clean, and cut them small and cut three Large Carrots cut thin put them in and cover the Cauldron close and set it on a moderate fire and Let it boil slowly for four Hours, but first when the gravy begins to draw, keep taking it out 'till you have got it all out, then put in as much water as will cover the meat, and Let it boil slowly for four Hours, then Strain it through a Hair Seive and put it into a Clean pan, and Let it boil three parts away and then put in the Gravy you drew from the meat strain it and Let it boil gently and Skim it clean till it Looks Like Glew, take great care it dos not burn: put in Cayen pepper to your taste and Salt pour it in to flat earthen Dishes a quarter of an Inch thick, the next day cut them in to small thin peices and set them in the Sun or in a cool oven to dry. The Soup will answer best to be made in frosty weather when the cakes are dry put them in a tin box with writing paper between them keep them in a dry place – when you want to use them put one in a Bason and pour Boiling water on it.

To make Coffee

To a quart of Boiling water put an Ounce of grownd Coffee if must be Turkey Coffee, for Plantation Coffee dos not go so far Let it just boil up, try that the spoot of your Coffee pot, be clear that it may pour out, after that Let it stand a few minutes that the grownds may settle, and it will be fitt to drink, some sweeten Coffee with Loaf, and some with Lisbon sugar, but Sugar Candy is the best, it is now very common for those who Like mustard, to put a teaspoonfull of Durham Flour of Mustard amongst the Coffee as soon as it is grownd it helps the flavour and is very wholsome, some break in an egg when it is boiling it helps to clear it.

To Stop a Bleeding of the Nose

Take a peice of Cap paper, and double it severall times and Lay it upon the Tongue, and press it against the roof of the Mouth till the Bleeding Stops – this was given to Captain Isaac Barras of Whitehaven when he was a Prisoner in France by an Old woman and as it is easyly try'd it is worth while to try it.

A Hint to prevent Bowell Complaints

To prevent Bowell Complaints now so prevalent an eminent Physician recomends a few pepper corns, to be put into the water in which greens are boiled, or any vegetables as it in part will corect the windyness.

For a Pin or Fish Bone in the throat

Make the person swallow the white of an egg, and if that will not do make them swallow an other and the second almost always carrys the Pin or Bone down with it, the experement is easy and has been successfull.

For the Gripes in a Horse

Two ounces of Rubarb – half an ounce of Laudanum – half a Pint of Gin mix them in half a Pint of warm water and give it to the Horse – good.

A Cement for China

Take a peice of Cheshire or Gloscester Cheese and boil it in three or four diferent waters, till it forms a soft & elastic mass, and while yet warm it must be rubbed upon a peice of marble: such as is used by Colourmen and as much unslacked Lime in powder as will be absorbed by the Cheese, without making it too hard – this forms one of the most impenetrable Cements if suffered to dry gradualy and slow it will stand fire as well as water.

To take Grease out of Silk or Stuff

Take a pound of Fullers earth dry it in an Oven & beat and Sift it very fine, a quarter of a pound of starch dry'd, beat and sifted, sixpenny worth of Camphor put it into a Jack of spirit of wine, then add to it a jack of Spirit of Turpentine, mix them well together and put it into a Bottle, cork it close and set it into a Cellar when you want it shake a Little out of the Bottle on the Spot.

To distroy Moths

Make a Powder of Sassafras Wood, the Flowers of Lavender and the dry'd Leaves of Rhue, Lay them in Small Sprinklings amongst your Linnen Cloths Silk or Linnens, scent your Drawer Trunks and Clossets with them but if they eat your Hangings but if you cannot get well to them with the Powder, then burn Sulpher and Storax in the Room the Doors and windows being Close shut, will uterly distroy them, without damaging the Hangings, and will keep them clear for Six Months smoaking the rooms is an exceeding good thing and ought to be done every year about Lammas – with Sulpher at Least.

To Prevent Milk from having a taste of Turneps

Dissolve two Ounces of Salt Petre in a Little warm water, and put it in a quart Bottle and fill it up with cold water, put a good teacupfull of it to ten or twelve quarts of milk as soon as it is brought in and stir it well together before you Sile it.

To preserve Arms from Rust

Take a pound of Hogs Lard, an Ounce of Camphor, and as much black Lead as will turn the mixture an Iron colour, melt it and when Cold rub it on the Arms and Let it be with a peice of Leather or woolen cloth – or some small shot in Oil of Olives or any other vegetable oil will make a tolerable good steel preservative.

Berry Bushes – infected with caterpillars

If your Berrybushes are infested with the Little Green Caterpillars, take a branch of Elder and dash them very much with it and Leave a small peice of Elder in every Bush, it is of great Service tho' perhaps not an effectual cure – it ought certainly to be try'd.

A NOTE ON LANGUAGE

When quoting from letters, newspapers and other sources I've kept original capitalizations and spellings, except where they obscure the meaning. In addition to pruning some long-winded passages, I've taken a few liberties with punctuation; to Bridget Atkinson's letters, in particular, I have added a sprinkling of full stops.

Slavery was a condition imposed upon millions of Africans against their will, and its terminology was devised to strip them of their dignity. Much of this language is today considered derogatory or offensive. Where possible, I have referred to 'enslaved' men and women, rather than 'slaves', to highlight their humanity and not simply the cruel status that was forced upon them.

A NOTE ON TYPE

The text is set in Bell, a typeface commissioned by the publisher John Bell, and created by the engraver Richard Austin in 1788.

A NOTE ON MONEY AND MEASUREMENTS

Under the old, pre-decimal system of pounds, shillings and pence, £1 consisted of 240 pence (denoted by the letter 'd' for the Latin *denarius*), with 12 pence making a shilling, and 20 shillings ('s' for *solidus*) making a pound. A guinea was worth 21 shillings, or £1 1s.

During the period covered by this book, Jamaican currency was worth less than its counterpart in Britain – £1 8s currency equalled £1 sterling. Monetary figures in the text are in pounds sterling, except where I have specified 'currency'.

It is impossible to estimate the modern value of historic sums with even the slightest accuracy, for the relative values of what money might buy – commodities, food, labour, manufactured goods, property – have fluctuated too greatly in the interim. Moreover, it depends on which yardstick you use – retail prices, say, or average earnings. MeasuringWorth.com, a useful resource on this subject, estimates the 2018 value of £1 from the years given below:

	using retail price index	using average earnings
1750	£155	£1,925
1775	£125	£1,650
1800	£79	£1,147
1825	£81	£841
1850	£105	£796

The gulf between these figures rather suggests the limitations of the exercise. When George Atkinson died in 1814, his fortune was valued at £140,000; according to these criteria, it would today either be worth £9.6 million, or £107 million.

Some container sizes, mostly taken from Johnson's *Dictionary*:

> Barrel: 36 gallons
> Bushel: 8 gallons
> Cask: a barrel of any size, smaller than a hogshead
> Chaldron: a measure of coals, 2000 lb in weight
> Firkin: ¼ barrel, 9 gallons
> Hogshead (Hhd): 60 gallons
> Pipe: 2 hogsheads
> Puncheon: 102 gallons
> Quarter: 8 bushels

BIBLIOGRAPHY

ABBREVIATIONS

AF	Atkinson Family
AP	Abergavenny Papers, Eridge Park
BA	Baring Archive, London
BC	Boston College, Chestnut Hill
BL	British Library, London
BLO	Bodleian Library, Oxford
CAE	Cambridgeshire Archives, Ely
CAK	Cumbria Archives, Kendal
CL	Caird Library, National Maritime Museum, Greenwich
CUL	Cambridge University Library, Cambridge
DM	Devonshire Manuscripts, Chatsworth
DUL	Durham University Library, Durham
EUL	Edinburgh University Library, Edinburgh
GM	*Gentleman's Magazine*
HA	Hertfordshire Archives, Hertford
HL	Huntington Library, San Marino
HRO	Hampshire Record Office, Winchester
ICWS	Institute of Commonwealth Studies, London
JA	Jamaica Archives, Spanish Town
KA	Kent Archives, Maidstone
KCUP	Kislak Center, University of Pennsylvania, Philadelphia
LSF	Library of the Society of Friends, London

NA	National Archives, Kew
NAM	National Army Museum, London
NAW	Northumberland Archives, Woodhorn
NHSN	Natural History Society of Northumbria, Newcastle
NJHS	New Jersey Historical Society, Newark
NJSA	New Jersey State Archives, Trenton
NLS	National Library of Scotland, Edinburgh
NLW	National Library of Wales, Aberystwyth
NRS	National Records of Scotland, Edinburgh
NYHS	New-York Historical Society, New York
RGDJ	Registrar-General's Department, Jamaica
RM	Ringwood Manor, New Jersey
SA	Staffordshire Archives, Stafford
SRO	Suffolk Record Office, Lowestoft
SV	Slave Voyages (see Digital Resources)
TWA	Tyne & Wear Archives, Newcastle
UNA	University of Nottingham Archives, Nottingham
WL	Wellcome Library, London
YUL	Yale University Library, New Haven

DIGITAL RESOURCES

The Burney Collection
(https://www.bl.uk/collection-guides/burney-collection)
The vast newspaper collection of the Rev. Charles Burney, now
digitized and searchable online. A tip for researchers: bear in mind
that during the eighteenth century a letter resembling 'f' was used
for an 's' at the start or in the middle of a word, so a word search
for 'Atkinfon' (for example) will yield many more results than
one for 'Atkinson'.

Founders Online (http://founders.archives.gov)
The correspondence and other writings of six founding fathers
of the United States – George Washington, Benjamin Franklin,
John Adams, Thomas Jefferson, Alexander Hamilton and James
Madison – searchable by date, author and recipient.

Legacies of British Slave-ownership (https://www.ucl.ac.uk/lbs/)
A centre for the study of colonial slavery and its legacy in
modern-day Britain. Its database identifies all the slave owners
in the British West Indies, the Cape and Mauritius who claimed
compensation following the abolition of slavery in 1833; it also
includes the ownership histories of thousands of estates.

National Library of Scotland: Maps of Jamaica
(https://maps.nls.uk/jamaica/)
James Robertson's map of Jamaica, published in 1804, is the most
detailed survey of the island at the height of its prosperity, showing
the location of more than eight hundred sugar plantations. Now
georeferenced, it can be viewed as a zoomable overlay on a modern
Google map – an invaluable resource for those tracking down
old estates.

The Papers of George Washington: Digital Edition
(https://rotunda.upress.virginia.edu)
The letters and diaries of the first President of the United States,
searchable within the text as well as by date, author and recipient.

Slave Voyages (https://www.slavevoyages.org)
A comprehensive database of the transatlantic slave trade, drawing
on British, Dutch, French, Portuguese and Spanish-language
archives around the Atlantic world. It shines light on more than
36,000 slave-trading voyages, giving details of itineraries, dates,
nationalities, names of ships, captains and shipowners, embarkation
numbers and mortality rates.

PRIMARY SOURCES

Acts of the Council and General Assembly of the State of New-Jersey
    (1784)
Almon, John: *Anecdotes of the Life of the Right Hon. William Pitt,*
    Earl of Chatham, Vol. 3 (1797 edition)
Almon, John: *The Parliamentary Register,* printed for J. Almon,
    opposite Burlington-House, in Piccadilly, Vols. 9–11 (1778–9)

Annesley, George (Earl of Mountmorris): *Voyages and Travels to India, Ceylon, the Red Sea, Abyssinia, and Egypt* (1811)

Archaeologia Aeliana, or, Miscellaneous Tracts Relating to Antiquity, published by the Society of Antiquaries of Newcastle upon Tyne, Vol. 1 (1822)

Aspinall, A., ed.: *The Correspondence of George, Prince of Wales,* Vol. 1, 1770–1789 (1963)

Atkinson, George Clayton: *Sketch of the Life and Works of the late Thomas Bewick* (1830)

Atkinson, John Nathaniel: 'Notes on the history of Temple Sowerby and of the Atkinson family' (AF: unpublished MS)

The Bankers' Magazine, and Statistical Register, Vol. 4 (1850)

Baring, Alexander: *Mr. Alexander Baring's Speech in the House of Commons on the 15th Day of May, 1823, on Mr. Buxton's Motion for a Resolution Declaratory of Slavery in the British Colonies Being Contrary to the English Constitution and to Christianity* (1823)

Baring, Francis: *Observations on the Establishment of the Bank of England, and on the Paper Circulation of the Country* (1797)

Barnard, Lady Anne: *Memoirs,* Vols. 1–6 (NLS: Crawford Papers: Acc 9769 27/4/14)

Barrett, Charlotte, ed.: *Diary & Letters of Madame D'Arblay* (1842)

Beche, H.T. de la: *Notes on the Present Condition of the Negroes in Jamaica* (1825)

Beckford, William: *A Descriptive Account of the Island of Jamaica* (1790)

Bewick, Thomas: *A History of British Birds* (1804)

Bigelow, John: *Jamaica in 1850: or, the Effects of Sixteen Years of Freedom on a Slave Colony* (1851)

Bleby, Henry: *Death Struggles of Slavery* (1853)

Boswell, James: *Boswell's London Journal, 1762–1763* (1951)

Bridges, G.W.: *The Annals of Jamaica* (1828)

Bridges, G.W.: *A Voice from Jamaica; in Reply to William Wilberforce, Esq.* (1823)

Brontë, Charlotte: *Jane Eyre* (1850)

Bruce, Gainsford: *The Life and Letters of John Collingwood Bruce* (1905)

Bruce, John Collingwood: *The Roman Wall* (1851)

Budge, E.A.W.: *An Account of the Roman Antiquities Preserved in the Museum at Chesters, Northumberland* (1907)

Camden Miscellany, Volume XXIII, Fourth Series, Vol. 7 (1969)

Catterall, H.T.: *Judicial Cases Concerning American Slavery and the Negro*, Vol. 1 (1926)

Christie, Octavius F., ed.: *The Diary of the Revd. William Jones, 1777–1821* (1929)

Clarkson, Thomas: 'Negro Slavery. Argument, That the colonial slaves are better off than the British peasantry. Answered, from the Royal Jamaica Gazette' (1824)

Clarkson, Thomas: *The History of the Rise, Progress, and Accomplishment of the Abolition of the African Slave Trade by the British Parliament* (1808)

Clerk, John: *An Essay on Naval Tactics, Systematical and Historical, with Explanatory Plates* (1827 edition)

Collections of the Massachusetts Historical Society, For the Year 1792, Vol. 1 (1859 edition)

The Corporation Annual; or, Recollections (not Random) of the First Reformed Town Council, of the Borough of Newcastle upon Tyne. Dedicated (without Permission) to T.E.H., Esq. Leader of the Clique (1836)

Cox, Francis A.: *History of the Baptist Missionary Society, from 1792 to 1842* (1842)

Cumberland, Richard: *Memoirs of Richard Cumberland* (1807)

Dallas, Robert: *The History of the Maroons* (1803)

The Debates in Parliament – Session 1833 – on the Resolutions and Bill for the Abolition of Slavery in the British Colonies (1834)

Defoe, Daniel: *A Tour Thro' the Whole Island of Great Britain: Divided into Circuits or Journeys* (1748 edition)

A Description of Brighthelmstone and the Adjacent Country, or, The New Guide for Ladies and Gentlemen resorting to that Place of Health and Amusement (1784)

Douglas, Sylvester (Lord Glenbervie): *Reports of Cases Argued and Determined in the Court of King's Bench, in the Twenty-Second, Twenty-Third, Twenty-Fourth, and Twenty-Fifth Years of the Reign of George III* (1831)

Edwards, Bryan: *The History, Civil and Commercial, of the British Colonies in the West Indies* (1793)

Elwin, Malcolm: *The Noels and the Milbankes: Their Letters for Twenty-five Years, 1767–1792* (1967)

Evans, Henry B.: *Our West Indian Colonies. Jamaica, A Source of National Wealth and Honour* (1855)

Falconbridge, Alexander: *An Account of the Slave Trade on the Coast of Africa* (1788)

The Festival of Wit; Or, Small Talker, being a Collection of Bon Mots, Anecdotes, &c. of the Most Exalted Character (1793 edition)

Foote, Samuel: *The Patron: A Comedy in Three Acts* (1764)

Fortescue, John, ed.: *The Correspondence of King George III, from 1760 to December, 1783* (1927–8)

Fox, William: *An Address to the People of Great Britain, on the Propriety of Abstaining from West India Sugar and Rum* (1792)

Franklin, Benjamin: *The Interest of Great Britain Considered with Regard to Her Colonies and the Acquisitions of Canada and Guadaloupe* (1760)

Fremantle, Anne, ed.: *The Wynne Diaries*, Vol. 3 (1940)

French, Gilbert J.: *The Life and Times of Samuel Crompton* (1859)

Gardner, William: *A History of Jamaica from its Discovery by Christopher Columbus to the Present Time* (1873)

Glasse, Hannah: *The Art of Cookery Made Plain and Easy* (1805 edition)

Greig, J.Y.T., ed.: *The Letters of David Hume*, Vol. 2: 1766–1776 (1932)

Grenville, Richard (Duke of Buckingham): *Memoirs of the Court and Cabinets of George the Third* (1853)

Grosley, Pierre Jean: *A Tour to London, or New Observations on England and its Inhabitants* (1765)

Gurney, Joseph John: *A Winter in the West Indies, described in Familiar Letters to Henry Clay, of Kentucky* (1841)

Hakewill, James: *A Picturesque Tour of the Island of Jamaica from Drawings made in the Years 1820 and 1821* (1825)

Hansard, T.C.: *The Parliamentary Debates from the Year 1803 to the Present Time*, published under the superintendence of T.C. Hansard, Old Series, Vol. 9 (1812)

Hansard, T.C.: *The Parliamentary Debates: Forming a Continuation of the Work entitled 'The Parliamentary History of England, from the Earliest Period to the Year 1803'*, published under the superintendence of T.C. Hansard. New Series, commencing with the Accession of George IV, Vol. 9 (1824)

Hansard, T.C.: *The Parliamentary History of England, from the Earliest Period to the Year 1803*, printed by T.C. Hansard, Peterborough-Court, Fleet-Street, Vols. 16–32 (1813–18)

Hardcastle, Daniel: *Banks and Bankers* (1842)

Harford, John S.: *Recollections of William Wilberforce during nearly Thirty Years* (1865)

Hawkesworth, John ed.: *An Account of the Voyages Undertaken by the Order of his Present Majesty for Making Discoveries in the Southern Hemisphere* (1773)

Hoare, Prince: *The Memoirs of Granville Sharp* (1820)

Hodgson, John: *A Topographical and Historical Description of Westmorland* (1810)

Hodgson, John et al.: *The Beauties of England and Wales: or, Original Delineations, Topographical, Historical, and Descriptive, of each County*, Vol. 15, Part 2 (1814)

Holroyd, John (Lord Sheffield): *Observations on the Commerce of the American States* (1784)

Howitt, William: *Visits to Remarkable Places* (1842)

Hutchinson, William: *An Excursion to the Lakes in Westmoreland and Cumberland; With a Tour Through Part of the Northern Counties, In the Years 1773 and 1774* (1776)

Hutton, William: *The History of the Roman Wall, which Crosses the Island of Britain, from the German Ocean to the Irish Sea* (1801)

An Impartial History of the Town and County of Newcastle upon Tyne and its Vicinity (1801)

Jackson, Donald, ed.: *The Diaries of George Washington*, Vol. 1 (1976)

Jackson, Robert: *A Treatise on the Fevers of Jamaica* (1791)

Johnson, Samuel: *A Dictionary of the English Language* (1805 edition)

Johnson, Samuel: *Taxation no Tyranny: An Answer to the Resolutions and Address of the American Congress* (1775)

Journals of the House of Commons, from 10 January 1765 to 16 September 1766, Vol. 30 (1803)

Journals of the House of Commons, from 26 November 1772 to 15 September 1774, Vol. 34 (1804)

Journals of the House of Commons, from 29 November 1774 to 15 October 1776, Vol. 35 (1803)

Journals of the House of Commons, from 31 October 1780 to 10 October 1782, Vol. 38 (1803)

Knight, William, ed.: *Letters of the Wordsworth Family from 1787 to 1855* (1969)

Knox, William: *Extra Official State Papers, Addressed to the Right Hon. Lord Rawdon, and the Other Members of the Two Houses of Parliament* (1789)

Laprade, William T.: *Parliamentary Papers of John Robinson, 1774–1784* (1922)

Lawrence-Archer, James: *Monumental Inscriptions of the British West Indies* (1875)

Lenta, Margaret and Le Cordeur, Basil, eds: *The Cape Diaries of Lady Anne Barnard, 1799–1800* (1999)

A Letter to a Merchant of Bristol; concerning a Petition of S. T. Esq. (S. Touchet) to the King, for an Exclusive Grant to the Trade of the River Senegal. By a Merchant of London (1762)

Lewis, Matthew G.: *Journal of a West-India Proprietor, 1815–17* (1929)

Lindsay, Alexander (Earl of Crawford): *Lives of the Lindsays* (1849)

A List of the Liverymen of London, who voted for Mr. Alderman Sawbridge, and Richard Atkinson Esq., at the late election for Members of Parliament for the City of London, Carefully Corrected from the Sheriff's Attested Copies of the Poll (1784)

Long, Edward: *The History of Jamaica: or, General Survey of the Antient and Modern State of that Island* (1774)

Lustig, I.S. and Pottle, F.A., eds: *Boswell: The English Experiment, 1785–1789* (1986)

Mackenzie, Eneas, ed.: *An Historical, Topographical, and Descriptive View of the County of Northumberland* (1825)

Madden, Richard: *A Twelvemonth's Residence in the West Indies, during the Transition from Slavery to Apprenticeship* (1835)

Manuscripts of Captain Howard Vicente Knox: Report on Manuscripts in Various Collections, Vol. 6 (1909)

Martin, R.M.: *The British Colonies, Vol. 4: Africa and the West Indies* (1853)

Moore, Thomas: *Works of Lord Byron: With His Letters and Journals, and His Life* (1832)

Moorman, Mary, ed.: *Journals of Dorothy Wordsworth: The Alfoxden Journal 1798, The Grasmere Journals 1800–1803* (1971)

Moreton, J.B.: *West India Customs and Manners* (1793)

Nicolson, Joseph and Burn, Richard: *The History and Antiquities of the Counties of Westmorland and Cumberland, in Two Volumes* (1777)

Papers presented to the House of Commons on the 7th May 1804, Respecting the Slave-Trade; &c. &c. (1804)

Peach, W.B. and Thomas, D.O., eds: *The Correspondence of Richard Price* (1983–94)

Peel, Robert: *Six Speeches: The Tamworth Election* (1841)

Phillimore, J., ed.: *Reports of Cases Argued and Determined in the Ecclesiastical Courts at Doctors' Commons*, Vol. 2 (1812–18)

Phillippo, James: *Jamaica: Its Past and Present State* (1843)

The Picture of Newcastle upon Tyne, containing a Guide to the Town and Neighbourhood, an Account of the Roman Wall, and a Description of the Coal Mines, etc (1807)

The Poll for Knights of the Shire, To represent the County of Westmorland, Taken at Appleby, On Thursday, Friday, Saturday, Monday, and Tuesday, the 13th, 14th, 15th, 17th and 18th Days of October, 1774 (1774)

Postlethwayt, Malachy: *The African Trade the Great Pillar & Support of the British Plantation Trade in America* (1745)

Postlethwayt, Malachy: *The Universal Dictionary of Trade and Commerce* (1774 edition)

The Proceedings of the Governor and Assembly of Jamaica, in Regard to the Maroon Negroes (1796)

Proceedings of the Society of Antiquaries of Newcastle-upon-Tyne, Vol. 3 (1889)

Quine, David A., ed.: *Expeditions to the Hebrides by George Clayton Atkinson in 1831 and 1833* (2001)

Raine, James: *A Memoir of the Rev. John Hodgson* (1857)

Register of Ships, Lloyd's (1764)

The Remarkable Case of Peter Hasenclever, Merchant: formerly one of the proprietors of the iron works, pot-ash manufactory, &c. established, and successfully carried on under his direction, in the provinces of New York, and New Jersey, in North America, 'till November 1766 (1773)

Renny, Robert: *An History of Jamaica* (1807)

Reports from Committees of the House of Commons, Vol. XI, Miscellaneous Subjects: 1782–1799 (1803)

Rochefoucauld, François: *A Frenchman's Year in Suffolk: French Impressions of Suffolk Life in 1784* (1988)

Russell, Richard: *A Dissertation on the Use of Sea-Water in the Diseases of the Glands; particularly the Scurvy, Jaundice, King's-Evil, Leprosy, and the Glandular Consumption* (1752)

Sainsbury, W.N. and Fortescue, J.W., eds: *Calendar of State Papers, Colonial Series, Vol. 10, America and West Indies, 1677–80* (1896)

Scoresby-Jackson, Robert E.: *Medical Climatology: or, A Topographical and Meteorological Description of the Localities Resorted to in Winter and Summer by Invalids of Various Classes, Both at Home and Abroad* (1862)

Seaton, A.V., ed.: *Journal of an Expedition to the Feroe and Westman Islands and Iceland, 1833, by George Clayton Atkinson* (1989)

Second Series of Recollections (not Random) of the Reformed Town Council of Newcastle-upon-Tyne (1855)

Sheridan, Richard Brinsley: *Clio's Protest* (1819)

Sheridan, Thomas: *A Course of Lectures on Elocution* (1762)

Sketches of Public Men of the North (1855)

Skinner, John: *Hadrian's Wall in 1801: Observations on the Roman Wall* (1978)

Smith, Adam: *An Inquiry into the Nature and Causes of the Wealth of Nations* (1776)

Stanhope, Philip: *Life of the Right Honourable William Pitt* (1861)

The State of the Nation, with Respect to its Public Funded Debt, Revenue, and Disbursement; comprised in the Reports of the Select Committee on Finance, Vol. 2 (1798)

The Statutes of the United Kingdom of Great Britain and Ireland, 1 & 2 Victoria (1838)

Stephen, George: *Anti-Slavery Recollections: In a Series of Letters addressed to Mrs. Beecher Stowe, written by Sir George Stephen, at Her Request* (1854)

Stewart, J.: *An Account of Jamaica and its Inhabitants* (1808)

Stewart, J.: *A View of the Past and Present State of the Island of Jamaica* (1823)

Stockdale, John: *The Parliamentary Register . . . in Seventeen Volumes*, reprinted for John Stockdale, Piccadilly, Vol. 2 (1802)

Sturge, Joseph and Harvey, Thomas: *The West Indies in 1837: Being the Journal of a Visit to Antigua, Montserrat, Dominica, St. Lucia, Barbados, and Jamaica* (1838)

Terrill, Anne E.: *Memorials of a Family in England and Virginia, 1771–1851* (1887)

Thomson, Thomas: *Annals of Philosophy: or, Magazine of Chemistry, Mineralogy, Mechanics, Natural History, Agriculture, and the Arts*, Vol. 4 (1814)

Tooke, John Horne: *Facts Addressed to the Landholders* (1780)

Toynbee, Mrs Paget: *The Letters of Horace Walpole, Fourth Earl of Orford* (1903–5)

The Transactions of the Jamaica Society of Arts, Vol. 1 (1855)

Transactions of the Natural History Society, of Northumberland, Durham, and Newcastle upon Tyne, Vol. 1 (1831)

Transactions of the Natural History Society, of Northumberland, Durham, and Newcastle upon Tyne, Vol. 2 (1838)

Walpole, Horace: *Memoirs of the Reign of King George III* (1845)

Walpole, Horace: *The Last Journals of Horace Walpole during the Reign of George III, from 1771–1783* (1910)

Welford, Richard: *Men of Mark 'twixt Tyne and Tweed* (1895)

Wilberforce, R. and Wilberforce, S.: *The Life of William Wilberforce* (1838)

Wraxall, Nathaniel: *Historical Memoirs of His Own Time* (1836)

Wraxall, Nathaniel: *Posthumous Memoirs of His Own Time* (1836)

Wright, Philip, ed.: *Lady Nugent's Journal of her Residence in Jamaica from 1801 to 1805* (1966)

Young, Arthur: *Annals of Agriculture, and Other Useful Arts* (1784–1815)

SECONDARY SOURCES

Ashton, T.S.: *An Economic History of England: The Eighteenth Century* (London, 1964)

Ashton, T.S.: *The Industrial Revolution, 1760–1830* (Oxford, 1948)

Ashton, T.S.: *Iron and Steel in the Industrial Revolution* (Manchester, 1951)

Austin, Peter E.: *Baring Brothers and the Birth of Modern Finance* (London, 2015)

Baker, Norman: *Government and Contractors: The British Treasury and War Supplies, 1775–1783* (London, 1971)

Baker, Norman: 'The Treasury and Open Contracting, 1778–1782', *The Historical Journal*, Vol. 15, No. 3, pp. 433–54 (1972)

Black, Jeremy: *A Brief History of Slavery* (London, 2011)

Black, Jeremy: *Eighteenth-century Britain, 1688–1783* (Basingstoke, 2008)

Bouch, C.M.L. and Jones, G.P.: *A Short Economic and Social History of the Lake Counties, 1500–1830* (Manchester, 1961)

Bowler, R. Arthur: *Logistics and the Failure of the British Army in America, 1775–1783* (Princeton, 1975)

Brathwaite, Edward: *The Development of Creole Society in Jamaica, 1770–1820* (Oxford, 1971)

Brewer, John: *The Sinews of Power: War, Money and the English State, 1688–1783* (London, 1989)

Buckley, Roger N.: *Slaves in Red Coats: The British West India Regiments, 1795–1815* (New Haven, 1979)

Buel, R.: *Dear Liberty: Connecticut's Mobilization for the Revolutionary War* (Middletown, 1980)

Burn, William L.: *Emancipation and Apprenticeship in the British West Indies* (London, 1937)

Burns, Alan: *History of the British West Indies* (London, 1954)

Cannon, John: *The Fox-North Coalition* (Cambridge, 1969)

Carrington, Selwyn H.H.: *The Sugar Industry and the Abolition of the Slave Trade, 1775–1810* (Gainesville, 2002)

Christie, Ian R.: *Crisis of Empire: Great Britain and the American Colonies, 1754–1783* (London, 1966)

Christie, Ian R.: *The End of North's Ministry, 1780–1782* (London, 1958)

Christie, Ian R.: 'The political allegiance of John Robinson, 1770–1784', *Historical Research*, Vol. 29, Issue 79, pp. 108–22 (1956)

Clapham, J.H.: *The Bank of England: A History* (Cambridge, 1958)

Colley, Linda: *Britons: Forging the Nation, 1707–1837* (New Haven, 1992)

Collins, Rob and McIntosh, Frances, eds: *Life in the Limes: Studies of the People and Objects of the Roman Frontiers* (Oxford, 2014)

Connell, Andrew: 'John Robinson (1727–1802), Richard Atkinson (1739–85), Government, Commerce and Politics in the Age of the American Revolution: "From the North"', *Northern History*, Vol. 50:1, pp. 54–76 (2013)

Cundall, Frank: *Historic Jamaica* (London, 1915)

Derry, John W.: *Politics in the Age of Fox, Pitt and Liverpool* (Basingstoke, 1990)

Dickerson, Oliver M.: *The Navigation Acts and the American Revolution* (Philadelphia, 1951)

Donoughue, Bernard: *British Politics and the American Revolution: The Path to War 1773–1775* (New York, 1964)

Draper, Nicholas: *The Price of Emancipation: Slave-ownership, Compensation and British Society at the End of Slavery* (Cambridge, 2010)

Drescher, Seymour: *Abolition: A History of Slavery and Antislavery* (Cambridge, 2009)

Duffy, Michael: *Soldiers, Sugar, and Seapower: The British Expeditions to the West Indies and the War against Revolutionary France* (Oxford, 1987)

Ehrman, John: *The Younger Pitt: The Years of Acclaim* (London, 1969)

Eisner, Gisela: *Jamaica, 1830–1930: A Study in Economic Growth* (Manchester, 1961)

Fell, Alfred: *The Early Iron Industry of Furness and District, 1726–1800* (Ulverston, 1908)

Ferguson, Niall: *Empire: How Britain Made the Modern World* (London, 2004)

Fetherstonhaugh, Robert C.: *The 13th Battalion Royal Highlanders of Canada, 1914–1919* (Montreal, 1925)

Furber, Holden: 'The East India Directors in 1784', *The Journal of Modern History*, Vol. 5, No. 4, pp. 479–95 (1933)

Geggus, David: 'Jamaica and the Saint Domingue Slave Revolt, 1791–1793', *The Americas*, Vol. 38, No. 2, pp. 219–33 (1981)

Geggus, David: *Slavery, War and Revolution: The British Occupation of Saint Domingue 1793–1798* (Oxford, 1982)

George, M.D.: *Catalogue of Political and Personal Satires Preserved in the Department of Prints and Drawings in the British Museum* (London, 1952)

George, M.D.: *London Life in the Eighteenth Century* (London, 1996)

Gerzina, Gretchen: *Black England: Life before Emancipation* (London, 1995)

Green, William A.: *British Slave Emancipation: The Sugar Colonies and the Great Experiment, 1830–1865* (Oxford, 1976)

Hague, William: *William Pitt the Younger* (London, 2004)

Hall, C., Draper, N. and McClelland, K.: *Emancipation and the Remaking of the British Imperial World* (Manchester, 2014)

Hall, Catherine et al.: *Legacies of British Slave-ownership: Colonial Slavery and the Formation of Victorian Britain* (Cambridge, 2016)

Hall, Douglas: *A Brief History of the West India Committee* (Barbados, 1971)

Hall, Douglas: *In Miserable Slavery: Thomas Thistlewood in Jamaica, 1750–1786* (London, 1989)

Heusser, Albert H.: *George Washington's Map Maker: A Biography of Robert Erskine* (New Brunswick, 1966)

Hibbert, Christopher: *Redcoats and Rebels: The War for America 1770–1781* (London, 1990)

Higman, B.W.: *Jamaica Surveyed: Plantation Maps and Plans of the Eighteenth and Nineteenth Centuries* (Jamaica, 1988)

Higman, B.W.: *Plantation Jamaica 1750–1850: Capital and Control in a Colonial Economy* (Jamaica, 2005)

Higman, B.W.: *Slave Population and Economy in Jamaica, 1807–1834* (Cambridge, 1976)

Hochschild, Adam: *Bury the Chains: The British Struggle to Abolish Slavery* (London, 2005)

Holmes, Richard: *Redcoat: The British Soldier in the Age of Horse and Musket* (London, 2001)

Howard, D.S.: *Chinese Armorial Porcelain*, Vol. 2 (Chippenham, 2003)

Hudleston, C. Roy: 'The Dalstons of Acornbank', *Transactions of the Cumberland & Westmorland Antiquarian & Archaeological Society*, Series 2, Vol. 58, pp. 140–79 (1958)

Ingram, Kenneth E.: *Sources of Jamaican History, 1655–1838: A Bibliographical Survey with Particular Reference to Manuscript Sources* (London, 1976)

Inikori, Joseph E.: 'Slavery and the Revolution in Cotton Textile Production in England', *Social Science History*, Vol. 13, No. 4, pp. 343–79 (1989)

James, C.L.R.: *The Black Jacobins: Toussaint L'Ouverture and the San Domingo Revolution* (London, 1980)

Johnson, Carol, ed.: 'Robert Erskine's letters of 1770 about the British iron and steel industry', *Historical Metallurgy*, Vol. 43, pp. 75–97 (2009)

Kup, A.P.: 'Alexander Lindsay, 6th Earl of Balcarres, Lieutenant Governor of Jamaica 1794–1801', *Bulletin of the John Rylands Library*, Vol. 57, Issue 2, pp. 327–65 (1975)

Leach, Stephen and Whitworth, Alan: *Saving the Wall: The Conservation of Hadrian's Wall, 1746–1987* (Stroud, 2011)

Logan, Rayford W.: *Haiti and the Dominican Republic* (Oxford, 1968)

Mackesy, Piers: *The War for America, 1775–1783* (London, 1964)

Mintz, Sidney W.: *Sweetness and Power: The Place of Sugar in Modern History* (London, 1985)

Monteith, Kathleen E.A. and Richards, Glen: *Jamaica in Slavery and Freedom* (Barbados, 2002)

Namier, Lewis: *England in the Age of the American Revolution* (London, 1930)

Namier, Lewis: *The House of Commons, 1754–1790* (London, 1964)

Nelson, Louis P.: *Architecture and Empire in Jamaica* (New Haven, 2016)

O'Shaughnessy, Andrew J.: 'The Formation of a Commercial Lobby: The West India Interest, British Colonial Policy and the American Revolution', *The Historical Journal*, Vol. 40, No. 1, pp. 71–95 (1997)

O'Shaughnessy, Andrew J.: *An Empire Divided: The American Revolution and the British Caribbean* (Philadelphia, 2000)

O'Shaughnessy, Andrew J.: *The Men Who Lost America: British Command during the Revolutionary War and the Preservation of the Empire* (London, 2013)

Pares, Richard: *King George III and the Politicians* (London, 1967)

Pares, Richard: *War and Trade in the West Indies, 1739–1763* (Oxford, 1936)

Parker, Matthew: *The Sugar Barons* (London, 2011)

Penson, Lillian M.: 'The London West India Interest in the Eighteenth Century', *The English Historical Review*, Vol. 36, No. 143, pp. 373–92 (1921)

Perry, Keith: *British Politics and the American Revolution* (Basingstoke, 1990)

Petley, Christer: *Slaveholders in Jamaica: Colonial Society and Culture during the Era of Abolition* (London, 2015)

Philips, C.H.: *The East India Company, 1784–1834* (Manchester, 1961)

Phillips, Maberly: *A History of Banks, Bankers, and Banking in Northumberland, Durham, and North Yorkshire* (London, 1894)

Picard, Liza: *Dr Johnson's London* (London, 2000)

Porter, Roy: *English Society in the Eighteenth Century* (London, 1982)

Pressnell, Leslie S.: *Country Banking in the Industrial Revolution* (Oxford, 1956)

Ragatz, Lowell J.: *The Fall of the Planter Class in the British Caribbean, 1763–1833* (London, 1928)

Robertson, James: *Gone is the Ancient Glory: Spanish Town, Jamaica 1534–2000* (Jamaica, 2005)

Roebuck, Peter: *Cattle Droving through Cumbria, 1600–1900* (Carlisle, 2016)

Rubinstein, W.D.: *Who Were the Rich?: A Biographical Dictionary of British Wealth-holders* (London, 2009)

Ryden, David B.: *West Indian Slavery and British Abolition, 1783–1807* (Cambridge, 2009)

Sheridan, Richard B.: 'The British Credit Crisis of 1772 and the American Colonies', *The Journal of Economic History*, Vol. 20, No. 2, pp. 161–86 (1960)

Sheridan, Richard B.: 'The Wealth of Jamaica in the Eighteenth Century', *The Economic History Review*, New Series, Vol. 18, No. 2, pp. 292–311 (1965)

Sheridan, Richard B.: *Sugar and Slavery: An Economic History of the British West Indies, 1623–1775* (Baltimore, 1974)

Sutherland, Lucy S.: *The East India Company in Eighteenth-century Politics* (Oxford, 1962)

Sutherland, Lucy S.: *Politics and Finance in the Eighteenth Century* (London, 1984)

Sutton, Jean: *Lords of the East: The East India Company and its Ships* (London, 1981)

Syrett, David: *Shipping and the American War, 1775–83* (London, 1970)

Tattersfield, Nigel: *Bookplates by Beilby & Bewick, 1760–1849* (London, 1999)

Taylor, Stephen: *Defiance: The Life and Choices of Lady Anne Barnard* (London, 2016)

Thomas, Hugh: *The Slave Trade: The History of the Atlantic Slave Trade, 1440–1870* (London, 1997)

Thomas, Peter D.G.: *British Politics and the Stamp Act Crisis* (Oxford, 1975)

Thomas, Peter D.G.: *Lord North* (London, 1976)

Thompson, A.S. & Frentzos, C.G., ed.: *The Routledge Handbook of American Military and Diplomatic History: The Colonial Period to 1877* (New York, 2015)

Thomson, Ian: *The Dead Yard: Tales of Modern Jamaica* (London, 2009)

Tyson, Blake: 'Oak for the Navy: A Case Study, 1700–1703', *Transactions of the Cumberland & Westmorland Antiquarian & Archaeological Society*, Series 2, Vol. 87, pp. 117–26 (1987)

Tyson, Blake: 'Two Appleby Houses in the 18th Century: A Documentary Study', *Transactions of the Cumberland & Westmorland Antiquarian & Archaeological Society*, Series 2, Vol. 85, pp. 193–218 (1985)

Uglow, Jenny: *In These Times: Living in Britain through Napoleon's Wars, 1793–1815* (London, 2014)

Uglow, Jenny: *Nature's Engraver: A Life of Thomas Bewick* (London, 2006)

Wadsworth, Alfred P.: *The Cotton Trade and Industrial Lancashire, 1600–1780* (Manchester, 1931)

Wake, Thomas: 'The Society's Fifteenth Century Fede-ring Brooch', *Proceedings of the Society of Antiquaries of Newcastle upon Tyne*, Fourth Series, Vol. 6, pp. 172–4 (1935)

Walvin, James: *England, Slaves and Freedom, 1776–1838* (Basingstoke, 1986)

Walvin, James: *A Short History of Slavery* (London, 2007)

White, Jerry: *London in the Eighteenth Century: A Great and Monstrous Thing* (London, 2012)

Wilkes, Lyall and Dodds, Gordon: *Tyneside Classical: The Newcastle of Grainger, Dobson and Clayton* (London, 1964)

Williams, Eric: *Capitalism and Slavery* (London, 1964)

Woodside, Robert and Crow, James: *Hadrian's Wall: An Historic Landscape* (London, 1999)

Ziegler, Philip: *The Sixth Great Power: Barings 1762–1929* (London, 1988)

NOTES

1 A Tangled Inheritance

1 AF: JLA to JREA, 29 Jul 1968

2 The Tanner's Wife

1 Nicolson & Burn, Vol. 1, p. 8
2 CAK: WDX 82
3 Hudleston, p. 160
4 AF: WA's will, 17 May 1645
5 Defoe, Vol. 3, p. 258
6 NA: E 179/195/73
7 AF: JA's will, 18 Oct 1680
8 Hodgson, *A Topographical and Historical Description*, p. 106
9 Tyson, 'Oak for the Navy', p. 120
10 Tyson, 'Two Appleby Houses', p. 198
11 CAK: WPR 81
12 Nicolson & Burn, Vol. 1, p. 10
13 CAK: WDX 82
14 NA: IR 1/20
15 *Public Advertiser*, 22 Apr 1756
16 NAW: ZAL 95/7/2: BM to GA, 7 Jul 1756
17 NAW: ZAL 95/7/3: JT to BM, 29 Jul 1756
18 NAW: ZAL 96/2/6: BS to BM, 5 Sep 1756
19 NRS: CS96/2154
20 NAW: ZAL 96/2/7: GA to JM, 4 Mar 1757
21 NAW: ZAL 95/7/5: BA to JM, 13 Jan 1758
22 NAW: ZAL 95/7/6: BT to DM, BA to DM, 13 Jan 1758
23 *GM*: Vol. 28, p. 46
24 NAW: ZAL 95/7/7: BA to GA, 13 Jul 1758
25 NAW: ZAL 96/2/9: BA to JM, 12 Jan 1759
26 NAW: ZAL 95/7/8: BA to JM, 28 Jan 1759
27 NAW: ZAL 95/7/9: GA to JM, 3 Mar 1761
28 NAW: ZAL 95/3/7: MT to JA, nd

3 Atlantic Empire

1 Grosley, Vol. 1, p. 37
2 Ibid., Vol. 1, p. 35
3 French, p. 254
4 Postlethwayt, *The African Trade*, p. 2
5 NA: T 70/1523: Thomas Melvil to Committee, 10 Aug 1754
6 Falconbridge, p. 34
7 SV: Voyages 77616, 77617, 90647
8 SV: Voyage 90839
9 Postlethwayt, *Universal Dictionary*, Vol. 2, 'Privateers and Prizes'
10 NA: HCA 26/6, fo. 68

11 Sheridan, T., p. 30
12 Ibid., p. 24
13 *London Chronicle*, 26 Feb 1761
14 BL: Add MS 32923, fo. 282: JW to Newcastle, 28 May 1761
15 HRO: 92M95/NP3/1/8: EB to FB, 31 Mar 1766
16 BA: HC 5.3.4/18: Nathaniel Clayton to Alexander Baring, 4 Dec 1822
17 Foote, pp. 5, 6, 13
18 SV: Voyages 75031, 75095, 75781, 75975, 77099, 77771, 77773, 77817
19 Greig, p. 52: DH to Richard Davenport, Jun 1766
20 Almon, *Anecdotes*, p. 222
21 Franklin, pp. 14–15
22 Hibbert, *Redcoats and Rebels*, p. xvii
23 *Collections of the Massachusetts Historical Society*, p. 83
24 *Providence Gazette*, 27 Oct 1764
25 BL: Add MS 38202, fo. 368: RA to CJ, 29 Jun 1764
26 Hansard, *Parliamentary History*, Vol. 16, cols. 37–8
27 *Halifax Gazette*, 13 Feb 1766
28 BL: Add MS 33030, fo. 166
29 *Camden Miscellany*, p. 318
30 *Journals of the House of Commons*, Vol. 30, p. 790
31 CAE: R 55/7/122(0)4: RA to JT, 13 Jul 1767
32 CAE: R 55/7/122(0)4: MSA to JT, 15 Nov 1767
33 *GM*: Vol. 34, p. 493
34 Sainsbury & Fortescue, p. 120
35 Catterall, p. 9
36 Ibid., pp. 12, 13
37 Hoare, p. 35

4 Four Dice

1 *Founders Online*: BF to William Brownrigg, 7 Nov 1773
2 NJHS: MG 199: 'An Account of some of the Uses of the Patent Centrifugal Hydraulic Engine'
3 NYHS: American Iron Co. MSS: Trustees to Messrs R&Y, 30 Jan 1770
4 NJSA: RE to RA, 16 Sep 1770
5 RM: Erskine Papers: RE to RA, 18 Oct 1770; NJSA: PHEUS001: RE to RA, 20 Oct 1770
6 NJSA: PHEUS001: RE to RA, 27 Oct 1770
7 NJHS: MG 199: RE to RA, nd
8 *Scots Magazine*, Vol. 34, p. 421
9 *Middlesex Journal*, 13 Jun 1772
10 NLS: MS.4944: RA to Baron Mure, 2 Apr 1768
11 Young, A., Vol. 18 (1792), pp. 164–8
12 Sheridan, R.B., *Clio's Protest*, pp. 17–18
13 Lindsay, Vol. 2, p. 332
14 Knight, Vol. 3, p. 25: WW to Alexander Dyce, 4 Dec 1833
15 Barnard, Vol. 2, pp. 2–3
16 Ibid., Vol. 2, pp. 5–6
17 Ibid., Vol. 2, pp. 2–4
18 Ibid., Vol. 2, pp. 3–4
19 Ibid., Vol. 1, pp. 162–3
20 Ibid., Vol. 2, pp. 5–10
21 Ibid., Vol. 2, pp. 56–7
22 Ibid., Vol. 2, pp. 50–1
23 NA: B 3/3675
24 Barnard, Vol. 2, pp. 50–1
25 Ibid., Vol. 2, pp. 53–4
26 *Scots Magazine*, Vol. 34, p. 311
27 Smith, Vol. 1, p. 388
28 Barnard, Vol. 2, pp. 81–3

29 *GM*: Vol. 42, p. 293
30 Toynbee, Vol. 8, Letter 1413, p. 178: HW to Sir Horace Mann, 1 Jul 1772
31 Greig, p. 463: DH to AS, 27 Jun 1772
32 Barnard, Vol. 2, pp. 91–2
33 Ibid., Vol. 2, pp. 92–4
34 Ibid., Vol. 2, pp. 95–6
35 Ibid., Vol. 2, pp. 97–9
36 *Public Ledger*, 22 Aug 1772
37 *London Evening Post*, 15 Sep 1772
38 *Morning Chronicle*, 14 Sep 1772
39 *London Chronicle*, 15 Sep 1772
40 *The Festival of Wit*, p. 144
41 Holroyd, p. 201
42 NYHS: American Iron Co. MSS: Trustees to Messrs R&Y, 2 Dec 1772

5 All the Tea in Boston

1 *Evening Post*, 22 Sep 1772
2 *Boston Evening-Post*, 20 Dec 1773
3 DM: CS4/1134: Sir Anthony Abdy to Devonshire, 3 Jun 1759
4 UNA: Pw F 3269: WD to Portland, 24 Feb 1769
5 Walpole, *Memoirs*, Vol. 4, p. 78
6 BL: Add MS 38206, fo. 285: JR to Charles Jenkinson, 26 Sep 1770
7 *Journals of the House of Commons*, Vol. 34, p. 345
8 *GM*: Vol. 44, pp. 40–1
9 Hansard, *Parliamentary History*, Vol. 17, col. 1165
10 Ibid., Vol. 17, col. 1169
11 NJHS: MG 199 (K26.31 & K26.32): RE to RA, 2 Nov 1773
12 NJHS: MG 199 (K26.31 & K26.32): RE to RA, 1 Jun 1774

13 *GM*: Vol. 44, pp. 40–1
14 NA: T 1/500, fo. 56
15 NA: T 1/500, fo. 48
16 Fell, pp. 339–40
17 *The Poll for Knights of the Shire*, p. 2
18 NJHS: MG 199 (K26.31 & K26.32): RE to RA, 5 Oct 1774
19 *Evening Post*, 19 Jan 1775
20 ICWS: M915: West India Committee, Mar 1775
21 Hawkesworth, Vol. 2, pp. 80–1
22 NA: CO 5/92, fo. 123: TG to Dartmouth, 28 Mar 1775
23 NJHS: MG 199 (K26.31 & K26.32): RE to Trustees, 3 May 1775
24 Stockdale, *Parliamentary Register*, Vol. 2, p. 89; NA: CO 5/92, fo. 187: TG to Dartmouth, 25 Jun 1775
25 Almon, *Parliamentary Register*, Vol. 9, Appendix No. 1: TG to Grey Cooper, 19 May 1775
26 Fortescue, Vol. 3, Letter 1682, p. 234: North to King, 26 Jul 1775
27 Almon, *Parliamentary Register*, Vol. 9: Report from the Select Committee, p. 12
28 NA: T 1/513, fo. 140: MSA to William Howe, 25 Sep 1775
29 BL: Add MS 38206, fo. 179: JR to CJ, 19 Sep 1775
30 NA: T 1/513, fos. 140–5: RA to WH, 25 Sep 1775
31 Ibid.
32 BL: Add MS 37833, fo. 18: JR to King, 2 Nov 1775
33 *Evening Advertiser*, 5 Oct 1775
34 NJHS: MG 199 (K26.31 & K26.32): RE to RA, 10 Oct 1775

35 NJHS: MG 199 (K26.31 & K26.32): RE to RA, 23 May 1775
36 NJHS: MG 199 (K26.31 & K26.32): RE to RA, 6 Dec 1775
37 NA: T 64/108, fo. 34: WH to JR, 31 Dec 1775
38 NA: T 64/108, fo. 38
39 NA: CO 5/93, fo. 172

6 The Rum Contracts

1 Bowler, p. 3
2 NA: T 29/45, fo. 27: 22 Feb 1776
3 Ibid.
4 NA: CO 5/147, fo. 226: RA to JR, 10 Apr 1776
5 CAK: WD/Ho, Plan 25
6 Hutchinson, Vol. 2, p. 43
7 NAW: ZAL 95/27/2: BA to DA, 26 May 1776
8 NAW: ZAL 96/2/11: William Borradaile to BA, 18 Jul 1776
9 *Bibliotheca Nautica*, Part III, No. 585, Maggs Bros, 1933: GD to George Atkinson, 24 Nov 1776
10 AF: BA pocket journal, 1776
11 WL: MS.5231, fo. 2: 1 Dec 1772
12 NAW: ZAL 95/7/11: BA to GA, nd
13 Hansard, *Parliamentary History*, Vol. 18, cols. 1365–6
14 Library of Congress, United States & Continental Congress Broadside Collection
15 Johnson, S., *Taxation no Tyranny*, p. 89
16 NJSA: PHEUS001
17 Almon, *Parliamentary Register*, Vol. 11, p. 361: WH to Lord George Germain, 30 Nov 1776
18 Library of Congress, *George Washington Papers, Series 4, General Correspondence, 1697–1799*: GW to John Augustine Washington, 18 Dec 1776
19 NA: CO 5/93, fo. 228: WH to Lord George Germain, 6 Aug 1776
20 NA: T 64/106, fo. 62: RA to William Howe, 14 Sep 1776
21 BL: Add MS 21687, fo. 304: RA to GC, 20 Sep 1776
22 BL: Add MS 37833, fo. 32: King to JR, 16 Sep 1776
23 Hansard, *Parliamentary History*, Vol. 19, col. 56
24 Ibid., Vol. 19, col. 266
25 *Morning Post*, 20 May 1777
26 NA: T 1/537, fo. 24: RA to WH, 14 Jan 1777
27 SA: Dartmouth MSS 1732: RA to JL, 14 Jan 1777
28 NA: T 38/269, fos. 1–11
29 NA: T 64/108, fo. 105: WH to JR, 5 Apr 1777
30 NA: T 1/535, fo. 368: Agreement, 1 Apr 1777
31 NA: T 29/46, fo. 90: 18 Jun 1777
32 NA: T 1/538, fo. 199: RA to JR, 12 Aug 1777
33 SA: Dartmouth MSS 1772: RA to Treasury, 23 Jul 1777
34 NA: T 1/534, fo. 179: RA to Treasury, 15 Aug 1777
35 *Founders Online*: GW to the Congress Committee to Inquire into the State of the Army, 19 Jul 1777
36 *The Papers of George Washington Digital Edition*: Robert Erskine to George Washington, 1 Aug 1777
37 *Acts of the Council*, p. 271
38 BL: Add MS 37833, fo. 200: King to JR, 24 May 1777

39 AP: Abergavenny MSS 147: North to Mr Forth, 25 Sep 1777

40 NA: SP 78/305, fo. 186: Stormont to Weymouth, 10 Dec 1777

41 NA: T 64/108, fo. 154: WH to John Robinson, 30 Nov 1777

42 NA: T 1/546, fo. 379: RA to John Robinson, 12 Jan 1778

43 SA: Dartmouth MSS 1828: RA to Treasury, 22 Jan 1778

44 SA: Dartmouth MSS 1830: RA to Treasury, 24 Jan 1778

45 *Morning Post*, 13 Feb 1778; *Gazetteer*, 14 Feb 1778

46 *Evening Post*, 5 Mar 1778

47 Hansard, *Parliamentary History*, Vol. 19, cols. 901–8

48 Johnson, S., *Dictionary*, Vol. 2, 'Job'

49 Hansard, *Parliamentary History*, Vol. 19, cols. 972–80

50 NA: T 1/548, fo. 31: HH to JR, 27 Jan 1779

51 HRO: 75M91/A25/7: RA to Contractors, 13 Jun 1778

52 KA: U1350 O86/5: WK to Amherst, 18 Jun 1778

53 KA: U1350 O86/9: WK to Amherst, 23 Jun 1778

54 *Evening Post*, 23 Jul 1778

55 BL: Add MS 38343, fo. 75

7 Jamaica Imperilled

1 NA: T 1/540, fo. 165: TS to RA, 14 Jul 1778

2 NA: T 29/47, fo. 143: 29 Jul 1778

3 NA: T 1/546, fo. 404: RA to JR, 13 Oct 1778

4 BL: Add MS 37834, fo. 39: King to JR, 6 Nov 1778

5 NA: CO 5/97, fo. 28: HC to Germain, 15 Dec 1778

6 NA: CO 5/151, fo. 122: RA to JR, 25 Feb 1779

7 NA: T 27/32, fos. 360–1: JR to RA, 13 Nov 1778

8 NA: T 29/48, fo. 141: 27 May 1779

9 NA: T 29/48, fo. 185: 20 Jul 1779

10 NA: T 1/552, fo. 128: RA to Treasury, 21 Jul 1779

11 Fortescue, Vol. 4, Letter 2241, p. 73: North to King, 23 Mar 1778

12 Ibid., Vol. 4, Letter 2657, p. 356: King to North, 15 Jun 1779

13 Wraxall, *Historical Memoirs*, Vol. 1, p. 318

14 BL: Add MS 38212, fos. 248–53: JR to CJ, 28 Nov 1779

15 Fortescue, Vol. 4, Letter 2773, p. 433: King to Sandwich, 13 Sep 1779

16 *London Chronicle*, 3 Dec 1778

17 Christie, O.F., p. 61

18 BC: Fuller Letterbook, p. 109: Stephen Fuller to Germain, 23/24 Dec 1778

19 *Morning Post*, 18 Oct 1779

20 *Manuscripts of Captain Howard Vicente Knox*, p. 163: RA to WK, 28 Oct 1779

21 *Evening Post*, 11 Nov 1779

22 NA: WO 34/122, fo. 26: Germain to SF, 13 Dec 1779

23 BL: Add MS 37835, fo. 77: King to JR, 15 Dec 1779

24 KA: U1350 O76/19: Memorandum

25 Hansard, *Parliamentary History*, Vol. 20, cols. 1383–9

26 BC: Fuller Letterbook, p. 169: Minutes, 17 Dec 1779

27 *Whitehall Evening Post*, 10 Feb 1780; *GM*: Vol. 50, p. 352

28 Toynbee, Vol. 11, Letter 2137, p. 368: HW to Lady Ossory, 14 Jan 1781

29 Hansard, *Parliamentary History*, Vol. 21, col. 72

30 *London Courant*, 30 Mar 1780

31 *Morning Chronicle*, 5 Jun 1780

32 NA: CO 5/152, fo. 238: RA to WK, 4 Jul 1780

33 NA: CO 5/152, fo. 234: RA to WK, 12 Sep 1780

34 NA: T 29/49, fo. 190: 20 Sep 1780

35 BL: Loan MS 72/29, fo. 75: JR to CJ, 3 Oct 1780

36 Knox, pp. 15–16

37 *Journals of the House of Commons*, Vol. 38, pp. 827–8

38 Ibid., Vol. 35, p. 611

39 Buel, p. 349

40 *Founders Online*: GW to John Cadwalader, 5 Oct 1780

41 NA: T 29/49, fo. 256: 21 Dec 1780

42 AF: Ledger, pp. 19, 62

43 Hansard, *Parliamentary History*, Vol. 22, col. 1345

44 *London Chronicle*, 7 Mar 1782

8 A Heartbreaking Letter

1 Barnard, Vol. 2, pp. 119–21

2 Ibid., Vol. 2, pp. 157–8

3 Ibid., Vol. 2, pp. 209–10

4 *Whitehall Evening Post*, 22 Jan 1782

5 Barrett, Vol. 2, p. 149

6 Barnard, Vol. 2, pp. 206–7

7 Ibid., Vol. 2, pp. 206–7

8 Ibid., Vol. 2, pp. 218–19

9 Ibid., Vol. 2, pp. 244–5

10 Ibid., Vol. 3, pp. 101–2

11 NA: C 104/76: HM to PB & RA, 31 Dec 1780

12 SRO: 741/HA12/B1/5/92: HM to RM & RA, 20–21 Apr 1781

13 Hansard, *Parliamentary History*, Vol. 21, cols. 1342–9; *London Chronicle*, 8 Mar 1781

14 Ibid., Vol. 21, cols. 1342–9

15 Ibid., Vol. 21, cols. 1349–62

16 Barnard, Vol. 3, pp. 1–2

17 Ibid., Vol. 3, pp. 3–5

18 Ibid., Vol. 3, pp. 4–6

19 NLS: Acc 9769 27/2/3: AL to RA, nd

20 *Gazetteer*, 26 Mar 1781

21 *Gazetteer*, 27 Mar 1781

22 Hansard, *Parliamentary History*, Vol. 22, col. 11

23 Barnard, Vol. 3, pp. 5–6

24 Ibid., Vol. 3, pp. 18–19

25 NA: T 1/569, fo. 63

26 *Journals of the House of Commons*, Vol. 38, p. 828

27 Barnard, Vol. 3, pp. 21–2

28 Ibid., Vol. 3, pp. 23–4

29 Ibid., Vol. 3, pp. 23–4

30 NLS: Acc 9769 27/2/3: RA to AL, nd

31 Barnard, Vol. 3, pp. 30–2

32 NLS: Acc 9769 27/2/3–4: AL to RA, nd

33 Barnard, Vol. 3, pp. 35–6

34 NLS: Acc 9769 27/2/7: RA to AL, nd

35 NLS: Acc 9769 27/2/5: RA to AL, nd

9 Mortal Thoughts

1 NLS: Acc 9769 27/2/11: RA to AL, 22 Aug 1781

2 Barnard, Vol. 3, pp. 42–3

3 Ibid., Vol. 3, pp. 22–3

4 Reprinted in *Penrith Observer*, 12 Jan 1926

5 NLS: Acc 9769 27/2/10: RA to AL, 13 Aug 1781

6 Wraxall, *Historical Memoirs*, Vol. 2, p. 435

7 *Public Advertiser*, 24 Sep 1781

8 NA: PRO 30/20/17

9 Wraxall, *Historical Memoirs*, Vol. 2, p. 468

10 *General Advertiser*, 22 Feb 1782

11 NLS: Acc 9769 27/2/13: RA to AL, 23 Feb 1782

12 Barnard, Vol. 3, pp. 65–6

13 *Morning Chronicle*, 5 Mar 1782

14 Toynbee, Vol. 12, Letter 2283, p. 190: Horace Walpole to Sir Horace Mann, 11 Mar 1782

15 *London Courant*, 11 Mar 1782

16 Fortescue, Vol. 5, Letter 3560 (enc), p. 389: JR to Charles Jenkinson, 16 Mar 1782

17 Wraxall, *Historical Memoirs*, Vol. 2, p. 607

18 Barnard, Vol. 3, pp. 67–8

19 Fortescue, Vol. 5, Letter 3584, p. 415: North to King, 26 Mar 1782

20 Ibid., Vol. 5, Letter 3594, p. 421: King to North, 27 Mar 1782

21 Ibid., Vol. 5, Letter 3593, p. 421: King to North, 27 Mar 1782

22 Hansard, *Parliamentary History*, Vol. 22, cols. 1346–7

23 *London Courant*, 3 Jan 1782

24 Clerk, pp. xxxvi–xxxvii

25 Cumberland, Vol. 1, p. 407

26 *The United Service Journal*, 1829, Part 2, pp. 562–74

27 BL: IOR B/95, p. 637: Court of Directors, 10 Apr 1780

28 Barnard, Vol. 3, pp. 67–8

29 Lindsay, Vol. 2, p. 343

30 HA: DE/HCC/27730: Settlement, 12 Jul 1782

31 *Morning Herald*, 31 Jul 1782

32 Barnard, Vol. 3, pp. 70–3

33 Elwin, p. 204: Wentworth to Judith Milbanke, 20 Aug 1782

34 NLS: Acc 9769 27/2/162: 'Leon' to AL, 9 Jan 1783

35 NLS: Acc 9769 27/2/162: RA to 'Leon', 16 Jan 1783

36 *Morning Herald*, 5 Feb 1783

37 Barnard, Vol. 3, pp. 89–90

38 Ibid., Vol. 3, pp. 81–2

39 NLS: Acc 9769 27/2/21: RA to AL, 22 Dec 1782

10 A Royal Coup

1 BL: IOR/L/MAR/B/259A–B: Bessborough Journal, 26 Dec 1776 to 31 Oct 1781

2 YUL: MS 58: RA to JB, 15 Feb 1782

3 Howard, D.S., p. 512

4 CL: HMN/142

5 CL: HMN/143

6 BL: IOR/L/AG/14/5/18: East India Company Stock Ledger A–K, 1769–1774

7 NA: C 104/76

8 BL: Add MS 29154, fo. 134: JM to WH, 22 Apr 1782

9 Thompson & Frentzos, p. 117

10 AP: Abergavenny MSS 493: JR to North (draft), 1 Feb 1783

11 AP: Abergavenny MSS 494: RA to JR, 6 Feb 1783

12 Hansard, *Parliamentary History*, Vol. 22, col. 1106

13 Toynbee, Vol. 11, Letter 2176, p. 449: Horace Walpole to Sir Horace Mann, 17 May 1781

14 Fortescue, Vol. 6, Letter 3871, p. 97: King to John Robinson, 7 Aug 1782

15 NA: PRO 30/8/12, fos. 201–2: WP to Lady Chatham, Nov 1780

16 Fortescue, Vol. 6, Letter 4133, p. 249: King to Thurlow, 24 Feb 1783

17 NA: PRO 30/8/12, fos. 286–7: WP to Lady Chatham, 25 Feb 1783

18 BL: Loan MS 72/29, fo. 130: JR to Charles Jenkinson, 14 Mar 1783

19 Barnard, Vol. 3, pp. 87–8

20 BL: Loan MS 72/29, fo. 130: JR to CJ, 14 Mar 1783

21 Ibid.

22 NA: PRO 30/8/103, fo. 1: King to WP, 20 Mar 1783

23 BL: Add MS 37835, fo. 202: RA to JR, 21 Mar 1783

24 AP: Abergavenny MSS 506: RA to JR, 25 Mar 1783

25 Aspinall, p. 104: King to Prince of Wales (draft), nd

26 BL: Add MS 38567, fo. 145: JR to Charles Jenkinson, 1 Apr 1783

27 Barnard, Vol. 3, pp. 99–100

28 BL: Add MS 34523, fos. 371–3: King to Shelburne, 2 Apr 1783

29 Hansard, *Parliamentary History*, Vol. 23, col. 1200

30 Stanhope, Vol. 1, pp. 140–1: William Pitt to Rutland, 22 Nov 1783

31 Hansard, *Parliamentary History*, Vol. 23, col. 1224

32 Ibid., Vol. 23, col. 1247

33 Ibid., Vol. 23, cols. 1263, 1272

34 Ibid., Vol. 23, col. 1280

35 *English Chronicle*, 27 Nov 1783

36 BL: Add MS 88906/1/1, fo. 106: FB to Shelburne, 30 Nov 1783

37 *London Chronicle*, 6 Dec 1783

38 Grenville, Vol. 1, pp. 288–9

39 AP: Abergavenny MSS 520: RA to JR, 3 Dec 1783

40 BL: Add MS 38567, fo. 167: JR to CJ, 7 Dec 1783

41 Laprade, pp. 66–105

42 AP: Abergavenny MSS 525: RA to JR, 8 Dec 1783

43 BL: Add MS 38567, fos. 169–70: JR to Charles Jenkinson, 9 Dec 1783

44 AP: Abergavenny MSS 526: RA to JR, 12 Dec 1783

45 AP: Abergavenny MSS 530: RA to JR, 15 Dec 1783

46 AP: Abergavenny MSS, Box 2 A/5, Part One

47 AP: Abergavenny MSS 535: RA to JR, 17 Dec 1783

48 AP: Abergavenny MSS 541: RA to JR, 18 Dec 1783

49 Fortescue, Vol. 6, Letter 4546, p. 476: King to North, 18 Dec 1783

11 Secret Influence

1 Barnard, Vol. 3, pp. 100–1

2 Laprade, p. xx

3 BL: Add MS 47570, fo. 156: CJF to Elizabeth Armistead, nd

4 Wraxall, *Historical Memoirs*, Vol. 4, p. 664

5 *Morning Chronicle*, 3 Jan 1784

6 *Public Advertiser*, 29 Dec 1783

7 *Public Advertiser*, 30 Dec 1783

8 AP: Abergavenny MSS 551: RA to JR, 31 Dec 1783

9 *Morning Chronicle*, 13 Jan 1784

10 NLS: Acc 9769 23/2/13: RA to Balcarres, 12 Jan 1784

11 Hansard, *Parliamentary History*, Vol. 24, col. 318

12 AP: Abergavenny MSS 568: North to JR, 27 Jan 1784

13 NLS: Acc 9769 23/2/14: RA to Balcarres, 27 Jan 1784

14 *GM*: Vol. 54, Part 1, p. 70

15 NLS: Acc 9769 27/1/340

16 Barnard, Vol. 3, pp. 102–3

17 NAW: ZAL 95/3/6: DA to BA, 2 Mar 1784

18 AP: Abergavenny MSS Box 2 A/5, Part One (see also Laprade, pp. 114–18, 124–9)

19 Hansard, *Parliamentary History*, Vol. 24, cols. 734–5

20 Barnard, Vol. 3, pp. 100–1

21 *Gazetteer*, 30 Mar 1784

22 AP: Abergavenny MSS 599: RA to JR, 29 Mar 1784

23 *London Chronicle*, 30 Mar 1784

24 *Gazetteer*, 30 Mar 1784

25 AP: Abergavenny MSS 600: RA to JR, 31 Mar 1784

26 *Morning Chronicle*, 2 Apr 1784

27 *St James's Chronicle*, 1 Apr 1784

28 Wraxall, *Posthumous Memoirs*, Vol. 1, pp. 117–21

29 *Morning Herald*, 7 Apr 1784

30 *Morning Post*, 20 Apr 1784

31 NA: PRO 30/8/355, fo. 271: RA to Henry Dundas, nd; BL: Add MS 88906/1/1, fo. 122: Francis Baring to Shelburne, 26 Apr 1784

32 AP: Abergavenny MSS 602: RA to JR, 15 Apr 1784

33 BLO: Ms. Eng. hist. b.190, fos. 32–7: LS to Richard Sulivan, 20 Nov 1784

34 *Evening Post*, 24 Apr 1784

35 *St James's Chronicle*, 24 Apr 1784

36 *Evening Post*, 1 May 1784

37 *Morning Herald*, 6 May 1784

38 BL: Add MS 88906/1/1, fo. 127: FB to Shelburne, 18 May 1784

39 Walpole, *Last Journals*, Vol. 2, p. 280

40 NA: PRO 30/8/129, fo. 127: ED to WP, 24 Sep 1794

41 *Morning Herald*, 11 May 1784

12 A Dose of Vitriol

1 *Morning Herald*, 18 Jun 1784

2 NA: PRO 30/8/355: Report, 31 May 1784

3 *Public Advertiser*, 25 Jun 1784; *Evening Post*, 24 Jun 1784

4 NA: PRO 30/8/356, fos. 10–18: Report (margins numbered by RA); NA: PRO 30/8/355, fos. 216–39: RA's rebuttal

5 AP: Abergavenny MSS 613: RA to JR, 1 Jul 1784

6 Barnard, Vol. 3, pp. 97–8

7 Ibid., Vol. 3, pp. 106–7

8 NLS: Acc 9769 27/2/23: RA to AL, 2 Jul 1784

9 Barnard, Vol. 3, pp. 109–12

10 *Morning Chronicle*, 15 Jul 1784

11 NA: PRO 30/8/283, fo. 148

12 *Reports from Committees*, p. 284

13 NA: PRO 30/8/294, fos. 171, 182, 186, 220

14 *St James's Chronicle*, 21 Sep 1784

15 NLS: Acc 9769 27/2/22: RA to AL, 21 Jul 1784

16 NA: PRO 30/8/103, fo. 119: King to WP, 29 Jul 1784

17 *Morning Chronicle*, 31 Jul 1784

18 AP: Abergavenny MSS 615: RA to JR, 30 Jul 1784

19 NLS: Acc 9769 27/2/24: RA to AL, 3 Aug 1784

20 NLS: Acc 9769 27/2/26: RA to AL, 17 Aug 1784

21 AP: Abergavenny MSS 616: RA to JR, 16 Aug 1784

22 Glasse, p. 227

23 BL: Add MS 29166, fo. 368: John Scott to Warren Hastings, 30 Oct 1784

24 BL: Add MS 12567, fo. 104: 6 Oct 1784

25 AP: Abergavenny MSS 622: RA to John Robinson, 29 Sep 1784

26 *Morning Post*, 6 Oct 1784

27 NLS: Acc 9769 27/2/28: RA to AL, 12 Oct 1784

28 NA: PRO 30/8/181, fo. 218: Sydney to WP, 24 Sep 1784

29 NLS: Acc 9769 23/2/17: RA to Balcarres, 29 Oct 1784

30 *Gazetteer*, 17 Nov 1784

31 AP: Abergavenny MSS 626: RA to JR, 2 Dec 1784

32 KCUP: Ms. Coll. 888: RA to HD, 31 Jan 1785

33 *Gazetteer*, 19 Feb 1785

34 BL: Add MS 29168, fo. 79: John Scott to Warren Hastings, 18 Feb 1785

35 Ibid.

36 *Gazetteer*, 19 Feb 1785

37 *Gazetteer*, 5 Mar 1785

38 Hansard, *Parliamentary History*, Vol. 25, cols. 174, 180

39 Ibid., Vol. 25, col. 251

40 Ibid., Vol. 25, cols. 249–50

41 Wraxall, *Posthumous Memoirs*, Vol. 1, p. 261

42 Barnard, Vol. 3, pp. 189–91

43 Ibid., Vol. 3, pp. 189–91

44 Ibid., Vol. 4, pp. 6–7

45 NAW: ZAL 95/7/14: BA to DA, 19 Apr 1785

46 NA: PRO 30/8/353, fos. 76–7: 22 Apr 1785

47 NLS: Acc 9769 27/1/282: Elizabeth Yorke to Anne Lindsay & Margaret Fordyce, 30–31 May 1785

13 The Newcastle Attorney

1 Wraxall, *Posthumous Memoirs*, Vol. 1, p. 120

2 NLS: Acc 9769 27/1/282: EY to AL & MF, 30–31 May 1785

3 Barnard, Vol. 4, pp. 14–17

4 RGDJ: LOS Deeds 337, fo. 27: 1 May 1785

5 NLS: Acc 9769 27/2/21: RA to AL, 22 Dec 1782

6 Peach & Thomas, Vol. 2, p. 281: RP to Lansdowne, 2 Jun 1785

7 *Morning Chronicle*, 9 Jun 1785

8 *Public Advertiser*, 23 Jun 1785

9 NLS: Acc 9769 27/1/282: EY to AL & MF, 30–31 May 1785

10 NLS: Acc 9769 27/1/102: Balcarres to AL, 20 Jun 1785

11 *Public Advertiser*, 14 Jun 1785

12 NLS: Acc 9769 27/1/339

13 NLS: Acc 9769 27/1/340

14 Barnard, Vol. 4, pp. 7–8

15 Rochefoucauld, p. 103

16 NLS: Acc 9769 23/9/379: RM to Balcarres, 3 Jun 1785

17 NLS: Acc 9769 23/9/385: RM to Balcarres, 20 Aug 1785

18 AF: 1 Nov 1783

19 Barnard, Vol. 4, pp. 16–17

20 NAW: ZAL 95/7/15: DA to BA, 31 Mar 1786

21 NAW: ZAL 95/7/16: DA to BA, nd

22 *Morning Herald*, 22 Apr 1786; 10 May 1786
23 Barnard, Vol. 4, pp. 32–3
24 Ibid., Vol. 4, pp. 34–5
25 AF: Victoria Atkinson notes
26 NAW: ZAL 95/7/17: NC to DA, nd
27 NAW: ZAL 95/7/18: NC to DA, nd
28 NAW: ZAL 95/7/20: NC to DA, nd
29 NAW: ZAL 95/3/3: DA to BA, nd
30 NAW: ZAL 95/7/21: BA to DA, 29 Oct 1786
31 NAW: ZAL 95/27/4: NC to DA, 17 Nov 1786
32 NAW: ZAL 95/3/5: Dorothy Clayton to Bridget Atkinson, nd
33 NAW: ZAL 95/27/5: DC to BA, nd
34 NAW: ZAL 96/1/3: DC to BA, 8 Jan 1787
35 NAW: ZAL 95/6/2: NC to DC, 30 Jun 1787
36 NAW: ZAL 96/1/4: NC to BA, 17 Aug 1787
37 NAW: ZAL 95/1/12: Nathaniel Clayton to Bridget Atkinson, nd
38 NAW: ZAL 95/1/1: Nathaniel Clayton to Bridget Atkinson, 11 May 1788
39 NAW: ZAL 95/1/12: NC to BA, nd
40 Lustig & Pottle, p. 203
41 YUL: Gen MSS. M 190: 1 May 1788
42 Barnard, Vol. 3, pp. 81–2
43 Ibid., Vol. 4, pp. 36–7
44 NLS: Acc 9769 30/1/485: RL to AL, 27 Dec 1789
45 AP: Abergavenny B14 bundle: 'Plan of Arrangement', nd
46 NLS: Acc 9769 27/1/340
47 Barnard, Vol. 4, pp. 117–18

14 Taking Possession

1 *Morning Chronicle*, 18 Mar 1783
2 SV: Voyage 84106
3 Douglas, Vol. 3, p. 232
4 Hoare, p. 241
5 Harford, p. 139
6 Clarkson, *History of the Rise*, Vol. 1, pp. 286–7
7 Ibid., Vol. 1, p. 418
8 NA: CO 137/87, fo. 260: SF to Sydney, 25 Jun 1788
9 Clarkson, *History of the Rise*, Vol. 2, pp. 24–5
10 NA: PRO 30/8/349, fo. 135: SF to Hawkesbury, 16 Apr 1788
11 BL: Add MS 38416, fo. 73: Rodney to Hawkesbury, Mar 1788
12 Clarkson, *History of the Rise*, Vol. 2, p. 48
13 SV: Voyage 80666
14 Hansard, *Parliamentary History*, Vol. 28, col. 42
15 Ibid., Vol. 28, col. 76
16 Sotheby's, Catalogue, 9 Dec 1981, p. 58
17 NAW: ZAL 95/7/22: RA to BA, 6 Sep 1789
18 AF: Victoria Atkinson notes
19 NAW: ZAL 96/2/14: Bridget Atkinson to Nathaniel Clayton, 29 Oct 1789
20 Ibid.
21 BL: Eur C307/4: Nathaniel Wraxall to Paul Benfield, 27 Oct 1789
22 BL: Eur C307/4: NW to PB, 3 Dec 1789

23 BL: Eur C307/4: Nathaniel Wraxall to Paul Benfield, 8 Apr 1790

24 BA: NP1.A15.2: Agreement, 28 May 1791

25 Hansard, *Parliamentary History*, Vol. 29, col. 278

26 Elwin, p. 230: Wentworth to Judith Milbanke, 21 Feb 1784; Hansard, *Parliamentary History*, Vol. 29, col. 281

27 Hansard, *Parliamentary History*, Vol. 29, col. 343

28 Toynbee, Vol. 14, Letter 2793, p. 418: HW to Mary Berry, 23 Apr 1791

29 NLW: Slebech Papers, MS. 8386: Thomas Barritt to Nathaniel Phillips, 8 Dec 1791

30 Fox, pp. 4–5

31 LSF: Wilkinson MSS 114/3: TC to Thomas Wilkinson, 1 Mar 1792

32 Hansard, *Parliamentary History*, Vol. 29, cols. 1105, 1110

33 Moreton, p. 81

34 Beckford, Vol. 1, p. 14

35 Ibid., Vol. 2, p. 1

36 Ibid., Vol. 2, p. 120

37 Renny, p. 128

38 AF: GA to FB, 13 Feb 1792

39 Beckford, Vol. 1, p. 20

40 Moreton, p. 34

41 AF: GA to FB, 11 Jun 1792

42 AF: GA to Nathaniel Clayton, 11 Jun 1792

15 Fevered Isle

1 *Evening Post*, 26 Feb 1793

2 NAW: ZAL 96/1/9: DC to BA, 20 Mar 1793

3 NAW: ZAL 96/1/10: DC to BA, nd

4 NAW: ZAL 96/3/17: DC to BA, 5 May 1793

5 BA: HCOS 126/5–7/126: NC to Francis Baring, 15 Jul 1792

6 AF: DC to Matt Atkinson, 26 Dec 1820

7 Edwards, Vol. 2 (1801 edition), p. 586

8 AF: NC to GA, 1 Apr 1793

9 AF: GA to NC, nd

10 NAW: ZAL 96/3/19: NC to BA, 5 Jun 1793

11 Jackson, D., p. 281: 19 May 1760

12 Renny, p. 198

13 Jackson, R., p. 261

14 Annesley, p. 51

15 NAW: ZAL 95/21/48: JA to Matt Atkinson, 9 Apr 1791

16 NAW: ZAL 96/3/24: JA to BA, nd

17 NAW: ZAL 95/21/49: JA to Jane Atkinson, nd

18 CUL: Add. 8908/2: CW to Christopher Crackanthorp, 12 May 1793

19 NAW: ZAL 96/3/21: JA to BA, 29 Jul 1793

20 NAW: ZAL 96/1/15: NC to BA, 14 Oct 1793

21 NAW: ZAL 96/1/16: NC to BA, 15 Oct 1793

22 NAW: ZAL 96/1/17: NC to BA, 20 Oct 1793

23 NA: CO 137/91, fo. 327: Adam Williamson to Henry Dundas, 18 Oct 1793

24 NA: CO 137/92, fos. 49–50: George Bogle to Adam Williamson, 18 Nov 1793

25 BA: HCOS 126/1/118: WM to HD, 14 Sep 1793

26 BA: HCOS 126/1/119: HD to FB, 19 Sep 1793
27 BA: HCOS 126/2–4/9: GA to Francis Baring, 20 Jan 1794
28 BA: HCOS 126/1/116: NC to FB, 3 Jan 1794
29 NAW: ZAL 95/2/1: NC to BA, 3 Jan 1794
30 *Morning Chronicle*, 21 Feb 1794
31 NAW: ZAL 95/2/6: NC to BA, 25 Mar 1794
32 *GM*: Vol. 64, Part 2, p. 771
33 BA: HCOS 126/12–14/291: Memorandum, Dec 1798
34 www.baringarchive.org.uk
35 EUL: Laing Collection: La.II/481: Agreement, 22 Mar 1781
36 Long, Vol. 1, p. 82
37 Stewart, *An Account of Jamaica*, p. 35
38 NAW: ZAL 95/2/23: NC to Bridget Atkinson, nd
39 BL: Loan 57/107: HD to Richmond, 8 Jul 1793
40 BA: HCOS 126/2–4/12: GA to FB, 8 Feb 1794
41 NAW: ZAL 95/2/6: NC to BA, 25 Mar 1794
42 NA: CO 318/13, fo. 203
43 BA: HCOS 126/2–4/14: GA to Francis Baring, 4 Apr 1794
44 NA: CO 318/13, fo. 283: Charles Grey to Evan Nepean, 23 Apr 1794
45 BA: HCOS 126/2–4/18: GA to FB, 29 Apr 1794

16 Maroon War

1 BA: HCOS 126/2–4/20: GA to FB, 17 May 1794
2 BA: HCOS 126/2–4/24: GA to FB, 15 Jun 1794
3 BA: DEP41: Francis Baring Atkinson to F.H. Atkinson (transcript), 28 Jan 1863
4 NAW: ZAL 95/2/20: NC to BA, 18 Nov 1794
5 NAW: ZAL 95/2/24: JA to Jane Atkinson, nd
6 Edwards, Vol. 3 (1807 edition), p. 174
7 BA: HCOS 126/2–4/35: GA to FB, 17 Nov 1794
8 NA: T 1/740, fos. 8–9
9 *The State of the Nation*, p. 311
10 Ibid., p. 300
11 BA: HCOS 126/2–4/56: GA to FB, 5 Jul 1795
12 BA: HCOS 126/2–4/48: Francis Baring to AMB & Co, 6 May 1795
13 NAW: ZAL 95/4/1: JA to BA, nd
14 BA: HCOS 126/2–4/42: GA to FB, 4 Feb 1795
15 NA: CO 137/95, fo. 51: Balcarres to Portland, 30 May 1795
16 Lindsay, Vol. 3, p. 35: Magistrates to Balcarres, 18 Jul 1795
17 Ibid., Vol. 3, p. 48
18 Terrill, p. 88: Mary Yates to John Yates, 31 Dec 1795
19 NA: CO 137/95, fo. 107
20 NA: WO 1/92, fo. 58: Balcarres to Henry Dundas (in George Atkinson's hand), 24 Aug 1795
21 NLS: Acc 9769 23/11/103: GW to Balcarres, 20 Sep 1795
22 BA: HCOS 126/2–4/67: GA to Francis Baring, 29 Nov 1795
23 NA: WO 1/92, fo. 149: Balcarres to HD, 16 Nov 1795

24 NA: CO 137/96, fo. 58: Balcarres to Portland, 29 Dec 1795

25 *The Proceedings . . . in Regard to the Maroon Negroes*, p. 12: GW to Balcarres, 22 Dec 1795

26 NLS: Acc 9769 23/1/332: Balcarres to Elizabeth Lindsay, 13 Jan 1796

27 NA: CO 137/96, fo. 112: Balcarres to Portland, nd

28 *The Proceedings . . . in Regard to the Maroon Negroes*, p. 78: GW to Balcarres, 5 Mar 1796

29 Ibid., p. 82: GW to Balcarres, 11 Mar 1796

30 NLS: Acc 9769 23/11/3: GA to Balcarres, 17 Apr 1796

31 NLS: Acc 9769 23/10/595: HP to Balcarres, 3 May 1796

32 JA: IB/5/1/42, fo. 143: House of Assembly Journals, Nov 1796–Nov 1797

33 Hansard, *Parliamentary History*, Vol. 32, col. 924

34 NA: WO 1/92, fo. 273: HD to Balcarres, 21 Feb 1796

35 NLS: Acc 9769 23/11/155: Balcarres to Charles Yorke, 2 May 1796; NA: CO 137/96, fo. 262: *Royal Gazette*, 7 May 1796

36 NA: CO 137/96, fo. 270: Balcarres to Portland, 9 May 1796

37 BA: HCOS 126/2–4/64: GA to Francis Baring, 27 Oct 1795

38 BA: HCOS 126/5–7/92: FB to AMB, 4 Dec 1795

39 BL: Add MS 35916, fo. 202: Balcarres to Hardwicke, 6 Jun 1796

40 Baring, F., pp. 53–4

41 NLS: Acc 9769 23/10/26: GA to Balcarres, 3 Jun 1798

42 BA: HCOS 126/12–14/291: Memorandum, Dec 1798

43 BA: HCOS 126/5–7/160–2: GA to FB, 28 Aug 1798

44 BA: HCOS 126/5–7/158: NC to FB, 31 Jul 1798

45 NA: WO 1/70, fo. 20: Balcarres to TM, 6 Jul 1798

46 NA: WO 1/70, fo. 85: Thomas Maitland to Henry Dundas, 28 Aug 1798

47 NLS: Acc 9769 23/10/37: JA to Balcarres, 1 Sep 1798

48 NLS: Acc 9769 23/10/853: Balcarres to JA, 1 Sep 1798

17 Black Pioneers

1 Skinner, p. 35

2 NAW: ZAL 95/5/2: NC to JA, 6 Apr 1798

3 *An Impartial History*, p. 123

4 NAW: ZAL 96/1/28: JA to Bridget Atkinson, 22 Jan 1800

5 NAW: ZAL 96/1/29: NC to BA, 1 Feb 1800

6 NAW: ZAL 95/5/2: NC to JA, 6 Apr 1798

7 Budge, pp. 15–16: John Clayton to W. Campbell, 24 Jul 1889

8 NAW: ZAL 95/27/6: NC to BA, 29 Mar 1799

9 NAW: ZAL 96/2/16: BA to DC, 27 Oct 1799

10 NLS: Acc 9769 23/10/27: GA to Balcarres, 4 Nov 1798

11 BA: HCOS 126/8–11/177: FB to George Bogle, 17 Nov 1798

12 BA: HCOS 126/8–11/181: Memorandum, 1 Dec 1798

13 BA: HCOS 126/12–14/291: Memorandum, Dec 1798

14 NAW: ZAL 95/2/8: DC to BA, 29 May 1794

15 NLS: Acc 9769 23/10/27: GA to Balcarres, 4 Nov 1798

16 NLS: Acc 9769 23/8/3: GA to Balcarres, 3 Feb 1799

17 BA: HCOS 126/5–7/167: MA to FB, 10 Feb 1799

18 NLS: Acc 9769 23/8/189: James Mackintosh to MA, 24 Sep 1799

19 BA: HCOS 126/5–7/167: MA to FB, 10 Feb 1799

20 *Papers presented to the House of Commons on the 7th May 1804*: G. pp. 26, 37

21 BA: HCOS 126/8–11/184: FB to MA, 12 Aug 1799

22 NAW: ZAL 96/1/27: NC to DC, 7 Dec 1799

23 NA: CO 137/98, fo. 150: Balcarres to Portland, 28 Jan 1797

24 NLS: Acc 9769 23/10/1167: Balcarres to War Office, 13 Sep 1800 (not sent)

25 NAM: 6807-183-1, fo. 163; NLS: Acc 9769 23/10/1770

26 NA: WO 1/71, fo. 255: Maitland memorandum, 20 Apr 1799

27 NA: WO 1/72, fo. 27: Grant to Thomas Maitland, 14 Jul 1799

28 NA: WO 1/71, fo. 440: TM to Balcarres, 20 Jun 1799

29 NA: WO 1/71, fo. 438: Thomas Maitland to Balcarres, 17 Jun 1799

30 NA: WO 1/71, fo. 493: HC to Grant, 26 Nov 1799

31 NA: CO 137/103, fo. 204

32 NLS: Acc 9769 23/1/380: Balcarres to Lady Balcarres, 6 Jan 1800

33 NA: WO 1/74, fo. 77: John Wigglesworth to John King, 20 Dec 1799

34 BA: HCOS 126/8–11/216: HC to GA, 12 Jun 1800

35 BA: HCOS 126/8–11/187: FB to GMA, 5 Oct 1799

36 SV: Voyage 82553

37 BA: HCOS 126/8–11/199: JH to FB, 23 Mar 1800; SV: Voyage 84028

38 BA: HCOS 126/8–11/204: FB to JH, 9 May 1800; SV: Voyages 83515, 84102, 80741, 82374

39 BA: HCOS 126/8–11/211: FB to JH, 8 Aug 1800

40 BA: HCOS 126/12–14/317: GA to MA, JH & HC, Aug 1800

41 BA: HCOS 126/8–11/223: GB to FB, 2 Jan 1801

42 BA: HCOS 126/8–11/225: GB to FB, 27 Jan 1801

43 BA: HCOS 126/8–11/245: MA to FB, 28 Jan 1801

44 Stewart, *An Account of Jamaica*, p. 58

45 BA: HCOS 126/8–11/268: George Bogle to Francis Baring, 1 Nov 1801

46 BA: HCOS 126/8–11/254: GB to George Atkinson, 20 Jun 1801

47 BA: HCOS 126/8–11/261–3: Memorandum, 17 Jul 1801

48 Wright, p. 10: 29 Jul 1801

49 Fremantle, p. 26

50 Wright, pp. 11–12: 31 Jul 1801

51 NLS: Acc 9769 23/8/20: MA to Balcarres, 18 Nov 1802

52 NLS: Acc 9769 23/8/33: MA to Balcarres, 7 Oct 1804

53 NLS: Acc 9769 23/1/62: Lady Balcarres to Balcarres, 4 Jan 1802

18 The Nabob's Return

1 Barnard, Vol. 5, pp. 67–8
2 Lenta & Le Cordeur, Vol. 1, pp. 19–20: 15 Jan 1799
3 BL: Add MS 88906/1/1, fo. 106: FB to Shelburne, 30 Nov 1783
4 AP: Abergavenny B14 bundle: WD to JR, 15 Jun 1801
5 AP: Abergavenny B14 bundle: GA to JR, 13 Jan 1802
6 Wright, pp. 29–30: 2 Oct 1801
7 Ibid., p. 33: 21 Oct 1801
8 Ibid., p. xx
9 NLS: Acc 9769 23/8/19: MA to Balcarres, 28 Jun 1802
10 *Lettres du Général Leclerc*, 256, no. 145: Leclerc to Napoleon Bonaparte, 7 Oct 1802
11 NA: CO 137/111, fo. 353: 24 Mar 1804 (unnamed)
12 BA: NP1.A4.4: FB to P.C. Labouchère, 15 Feb 1803
13 BA: NP1.A4.28: HA to FB, 16 Dec 1803
14 BA: HCOS 126/12–14/297: MA to GA, 11 Mar 1804
15 BA: HCOS 126/12–14/297: Matt Atkinson to George Atkinson, 15 Jan 1804
16 Ibid.
17 BA: HCOS 126/12–14/297: MA to GA, 11 Mar 1804
18 Ibid.
19 BA: HCOS 126/12–14/298: GA to FB, 30 Apr 1804
20 *Morning Post*, 23 May 1804
21 AF: Bridget Atkinson to Matt Atkinson, 2 Jul 1804
22 Ibid.
23 Ibid.
24 AF: JA to MA, 2 Jul 1804
25 AF: Bridget Atkinson to Matthew Atkinson, 30 Dec 1804
26 RGDJ: Kingston, Register of Baptisms, Vol. 2, 1793–1825, p. 86
27 RGDJ: Kingston, Register of Baptisms, Vol. 2, 1793–1825, p. 128
28 JA: IB/11/6/25, fo. 220
29 RGDJ: Kingston, Register of Baptisms, Vol. 2, 1793–1825, p. 105
30 RGDJ: Kingston, Register of Baptisms, Vol. 1, 1722–92, p. 348
31 RGDJ: Kingston, Register of Baptisms, Vol. 2, 1793–1825, p. 105
32 RGDJ: Kingston, Register of Baptisms, Vol. 2, 1793–1825, p. 136
33 Renny, p. 324
34 Wright, p. 65: 5 Mar 1802
35 NA: CO 137/91, fo. 146: BE to Henry Dundas, 16 May 1793
36 Stewart, *An Account of Jamaica*, p. 296
37 *The Times*, 7 Mar 1806: MA to MA, 29 Jul 1804
38 AF: BA to MA, 30 Dec 1804
39 CUL: MS Add. 9723: Bridget Atkinson waste book
40 *The Times*, 7 Mar 1806
41 Ibid.
42 Ibid.
43 AF: JA to MA, 2 Jul 1804
44 BA: HCOS 126/12–14/322: Nathaniel Clayton to George Atkinson, 19 Nov 1806
45 RGDJ: Kingston, Register of Baptisms, Vol. 2, 1793–1825, p. 158
46 AF: RR to MA, 24 Apr 1807
47 Hansard, *Parliamentary Debates*, Old Series, Vol. 9, col. 170
48 ICWS: ICS 120, 1/I/24: ST to George Hibbert, 22 Apr 1807

19 End of an Era

1 *The Picture of Newcastle upon Tyne*, pp. 100–1
2 BA: HCOS 126/12–14/301: GA to FB, 7 Feb 1805
3 *The Picture of Newcastle upon Tyne*, p. 98
4 Thomson, T., p. 232
5 Mackenzie, p. 382
6 NAW: ZAL 95/5/4: NC to BA, 6 Jan 1807
7 *The Times*, 20 Apr 1808
8 NAW: ZAL 96/1/40: Dorothy Clayton to Bridget Atkinson, 18 May 1809
9 NAW: ZAL 95/5/5: JA to Dorothy Clayton, 17 Jan 1822
10 NAW: ZAL 96/1/40: Dorothy Clayton to Bridget Atkinson, 18 May 1809
11 NA: TS 25/3, fos. 421–2: 22 Nov 1809; NA: TS 25/5, fos. 424–38: 17 Jun 1812
12 BA: NP1.A4.67: FB to P.C. Labouchère, 9 Oct 1804
13 *The Bankers' Magazine*, p. 882
14 *GM*: Vol. 80, Part 2, p. 293
15 *Evening Post*, 22 Mar 1770
16 NAW: ZAL 96/1/36: Dorothy Clayton to Bridget Atkinson, 15 Mar 1809
17 Raine, Vol. 1, p. 17
18 Ibid., Vol. 1, pp. 80–1: JH to Jane Hodgson, 2 May 1811
19 Ibid.
20 AF: BA to DC, 28 Jun 1812
21 NAW: SANT/ADM/4/1/1/12
22 *Archaeologia Aeliana*: Donations, p. 3
23 NA: TS 25/5, fos. 424–38: 26 Feb 1813

24 AF: GA to MA, 24 May 1813
25 Ibid.
26 AF: NC to Henry Tulip, 28 Jun 1813
27 AF: MA to NC, 5 Jul 1813
28 NAW: ZAL 95/27/8: NC to BA, 7 Jan 1805
29 CUL: MS Add. 9723: Bridget Atkinson waste book
30 NAW: SANT/BEQ/18/11/13
31 NAW: SANT/BEQ/18/11/3/66–8: BA to MA, 25 Oct 1813
32 Ibid.
33 Ibid.
34 NAW: ZAL 95/21/3: NC to DC, 13 Mar 1814
35 AF: Scrapbook
36 NA: PROB 11/1620/355
37 AF: MA to (cousin) Matthew Atkinson, 29 Jun 1814
38 NLS: Acc 9769 23/8/73: Matt Atkinson to Balcarres, 16 Aug 1814
39 AF: MA to MA, 29 Jun 1814
40 NLS: Acc 9769 23/8/73: MA to Balcarres, 16 Aug 1814
41 Rubinstein, p. 87

20 Settling Scores

1 AF: JA to MA, 14 Mar 1815
2 AF: JA to (cousin) Matthew Atkinson, 14 Mar 1815
3 Phillimore, pp. 316–20
4 Barnard, Vol. 6, p. 114
5 NLS: Acc 9769 27/2/318: AB to B.W. van Rijneveld, 27 Aug 1809
6 NLS: Acc 9769 27/1/340
7 NLS: Acc 9769 23/1/21: AB to Balcarres, 24 Mar 1816
8 Lenta & Le Cordeur, Vol. 2, p. 112: 22 Apr 1800
9 Barnard, Vol. 1, p. 2
10 Ibid., Vol. 1, p. 2

11 Ibid., Vol. 1, p. 10

12 NLS: Acc 9769 23/8/61: AB &
Co to Balcarres, 6 Oct 1810

13 NLS: Acc 9769 23/8/246:
Balcarres to George Atkinson,
4 Jan 1813

14 *The Jamaica Almanack*, 1821

15 NAW: ZAL 95/20/2: NC to
Sarah Clayton, 2 Feb 1816

16 NLS: Acc 9769 23/8/87: EA to
Balcarres, 25 Feb 1817

17 NLS: Acc 9769 23/8/91: EA to
Balcarres, 1 Aug 1817

18 NLS: Acc 9769 23/8/256:
Balcarres to EA, nd

19 NLS: Acc 9769 23/8/93: EA to
Balcarres, 17 Aug 1817

20 NLS: Acc 9769 23/8/96: EA to
Balcarres, 1 Nov 1817

21 *The Colonial Journal*, Vol. 1,
Jan–Jul 1816, p. 246

22 Bridges, *A Voice from Jamaica*, p. 27

23 Beche, p. 27

24 RGDJ: Westmoreland Parish,
Baptisms, Marriages, Burials
1739–1825, Vol. 1, pp. 350–3

25 NLS: Acc 9769 23/9/608: AR &
Co to Barings, 7 Oct 1820

26 NLS: Acc 9769 23/9/38: MA to
Balcarres, 16 Oct 1818

27 NLS: Acc 9769 23/9/519:
Balcarres to MA, 30 Oct 1818

28 CUL: MS Add. 9723: Michael
Clayton to (cousin) Matthew
Atkinson, 19 Jan 1819

29 NLS: Acc 9769 23/1/25: AB to
Balcarres, 26 Jan 1819

30 *The Times*, 2 Aug 1821

31 AF: NC to MA, 6 Nov 1821

32 NAW: ZAL 96/1/50: NC to DC,
21 Nov 1821

33 AF: Affidavits, nd

34 NAW: ZAL 95/5/5: Jane
Atkinson to Dorothy Clayton,
17 Jan 1822

35 NAW: ZAL 96/1/51: MC to DC,
13 Jul 1822

36 CUL: MS Add. 9723: Michael
Clayton to (cousin) Matthew
Atkinson, 24 Jan 1823

37 AF: Memorandum, nd

38 AF: Victoria Atkinson
transcript: MA to SC, nd

39 NLS: Acc 9769 23/1/26: AB to
Balcarres, 18 May 1823

40 NLS: Acc 9769 27/2/3

41 NLS: Acc 9769 27/2/21

42 NLS: Acc 9769 27/2/6

43 NLS: Acc 9769 23/9/198: MC to
Balcarres, 18 Nov 1823

44 AF: JT to (cousin) Matthew
Atkinson, 10 Mar 1824

45 *The Times*, 26 Mar 1825

46 AF: Robert Robertson to George
Atkinson, 4 May 1825

21 Human Relics

1 AF: GCA, childhood description

2 Ibid.

3 AF: Victoria Atkinson
transcript: Matthew Atkinson
to Sophia Cator, nd

4 AF: NC to MA, 5 Mar 1816

5 AF: MA to NC, 7 Mar 1816

6 AF: MA to NC, 11 Mar 1816

7 AF: NC to MA, 13 Mar 1816

8 Raine, Vol. 2, p. 214

9 Moorman, p. 109: 15 Apr 1802

10 AF: GCA, childhood description

11 Brontë, Vol. 1, p. 4

12 Atkinson, G.C., p. 16

13 NHSN: NEWHM: 2006.H3.1:
British Land Birds, Thomas

Bewick, Vol. 1 (inc. draft memoir by GCA)

14 Atkinson, G.C., p. 18

15 NHSN: NEWHM: 2006.H3.1: *British Land Birds*, Thomas Bewick, Vol. 1 (inc. draft memoir by GCA)

16 Atkinson, G.C., p. 24

17 NHSN: NEWHM:1994–H6 (tooth and wrapping)

18 NAW: ZAL 96/4/1/32: Michael Clayton to Nathaniel Clayton, 12 Jul 1826

19 AF: FBA to (cousin) Matthew Atkinson, 19 Dec 1825

20 Ibid.

21 AF: RR to MA, 28 Sep 1827

22 NAW: ZAL 96/1/61

23 AF: GCA to Isaac & Richard Atkinson, 7 Oct 1828

24 AF: EW to Thomas Littledale, 9 Oct 1828

25 *Newcastle Courant*, 24 Jan 1829

26 *Newcastle Courant*, 3 Oct 1829

27 *Transactions of the Natural History Society*, Vol. 1, Presents and Purchases, p. 13

28 DUL: DPRI/1/1831/A16/1–6

29 Clarkson, *History of the Rise*, Vol. 2, p. 464

30 HL: Thomas Clarkson Papers: CN 73

31 Hansard, *Parliamentary Debates*, New Series, Vol. 9, cols. 274–5

32 Baring, A., p. 6

33 Bridges, *A Voice from Jamaica*, p. 36

34 RGDJ: Westmoreland Parish, Baptisms, Marriages, Burials 1739–1825, Vol. 1, pp. 347–50

35 Clarkson, 'Negro Slavery', p. 1

36 AF: Francis Baring Atkinson to (cousin) Matthew Atkinson, 2 Jan 1826

37 *Morning Chronicle*, 17 May 1830

38 NAW: ZAL 95/21/7: BC to JA, 10 Nov 1830

39 NLS: Acc 9769 25/11/523: Balcarres to Robertson, Brother & Co, 31 Dec 1826

40 NLS: Acc 9769 25/11/8: EA to Balcarres, 20 Aug 1825

41 NLS: Acc 9769 25/11/74: Thomas Fowlis to Balcarres, 4 Oct 1828

42 NLS: Acc 9769 25/11/570: Balcarres to Thomas Fowlis, 4 Jan 1832

43 NLS: Acc 9769 25/11/76: Thomas Fowlis to Balcarres, 9 Dec 1828

44 NLS: Acc 9769 25/11/27: GA to Balcarres, 1 Jan 1830

45 NLS: Acc 9769 25/11/28: EA to Balcarres, 22 Feb 1830

46 NLS: Acc 9769 25/11/32: Balcarres to Thomas Fowlis, 6 Feb 1831

47 NLS: Acc 9769 25/11/533: Balcarres to Atkinson & Hosier, 16 May 1831

48 NLS: Acc 9769 25/11/34: GA to Balcarres, 24 Oct 1831

49 NLS: Acc 9769 25/11/649: Balcarres, nd

50 NLS: Acc 9769 25/11/530: Balcarres to GA, 4 Mar 1830

51 NLS: Acc 9769 25/11/29: GA to Balcarres, 14 Jun 1830

52 NLS: Acc 9769 25/11/30: EA to Balcarres, 7 Aug 1830

53 *Accounts and Papers, Eighteen Volumes*, Session 6, December 1831–16 August 1832, Vol. 31, p. 284

54 Stewart, *A View of the Past and Present State*, p. 352

55 Cox, Vol. 2, p. 83

56 Bleby, p. 26

57 Ibid., p. 116

58 Stephen, p. 197

59 *The Debates in Parliament – Session 1833*, p. 81

60 Ibid., p. 462

61 Ibid., p. 501

62 Ibid., p. 657

63 Wilberforce, Vol. 5, p. 368

22 A Spice of the Devil

1 Moore, Vol. 1, p. 63

2 NAW: ZAL 95/12/5: NC to NC, 2 Oct 1831

3 AF: GCA to Richard Atkinson, 10 Dec 1833

4 *The Corporation Annual*, p. 71

5 *Cobbett's Weekly Register*, Vol. 43, No. 1, cols. 21–2, 6 Jul 1822

6 Quine, pp. 3, 37

7 Ibid., p. 36

8 Ibid., p. 42

9 *Transactions of the Natural History Society*, Vol. 2, pp. 215–25

10 Quine, p. 50

11 Ibid., p. 58

12 AF: GCA to RA, 10 Dec 1833

13 AF: IA to RA, 24 Jan 1834

14 NLS: Acc 9769 25/11/651

15 NA: CO 137/193, fo. 304: Sligo to TSR, 18 Nov 1834

16 AF: GA to (cousin) Matthew Atkinson, 29 Dec 1834

17 *London Gazette*, 18 Apr 1834

18 NLS: Acc 9769 25/11/583: Balcarres to Thomas Fowlis, 13 Jan 1835

19 NLS: Acc 9769 25/11/38: George Atkinson to Balcarres, 11 May 1833

20 NLS: Acc 9769 25/11/549: Balcarres to GA, 22 Jul 1835

21 NLS: Acc 9769 25/11/555: Balcarres to GA, 8 Jan 1836

22 NLS: Acc 9769 25/11/43: GA to Balcarres, 8 Aug 1835

23 NLS: Acc 9769 25/11/46: GA to Balcarres, 28 Sep 1835

24 NA: T 71/703, claim 694

25 NA: T 71/74, fo. 188

26 NAW: ZAL 95/21/10: GA to Jane Atkinson, 20 Jun 1835

27 NAW: ZAL 95/21/21: GA to JA, 1 Feb 1840

28 NAW: ZAL 95/21/15: GA to JA, 11 Jul 1836

29 NAW: ZAL 95/21/15: GA to JA, 11 Jul 1836

30 NAW: ZAL 95/21/18: RA to JA, 27 Sep 1837

31 AF: JD to RA, 30 Mar–2 Apr 1837

32 NAW: ZAL 95/21/18: RA to JA, 27 Sep 1837

33 NA: CO 140/115: p. 100

34 NA: CO 137/192, fo. 273: *Jamaica Despatch*, 24 May 1834

35 Sturge & Harvey, p. 176

36 *The Statutes of the United Kingdom*, p. 76

23 Farewell to Jamaica

1 AF: Charles Mills to Lonsdale, 3 Mar 1826

2 CUL: MS Add. 9723: JC to MA, 6 May 1837

3 Hardcastle, p. 258

4 AF: John Clayton to MA (draft reply), 4 Jan 1832

5 CAK: WDX 82

6 NAW: ZAL 95/21/23: GA to Jane Atkinson, 17 Apr 1841

7 NAW: ZAL 95/21/21: GA to JA, 1 Feb 1840

8 Gurney, p. 104

9 NAW: ZAL 95/21/25: GA to JA, 29 May 1843

10 Gurney, p. xiv

11 NAW: ZAL 95/21/25: GA to JA, 29 May 1843

12 AF: RA to George Clayton Atkinson, 9 Oct 1844

13 *GM*: New Series, Vol. 25, Part 1, p. 413

14 Peel, p. 6

15 NAW: ZAL 95/21/29: RA to JA, 7 Jun 1847

16 *The Transactions of the Jamaica Society of Arts*, p. 46

17 TWA: D/CG 39/17: Clayton & Dunn to RA, 30 Jun 1846

18 AF: RA to GCA, 7 Sep 1847

19 AF: RA to George Atkinson, 8 Nov 1847

20 RGDJ: LOS 895, fo. 181

21 AF: RA to George Atkinson, 22 Nov 1847

22 Scoresby-Jackson, p. 499

23 NAW: ZAL 95/21/28: RA to Jane Atkinson, 7 Feb 1846

24 NAW: ZAL 95/21/34: RA to Jane Atkinson, 27 Aug 1851

25 NAW: ZAL 95/21/35: RA to Jane Atkinson, 4 Sep 1851

26 NA: CO 137/330: Report of Richard Hill (1856)

27 Martin, p. 77

28 Evans, p. 7

29 Ibid., p. 11

30 *Daily News*, 19 May 1856

31 *Second Series of Recollections*, p. iii

32 *Newcastle Journal*, 31 May 1834

33 Howitt, p. 310

34 *Sketches of Public Men*, pp. 75–85

35 Budge, p. 6; Hutton, p. 202

36 AF: JA to Elisabeth Atkinson (GCA's second wife), 4 Dec 1875

37 AF: JA to Elisabeth Atkinson (GCA's second wife), 13 Dec 1875

38 *Proceedings of the Society of Antiquaries*, p. 28

39 Bruce, G., pp. 163–4

40 AF: Victoria Atkinson notes

41 *Madras Times*, 7 Jul 1914

42 Fetherstonhaugh, p. 167

43 AF: JNA to G.A. Atkinson, 21 Oct 1923

44 AF: JNA to G.A. Atkinson, 30 May 1928

45 AF: IC to JNA, 1 Nov 1923

46 Hampton & Sons, 18 Jun 1929

47 *The Times*, 3 Jan 1930

48 *Hexham Courant*, 13 Jan 1930

49 AF: JNA's diary, 6 Aug 1922

50 *Sunday Times*, 31 Jul 1932

51 AF: RLA to JLA, 15 Jan 1957

24 Distant Cousins

1 Lawrence-Archer, p. 106

Appendix I

1 NLS: Acc 9769 27/2/3: Richard Atkinson to Lady Anne Lindsay, nd

Appendix II

1 NLS: Acc 9769 27/1/330

PICTURE CREDITS

478

ACKNOWLEDGEMENTS

It has somehow taken me nearly a decade to write this book, and I wouldn't have managed it without the help of a great many people along the way. First, before singling out individuals, I'd like to express my gratitude to the multitude – family, friends, colleagues, complete strangers – who have been kind enough to show even a flicker of interest in my project. I really can't begin to articulate how much I have appreciated your support.

I've been fortunate to be able to draw on an astonishing range of primary sources for my research. Most of all, I'd like to thank the Earl of Crawford and Balcarres for allowing me access to his voluminous family papers; and Kenneth Dunn, who smoothed the way for my visits to the National Library of Scotland. I'd also like to thank the Marquess of Abergavenny for letting me see his ancestor John Robinson's correspondence; and Pat Stallwood and Arland Kingston, who made my outings to Eridge Park so enjoyable. I would often marvel, during my trips to the British Library and the National Archives, at the speed with which obscure documents were summoned up from the depths, and it would occur to me how lucky I am to live in a country where so much history is at hand. The curators and librarians at all the public and private archives I visited were unfailingly helpful; in particular, I'd like to thank Clara Harrow at the Baring Archive, June Holmes at the Natural History Society of Northumbria and Doug Oxenhorn at New Jersey Historical Society.

Julie Evans, Georgina Plowright, Andrew Connell, Irene Dunn and Andrea Stuart offered invaluable encouragement right at the beginning; while Frances McIntosh, Peter Roebuck, Ian Thomson,

Margaret Gowling, Frances Wilkins and the late Iain Bain gave generously of their knowledge further down the line. Ivan Day, amazingly, led me to another of Bridget's cookbooks. Bill Swainson was kind enough to show me some revealing family papers of his own. My former employers at Bloomsbury were extraordinary for keeping faith in me for so long; Alexandra Pringle and Natalie Bellos, especially, proved the warmest and most constant of colleagues. Valerian Freyberg accompanied me on a life-changing visit to Temple Sowerby. Bill and Karen Chaytor kept me wonderfully well fed and watered during my frequent research trips up north. Tom Gilkes and David Kellie-Smith helped decipher my family's old business ledger. In Jamaica, Peter Espeut, Audene Brooks, Dianne Frankson, Ann Sutton and James Robertson unlocked treasures, archival and archaeological, while Suzanne Francis-Brown gifted me the book's ending. Jonnie Cook and Whitney Mortimer were delightful travelling companions on the island. Chris Lloyd provided good cheer and wise counsel at times when I was struggling with my task. Stephen Taylor — Lady Anne Lindsay's biographer — was a most congenial fellow time traveller. Pascal Cariss hacked his way through my dense first draft with great fortitude, and inspired me to make my second draft a lot better. Jenny Uglow, Nicholas Draper, Jeremy Black, John Watherston, Gavin Hasselgren and Jasper Gerard-Sharp were also generous enough to read early versions of the manuscript, and the book would be the less without their perceptive comments.

It is no exaggeration to say that *Mr Atkinson's Rum Contract* wouldn't exist had not Claire Paterson Conrad hounded me to write the proposal, for which I must remain in her everlasting debt. My agent Rebecca Carter offered kind words of encouragement throughout the writing process, and saw the manuscript at a stage when it really shouldn't have been seen by anyone. By bizarre coincidence, it turned out that my editor Louise Haines had stayed the night at Temple Sowerby House before she even knew about my connection to the place. I could not be more grateful for the quiet persistence with which she has coaxed me to turn in my best work; and for the forbearance she has shown towards an author who delivered his manuscript *five years late*. I would also like to give special thanks to Steve Gove, for the extra polish he lent the manuscript; Sarah Thickett, for handling the editorial process (and my endless tweaks) with great poise; Rachel Smyth, for her elegant page layout; Julian Humphries, for his excellent cover design; Anne Rieley, for meticulous proofreading; Mark Wells, for methodical indexing; and Michelle Kane, for putting the word about. Many thanks, too, to Andrew Davidson for his beautiful woodcuts; David Atkinson (no relation, as far as I am aware) for his evocative maps; and Adrian Gibbs, Lucy Grange, Felicity Page, Peter Dawson, Alice Kennedy-Owen and Matt Livey for their help wrangling the pictures.

While writing this book I discovered a fair few cousins I had not realized I had, and getting to know them has been a joy. I will never forget the warmth with which Phillipa and her daughter Laura welcomed me into their lives. David Atkinson not only entrusted me with a mass of family papers, but offered unflagging support from the start. The Scandinavian branch of the family – Renira Müller, Karen and Tomas Tunemyr, Jon and Grete Müller, and Sigrun Müller-Steen – showed me great hospitality, involving memorable crayfish feasts. Closer to home, Anthea Guthrie, Ridley Scott, Hilary Vidnes, Caroline Garrett, Jenny Tyler and George Atkinson-Clark shared the contents of family scrapbooks and shoeboxes.

My final thanks, however, are saved for the three most important people in my life: my beloved mother Jane, whose difficult decision to sell Temple Sowerby House liberated me from a painful choice; my dearest sister Harriet, who is co-heir to the 'tangled inheritance' at the heart of this story; and my darling wife Sue, whose belief in me never wavered and who (together with T&T) has been my steadfast companion during this most exhilarating, and at times daunting, adventure of my life.

Richard Atkinson
London, January 2020

INDEX

Abbott, Lemuel, 236–7
Abbott, Sir Charles, 343
Abergavenny, 1st Earl of, 154, 178, 196
Abergavenny, 6th Marquess of, 183–4
Adam, Robert, 49
Adams, Edward, 318, 339–40, 354, 362, 363, 364
Addingham (Cumberland), 34
Addington, Henry, 306, 308
Allgood family of Nunwick Hall, 16–17
American colonies: and Navigation Acts, 40, 51; and post-Seven Years' War settlement, 50–1; and the Sugar Act (1764), 51–2, 54–5; and financing of British Empire, 51–3, 54–5, 77–9; rum distillers of New England, 51; and the Stamp Act (1765), 52–3, 55; and banking crisis (1772), 76; and 'Townshend duties', 77–9; Boston 'tea party' (16 December 1773), 79, 82; 'intolerable acts' (1774), 82–3, 85–7; 'Continental Congress' at Philadelphia (1774/75), 85–7, 88; resolutions of Congress (1774), 86–7; declaration of independence (4 July 1776), 101; alliance with France (February 1778), 113, 117, 118, 121
American Duties Act (1766), 54–5, 56
American War of Independence: provisioning of king's army, 10–11, 88–92, 93–4, 95–7, 103–8, 110–13, 115, 117–21, 130–1, 194; battles at Lexington and Concord (1775), 87; Bunker Hill (1775), 88, 89; companies of American militia, 92; occupation of Dorchester Heights (1776), 94; logistical minutiae of, 95; British advance (autumn 1776), 101–2;

Washington's victories at Trenton and Princeton, 103; French support for rebels, 109, 110, 113; British 1777 campaign, 110; Burgoyne's surrender at Saratoga, 110, 158; France enters (1778), 113, 117, 118, 121; Spain enters (1779), 121–2, 128, 129; French forces in Caribbean/America, 122, 123, 124, 125; British victory at Savannah (1779), 125; British public discontent, 126–7; Charleston surrenders to British (June 1780), 127–8; Rodney's capture of Saint Eustatius, 138, 149–50; British defeat at Yorktown (1781), 149–50; fighting near Ticonderoga, 158; Shelburne's peace treaty, 168–9
Amherst, General, 114, 123–4, 125
Ancestry, 10
Ancestry DNA, 409–10
Anglican church, 313, 340–1; Colonial Church Union, 365–6
Anson, Admiral, 45
anti-slavery campaign: Granville Sharp as father of, 60, 231; story of the *Zong*, 231–2; Somerset case (1772), 231; and William Wilberforce, 232–3, 234, 236, 239–40, 242–3, 319, 320, 338–9, 340, 358, 368; Clarkson's tract, 232; Clarkson's investigation, 233–4, 235; Committee for the Abolition of the Slave Trade, 233, 242; image of the 'kneeling slave', 233, 234; Quaker sympathizers, 233, 340; roots in Nonconformist Christianity, 233, 340, 365; Wedgwood's cameos, 233; Dolben's Act (1788), 234–5; Lord Hawkesbury's committee, 234, 235, 236;